WOMEN AND HUMAN RIGHTS

WOMEN AND HUMAN RIGHTS

M A KHAN

2007

SBS Publishers & Distributors Pvt. Ltd.
New Delhi

ISBN : 81-89741-02-0

Indian Price - Rs 875

First Published in India in 2006
Reprinted in 2007

Published by:
SBS PUBLISHERS & DISTRIBUTORS PVT. LTD.
2/9, Ground Floor, Ansari Road, Darya Ganj,
New Delhi - 110002, INDIA
Tel: 23289119, 41563911
Email: mail@sbspublishers.com

Printed at Chaman Enterprises, New Delhi - 110002.

Contents

Preface

Be it any platform, the issue of womenfolk has ever been of great interest, may be because of unconsciously triggered instinct of man for the opposite sex. But, most unfortunately, there seems to be no end to the woes of women. Locally or globally, violence against them in diverse forms is as clear as day light. From time to time, conventions and conferences always keep focusing on the issue with fire and fervour, but with the winding up of theirs, all the covenants and resolutions reach the back seat *ipso facto*.

Nevertheless, one should not lose heart. Agencies and societies of national and international repute are tirelessly endeavouring to bring relief to this troubled lot. The most important thing in this concern, is the process of inculcating moral values and esteem for women in the hearts of the young and the coming generation.

This research-based exclusive work on Women and Human Rights is an humble attempt towards the emancipation of women. Expectedly, it would prove to be a balm on the tortured psyche of the weaker sex, provided it is given due heed.

Also, it would be beneficial to a great extent for women-activists, striviting for the cause referred to.

Readers' comments and suggestions are anticipated and would be appreciated.

— **Author**

1

Concept and Perception

Till the end of World War II, there was no body of international human rights law to speak of. There were, to be sure, philosophies and theories, but the international rules that reflected them were absent. Today, through the United Nations and its half-century of enactments, an impressive body of human rights doctrine is embodied in international law.

Having come this far legally, why then should we still be concerned with the philosophical foundations of human rights? To philosophize, Plato taught, us to come to know oneself. Others say that the special function of philosophy is to discover true propositions or, at least, to deepen our understanding of truth. Still others see the philosopher as a judge, assessing the varieties of human experience and pronouncing on the claim to knowledge. But are there particular reasons for reflection on the philosophy of human rights? With due allowance for philosophical ardour, we suggest there are.

First, the justification of moral principles is an attempt to make coherent sense about the principles which govern and should govern the ways human beings treat one another. Our own attitudes towards the subject are likely to remain obscure unless we try to understand the philosophies which shape them. Moral principles influence, if not determine, the right modes of individual conduct and social institutions. Piaget's statement that 'morality is the logic of action' contains a striking insight.

Second, if we understand the moral force of human rights principles, we can reinforce the authority of the international law of human rights, which is particularly valuable for an arena still lacking in formal enforcement mechanisms. Put another way, we further fidelity to human rights law by understanding the moral justifications that underlie human rights laws.

Third, understanding the philosophical foundations of human rights helps us devise a translation formula which will permit men and women to speak to each other across the gulfs of creed and dogma, a necessary exercise if there is to be universal recognition of human rights principles.

Fourth, understanding the moral philosophy of human rights also helps us to delineate the structures of human thought in a manner which reveals the implications of thinking and speaking about rights in a particular way, the relationships of rights to one another, the hierarchical ordering of rights and the nature of the conflicts or tension among rights.

So let us take for granted that we can benefit from reflecting on the philosophical foundations of human rights. What then is the segment of philosophy we examine when we delve into human rights? The answer is that human rights are a set of moral principles and their justification lies in the province of moral philosophy. It is that field we explore here.

It bears emphasis, at this point, that, while the modern human rights theories we discuss have been articulated largely by Western philosophers, the moral concepts are not exclusively Western and find counterparts in non-Western thought as well. Of course, the truth of a philosophical principle should not depend on its geography but on the soundness of its foundation. Self-determination, for example, is a Western-originated concept, yet it has spawned the birth of many Third World states. It is significant that the key human rights instruments starting with the Universal Declaration of Human Rights were not drafted by Western states alone and, in any event, the instruments have been endorsed by nations around the world. It is hoped that the theories and concepts dealt with here will be appraised objectively in the calculus of reason.

We shall approach our task, first, by addressing the historical sources of human rights justifications, then surveying key modern human rights theories and analysing some of the current conflicts in human rights theory. At best, we can only touch on the teachings in a field which is complex, vast and, too often, obscure.

General Notion

One of the initial questions in any philosophical inquiry is what is meant by human rights. The question is not trivial. Human beings, as Sartre said, are 'stalkers of meaning'. Meaning tells us 'why'. Particularly in the international sphere, where diverse cultures are involved, where positivist underpinnings are shaky and where implementation mechanisms are fragile, the issue of definition can be crucial. Indeed, some philosophical schools assert that the entire task of philosophy centres on meaning. How we understand the meaning of human rights will influence our judgments on such issues where rights are regarded as absolute, which are universal, which should be given priority which can be overruled by other interests, which call for international pressures, which can demand programmes for implementation and which will be fought for.

We turn first to the question, what do we mean by human 'rights'? Let us focus initially on the word 'human'. To speak of 'human' rights requires a conception of what rights one possesses by virtue of being human. Of course, we are not speaking here of human rights in the self-evident sense that those who have them are human, but in the sense that, in order to have them, one need only be human. Put another way, are the rights that human beings have simply because they are human beings, and independent of their varying social circumstances and degrees of merit? The answers which individuals and states provide to this question have great bearing on their attitudes and their vigour with respect to protecting human rights.

Some scholars identify human rights as those which are 'important', 'moral' and 'universal'. It is comforting to adorn human rights with those characteristics, but such attributes themselves contain ambiguities. For example, when we say a right is 'important' enough to be a 'human' right, we may be speaking of one or more of the following qualities: (1) intrinsic value, (2) instrumental value, (3) value in a scheme of rights, (4) importance in not being outweighed by other considerations, or (5) importance as structural support for the system of the good life. 'Universal' and 'moral' are perhaps even more complicated words. What makes certain rights universal, moral and important, and who decides? This is another way, perhaps, of getting at the question of what is the source or authority for human rights, or how they can be established or justified.

Approaches to these questions vary widely. Intuitive moral philosophers claim that definitions of human rights are futile because they involve moral judgments which must be self-evident and are not further explicable. Other moral philosophers, faced with the instability of meaning, focus on the consequences of human rights, or what they are for. A refinement on this process, advanced by the prescriptivist school, says that we should not be concerned with what is sought to be achieved by issuing a moral (human rights) utterance but with what is actually done in issuing it: that is what act is accomplished, what facts are brought into existence. We shall explore some of these questions in discussing the various schools of moral philosophy.

The definitional process does not become easier when we examine the second word in the term human 'rights'. Certainly, 'rights' is a chameleon-like term which can describe a variety of legal relationships. Sometimes, 'right' is used in its strict sense of the right-holder being entitled to something with a correlative duty in another. Sometimes, 'right' is used to indicate an immunity from having a legal status altered. Sometimes it indicates a privilege to do something. Sometimes, it refers to a power to create a legal relationship. Although all of these terms have been identified as rights, each invokes different protections and produces variant results.

For example, when we speak of an inalienable right, do we mean a right on which no expectations or limitations are valid? Or do we mean a prima facie right with a special burden on the proponent of any limitation? Or do we mean a principle which must be followed unless some other moral principle weighty enough to allow abridgment arises?

If we classify a right as a claim against a government to refrain from certain acts, such as not to torture its citizens or deny them freedom of speech, religion or emigration, then other complexities arise. If a particular claim stems from a metaphysical concept such as the nature of humanity, or from a religious concept such as the divine will, or from some other *a priori* concept, then the claim may really be an immunity to which normative judgments should not apply. If, however, the claim is based on certain interests such as the common good, other problems arise, such as the need to determine the common good, or the need to balance other societal interests, which may allow a wide variety of interpretations not supportive of individual human rights demands.

If we speak of the 'rights' in the International Covenant on Economic, Social and Cultural Rights, such as the right to favourable conditions of work, social security, health, education, fair wages, a decent standard of living, and even holidays with pay, what do we intend? Are these rights which individuals can assert? Or are they only aspirational goals? If they are rights, on whom are the correlative duties?

If we speak of privileges, there are other concerns. If the privileges are granted by the state, then presumably the state is entitled to condition them. Does the right of a state to derogate from rights in an international covenant mean that the rights are only privileges? Here, too, the answer is connected to the moral strength and inviolability of the 'right' or 'privilege' that is involved.

The definitional answers to these many questions are complex. And part of the complexity is that in defining we must confront the conflicts between utilitarian and anti-utilitarian philosophy, between values of equality and liberty, between absolute and relativist conceptions of rights, all issues of moral justification.

To summarize at this point, even where international law has established a conventional system of human rights, a philosophical understanding of the nature of rights is not just an academic exercise. Understanding the nature of the 'right' involved can help clarify our consideration of the degree of protection available, the nature of derogations or exceptions, the priorities to be afforded to various rights, the question of the hierarchical relationships in a series of rights, the question of whether rights 'trump' competing claims based on cultural rooting, and similar problems. To be sure, the answer to these questions may evolve over time through legal rulings, interpretations, decisions and pragmatic compromises. But how those answers emerge will be influenced, if not driven, by the moral justifications of the human rights in issue. We proceed therefore to examine the sources of human rights claims. Where do we derive the moral justifications which can be urged for or against human rights? What is their scope or content and how compelling are they?

The Basis

The term 'human rights' as such is not found in traditional religions. Nonetheless, theology presents the basis for a human rights theory stemming from a law higher than the state and whose source is the Supreme Being. Of course, this theory presupposes an acceptance of revealed doctrine as the source of such rights.

If one accepts the premise of the Old Testament that Adam was created in the 'image of God', this implies that the divine stamp gives human beings a high value of worth. In similar vein, the Koran says: 'Surely we have accorded dignity to the Sons of Man.' So too, in the Bhagavad-Gita:

> Who sees his Lord
> Within every creature
> Deathlessly dwelling
> Amidst the mortal: That man sees truly...

Put another way, in a religious context, every human being is considered sacred. Accepting a universal common father gives rise to a common humanity and from this flows a universality of certain rights. Since the rights stem from a divine source, they are inalienable by mortal authority. This concept is found not only in the Judaeo-Christian tradition but in Islam and other religions with a deistic base.''

Even if one accepts the revealed truth of the fatherhood of God and the brotherhood of all human beings, the problem remains as to which human rights flow therefrom. Equality of all human beings in the eyes of God would seem a necessary development from the common creation by God, but freedom to live as one prefers is not. Indeed, religions generally impose severe limitations on individual freedom. For most religions, the emphasis falls on duties rather than rights. Moreover, revelation is capable of differing interpretations even as to equality, and some religions have been quite restrictive towards slaves, women and non-believers, even though all are God's creations. Thus, at least as practised, there are serious incompatibilities between various religious practices and the scope of human rights structured by the United Nations.

However, religious philosophers of all faiths are engaged in the process of interpreting religious doctrines towards the end of effecting a reconciliation with basic human rights prescriptions.

This process is largely through hermeneutic exercise, namely reinterpretation of a religion's sacred texts through both historical explication and a type of prophetic application to modern conditions.

Hence, despite the problems in the theological approach, religious doctrine offers a promising but still largely undeveloped possibility of selecting elements of various religious traditions to construct a broad intercultural rationale which supports the various fundamental principles of equality and justice which underlie international human rights. Indeed, once the leap to belief has been made, religion may be the most attractive of the theoretical approaches. When human beings are not visualized in God's image then their basic rights may well lose their metaphysical *raison detre*. On the other hand, the concept of human beings created in the image of God certainly endows men and women with a worth and dignity from which can logically flow the components of a comprehensive human rights system.

Right to be Born

Philosophers and jurists did not leave human rights solely to theologians. In their search for a law which was higher than positive law, they developed the theory of natural law. Natural law theory has underpinnings in Sophocles and Aristotle, but it was first elaborated by the stoics of the Greek Hellenistic period and later of the Roman period. Natural law, they believed, embodied those elementary principles of justice which were right reason, that is in accordance with nature, unalterable and eternal. A classic example is that of Antigone, who defied Creon's command not to bury her slain brother by claiming that she was obeying immutable laws higher than the ruler's command.

Mediaeval Christian philosophers, such as Thomas Aquinas, put great stress on natural law, as conferring certain immutable rights upon individuals as part of the law of God. But there were critical limitations in the mediaeval concepts which recognized slavery and serfdom, thus excluding central ideas of freedom and equality.

As feudalism declined, modern secular theories of natural law arose, particularly as enunciated by Hugo Grotius and Samuel von Pufendorf. Their philosophy detached natural law from religion, laying the groundwork for the secular, rationalistic version of modern natural law. According to Grotius, a natural characteristic of human beings is the social impulse to live peacefully and in harmony with others. Whatever conformed to the nature of men and women as rational, social beings was right and just; whatever opposed it by disturbing the social harmony was wrong and unjust. Grotius defined natural law as a 'dictate of right reason'; that is, an act, according to whether it is or is not in conformity with rational nature, has in it a quality of moral necessity or moral baseness.

Grotius, it should be noted, was also a father of modern international law. He saw the law of nations as embodying both laws which have as their source the will of man and laws derived from the principles of the law of nature. This theory, of course, has immense importance for the status and legitimacy of human rights as part of a system of international law.

Natural law theory led to natural rights theory, the theory most closely associated with modern human rights. The chief exponent of this theory was John Locke, who developed his philosophy within the framework of seventeenth-century humanism and political activity, known as the Age of Enlightenment. Locke imagined the existence of human beings in a state of nature. In that state, men and women were in a state of freedom, able to determine their actions and also in a state of equality in the sense that no one was subjected to the will or authority of another. However, to end the hazards and inconveniences of the state of nature, men and women entered into a social contract' by which they mutually agreed to form a community and set up a body politic. However, in setting up that political authority, individuals retained the natural rights of life, liberty and property which were their own. Government was obliged to protect the natural rights of its subjects and, if government neglected this obligation, it would forfeit its validity and office.

In practice, natural rights theory was the philosophical impetus for the wave of revolt against absolutism during the late eighteenth century. It is seen in the French Declaration of the Rights of Man, in the United States Declaration of Independence, and later in the constitutions of numerous states created upon liberation from colonialism and, still later, in the principal United Nations human rights documents.

Natural rights theory makes an important contribution to human rights. It affords an appeal from the realities of naked power to a higher authority which is asserted for the protection of human rights. It identifies with human freedom and equality from which other human rights easily flow. And it provides properties of security and support for a human rights system, both domestically and internationally.

From a philosophical viewpoint, the critical problem which natural rights doctrine faced is how to determine the norms that are to be considered as part of the law of nature and therefore inalienable, or at least prima facie inalienable.

Under Locke's view of human beings in the state of nature, all that was needed was the opportunity to be self-dependent; life, liberty and property were the inherent rights which met this demand. But what of a world unlike the times of Locke, in which there are not ample resources to satisfy human needs? Does natural law theory have the flexibility to satisfy new claims based on contemporary conditions and modern human understanding? Perhaps it does, but that very potential for flexibility has been the basis for the chief criticism of natural rights theory. Critics pointed out that most of the norm setting of natural rights theories contain *a priori* elements deduced by the norm setter. In short, the principal problem with natural law is that the rights considered to be natural can differ from theorist to theorist, depending upon their conceptions of nature.

Because of this and other difficulties, natural rights theory became unpopular with legal scholars and philosophers. However, in revised form, natural rights philosophy had a renaissance in the aftermath of the Second World War, as we shall discuss shortly.

Government's Role

The assault upon natural law intensified during the nineteenth and twentieth centuries. John Stuart Mill claimed that rights are founded on utility. Karl von Savigny in Germany and Sir Henry Maine in England claimed that rights are a function of cultural variables. But the most serious attack on natural law came from a doctrine called legal positivism. This philosophy came to dominate legal theory during most of the nineteenth century and commands considerable allegiance in the twentieth.

Classical positivist philosophers deny an *a priori* source of rights and assume that all authority stems from what the state and officials have prescribed. This approach rejects any attempt to discern and articulate an idea of law transcending the empirical realities of existing legal systems. In its essence, this view negates the moral philosophical basis of human rights. Under positivist theory, the source of human rights is to be found only in the enactments of a system of law with sanctions attached to it. Views on what the law 'ought' to be have no place in law and are cognitively worthless. The need to distinguish with maximum clarity law as it is from what it ought to be is the theme that haunted positivist exponents, and they condemned natural law thinkers because they had blurred this vital distinction.

A principal criticism of this theory is that, under positivism, the law is no better than the source of its authority, an authority whose tradition may embody concepts which do not further human rights and which are, indeed, anti-human rights. By philosophically divorcing a legal system from the ethical and moral foundations of society, positive law encourages the belief that law must be obeyed, no matter how immoral it may be or however it disregards the world of the individual. The anti-Semitic edicts of the Nazis, although abhorrent to moral law, were obeyed as positive law. The same is true of the immoral apartheid practices which prevailed in South Africa for many years. The fact that positivist philosophy has been used to justify obedience to iniquitous laws has been a central focus for much of the modern criticism of that doctrine. Critics of positivism maintain that unjust laws not only lack a capacity to demand fidelity but also do not deserve the name of law because they lack internal morality.

Even granting the validity of the criticism, the positivist contribution can still be significant. If the state's processes can be brought to bear in the protection of human rights, it becomes easier to focus upon the specific implementation which is necessary for the protection of particular rights. Indeed, positivist thinkers such as Bentham and Austin were often in the vanguard of those who sought to bring about reform in the law. A positivist system also offers flexibility to meet changing needs, since it is always under human control.

The methodology of the positivist jurists in the technical building of legal conceptions is also pragmatically useful in developing a system of rights in international law. For example, the human rights treaties adopted by the United Nations reflect a positive set of rights, that is rules developed by the sovereign states themselves and then made part of a system of international law. While many states may differ on the theoretical basis of these rules, the rules themselves remain to provide a legal grounding for human rights protection. On other hand, in theory, positivism tends to undermine an international basis for human rights because of the emphasis positivists place on the supremacy of national sovereignty without accepting the restraining influence of an inherent right above the state. Under this view, rules of international law are not law but merely rules of positive morality set or imposed by opinion.

Furthermore, by emphasizing the role of the nation-state as the source of law, the positivist approach produces the view that the individual has no status in international law.

Social Aspects

Contrasted with natural law is Marxist theory an approach which is also concerned with the nature of human beings. However, here the view of men and women is not of autonomous individuals with rights developed from either a divine or inherent nature, but of men and women as 'specie beings'.

While the influence of Marxism has diminished considerably since the fall of communism in Eastern Europe, Marxism, which was a dominant philosophy in much of the world for many years and in variant forms, is not without influence still, particularly in assigning values to social and economic rights.

Marx regarded the law of nature approach to human rights as idealistic and historical. He saw nothing natural or inalienable about human rights. In a society in which capitalists monopolize the means of production, he regarded the notion of individual rights as a bourgeois illusion. Concepts such as law, justice, morality, democracy, freedom, and so on were considered as historical categories, whose content is determined by the material conditions and the social circumstances of a people. As the conditions of life change, so the content of notions and ideas may change.

Marxism sees a person's essence as the potential to use one's abilities to the fullest and to satisfy one's needs. Since, in capitalist society, production is controlled by a few, such a society cannot satisfy those individual needs. An actualization of potential is contingent on the return of men and women to themselves as social beings which occurs in a Communist society devoid of class conflict. However, until that stage is reached, the state is a social collectivity and is the vehicle for the transformation of society. Such a conceptualization of the nature of society precludes the existence of individual rights rooted in the state of nature which are prior to the state. Only rights which are granted by the state exist, and their exercise is contingent on the fulfilment of obligations to society and to the state.

The Marxist system of rights has often been referred to as 'parental', with the authoritarian political body providing the sole guidance in value choice. Marxism, as applied in communist doctrine, claims further that, no matter what the actual wishes of men and women may be, their true choice is to choose the goals the state sets.' The creation of such a 'specie being' is a type of paternalism which not only ignores transcendental reason but negates individuality. In practice, pursuit of the prior claims of society as reflected by the interests of the communist state has resulted in systematic suppression of individual civil and political rights.

On an international level, Marxist theory has proved incompatible with a functioning universal system of human rights. The prior claims of a communist society do not recognize overruling by international norms. While communist governments may admit a theoretical recognition of the competence of the international community to establish transnational norms, the application of those norms is held to be a matter of exclusive domestic jurisdiction. The repeated assertions over the years by communist states in international fora that their alleged abuse of human rights is a matter of exclusive domestic jurisdiction is not just a matter of protecting sovereignty or avoiding the embarrassment of international examination. It may be such, but it also reflects communist theory on the unlimited role of the state to decide what is good for the 'specie beings'. Be that as it may, the influence of Marxism on human rights concepts has declined, as Marxism itself has ironically become a historical category with lessening philosophical impact.

To many scholars, each of the theories of rights discussed so far is deficient. Moreover, the twentieth century is quite a different place from the nineteenth. Natural and social sciences developed and began to increase understanding about people and their cultures, their conflicts and their interests. Anthropology, psychology and other disciplines lent their insights. These developments inspired what has been called the sociological school of jurisprudence. 'School' is perhaps a misnomer, since what has evolved is a number of disparate theories which have the common denominator of trying to line up the law with the facts of human life in society Sociological jurisprudence tends to move away from both *a priori* theories and analytical types of jurisprudence. This approach, insofar as it relates to human rights, sometimes directs attention to the questions of institutional development; sometimes focuses on specific problems of public policy which have a bearing on human rights; sometimes aims at classifying behavioural dimensions of law and society. In a human rights context, the approach is useful in that it identifies the empirical components of a human rights system in the context of the social process.

A primary contribution of the sociological school is its emphasis on obtaining a just equilibrium of interests among prevailing moral sentiments and the social and economic conditions of time and place. In many ways this approach can be said to build on William James's pragmatic principle that 'the essence of good is simply to satisfy demand'. This approach also was related to the development in twentieth-century society of increased demands for a variety of wants beyond classical civil and political liberties: such matters as help for the unemployed, the handicapped, the underprivileged, minorities and other elements of society.

It is not possible here to outline the particular approaches of the leading sociological thinkers, but Roscoe Pound's analysis merits special reference. Pound pointed out that, during the nineteenth century, the history of the law was written largely as a record of an increasing recognition of individual rights. In the twentieth century, however, this history should be written in terms of a continually widening recognition of human wants, human demands and social interests. Pound catalogued the interests as individual, public and social. He did not try to give value preferences to these interests. His guiding principle was one of 'social engineering'; that is, the ordering of human relations through politically organized society so as to secure all interests insofar as this was possible with the least sacrifice of the totality of interests.

The approach of Pound and his progeny usefully enlarges our understanding of the scope of human rights and their correlation with demands. His identification of the interests involved takes into account the realities of the social process; he shows us how to focus on rights in terms of what people are concerned about and what they want. He makes us 'result-minded, cause-minded and process-minded'.

However, an approach which merely catalogues human demands is deficient in failing to focus on how rights are interrelated or what the priorities should be. The sociological school does not answer the logical question of how a normative conclusion about rights can be empirically derived from factual premises such as having interests. A descriptive science in the social human rights field is helpful but not enough to satisfy the need of goal identification. The sociological approach thus provides a useful method, but a method in need of a philosophy. Nonetheless, by providing a quantitative survey of the interests which demand satisfaction, this school sharpens perceptions of the values involved and the policies necessary to achieve them.

Recent Trends

Rights Based on Natural Rights: Core Rights : The aftermath of the Second World War brought about a revival of natural rights theory. Certainly, this was due in part to the revulsion against Nazism which revealed the horrors that could emanate from a positivist system in which the individual counted for nothing. It was not surprising that there should emerge a renewed search for immutable principles which would protect humanity against such brutality.

There is, of course, a large variety of presentations and analyses among scholars addressing theories of moral philosophy." While the new rights philosophers do not wear the same metaphysical dress as the early expounders of the Rights of Man, most adopt what may be called a qualified natural law approach, in that they try to identify the values which have an eternal and universal aspect. They agree that only a positive legal system which meets those values can function as an effective legal system. In a larger sense, the object of much of revived natural rights thought can be viewed as attempts to work out the principles which might reconcile the 'is' and the 'ought' in law.

The common theme which has emerged from a huge family of theories is that a minimum absolute or core postulate of any just and universal system of rights must include some recognition of the value of individual freedom or autonomy. Underlying such foundational or core rights theory is the omnipresence of Immanuel Kant's compelling ethic. Kant's ethic maintains that persons typically have different desires and ends, so any principle derived from them can only be contingent. But the moral law needs a categorical foundation, not a contingent one. The basis for moral law must be prior to all purposes and ends. The basis is the individual as a transcendental subject capable of an autonomous will. Rights then flow from the autonomy of the individual in choosing his or her ends, consistent with a similar freedom for all.

In short, Kant's great imperative is that the central focus of morality is 'personhood', namely the capacity to take responsibility as a free and rational agent for one's system of ends. A natural corollary of this Kantian thesis is that the highest purpose of human life is to will autonomously. A person must always be treated as an end and the highest purpose of the state is to promote conditions favouring the free and harmonious unfolding of individuality. Kant's theory being transcendental, *a priori* and categorical (all amount to the same thing) overrides all arbitrary distinctions of race, creed and custom and is universal in nature."

In variant forms, modern human rights core theories seem to

be settling for concepts of natural necessity, that is, necessity in the sense of prescribing a minimum definition of what it means to be human in any morally tolerable form of society.

Put another way, some modes of treatment of human beings are so fundamental to the existence of anything we would be willing to call a society that it makes better sense to treat an acceptance of them as constitutive of man and woman as social beings rather than as artificial conventions. This view does not entail verified propositions, as science requires. Rather, it views human life as encompassing certain freedom and sensibilities without which the designation 'human' would not make sense. To use a linguistic metaphor, humanity has a grammatical form of which certain basic human rights are a necessary part. This concept of what we take human beings to be is a profound one, even if it is deemed self-evident.

To be sure, there is a certain aspect of vindication to many of the new individualist theories. They can be viewed as saying that, if we adopt certain human rights (freedom of thought, equality) as norms, we can produce a certain kind of society; and, if one finds that kind of society desirable, one should adopt the norms and call them absolute principles. This, of course, is a type of tautology. Then, again, tautologies can be significant, if society is willing to accept them.

The renaissance of qualified or modified natural rights or core theories has had a seminal influence on conventional international human rights norms. A reflection of that influence is found in the Universal Declaration of Human Rights itself, which begins with the following concept: 'Whereas recognition of the inherent dignity and of the equal and inalienable rights of all members of the human family is the foundation of freedom, justice and peace in the world'. In a similar vein, Article 1 provides: 'All human beings are born free and equal in dignity. They are endowed with reason and conscience and should act toward one another in a spirit of brotherhood.' The debt that 'inherent dignity' and 'inalienable rights' owe to natural law philosophy is obvious. The key human rights treaties also reflect quite directly the moral universalist foundations we have just discussed.

The philosophical justification and affirmation of the core principles of human rights as universal principles are, of course, highly significant and reassuring for the vitality of human rights in rules for the world of nations. Rights which preserve the integrity of the person flow logically from the fundamental freedom and autonomy of the person. So does the principle of non-discrimination which must attach to any absolute concept of autonomy. However, affirming such basic or core principles is one thing; working out all the other elements of a complete system of rights such as international law seeks to provide, is something else. What rights derive from those we deem core rights? How are they developed with generic consistency? By what theory do we test the legitimacy of an overall system? In the next sections, we shall discuss some of the leading rights theories which have wrestled with the methodology and justification of an overall system of rights.

Practical Views

'Consequentialism' is a school of modern moral philosophy which embraces the family of utilitarian theories. Generally, it may be described as holding that actions and other objects of moral assessment are justified only if their consequences have more intrinsic value than alternative actions. Classic utilitarianism, the most explored branch of this school, is a moral theory that judges the rightness of actions which affect outcomes in terms of securing the greatest happiness to all concerned. Utilitarian theory played a commanding role in the philosophy and political theory of the nineteenth century and continues with vigour in the twenty first.

The approach to the problem of rights through theories of values has an obvious attraction. Utilitarian theories have a teleological structure; that is, they seek to define notions of right solely in terms of tendencies to promote certain specified ends. An ontological commitment may not be necessary here (at least, it is not so evident), since values (equality, happiness, liberty, dignity, respect, and so on) concern behaviour and are not known in a metaphysical sense but rather are accepted and acted upon.

Jeremy Bentham, who expounded classical utilitarianism, believed that every human decision was motivated by some calculation of pleasure and pain. He thought that every political decision should be made on the same calculation, that is to maximize the net produce of pleasure over pain. Hence, both governments and the limits of governments were to be judged not by reference to abstract individual rights but in terms of what tends to promote the greatest happiness of the greatest number.

Under utilitarian doctrine, all count equally at the primary level and any of us may have to accept sacrifices if the benefits they yield to others are large enough to outweigh them. In short, utilitarianism is a maximizing and collectivizing principle which requires governments to maximize the total net sum of the happiness of all their subjects. This principle is in contrast to natural rights theory, which is a distributive and individualizing principle that assigns priority to the specific basic interests of each individual subject.

Bentham's happiness principle enjoyed enormous popularity and influence during the first half of the nineteenth century, when most reformers spoke the language of utilitarianism. Nonetheless, Bentham's principle met with no shortage of criticism. His 'felicific calculus'; that is, adding and subtracting the pleasure and pain units of different persons to determine what would produce the greatest net balance of happiness, has come to be viewed as a practical, if not a theoretical, impossibility.

Later utilitarian thinkers have restated the doctrine in terms of 'revealed preferences'. Here, the rule-utilitarian guide for governmental conduct would not be pleasure or happiness but an economically focused value of general welfare, reflecting the maximum satisfaction and minimum frustration of wants and preferences.

Such restatements of utilitarian theory have an obvious appeal in the sphere of economic decision making. Even then, there are conceptual and practical problems which plague utilitarian value theory, such as the ambiguities of the welfare concept, the nature of the person who is the subject of welfare, the uncertain basis of individual preference whose satisfaction is at issue, and other problems inherent in the process of identifying the consequences of an act and in estimating the value of the consequences.

For our discussion here, what is particularly relevant is the modern criticism of utilitarianism on the ground that it fails to recognize individual autonomy or, put another way, it fails to take rights seriously. The criticism is along the following lines: utilitarianism, however refined, retains the central principle of maximizing the aggregate desires or general welfare as the ultimate criterion of value.

While utilitarianism treats persons as equals, it does so only in the sense of including them in the mathematical equation, and not in the sense of attributing to each individual worth. Under the utilitarian equation, one individual's desires or welfare may be sacrificed as long as aggregate satisfaction or welfare is increased. Utilitarianism thus fails to treat persons as equals, in that it literally dissolves moral personality into utilitarian aggregates. Moreover, the mere increase in aggregate happiness or welfare, if abstracted from questions of distribution and worth of the individual, is not a real value or true moral goal.

Hence, despite the egalitarian pretensions of utilitarian doctrine, it has a sinister side in which the well-being of the individual may be sacrificed for what are claimed to be aggregate interests, and justice and right do not have a secure place. Utilitarian philosophy thus leaves liberty and rights vulnerable to contingencies and therefore at risks. In an era characterized by inhumanity, the dark side of utilitarianism made it too suspect to be accepted as a prevailing philosophy. Indeed, most modern moral theorists seem to have reached an anti-utilitarian consensus, at least in recognizing certain basic individual rights as constraints on any maximizing aggregative principle. In Ronald Dworkin's felicitous phrase, rights must be 'trumps' over countervailing utilitarian calculations.

Equality in Society

The monumental thesis of modern philosophy is John Rawl's. *A Theory of Justice* 'Justice is the first virtue of social institutions,' says Rawls. Human rights, of course, are an end of justice; consequently, the role of justice is crucial to understanding human rights. No theory of human rights for a domestic or international order in modern society can be advanced today without considering Rawls's thesis, and we discuss this theory here more than any other contemporary ones.

Principles of justice, according to Rawls, prcvide a way of assigning rights and duties in the basic institutions of society. These principles define the appropriate distribution of the benefits and burdens of social cooperation. Rawl's thesis is that each person possesses 'an inviolability founded on justice' which even the welfare of society as a whole cannot override. 'Justice denies that the loss of freedom for some is made right by a greater good shared by others. Therefore, in a just society the liberties of equal citizenship are settled; the rights secured by justice are not subject to political bargaining or to the calculus of social interests.'

But what are the rights of justice? Put another way, what are the principles of morality or the foundation of rules which would be agreed upon by all members of a society? Rawls assumes that the principles of justice (morality) are not self-evident to our common sense but that they can be formulated through the tradition of the social contract in moral and political philosophy.

To set the stage for ascertaining the principles of justice, Rawls imagines a group of men and women who have come together to form a social contract. He conceives the contractors in an original position. What is this original position? It is one of equality of the contractor with respect to power and freedom. It is taken for granted that all know the general principles of human psychology, sociology, economics, social organization and the theory of human institutions. However, the contractors are under a 'veil of ignorance' as to the particular circumstances of their own society or of their individual race, sex, social position, wealth, talents, opinions, aspirations and tastes. Therefore they are prevented from making a self-interested decision, which otherwise would corrupt the fairness of their judgment. In that hypothetical original position, all of the contractors would consider only their own self-interest, which is to acquire a sufficiency of primary human goods, namely fundamental liberties, rights and opportunities of income and wealth, and as social bases of self-esteem. Hence, in the original position, contractors would choose a basic structure for society fairly, because they would be abstracted from knowing the detailed facts about their own condition in the real world.

Rawls then tries to show that, if these men and women were rational and acted only in their self-interest under a 'veil of ignorance', they would choose principles which would be good for all of the members, not simply to the advantage of some. The answers given by those in the original position may then be taken as a blueprint or as a pattern for the establishment of laws which are worthy of the universal assent of citizens everywhere. In other words, their choices would be the basis for the ordering of a just society in any time or place. Rawl's system thus allows us to derive universal principles of justice (morality) acceptable to all rational human beings.

What particular principles would be chosen? Rawls claims that, if the contractors in the original position are rational and act in a condition of disinterestedness or ignorance of their own status and prospects, they will choose two principles of justice.

Rawls's First Principle is that 'each person is to have an equal right to the most extensive total system of equal basic liberties compatible with a similar system of liberty for all' (para. 47).

Sensible persons would choose a society founded on such a principle, because under a veil of ignorance they would calculate that such a rule would best allow them to pursue their own interests.

Rawls's Second Principle deals with distributive justice. It holds that 'Social and economic inequalities are to be arranged so they are both (a) to the greatest benefit of the least advantaged, consistent with a just savings principle and (b) attached to positions and offices open to all under condition of fair equality of opportunity' (ibid.). The general conception of justice behind these two principles reached in the original position is one of 'fairness'.

Rawls's principles of justice are arranged in a hierarchy The first priority is that of liberty. Liberty can be restricted only for the sake of liberty. There are two such cases: (1) a less extensive liberty must strengthen the total system of liberty shared by all, and (2) a less than equal liberty must be acceptable to those citizens with the lesser liberty.

The First Principle focuses on the basic liberties. Which are they? Rawls does not enumerate them precisely but indicates, roughly speaking, that they include political liberty, freedom of speech and assembly, liberty of conscience and thought, freedom of the person (along with the right to hold personal property) and freedom from arbitrary arrest and seizure. These liberties are all required to be equal by the First Principle, since citizens of a just society are to have the same basic rights. Rawls applies a value criterion in determining basic liberties. He believes that a liberty is more or less significant depending on whether it serves the full, informal and effective exercise of the moral powers.

Rawls's Second Principle focuses on the problem of distributive justice. Clause (a) states Rawls's Difference Principle, a strongly egalitarian conception which holds that, unless there is a distribution which makes both groups better off, an equal distribution is preferred. Thus, the higher expectations of those better situated are just only if they are part of a scheme which improves the expectations of the least advantaged, In Rawls's theory, the Difference Principle is the most egalitarian principle which it would be rational to adopt among the various available alternatives.

Rawls recognizes that a person may be unable to take advantage of rights and opportunities as a result of poverty and ignorance and a general lack of means. These factors, however, are not considered to be constraints on liberty; rather, they are matters which affect the 'worth' or 'value' of liberty. Liberty is represented by the complete system of the liberties, while the worth of liberty to persons and groups is proportional to their capacity to advance their ends within the framework the system defines. The basic liberties must be held equally. But the worth of liberty may vary, because of inequality in wealth, income or authority. Therefore some have greater means to achieve their aims than others. However, the lesser worth of liberty is compensated for by the Difference Principle discussed above. Rawls, in short, builds a two-part structure of liberty which allows a reconciliation of liberty and equality.

This, of course, is highly abstract philosophy and not easily digested. When one tries to apply Rawls's principles to the non-metaphorical world, some difficult empirical questions arise.

Consider, for example, the basic civil and political liberties identified by Rawls which involve recognition of individual autonomy. The demands made are of a negative sort; they principally involve non-interference with the equal sharing of basic liberties by individuals. Rawls's overriding principle of justice requires that all citizens share these liberties equally, as indeed international law provides. Here the respective positions of modern utilitarian, egalitarian and natural rights philosophy all equally seem to be in general agreement. Moreover, groupings are not empirically difficult. The inclusion of all persons in these liberties does not negate or reduce the share of any, hence there is probably the least chance of a clash with other values. In constructing a rights system, it is therefore appropriate to impose a heavy burden on those who would treat persons unequally by denying any of them basic liberties.

But, in the real world, will there not be clashes between liberty and other interests, such as public order and security, or efficient measures for public health and safety? To solve this conflict, Rawls suggests a Principle of Reconciliation under which basic liberties may be restricted only when methods of reasoning acceptable to all make it clear that unrestricted liberties will lead to consequences generally agreed to be harmful for all. This Principle of Reconciliation is that of the common interest. Put another way, a basic liberty may be limited only in cases where there would be an advantage to the total system of basic liberty.

With respect to Rawls's Second Principle (Clause (b)), the problems are more complex. Here Rawls holds that a condition of distributive justice is fair equality of opportunity. Opportunity, stated as a principle of non-discrimination, is easy to put into legal precept and, in fact, international human rights covenants and many domestic constitutions provide that there should be no discrimination by virtue of sex, race, religion or national origin. However, empirical knowledge tells us that equality of opportunity is not enough because society creates the conditions of the pursuit, thereby affecting the outcome.

For example, a person who grows up under conditions of discrimination and deprivation has less opportunity to get into a college than someone from the mainstream of society with a good elementary and secondary education. Hence, to provide equality of opportunity it is necessary to compensate for unequal starting points. But the opportunities of others also should be protected. Our object, therefore, is to give those who have had an unequal start the necessary handicap points and yet not denigrate the opportunities of others. Whether we utilize subsidies, special courses, quotas or affirmative action programmes depends on how compelling we view the obligation to provide equality of opportunity. Here there may be substantial differences between a utilitarian and egalitarian approach. In some democratic states, for example, affirmative action programmes for minorities have met a utilitarian backlash. It is not easy to resolve the differences, but understanding the moral conceptions enables us to focus on reconciliation of competing views.

With respect to a more equal apportionment of economic benefits derived under Rawls's Second Principle and the Difference Principle, even more difficult problems arise since the demands on society are heavier. Economic benefits may range from modest ones, such as free education, aid to the elderly and to the handicapped, social security, and so on, to major redistributions of wealth. But obviously, such benefits are not achieved merely by a negative restraint on government; tinkering with distribution is required. But how much tinkering with the distribution system is suitable, and to what desirable ends? As reasonable moral persons interested in both the well-being of the individual and the common good, we might recognize that certain economic needs of those at the bottom strata of society present so imperative a claim for relief that they outweigh a larger aggregate of benefits to those higher on the economic scale. One's moral theory affects what one is willing to accept as relevant facts, as well as the degree of sacrifice one is willing to accept to further egalitarian goals.

Rawls's Difference Principle addresses this issue. But if we acknowledge the claims for more equitable distribution of economic benefits, we still have to decide at what point on the spectrum we draw the line and say that the claims for equality do not outweigh the competing values of liberty or the utilitarian, aggregate benefits which will be decreased by meeting the claims. It may be that, in any particular social structure, the inequalities allowed under the Difference Principle would produce a minimum distribution of goods and benefits too small to satisfy the reasonable demands of the least advantaged, or too large to command acceptance by the advantaged.

Rawls's thesis presents still more difficult moral issues of distributive justice in the international context. For example, many developing nations are economically disadvantaged and their disadvantages can only be redressed by substantial transfer to them of resources, technology and other benefits from developed countries. The sources of those inequalities compete for dominance in determining the appropriate moral response.

One basis put forward for the disadvantages suffered by developing nations is that developed countries caused the disadvantages through colonialism, imperialism, racism and other exploitation. If developed states accept that claim, the moral response should be that the entity which caused the harm should remedy it or, at least, contribute substantially to the remedy. If, however, the accusation is rejected (as unfair, too old, inaccurate and so on), the moral justification for a response is different. The developed countries may still be willing to help lessen international economic inequality, but that task may be undertaken not out of guilt or the need to make reparations but out of a utilitarian calculus that includes such values as increasing markets, creating alliances or lessening tension.

However, the utilitarian calculation may not warrant any substantial reallocation. Or the response may be elicited through the moral obligation to advance a just world order along the Rawlsian Difference Principle. But here the Rawlsian concept may impose conditions: for example, in the latter case, donor states may require the receiving states to accommodate certain civil and political liberties which are part of the donors' concept of justice, as a reciprocal element of (or the price for) a more just international system.

These issues are obviously quite complicated, with numerous considerations of realpolitik intersecting. But even this short discussion shows that the tough issues of fulfilling economic and social rights, on both a domestic and international level, cannot be divorced from the moral issues which swirl around modern moral and political philosophy. The contribution of moral theories to solutions of problems in the legal and political order may be impeded by lack of comprehension or inept articulation, but the interlacing is not barred by triviality or irrelevance.

Critics of Rawls's theory maintain that it was designed to support the institutions of modern democracy in a domestic state context. But even if that were the case, it does not refute his moral thesis, or an international extension of it. Indeed, even if Rawls's theory was intended as a model for domestic states, its duplication can further an international just order. This is because, in the real world, state parties only reach questions of international justice after dealing, first, with the basic structure of the state's institutions and, second, with the rights and duties of individual members. If Rawls's moral principles produce justice for individuals in a domestic state, that is a long step towards gaining the domestic state's endorsement of and adherence to international human rights principles. In this regard, the international world order is no greater than the sum of its state parts. Hence, if the Rawlsian moral schemata contributes to a realization of domestic justice by the various state parts, the prescriptions of international human rights will invariably be served.

Rawls himself has suggested that his model can be applied to a world order, if one extends the concept of the original position and thinks of the parties as representatives of different states which must choose together the fundamental principles to adjudicate claims among states (para. 57). However, as Thomas M. Franck has pointed out, once the actors in the original position are representatives of states, the dynamic changes, and it is not clear that they would opt for moral principles which further human rights unless they themselves are representatives of just states. It is a fair point that the implications of Rawls's model on an international level still need to be worked through. In any event, Rawls's moral structure, showing how the values of liberty and equality underlying the nature of the autonomous human can be realized in open institutional forms, should at least be morally compelling for a world in which large segments of humanity suffer oppression and poverty and deprivation of civil, political, social and economic rights.

One cannot cover Rawls's highly complex neo-Kantian theory or deal with the considerable critical analysis of it in a few pages, but even brief discussion shows the importance of his theory for the moral justification of a rights-based system of government under a participatory structure. Rawls effects a reconciliation of tensions between egalitarianism and non-interference, between demands for freedom by the advantaged and demands for equality by the less advantaged. His structure of social justice maximizes liberty and the worth of liberty to both groups. One may also consider whether Rawls's thesis is reflected in the consensus on human rights to be found in the international human rights covenants, and whether, in fact, most of the nations have tacitly agreed to a social contract in this area. Rawls's theory is obviously comforting for the construct of constitutional democracy as well as for the concept of the universality of human rights.

Expedition against Suppression

At least brief mention should be made of Professor Edmund Cahn's theory of justice. While Cahn's theory no longer has the influence it once enjoyed, it has a particular appeal to human rights activists. Cahn asserts that, although there may be universal *a priori* truths concerning justice from which rights or norms may be deduced, it is better to approach justice from its negative rather than its affirmative side. In other words, it is much easier to identify injustice from experience and observation than it is to identify justice. Furthermore, says Cahn, where justice is thought of in the customary manner as an ideal mode or condition (for example, Rawls), the human response will be contemplative and 'contemplation bakes no loaves'. But the response to a real or imagined instance of injustice is alive with movement and warmth, producing outrage and anger. Therefore, he concludes, justice is the active process of remedying or preventing what arouses the sense of injustice. An examination of the instances which will be considered injustice thereby allows a positive formulation of justice.

This concept of the need to right wrong has the capacity to produce action. The practical starting point may well be the strongly felt response to words which move one with emotional force and practical urgency to press for the satisfaction or repair of some need, deprivation, threat or insecurity. Such an approach obviously will find a response in human rights advocates anxious to focus public attention on the injustice of the wide variety of egregious human rights abuses which remain prevalent.

However, when we get to the more sophisticated kinds of entitlements arising from considerations of social justice, there is less agreement on what constitutes injustice, and Cahn's insight offers less help. Here we need an overall structure of the type presented by moral philosophers such as Rawls, Ackerman or Gewirth. Still, Cahn's insight is useful; in the end it may well be that we will secure only those rights for which we are aroused to fight.

***Rights Based on Dignity*:** A number of human rights theorists have tried to construct a comprehensive system of human rights based on a value-policy oriented approach founded on the protection of human dignity. Some religious philosophers, finding dignity the inherent quality of the sacredness of human beings, believe that an entire rights system can flow from that concept. A secular exposition of that theory is best presented by McDougal, Lasswell and Chen, who proceed on the premise that demands for human rights are demands for wide sharing in all the values upon which human rights depend and for effective participation in all community value processes. The interdependent values, which can all fall under the rubric of human dignity, are the demands relating to : (1) respect, (2) power, (3) enlightenment, (4) well-being, (5) health, (6) skill, (7) affection, and (8) rectitude. The authors assemble a huge catalogue of the aemands which satisfy these eight values, as well as all of the ways in which they are denigrated.

McDougal et al., find a great disparity between the rising common demands of people for human dignity values and the achievement of them. This disparity is due to 'environmental' factors, such as population, resources and institutional arrangements, and also to 'predispositional factors'; that is, special interests seeking 'short-term payoffs' in defiance of the common interests which would further human rights values. The ultimate goal, as they see it, is a world community in which a democratic distribution of values is encouraged and promoted, all available resources are utilized to the maximum, and the protection of human dignity is regarded as a paramount objective of social policy. While they call their approach a policy-oriented perspective, their choice of human dignity as the super-value in the shaping and sharing of all other values has a natural rights ring to it.

Their approach too has been criticized as having a Western orientation which it does, but that does not mean it is wrong. A more telling criticism is the difficulty in making use of their system. Their list of demands is huge, there is no hierarchical order, both trivial and serious claims are intertwined, and it has a utopian aspect which belies reality. Still, McDougal et al., have shown how a basic value such as dignity - a value on which most people would agree - can be a springboard for structuring a rights system. Even if one disagrees with their formulation, they have opened the door to a more simple and useful construction built on their insights.

Self-honour

A striking aspect of modern theorists is their pronounced effort to reconcile different theories of rights. In this regard, in our discussion of modern theories, we must consider the work of Ronald Dworkin, who offers a promising reconciliation theory between natural rights and utilitarian theories. Dworkin proceeds from the postulate of political morality; that is, that governments must treat all their citizens with equal concern and respect. In the absence of such a premise, there is a lack of a basis for any valid discourse on rights and claims. So far so good.

Dworkin next endorses the egalitarian character of the utilitarian principle that 'everybody can count for one, nobody for more than one, a practical political application of this principle being participatory democracy. Under this principle he believes that the state may exercise wide interventionist functions in order to advance social welfare.

Dworkin believes that a right to liberty in general is too vague to be meaningful. However, certain specific liberties, such as freedom of speech, freedom of worship, rights of association and personal and sexual relations, do require special protection against government interference. This is so not because these preferred liberties have some special substantive or inherent value (as most rights philosophers hold), but because of a kind of procedural impediment which these preferred liberties might face. The impediment is that, if those liberties were left to a utilitarian calculation, that is, an unrestricted calculation of the general interest, the balance would be tipped in favour of restrictions.

Why is there such an impediment? Dworkin says that, if a vote were truly utilitarian, all voters would desire the liberties for themselves and the liberties would be protected under a utilitarian calculation. However, a vote on these liberties would not be truly utilitarian, nor would it afford equal concern about and respect for liberties solely by reflecting personal wants or satisfactions of individuals and affording equal concerns to others. This is because external preferences, such as prejudice and discrimination against other individuals deriving from the failure to generally treat other persons as equals, would enter into the picture. These external preferences would corrupt utilitarianism by causing the individual to vote against assigning liberties to others.

Accordingly, the liberties to be protected against such external preferences must be given a preferred status. By doing so, we can protect the fundamental right of citizens to equal concern and respect because we prohibit 'decisions that seem, antecedently, likely to have been reached by virtue of the external components of the preferences democracy reveals'.

The argument is attractive because Dworkin (like Rawls, but in a different way) has minimized the tension between liberty and equality. Dworkin does so without conceding a general right to liberty (which might exacerbate the tension) but by specifying particular basic liberties which must be protected to prevent corruption of a government's duty to treat persons as equals.

Dworkin's theory seems to retain both the benefits of natural rights theory without the need for an ontological commitment and the benefits of utilitarian theory without the need to sacrifice basic individual rights. His resplendent universe thus seems to accommodate the two major planets of philosophical thought. Dworkin's theory is also valuable in focusing on the relational rather than the conflicting aspects of liberty and equality. Even if one is not fully convinced at this stage by Dworkin's analysis, one has the feeling that his reconciling approach should work within the institutions of a participatory democracy.

Cultural Issues

An issue which has an impact on the moral foundations of human rights is the clash between those who evaluate human rights from the perspective of cultural relativism and those who view human rights from the universalist or individualist perspective. This clash immerses one in the vortex of modern human rights politics.

At the outset, we should make clear that the issue is not over the cultural rights dealt with in the International Covenant on Economic, Social and Cultural Rights, which encourages and protects cultural, scientific and educational knowledge and development, rights which are part of the universal system of human rights. Rather, the issue here concerns those practices which contravene universal human rights, and which practices are sought to be justified on grounds of moral or cultural relativism. It is that thesis we address here.

Cultural relativism, as a concept to justify human rights abuses on cultural grounds, has scant claim to moral validity. Still, because cultural relativism has been given the trappings of philosophical credentials even in United Nations circles, we shall analyse the concept seriously and analytically from a philosophical perspective.

As presented earlier, the universalist (foundationalist, individualist) thesis is that human rights are universal, reflecting the autonomous, individual nature of the human being. What is cultural relativism? Essentially, it is an anthropological and sociological concept loosely grounded in the theory of moral relativism. Moral relativism is not very influential in modern philosophy, but 'cultural relativism' has been frequently used as an argument against the universality of human rights.

Cultural relativists, in their most aggressive conceptual stance, argue, that there are no human rights absolutes, that the principles which we may use for judging behaviour are relative to the society in which we are raised, that there is infinite cultural variability and that all cultures are morally equal or valid. Put into a philosophical calculus, the relativist says, 'Truth is just for a time or place' identified by the standards of one's cultural peers. Relativism thus shifts the touchstones by which to measure the worth of human rights practice. To suggest that fundamental rights may be overridden or adjusted in the light of cultural practices is to challenge the underlying moral justification of a universal system of human rights.

We discussed earlier the foundations and sources of universalism and how that moral philosophy developed. What are the sources of cultural relativism? Is it a philosophy at all? How should we analyse cultural relativism in the context of international human rights.

Moral relativism, the normative basis of cultural relativism, is said to derive from the famous aphorism (of dubious meaning) of the Greek philosopher Protagoras that 'Man is the measure of all things'. Plato's Theaetus states the Protagorean thesis in terms of the community (not the individual) as the measure of all things and Plato fairly decimates the concept. The Protagorean view had, at most, a feeble foothold in philosophical thought until the late eighteenth century when Johan Gottfried von Herder, dissenting from Enlightenment philosophy, claimed that all nations had a unique way of being; there were no absolute principles but only regional and contingent ones. Condemning universal values, he introduced the concept of Volksgeist, the spirit of the people. Herder's view influenced German romanticism and French counter-revolutionary writers who glorified the aggregate of local customs and prejudices, under an umbrella called ,culture'.

From time to time during the nineteenth and early twentieth century, the claims of Volksgeist arose mostly in the European political context of ultra-nationalism versus universalist principles of the Enlightenment philosophy. In time, with the rise of pan-Germanism, culture was reduced to the cult of origins. During the Nazi period, the Volksgeist theme revealed and realized its stark and tragic totalitarian potential.

During the nineteenth-century colonial period, many anthropologists, imbued with feelings of Western superiority, viewed other cultures as 'native', 'primitive' or 'barbaric', relegating those cultures to an inferior status. During the post-Second World War period, Western anthropologists and sociologists confessed error and embraced a concept of cultural relativism as a counterpoint to colonialization. In combating colonialization, with its implications of superiority of the colonists, the French anthropologist, Claude Levi-Strauss and others of his school argued for the separate, independent value of all cultures, and also that the West should stop extending its culture to the rest of the world. The goal of bringing about independence from colonialism was certainly worthy, but the anthropologists and sociologists went further and gave cultural relativism a moral or ethical stance. In restoring to other cultures the dignity stolen from them through Western imperialism, they argued that all cultures were morally equal and that universalist values (such as universal human rights) were dead.

For the new states, the theme of cultural identity was appealing: it helped break with Western imperialism and it permitted the colonialized to affirm their cultural differences, and to turn what colonializers had mocked into a subject of pride. It was logical that most new states wanted to make their own cultural traditions part of national life and to bind individuals to the integrity and cohesion of the socially minded spirit. But in some states, pursuit of cultural identity had deleterious effects. While it was a means of resistance under colonial rule, afterwards it turned out to have a repressive side by creating an obligatory homogeneity and diminishing the place of the individual in the calculus of identity politics.

With this background, let us examine the tenets of cultural relativism, particularly in the context of international human rights. What are the objectives of cultural relativism compared to those of universalism? What are the respective camps defending? A universal moral philosophy affirms principles which protect universal, individual human rights of liberty, freedom, equality and justice everywhere, giving them a non-transient, non-legal foundation. The relativists defend a cultural conditioning which supposedly reflects a set of wants and goods that members of disparate cultural groups share (and which may include various human rights goods), but are not ones arrived at by individual choices or preserved for individuals in the community as a matter of right.

Posing the contrast this way deflates the worth of the cultural relativist position in any objective value comparison with universalist principles. But cultural relativism cannot be dismissed so readily, if only because, in the real world, repressive rulers utilize the relativist claim as justification for their ruling practices. We can all cite examples of repressive rulers who seek to rationalize repressive practices by claiming that the culture of their society accepts those practices over universalist international human rights prescriptions, and that to criticize their society's human rights practices is to impose Western cultural imperialism over their local culture. Thus, cultural relativist arguments are used to justify limitations on speech, subjugation of women, female genital mutilation, amputation of limbs and other cruel punishment, arbitrary use of power, and other violations of international human rights conventions. It is no wonder that the doctrine that human rights are contingent on cultural practice has been called the 'gift of cultural relativists to tyrants'.

Philosophical analysis requires scrutiny of the foundation of any thesis. What is the basic tenet of cultural relativism? It is that cultures manifest so wide and diverse a range of preferences, motivations and evaluations that no human rights principles can be said to be self-evident and recognized in all times and all places. Does this relativist thesis withstand scrutiny? We believe it does not. We present the reasons for this conclusion on several levels.

First, John Finnis has cogently shown that those philosophers who have surveyed modern anthropological literature have found that the basic assumption which underlies the relativist approach is unwarranted. As Finnis points out:

> All human societies show a concern for the value of human life ... in none is the killing of other human beings permitted without some fairly definite justification. In all societies there is some prohibition of incest, some opposition to boundless promiscuity and to rape, some favour for stability and permanence in sexual relations. All human societies display a concern for truth ... all societies display a favour for the values of co-operation, of common over individual good, of obligation between individuals, and of justice

> within groups. All know friendship. All have some conception of title or property, and of reciprocity... All display a concern for powers or principles which are to be respected as suprahuman; in one form or another, religion is universal.

Here, in short, is a universality of basic moral requirements manifested in value judgments.

One, therefore, should not have to probe deeply to conclude that there is a universal cultural receptivity to such fundamental rights as freedom from torture, slavery and arbitrary execution, due process of law and freedom to travel. Moreover, any observer of state practice can cite example after example where repression which one authoritarian government excuses as cultural identity turns out not to be a cultural tradition at all, when a democratic government replaces the authoritarian one. Further, there are many examples of peoples of like cultures living virtually side by side, where one state condemns human rights abuses and a counterpart state creates abuses. Thus, most human rights abuses are not legitimately identified with the authentic culture of any society, only with authoritarian rulers of that society.

Indeed, even most confirmed relativist scholars are repulsed at practices which are highly coercive and abusive and accept that at least some human rights values are absolute. This is no more than a recognition, grudging or not, that suffering and abuse are not culturally authentic values and cannot be justified in the name of cultural relativism. In short, it is wrong to say that all cultures are equally valid; some cultures contain evil elements which have no rational, intuitive or empirical claim to moral equivalence with non-abusive cultures.

Second, cultural relativists often incorrectly perceive the attributes of cultural communities. Cultural relativists tend to look at cultures from a static, romanticized perspective in which traditional societies are defined as unchanging holistic entities, unaffected by human history or the dynamics of cultural change.

But this view fails to take into account the dynamism of culture which normally offers its members a range of development options, or is willing to accommodate varying individual responses to its norms, while preserving legitimate values of authentic tradition. Anthropologists acknowledge that culture is flexible and holds many possibilities of choice within its framework. To recognize the values held by a given people at a given time in no way implies that these values are a constant or static factor in the lives of current or succeeding generations of the same group.

Third, the dynamics of change have been accelerated in this technological, communicative age, with the result that many closed societies, once exposed to individualist benefits, seek to incorporate those values and interests in their culture, in fact, therefore, individualist values have a great appeal to all cultures once the values are perceived. Of course, a necessary element of bringing about such change is free discourse between cultures, so that the human rights benefits can be known. It is telling that authoritarian rulers try to prevent such discourse, which, at the least, reveals a lack of faith in their normative position.

Fourth, there is still another approach which, in part, renders moot the conflict between universalist and relativist theory. This consists of appreciation of what has transpired in international law. Even as theorists have continued to quarrel with each other, fundamental human rights principles have become universal by virtue of their entry into international law as *jus cogens*, customary law or by convention. In other words, the relativist argument has been overtaken by the fact that human rights have become hegemonic and therefore universal by fiat.

The relativist, of course, may reply that international law is not a decisive foundation for the relativist any more than an iniquitous positive law is for the universalist. This argument can be countered in relativist terms. Law creates societal pressure for adherence; adherence creates habit; habit creates custom; custom becomes a cultural attribute. Thus the legal standards convert to the very cultural standard which the cultural relativist advocates. To be sure, the normal process is for theory to turn into law, but, conversely, law creates the cultural attributes of a society. In any event, the broad acceptance by many nations across the globe of the principal human rights treaties can be taken, at least on the legal level (if not yet in practice), as a triumph of universalism over relativism.

Finally, it is revealing that the implications of the relativist position for human rights have obviously been troubling-to many relativist theorists who, in personal terms, would like to see human rights values firmly ensconced in world affairs. And so they search for justification other than the universalist theories to affirm human rights, a search which in itself speaks for the flimsy, if not spurious, foundations of cultural relativism.

For example, Jacob Raz grounds rights in interests which are themselves grounded in values. Richard Rorty argues that human rights activists should rely, not on reason and theory, but on passion and the courage of their convictions. Other theorists produce other rationales. It is still an open question among some theorists whether, at the end of the day, individualists and relativists will recommend the same policies but on different moral grounds. While such reconciliation may not satisfy the universalist thesis, human rights proponents should take comfort from the moral compulsion a good person feels to combat evil and to vindicate human rights. If enough feel that moral compulsion, the universalist goals will have then been fulfilled.

This brief description of modern theories of rights does not even begin to exhaust the complex and daunting literature and complexities of this subject. Moreover, the development of rights theory will certainly benefit from flourishing new philosophical and scientific exploration. Scholars such as Rawls, Ackerman, Coleman, Donagan, Donnelly, Dworkin, Finnis, Gewirth, Heller, Howard, Michelman, Nagel, Nozick, Raz, Richards, Rorty and Sumner, and others in many nations and from diverse backgrounds, are still adding insights to classic moral philosophy and developing or refining their own theories both in domestic and international contexts. It is the natural bent of theory analysis to raise queries and articulate doubts. The field is stirring and the potential for new insight remains large.

Long ago, Hume asked what authority any moral reasoning can have which leads to opinions so wide of the general practice of mankind. It remains a haunting point, as we view the gap between the international law of human rights and current practice. A more promising question may be whether moral reasoning can narrow the gap between moral principle and practice. It is hoped that the discussion here, will affirm faith in the meaningfulness and rationality of a just society of all human beings.

2

Basis of Human Rights

In order to comprehend the basic concepts of Human Rights, it's essentials to examine the broad array of universal and regional instruments and institutions for the protection of human rights. Already the term 'human rights' has been employed generously with little attempt to define it. From the preceding chapter, however, the reader may have glimpsed that the phenomenon known as human rights is connected not only with the protection of individuals from the exercise of state or governmental authority in certain areas of their lives, but that it is also directed towards the creation of societal conditions by the state in which individuals may develop to their fullest potential.

This description may reveal what human rights are intended to achieve in a teleological sense, but it does not reveal which human rights exist or what they are. This, of course, begs the question whether it is necessary in an enquiry into the institutions and the instrumentalities of human rights protection to attempt to define the nature of the phenomena under consideration. Surely it is appropriate simply to acknowledge that there now appears to be almost universal acceptance of human rights as identifiable; concrete, legal norms?. Indeed, commentators such as Wessbrodt and Vasak state unequivocally that human rights have become a universal ideology. If this were so, it would seem that the need for theoretical enquiry into the nature of human rights begins and ends here.

Even if one were to accept uncritically the proposition put forward by Wessbrodt and Vasak, it is none the less clear that their assertions raise a number of acute problems, Some of the problems may be posed in the form of the following questions:

> Are all three generations of rights 'human rights' in the true sense? If they are, are they all co-equal or is there some hierarchical relationship between them? Even within the category of civil and political rights, are all rights of an equal standing or are some more important than others? What differentiates civil and political rights from other kinds of rights anyway? Are human rights different from other kinds of rights? What is the relationship of rights to other kinds of rules? Are rights defeasible? Upon whom lies the obligation to 'prove' or 'disprove the existence of a right? Can their existence be proved objectively in any event? Do different cultures really have the same understanding of human rights? Are Chinese concepts of human rights the same Western, Islamic or African concepts? What would be the consequences if the concepts were shown to be fundamentally different?

All of these questions, and many more, are of fundamental importance, since perceptions about the existence, worth and relationship of rights one to another, and to legal norms in general, produce practical consequences as far as the protection of human rights is concerned. Take, for instance, the question of whether economic, social and cultural rights are true rights or simply aspirational targets. If they are the latter, then no human being can legitimately claim that his or her government is under an absolute, indefeasible obligation to accord those rights to him or her through a programme of progressive implementation. They are merely claims to a better life to which a government may give effect if economic conditions become more favourable at some undetermined future date. If they are rights, however, the government is under a positive obligation to accord them through the appropriate implementation mechanisms. Furthermore, do these rights exist independently of their reduction to positive law in an international instrument? If they do, are they inherent to individuals and therefore to be protected despite any unilateral binding commitment by the state.

The way in which we approach questions such as these depends upon our understanding of human rights within some form of theoretical framework. Even those who would deny that it is necessary to look beyond the positive law contained in the vast array of existing legal instruments have already implicitly adopted a theoretical stance, although they may be unaware of having done so. The function of theory, however, is to provide an analytical tool by which important questions such as those above may be posed and tentative answers offered. It permits the construction of paradigms which lend coherence and consistency to any debate about rights and a model against which putative rights may be measured. It also provides mechanisms by which it is possible to determine the precise ambit of the rights upon whose existence there may be agreement.

From the foregoing, it may be evident that two very broad categories of enquiry about human rights are implicit. The first, often referred to as analytical jurisprudence, raise questions about the nature and origin of rights and how it is possible to know that we have any rights at all. The second category of enquiry, which is sometimes called normative jurisprudence, poses questions about the specificities of rights which individuals are acknowledged to possess, and how such rights stand in relation to each other. While a substantial amount of work has been done in these fields by domestic jurists, international lawyers have concerned themselves little with such questions. International human rights theorists have tended to fall into one of two very broad schools of analytical jurisprudence - the natural and positive law schools - which we will examine shortly. It is in the field of normative jurisprudence that international theorists have been more active, but in the absence of sound analytical foundations, normative enquiry has assumed an air of unreality. This may be a reflection of the poor state of international legal theory, in general where commentators still have difficulty in adequately explaining the nature of legal obligation in international law.

It should not be thought, however, the domestic jurists are irrelevant to our inquiry into the analytical and normative aspects of human rights. There are two reasons for this. First, the protection of human rights is primarily a matter for domestic law. As we will see later in the book that it is only when domestic law falls short of the standards imposed by international law, that international mechanisms for individual protection become engaged. Thus, what domestic commentators say about rights within domestic systems has direct relevance to international lawyers. Second, the majority of human rights instruments create institutions to supervise the systems of which they are part. Very often these institutions function either in a judicial or quasi-judicial manner. The decision makers within these bodies are therefore required to apply what might be called traditional techniques of legal reasoning to questions concerning the rights under consideration and, in a sense, to behave like judges in domestic courts and tribunals. Indeed, many of the people who staff these international institutions concerned with human rights supervision are themselves lawyers and judges trained in the craft of domestic law who bring with them all the legal theories, assumptions and methodologies of their national systems. In analysing how these people make decisions, it is therefore appropriate to apply, by analogy, the theories of domestic jurists. One needs only to examine the extensive and detailed jurisprudence of the European Court of Human Rights to see the accuracy of the assertion.

In this chapter, it is possible to do little more than provide a cursory examination of some of the major theories which are of relevance to human rights. A caveat should be entered that such a brief treatment of these theories will lead inevitably to some inaccuracies and distortions and a loss of subtlety possessed by much of the writing under consideration. This chapter should, therefore, be taken only as a route map and must in no way be considered a complete topographical guide.

Natural Law

There can be little doubt that human rights are the rights of man as they were known as first progeny of the natural law school. As we saw in Chapter 1, the American Declaration of Independence and the French Declaration of the Rights of Man and the Citizen both had their origins in natural rights theory.

While precepts of natural law may be traced back to classical times, for present purposes it may be said that the modern school of natural law emerged in medieval times with the writings of the early Christian philosophers, foremost among whom was Saint Thomas Aquinas. The Thomistic view of natural law postulated that it was that part of God's perfect law which could be divined through the application of human reason. Part of early natural law philosophy was the idea that each person's station in life was determined by God, but that all people - whatever their status - were subject to the authority of monarchs constrained by divine rules, but that all human beings were endowed with a unique individual identity which was separate from the state. Indeed, this latter facet of natural law doctrine may be seen as containing the seen as of the natural rights idea that each person constituted an autonomous individual.

Of course, the basis of early natural law was entirely theistic, that is, it required belief in the Deity to render it coherent. The next stage in the development of natural law, however, was to sever it from its theistic origins and to make it a product of enlightened secular rational thought. This task was undertaken by Dutch jurist Hugo de Groot, who is usually known by his Latin name, Grotius, and who is generally acknowledged to be the 'father of international law'. In his treatise De lure Belli ac Pacis, Drotius argued that it was possible to rationalize the existence of natural law, which was the basis of all positive or written law, on a non-empirical basis by examining the axioms of geometry. Such a mathematical approach to the question of 'right reason' did not depend on the Deity for their validity. This rationalistic, secular approach to law appealed to post-Renaissance scholars, and from the application of Grotain 'right reason' it is possible to discern the development of individual or natural rights theory.

Throughout the seventeenth century, the Grotain view of natural law was refined and, eventually, transmuted into natural rights theory through which subjective, individual rights came to be recognized. Foremost among the proponents of natural rights doctrine was John Locke. Locke argued that all individuals were endowed by nature with the inherent rights to life, liberty and property which were their own and could not be removed or abrogated by the state. However, Locke also postulated that in order to avoid the uncertainties of life in a state of nature, mankind had entered into a social contract or voluntary association by which the exercise of their inalienable rights was transferred to the ruler of the state. Where the ruler of the state broke the social contract by violating the natural rights of the individual, subjects were free to remove the ruler and replace him or her with a government which was prepared to respect those rights.

Locke used his social contract theory to explain, and as an apology for the English Glorious Revolution of 1688. King James II, by violating the natural rights of his subjects, had forfeited his right to rule and had legitimated the consequent change in government. From the Lockean view of natural rights, two things are evident; first, the individual is an autonomous being capable of exercising choice and, second, the legitimacy of government depends not only upon the will of the people, but also upon the government's willingness and ability to protect those individual natural rights. While Lockean natural rights theory was clearly an artificial construct designed to explain the nature of man in political society, it nevertheless exercised a profound influence over political thinking in the seventeenth and eighteenth centuries. The language of both the American and French Revolutions, and the writings of French philosophe Jean-Jacques Rousseau and German moral philosopher Immanuel Kant, demonstrate the philosophical pedigree of natural law and natural rights.

While Rousseau followed the main thrust of Locke's social contract theory, he declared that far from creating individual natural rights, natural law, conferred inalienable sovereignty on the citizens of a state as a whole. Thus, whatever rights were derived from natural law dwelt within the people as a collectivity and could be identified by reference to the 'general will'. It will be readily apparent that the general will was not an absolute quality and could either transform itself or be transformed by a persuasive leader. While Rousseau's theory was therefore derived from natural precepts. It is obvious that it could be employed to justify demagoguery and totalitarianism. Indeed, it may be argued that the Terror of the French Revolution might be traced to a perversion of the 'general will' thesis.

Kant developed his ideas from a more general appreciation of the non-empirical natural law and natural rights tradition. The basis of Kant's theory was the categorical imperative, that is, the absolute moral good which is identifiable in the exercise of the virtuous will by all rational individuals. In Kant's theory, the categorical imperative operates on three levels; first, it specified universal acts of duty on all individuals; second, it provides systematic rules for determining these duties, and third, it specifies the relationship between freedoms and duties. Underlying the categorical imperative, however, is the idea that individuals are under a duty to develop their rational capacities and to employ them for the promotion of happiness in others. While the categorical imperative might be seen to be primarily duty-based, it has, as its correlative, a system of rights. Unlike the old natural law tradition, however, such rights are not prescribed, but flow from the consequences of the Kantian duty-based system. In a society of rational; self-determining human beings, Kant postulated that freedoms or rights would emerge as a consequence of the application of the categorical imperative. Such rights may therefore be described as consequential and non-relational in that they do not depend upon each other for their existence or worth. Unfortunately, because of the non-relational nature of rights in Kant's theory, it is particularly difficult to apply to concrete situations.

Although there has been something of a revival in the post-Second World War period, natural rights theory fell into general disrepute during the nineteenth century. The major criticism directed at natural rights theory was that it was not scientifically verifiable. How was it possible to know where rights came from, what they were and what content they had? Critics pointed to the a *priori* moral or value structures and assumptions derived from the personal preferences of the various theorists and declared that natural rights could have no objective existence. As English utilitarian Jeremy Bentham argued: 'Right is the child of law; from real laws come real rights, but from imaginary law, from "laws of nature", come imaginary rights .... Natural rights is simple nonsense: natural and imprescriptible rights, rhetorical nonsense upon stilts.'

Despite these criticisms of natural law and natural rights, however, sight must not be lost of the powerful influence which they have exercised over the emergence and development of human rights. Natural rights theory has the merit of providing the basis for a system of law which is allegedly superior to the law of the state and to which appeal may be made if it appears that the latter is unjust, arbitrary or oppressive. It may even be argued that the early revolutionary constitutional documents were 'natural rights' documents, and that following the barbarous excesses both prior to and during the Second World War, a revived natural rights movement led to the drafting of the major international human rights instruments. Of course, the view might be taken that although human rights had their origin in natural law, it took a system of positive law to provide a definite and systematic statement of the actual rights which people possessed.

Country's Laws

While natural law theorists derived their ideas of rights from God, reason or *a priori* moral assumptions, positivists argued that the existence and content of rights could be derived only from the laws of the state. While the approach of the natural law rights theorists was essentially non-empirical, the empirical methods adopted by the positivists reflected the scientific milieu of the 'Age of Enlightenment' of eighteenth-century Europe.

It was Scotsman David Hume who first raised the dichotomy between the naturalist and positivist schools of jurisprudence. Hume argued that inquiry into social phenomena could be divided into two distinct categories : First, the category of facts which could be proved to exist empirically and which could be demonstrated to be true or false. This was the 'is'. Second, there was the category of morality which could not be proved to exist objectively and about which people might have legitimate differences of opinion. This was the 'ought'. In Hume's view, it was only the 'is' - those matters which were empirically provable - that formed the basis of valid scientific enquiry. This had the consequence of severing the discussion of morality from the analysis of legal systems. Once this had been done, natural law appeared to be simply an argument about which moral position was; better than another. Furthermore, while natural law failed to demonstrate how a systematic legal system could be constructed from its precepts, positive law took as its starting point the existence of formal legal systems.

The apparent amoral starkness of Hume's position was given a humanitarian face by the development by Jeremy Bentham of a school of positivism known as utilitarianism. The central thesis of utilitarianism was that human existence was dominated by pleasure and pain, and that by increasing the former and diminishing the latter, the lot of mankind would be improved. The aim of utility, therefore, was to increase the overall stock of human pleasure, which could be calculated on a mathematical basis. The ultimate test of utility, therefore, was the implementation of rules which gave the greatest happiness to the greatest number of people—the maximization of felicity. It will be apparent that Bentham's utilitarianism was not amoral, but its morality was derived not from a metaphysical source; rather, its origins lay in the expression of the majority's personal preferences. Clearly this had the potential to lead to a tyranny of the majority and to the oppression of the minority in any given state. It is perhaps paradoxical, therefore, that Bentham and his followers employed utilitarianism as a potent vehicle for English flaw reform.

The main achievement of Hume and Bentham was to make law an autonomous field of scientific study separate and distinct from natural law inputs, and to pave the way for the more systematic approach of John Austin. Austin's empiricism led him to conclude that the only valid laws were the commands of the sovereign, or the ruling political power, which were accompanied by appropriate sanctions or remedies. From this position, it was possible to construct a rational system of interlocking and scientifically verifiable rules. The Austinian, legacy, however, has been, rightly or wrongly, to suggest that rights are simply those rules which the state has enacted for the protection of individuals and their property interests. In terms of Hohfeldian linguistic analysis of legal rights, it might be said that the Austinian position is that the state grants an immunity to individuals with a corresponding disability on the part of the state which prevents it from interfering with those immunities. The main criticism directed at this form of positivism are that it places no moral constraints on the rules adopted by states and individual only enjoy such rights as the state is prepared to grant them. Thus, the Nazi Nuremburg Laws on racial purity may have been immoral, but from a positivist point of view they were laws none the less, having been adopted by the government in power. Similarly, within a positivist framework, a law requiring all prisoners to be tortured would be legitimate despite its immoral quality.

The positivist position does, however, have certain advantages. It enables individuals to point to concrete norms and prescriptions that allow them to vindicate their rights. Professor H.L.A. Hart, a prominent and influential moral philosopher, has attempted to remove from positivism the less palatable aspects of its Austinian legacy. He has argued that although law and morality stand independently of each other, nevertheless the laws which a government adopts have been recognized and accepted by the community as a whole. This, therefore, provides legitimacy for the laws passed. Of course, Hart's theory is only as good as the system of government in power, so that the community standards and laws of Nazi Germany will be different to those of present-day Britain. It is also true of positivist approaches that may be possible to identify substantive rules for the protection of human rights within a legal system, but the reality of the situation may be that the social and institutional conditions are such as to deny the effective exercise of those rights.

Old Approach Invalidated

The central criticism of utilitarianism is that it sets as its priority the well being of the majority. Little thought is given to minorities or individuals within a state whose preferences are not represented by the majority and who may, in consequence, be severely disadvantaged or, in rights talk, deprived of their rights. Take, for example, the issue of homosexuality. The majority of people within a state might find the practice of homosexuality so abhorrent or abominable that would wish to prohibit it legislation. Clearly, this would satisfy the central axioms of utilitarianism by maximizing the happiness of the majority. The homosexuals, a minority whose practices would be forbidden, would be able to make no argument to gainsay the utilitarian position since, as a minority, their preferences would have to give way to the wishes of the majority.

Under a different theory, the treatment meted out to the homosexuals in our fictitious state might look like discrimination, or the consideration of a minority group as having less worth than the majority. Clearly, in a pluralistic, democratic state such a position would be untenable. Because of the tendency to a tyranny of the majority inherent in utilitarian focus.

Two of the most notable critics of utilitarianism are Dworkin and Nozick; but it is only in their criticism of utilitarianism that they are united. Each author starts from a different point of departure and arrives at starkly different conclusions. Nozick's rights theory flows from his general political philosophy which demands an ontological commitment to a particular species of morality and social organization. In his theory, he postulates a group of men and women in a state of nature who combine to form the minimal state.

The minimal state is not only based on certain moral precepts but is itself one of those moral precepts. To have more than a minimal state whose functions are limited to those of a 'night-watchman' would be to deprive its citizens of more liberty than necessary, which would in itself be immoral. The other moral bases of the minimal state are the right not to be killed, assaulted, robbed or defrauded; the right to acquire, retain and dispose of property; the right to performance of contracts and the right to do as one pleases so long as it does not violate the rights of others. Wrongdoing, therefore, corresponds only to violation of these rights. The role of the minimal state in such circumstances is limited to enforcement of the moral bases of the state by punishing violators, settling disputes and awarding compensation: the 'night-watchman' role. If the state were to transgress into other areas of activity such as providing welfare or redistributing wealth, it would exceed its function and become immoral by depriving citizens or their liberty to act. Nozick's main criticism of utilitarianism, therefore, is that it scarifies liberty of the individual for the sake of the majority; it takes no account of the fact that an individual's life is the only one she or he possesses.

Nozick's thesis is, of course, highly theoretical and application to forms of liberal democratic and capitalist state organization would simply have the effect of entrenching existing social inequalities. But what Nozick is seeking to do, is to construct a theory which would maximize the liberty available to all individuals without accepting the anarchist critique that maximum individual liberty is only possible without the state. With Nozick, the state remains a necessity, but one which must hardly encroach upon its citizens' freedom of action.

The Nozick's minimalist state strikes one as theoretically harsh and potentially populated by bleakly self-interested individuals. One might consider the other major contemporary critic of the utilitarian school whose anchor is firmly set in the Anglo-American liberal tradition: Gerald Dworkin. In Dworkin's view, rights are defined as political 'trumps' held by individuals 'when, for some reason, a collective goal is not a sufficient justification for denying them what they wish as individuals, to have or to do, or not a sufficient justification for imposing some loss or injury upon them'. In other words, rights perform the same function as trump cards in a game of bridge or whist where any trump card will always possess a higher value than the highest card of any other suit. In the same way a right will always defeat a policy designed to promote general welfare unless a good argument can be adduced for it not doing so. This definition of a right clearly counters the utilitarian thrust that individual preferences must always give way to those of the majority, since it says that in some circumstances the interests of the individual must take priority over those of society as a whole.

As a definition of rights, Dworkin's approach is unobjectionable, but it tells us nothing of where rights come from, what they are or where they stand in relation to each other. To answer these questions, it is necessary to understand that they are constructed on the foundation of Dworkin's commitment to the political doctrine of liberalism, one of the central tenets of which is that governments must treat individuals within their populations with equal respect and concern. Thus, although Dworkin's theory is anti-utilitarian this respect is shown because the individual cannot be sacrificed for the benefit of overall social welfare, he none the less accepts the Benthamite utilitarian credo that everybody counts for one, but nobody counts for more than one.

What he argues is that in aggregating the preferences of individuals, the utilitarians deviate from the central liberal proposition that individuals must be treated as individuals. It is therefore not the principle of one person one vote which is wrong, it is the mechanics of aggregation which are flawed. This is so, Dworkin argues, because in making decisions individuals are swayed by two types of preference; the first of which is acceptable, the second of which is not. First, individuals have personal preferences which rest on individual taste - a preference for Coke over Pepsi, for example. Such preferences are innate and do not involve preferences about other people's preferences. It is this second-preferences about other people's preferences which, Dworkin argues, distorts the utilitarian hedonic calculation.

This is so because, although in theory we would wish to assign the greatest number of liberties to everyone, our choices would be constrained by external preferences; by giving preference to those people whose preferences we would wish to see satisfied. This distinction leads, in Dworkin's view to a kind of double counting in favour of those whom we would wish to have their preferences fulfilled, which in turn, leads to a violation of the principle of equal respect and concern. Since, however, external preferences - preference about preferences - cannot be excluded from the calculation, but since they clearly violate the principle of equal respect and concern, a system of rights is necessary to 'trump' potential deviations in the hedonic calculation.

Dworkin's distinction between different kinds of preferences is extremely subtle, and it is doubtful whether it can be sustained in practice. Nevertheless, it is crucial to his understanding of rights in a liberal democratic society. At this point, it is possible to discern why rights are necessary and ought to be taken seriously in Dworkin's scheme, but it still does not tell us what rights we have, that is, the analytical side of the equation. Here Dworkin argues that there is no general right to liberty as such, since this would be meaningless, but that there are rights to specific liberties such as freedom of expression, association and religion, and freedom in personal and sexual relations. From whence, however, are these specific rights derived? In Dworkin's view that all derive from the fundamental right that everybody is entitled to 'treatment as an equal', which in turn is derived from the central tenet of liberalism that everybody must be treated with equal respect and concern. In what sense, however, is the right to treatment as an equal fundamental? It is because, argues Dworkin, it is the source both of the general authority of collective goals and of the special limitations on their authority that justify more particular rights'. Thus when a right is claimed it must be demonstrable that it is supported by the fundamental right to equal treatment.

While one can take issue with Dworkin's theory of rights at a number of levels, it is none the less useful because it attempts to reconcile societal goals with individual preferences and establish a hierarchical order of rights. The major problem with Dworkin in attempting to apply his theory to the international human rights field, however, is that his thesis is applicable only to the conditions of a liberal democracy possessing strong democratic institutions. In most states where gross human rights violations occur, they are not always endowed with either that form of political system not strong democratic institutions. This does not mean that Dworkin's thesis is wrong, but simply that it is has limited application. Nevertheless, both the Council of Europe and the inter-American systems for the protection of human rights explicitly require the prior existence of forms of representative democracy within their member states. It may well be that Dworkin's theory of rights might be fruitfully adopted and adapted to explain both the existence and application of rights within these systems at least.

Consideration of anti-utilitarian jurists cannot be deemed complete without a brief examination of Rawls Theory of Justice. In this work, he argues that justice is a way of distributing the rights, duties, benefits and burdens among individuals within society. He further posits, as distinct from utilitarians, that every person is inviolable and that even the welfare of society cannot displace this inviolability:

Justice denies that loss of freedom for some is made right by a greater good shared by others. Therefore, in a just society liberties of equal citizenship are settled; the rights secured by justice are not subject to political bargaining or to the calculus of social interest.

Like Nozick, but starkly different results, Rawls starts with the familiar social contract theory in which all persons are in an original position of equality as regards the distribution of freedom and power. Each, however, is endowed with a "veil of ignorance" about his or her own personal qualities and attributes. In this state, the rational person who is ignorant of their own potential will, in Rawls' view, chooses two principles of justice. The First Principle will be that everyone has an equal right to the most extensive total system of equal basic liberties compatible with the same system for others. The Second Principle is that social and economic inequalities are to be organized to that they are of the greatest benefit to the least advantaged and so that they provide a system of equal access to all offices and equality of opportunity. Thus, in Rawls' system, there is a general conception of fairness and equality in which all social primary goods such as liberty and opportunity, income and wealth are to be distributed equally unless an unequal distribution actually operates to the advantage of the least favoured.

Unlike Dworkin, who does not concede a general right to liberty, Rawls argues to the contrary, that liberty is the pre-eminent right and that all other rights are subsidiary to it. Within such a system, rights may only be restricted if, first, they would strengthen the total system of liberty shared by all or, secondly, if less than equal liberty were acceptable to the citizens so deprived. What then, are the rights comprehended by the First Principle? Among these Rawls would include political liberty, freedom of expression, conscience and thought, and freedom to integrity and inviolability of the person - including the freedom to hold property.

All such rights would be held equally by citizens in a just society. Rawls recognizes, however, that some citizens, although actually possessing the most extensive system of equal rights within society, might because of other factors, such as ignorance or poverty, be unable to take full advantage of their rights. Clearly, this does not affect the intrinsic value of rights possessed by individuals but it does hinder their enjoyment of those rights. In Rawls' terms, it affects the worth or value of the liberties held. How, then, is this disparity in the worth or value of liberty to be compensated for? Rawls' answer to this is by the application of the Difference Principle. This principle states that an equal distribution of resources is to be preferred unless it can be demonstrated that an unequal distribution would make both the advantaged and disadvantaged better off. Thus, this form of distributive justice should be implemented to ensure that each person enjoyed the full worth of his or her liberty.

Again it may be argued that Rawls' theory is acceptable in so far as it applies to liberal democratic societies, but that its application to other forms of political organization make it unrealistic. None the less, it is clear that even at a cursory glance Rawls' concepts could be applied to arguments in favour of the third generation right to development which demands a reallocation of the world's resources to maximize the wellbeing of those in the developing world.

Recent Approach

The explosion of regulatory activity in USA following President Roosevelt's economic 'New Deal' led a number of American jurists to consider new methods of attempting to explain the functions of law within a complex, highly regulated industrial society. In this task they were aided by the input of social scientific perspectives, particularly that of the then relatively modern discipline of sociology. Foremost among the legal realists were Karl Llewellyn and Roscoe Pound. Their major concern was, to paraphrase Llewellyn, to discover what law does rather than what law is. Because of their empirical framework, the legal realists had no general theory of rights as such, but considered them as forming part and parcel of their study of the processes and interaction of policy, law and legal institutions. Within this framework, rights might emerge as the end-product of such a process of interaction, thereby reflecting the prevailing moral values of society at any given time. In this sense, the realists provided a kind of 'snapshot' of rights as a temporary manifestation of an ongoing process. Although Pound devised a prescription for the validation of human wants, human demands and social interest through the principle of social engineering, he did not identify a mechanism or method by which individual rights might be prioritized both in relation to each other and in relation to societal goals. As Shestack points out, this lack of 'goal identification' renders Pound's approach deficient in assisting normative enquiry.

None the less, a contemporary development within the realist school perhaps addresses some of the criticisms directed at Pound. This is the Yale School of International Law, whose main proponent is Myres McDougal. He and his colleagues have developed a value-explicit and policy-orientated approach to human rights based on the 'super-value' of the protection of human dignity. Like other legal realists, McDougal, Lasswell and Chen argue that demands for the satisfaction of human rights derive from a broad based international sharing of values. These values are manifested by demands relating to such social goods as respect, power, enlightenment, well-being, health, skill, affection and rectitude. All of these values contribute towards, and are validated by,. The super-value of human dignity. The objective of the value-explicit policy-orientated approach is to offer a prescription for the world community in which all the values identified are shared through the application of democratic principles.

While the Yale School might be criticized on the ground that the concept of the 'super-value' of human dignity might not mean the same thing for all cultures at all times, nevertheless it does seem to represent an idea upon which a large core of consensus might be secured, especially since the humanitarian drive for many international human rights instruments has its origins in seeking protection and redress for individuals who are the subjects of inhumane treatment. Furthermore, the identification of a common goal or goals, again, as represented by the major human rights instruments, provides evidence of a minimum of shared values within the world community. This kind of approach avoids problems of metaphysical abstractions which characterizes a substantial amount of theoretical debate about human rights, but it still does not answer the question of whether human rights are immutable or whether - and this is a dangerous argument - they simply reflect prevailing social interests.

Marxist Approach

Before leaving our consideration of the theoretical schools which might help us to think in a coherent way about rights, it is probably pertinent to mention Marxist approaches to the issue. Marx, arguing from a scientific basis, claimed that the alleged law of nature was both idealistic and a historical, and as such the claim by seventeenth-and eighteenth-century bourgeois revolutionaries to the effect that rights were both inalienable and imprescriptibie was unsustainable and indefensible. Rights, Marx argued, were simply a bourgeois concept and a product of bourgeois-capitalist society, designed to maintain and reinforce the pre-eminent position of the ruling class. None the less, Marx was prepared to concede that even within the early stages of communist revolutionary state, rights, of a particular species, might still have an important role to play in the transformation of society. In order to understand this argument, it is necessary to consider the Marxist approach to the nature of the individual within both the capitalist and the communist state.

In Marxist theory, the essence of an individual is that of a social being who uses his or her abilities to satisfy his or her needs. The fulfilment of these needs in capitalist society, where the means of production are controlled by the ruling class, is impossible since it results in the alienation of the working class. The true potential of human beings, in Marxist doctrine, can only be realized if they are enabled to return to their true nature as social beings. This, however, can only be achieved in a truly communist society where all means of production are held in common and there is an absence of class conflict. Such a communist society can only come into being, however by a revolution of the industrial proletariat. This, in turn, will transform itself into a dictatorship of the proletariat and, though historical and economic forces; lead to the withering away of the state.

Until the state withers, however, the revolutionary party must occupy a vanguard position using the state and its institutions for the transformation of society. It is at this point that Marxist concepts of rights emerge. During the period of transformation there are no individual rights, since these are egoistic, bourgeois property-based 'right'; there are only legal rights, which are granted by the state and which are directed towards the transition from the communist state to communist society. These legal rights are, however, only contingent in that they are concerned simply with the mechanics of transformation. As such, these rights can only be social and economic, since they are directed towards the reduction of the means of production to common control. It is only this species of rights which contributes towards the Marxist objective of returning individuals to their status as social beings. Once the process of transformation has taken place, the need for rights disappears, since each individual will be in a free and spontaneous relationship with all other individuals. Within Marxist theory, therefore, rights are simply achieved, the tools are no longer needed and may be conveniently disposed of. Furthermore, rights have no transcendental or eternal value; they are positivistic in the sense that those rights which are deemed to exist are fixed solely by the state.

While some states such as China and North Korea still hold firm to teaching based on Marxist principles, other erstwhile communist states such as those comprising the Commonwealth of Independent States have abandoned not only Marxist economic theories, but also Marxist theories of rights. Indeed, a number of the old former communist bloc states, such as Hungary and Czechoslovakia, have become parties to human rights instruments that clearly give effect to individualistic civil and political rights. Nevertheless, the contribution of Marxist thought to the development of international instruments on social, cultural and economic rights have been pronounced and should be dismissed lightly.

Universal Laws

It was indicated earlier in this chapter that a great deal of debate about the juridical nature of humans in international law has tended to focus on the normative relationship between various alleged categories of rights. Some commentators, such as Cranston, take the view that only civil and political rights can properly be called human rights, and that economic and social rights are simply claims against the state which it is not obliged to fulfil. Other jurists, such as Tunkin, who are more predisposed to a socialist orientation, argue that only economic and social rights have any real meaning, since civil and political rights serve to reinforce the present unequal distribution of all social and material goods and impede the process of development. Such dogmatism tends to produce unfortunate effects, since, as we shall see below, it hinders appreciation of the fact that just as not all civil and political rights are individualistic, not all economic and social rights, are collectivist in orientation. However, even within supposed categories of rights, there is debate about whether the more fundamental rights and freedoms can be separated from those which are less fundamental.

The position of the UN General Assembly is clear on this issue. It has stated on a number of occasions that 'all human rights and fundamental freedoms are indivisible and interdependent and that equal attention and urgent consideration should be given to the implementation, promotion and protection of both civil and political and economic, social and cultural rights'

This statement, however, is not particularly useful, since it does not reflect the actual position as regards the different goals and implementation programmes of the various human rights instruments which we will be considering in detail later in this book. Furthermore, it might be questioned whether such an approach is also intellectually compelling, since different societal conditions might demand the setting of different priorities with regard to different classes of human rights. This is not to argue that certain rights may be regarded as less important than others on some kind of arbitrary hierarchical scale, rather that in an imperfect world with an imperfect allocation of resources, the priorities within different states may dictate a different allocation of such resources. None the less, it is possible, both as an intellectual exercise and as a matter of practicality, to adduce weighty arguments in favour of the contention that between different classes of rights, and even within classes of rights, there is some kind of hierarchical classification of rights.

Basic Rights

Are there some rights that might be regarded as more fundamental than others? Certainly, there is some support for this view in the wide variety of international human rights instruments now in force. The UN Charter, for example, states in its Preamble that the peoples of the UN are determined 'to reaffirm faith in fundamental human rights ....', apparently indicating that these fundamental human rights enjoyed an existence prior to their recognition by the Charter and prior to their reduction to positive law by the various UN instruments. Such rights have also been described as 'supra-positive' or 'elementary' rights by Theodoor van Boven who argues that their validity 'is not dependent on their acceptance by the subjects of law but which are at the foundation of the international community.' In referring to 'supra-positive' rights, the immediate impression is that Van Boven is claiming some kind of natural law origin for his fundamental rights, but throughout his discussion there is constant reference to human rights as a manifestation of international social order, thereby implying that rights, including supra-positive rights, have a sociological basis for their existence. As he says: 'These rights lie at the foundation of the international community as presently represented in United Nations and, in a more limited sense, in other important world-wide and regional organizations." This statement would seem to suggest that fundamental rights are not static but dynamic and that other human rights may be exalted of such a status. Indeed, Van Boven claims that this has been the case for such rights involving the prohibition of race and sex discrimination, since nearly all international human rights instruments take as their point of departure the need to ensure the absence of discrimination on these grounds.

Perhaps the most compelling argument in favour of treating some rights as fundamental lies is the fact that in the ICCPR as in the European, American and African regional human rights conventions, certain rights are characterized as inviolable in that they may not be derogated from even in times of war or other national emergency. Included in this list are the right to life; freedom from torture, inhuman and degrading treatment; freedom from slavery or servitude; freedom from *ex post facto* laws and freedom of thought, conscience and religion. Other rights, however, may be derogated from; under defined conditions. This would seem to imply that there is a difference between rights which may be derogated from and those which may not, the natural conclusion being that the former are to be regarded as more fundamental than the latter. Furthermore, the UN Convention Against Torture makes it clear that there can be no justification under any circumstances for the commission of the prohibited acts in that

Convention. It would therefore seem that an argument could be made that these non-derogable rights have the characteristics of *ius cogens*, that is, norms which can never be derogated from, and must, in that sense, be seen as fundamental both within the realm of international human rights law and international law in general. And if these non-derogable rights are indeed fundamental and do bear the characteristics of ius cogens, then it is possible to argue, as Van Boven does, that these rights are 'binding on States, even in the absence of any conventional obligation or of any express acceptance or comment'.

Negotiable Rights

It may be recalled from Chapter 1 that although the UDHR included reference to all categories of rights-civil, political, economic, social and cultural-within the framework of a single instrument, it proved impossible to secure agreement between the member states of the UN upon the drafting of a legally binding document embracing all of the rights contained in the Declaration. While some states argued that all types of rights constituted an indivisible and mutually self-supporting whole, others, particularly the US and the UK, took the view that whereas civil and political rights were immediately enforceable and justiciable, economic, social and cultural rights depended upon positive, programmatic implementation. These Western states, whose political and economic structures had been heavily influenced by the revolutionary constitutionalism of the seventeenth and eighteenth centuries, argued that only first-generation rights - freedoms from state interference - were all that international law could reasonably be expected to protect as a matter of immediacy. Economic, social and cultural rights were not amenable to such immediate protection and were best fulfilled through a progressive reporting system. The ultimate drafting of two separate Covenants dealing with the two broad categories of rights would seem to support the contentions adduced by the Western states. While the ICCPR provides for immediate protection by requiring states to 'respect and ensure to all individuals within its territory and subject to its jurisdiction the rights recognized'. The ICESCR, on the other hand requires only that states 'undertake to take steps ...to the maximum of their available resources, with a view to achieving progressively the full realization of the rights recognized.' The conclusion which is drawn by some commentators, such as Craston, from this differential implementation structure, is that whereas civil and political rights are human rights properly so - called, economic and social rights, do not enjoy such a status. If this position were taken to its logical conclusion, it would also mean that these second-generation rights do not require protection or implementation because they are not 'real' rights.

It is questionable, however, whether the drafting history and the arguments about implementation of the perceived categories of rights should determine decisively whether or not one category should be regarded as 'real' rights and the other not. At the theoretical level, it might be possible to argue that the right to education (which is classified as a social right) is of a different moral order to freedom of expression (a civil right), but this is an argument about the relational value of rights and not about the existence of such rights. Of course, whether we choose to accept economic, social and cultural rights as rights properly called, will depend upon our own preferred theoretical standpoint.

It we descent to the level of pragmatism, it also becomes clear that alleged distinctions between the two categories of rights often verges upon the arbitrary. Take, for instance., the argument that civil and political rights are capable of immediate protection, whereas economic, social and cultural rights require progressive implementation. While it is undeniable that the latter group of rights will probably require the spending of a higher proportion of a state's Gross Domestic Product (GDP) on such items as education, social security and health care, it is still obvious that civil and political rights also require a reasonably substantial element of public spending in order to ensure adequate protection. The right to a fair trial, for example, requires the maintenance of an effective justice system, the provision of publicly financed defenders, the payment of interpreters for individuals whose language is not that of state in which they are being tried, the provision of adequate security systems to enable the courts to be open to the public, and so on. While the costs associated with the implementation of such a system are probably not of the order of providing comprehensive social security for individuals within a state, none the less they will not be negligible and may impose a significant burden upon the treasuries of some states.

It should also be noted that the alleged division between civil and political rights, on the one hand and economic, social and cultural rights on the other, is largely arbitrary and cannot be entirely sustained by reference to the two UN Covenants. Both Covenants, for example, deal with rights involving freedom of association and family matters which may be categorized as hybrid rights, since they exhibit characteristics of both classes of rights. If one takes a selection of provisions from the ICCPR, it is possible to discern that they are not the 'freedom from' rights, which are normally associated with that Covenant, but 'rights to', which are usually regarded as second-generation rights. Article 24(1), for example, requires state intervention in order to ensure that a child is accorded 'the right to such measures of protection as are required by his status as a minor, on the part of.. The State'. Conversely, the ICESCR has a substantial number of provisions which would appear not to require state intervention for their protection. These are more of the 'freedom from' than the 'rights to' species and include the right to strike, the prohibition of the use of children in harmful work, and so on.

The existence of these hybrid rights makes it apparent that any classification and hierarchical ranking of rights in international law is not easy and that, indeed, it may be questionable whether there is any real utility in attempting to do so. Putting rights into particular categories tell us little about the value of a right; it simply provides fodder for moralizing or choosing a preferred political position in debates about human rights. This is not to deny that there may well be a certain utility in differentiating between the implementation measures attached to certain rights, since it permits determination of the varying degrees of state obligations with respect to all rights in general. Ultimately, however, whether rights are civil, political, economic, social or cultural in orientation makes little difference to their qualitative status as rights, but it may make a difference to the speed with which they are implemented by states.

The emergence of third-generation or solidarity rights is closely identified with the rise of Third World nationalism and the perception of developing states that the existing international order is loaded against them. It may also be seen as a claim by developing states for fairer treatment and for the construction of a world system that will facilitate distributive justice in the broadest Rawlian sense. The basis for these claims is not, however, simply moral, but can be identified as having a legal basis in a number of existing international instruments.

The UN Charter itself places human rights in a pivotal position to assist in the creation of a peaceful international order and economic development. Article I (2) of the Charter provides that one of the purposes of the UN is 'to develop friendly relations among nations based on the principle of equal rights and self-determination of people'. Article 1(3) further provides that another purpose of organization is 'to achieve international cooperation in solving international problems of economic, social, cultural or humanitarian character, and in promoting and encouraging respect for human rights and fundamental freedoms...'. These purposes are further reinforced by the substantive provisions of the Charter, particularly Articles 55 and 56, which clearly demonstrate that the creation of suitable international conditions is a prerequisite to the full social development of all individuals.

A number of other international instruments also support the view that the international community is obliged to establish a favourable global system for securing the better participation of developing states. The common Article 1 of the two International Covenants, for example, provide for both the political and economic right to self-determination. Article 1(2) provides :

> All people may, for their own ends, freely dispose of their natural wealth and resources without any prejudice to any obligations arising out of international economic cooperation, based upon the principle of mutual benefit, and international law. In no case may a people be deprived of its own means of subsistence.
>
> Article 2(1) of the ICESCR also provides that states parties are to 'take steps individually and through international assistance and cooperation, especially economic and technical, to the maximum of available resources, with a view of achieving progressively the rights recognized in the present Covenant by all available means'. These provisions, it is argued by some jurists, provide a clear basis; for a number of claimed solidarity rights.

What, then, are these third-generation or solidarity rights? Burns Weston identifies at least six categories of solidarity rights.

1. The right to economic, political, social and cultural self-determination.
2. The right to economic and social development.
3. The right to participate in and benefit from the Common Heritage of Mankind and other information and progress.
4. The right to peace.
5. The right to a healthy environment.
6. The right to humanitarian relief.

It is immediately apparent that these rights have two dominant characteristics: first, they are collective in nature and, second, they depend upon international cooperation for their achievement. It is also apparent that these rights build upon and develop existing categories of rights and in that sense they are, as Weston suggests, historically cumulative.

The fact that third-generation rights are collective in nature does not automatically mean that they should be thought of as less than 'real' right for that reason alone. While traditional liberal conceptions of rights emphasize their individualistic quality, it is none the less apparent that even within the category of rights which might be described as civil and political, certain rights are collective in nature. These include the right to exercise one's religion in community with others, the right of peaceful assembly and the right to freedom of association. The rights categorized as economic, social and cultural, which are contained in a variety of international instruments, are also largely collectivist in nature, but are nevertheless recognized by the parties to those instruments as positive rights.

The fact, however, that the new generation of rights depends for its implementation on international cooperation leads some authors to assert that they are little more than aspirational claims which do not possess the binding quality which; is the hallmark of rights proper. Others, such as Alston, however, argue that there is no need to resort to claiming new rights which may be categorized as third generation, since by and large the problems which they seek to address are dealt by existing instruments. Alston has also argued that claims for novel rights such as the 'right to tourism' obscures the need to properly develop existing rights, and more particularly, implementation programmes. He has also argued that there should be a system of procedures for granting a kind of approved origin mark to any 'new' rights proclaimed by the General Assembly.

As the foregoing discussion amply demonstrates, there is considerable debate about what rights are, where they come from, what their content is, how they relate to each other and how new rights might be properly identified. The proposed solutions to these questions may be as numerous as the questions themselves. It is, however, the identification of the questions which is of importance, since they act as signposts towards a coherent method of thinking about human rights. What is also apparent is that debate about human rights is not static, but is part of continuing dialectic process through which progress in the field might be, and manifestly has been, made.

Important Issues

The root of humanitarian disasters, refugee flows or mass exoduses often stems directly from violations of human rights. Addressing the cause is as essential to preventing humanitarian tragedies similar to those experienced in Rwanda or in the countries of the former Yugoslavia as it is to the search for comprehensive solutions. A continuum between human rights law and humanitarian law is necessary; protection of the victim should be the overriding concern of the United Nations and its agencies and programmes. Since 1948, the UN has developed a comprehensive body of international standards and norms for the promotion and protection of human rights, the major instrument being the international bill of human rights. In 1970, the General Assembly adopted a number of resolutions which recognized that fundamental human rights as accepted in international law and international instruments continue to apply in situations of armed conflict.

While the first World Conference on Human Rights held in Tehran in 1968 did not explicitly refer to humanitarian law in its proclamation, it affirmed that humanitarian principles must prevail during periods of armed conflict. The Vienna Declaration and Programme of Action, the concluding document of the 1993 World Conference on Human Rights, called on all States and parties to armed conflicts to adhere strictly to humanitarian law as well as to minimum standards for protection of human rights as laid down in international conventions. The Conference also recognized the gross violation of human rights as one of the major factors leading to the displacement of people and expressed grave concern over continuing violations of human rights in all parts of the world -in disregard of international standards - and the lack of adequate and effective remedies for the victims.

Human rights and humanitarian law, once clearly distinguishable segments of international law, are increasingly being viewed in an integrated and holistic manner, where the individual has a continuum of protection under human rights law as well as that provided under humanitarian law, as warranted by the specific circumstances.

The Office of the UN High Commissioner for Human Rights (OHCHR), as an institution devoted to the promotion and protection of all human rights, emphasizes the value of early warning and preventive action aimed at deterring human rights violations and defusing situations with the potential for humanitarian disasters. The information and findings of UN human rights experts (special rapporteurs, special representatives, experts of human rights treaty-based bodies), complemented by those submitted by UN human rights field offices, represent a valuable contribution to an early warning mechanism of the UN in this area.

OHCHR recognizes that the wealth of information at its disposal needs to be systematically organized and analyzed if it is to be an effective and useful tool. The objectives are to strengthen the early warning capacity of the UN in the humanitarian field, enhance the substantive exchanges between OHCHR, the Office for the Coordination of Humanitarian Affairs (OCHA) and other Departments and Programmes, and to integrate human rights concerns before crises arise, thus guaranteeing effective cooperation both in terms of preparedness and response.

Human Rights training should be considered part of the overall training background of all UN humanitarian staff. The Office of the High Commissioner is developing a human rights manual for all UN staff members which will be available soon. The manual will cooperate with the Complex Emergency Training Initiative

(CETI) as well as with the UN staff college in Turin on the question of initiatives aimed at familiarizing all UN staff with international human rights standards.

As possible immediate steps, contacts should be established with the Office of Human Resources Management (OHRM) and the UN Staff College Project with a view to integrating human rights into the courses held at Headquarters and at the College. Training of UN humanitarian staff in the field, as well as staff at Headquarters and new recruits, in human rights standards, monitoring methodology, technical cooperation procedures and other topics, should be given priority attention. A mechanism could be established so that all newly recruited staff undergo appropriate human rights training. In the case of field staff, one or more officers could be appointed as trainers and delegated the responsibility for providing on-site training to all field staff, based on OHCHR training materials.

In regard to the human rights aspects of UN humanitarian operations, it is important to learn from past experience and to attempt to integrate human rights concerns whenever possible, to include human rights experts in large-scale humanitarian operations, and to emphasize the protection and promotion of human rights, including the creation of viable national human rights institutions capable of preventing the recurrence of similar humanitarian crises.

When a humanitarian operation is considered, the human rights dimension should be part of the planning, requiring close cooperation between OCHA, the UN High Commissioner for Refugees (UNHCR) and OHCHR. While the need and opportunity for inclusion of human rights field officers or advisers within humanitarian operations will vary, an explicit human rights strategy would be pivotal to the planning of major humanitarian efforts. The strategy could be of an advisory nature and/or cover training and institution-building issues.

Humanitarian staff, particularly in the field, should be fully conversant with human rights standards and procedures. The effectiveness of the UN machinery and mechanisms in the field of human rights would be enhanced through more consistent use of these procedures by humanitarian workers, resulting in a greater degree of protection for individuals and other vulnerable groups. Procedures on how this information would be handled could be discussed in-depth between OHCHR and the various humanitarian actors so as to preserve their mandates, independence and specific missions.

OHCHR'S, global project for internally displaced persons (IDPs), in the context of its technical cooperation programme, is a good example of humanitarian and human rights interfacing. According to the Representative of the Secretary-General on IDPs, internally displaced persons are: "Persons or groups of persons who have been forced or obliged to flee or to leave their homes or places of habitual residence, in particular as a result of or in order to avoid the effects of armed conflict, situations of generalized violence, violations of human rights or natural or human-made disasters, and who have not crossed an internationally recognized State border".

Internal displacement constitutes one of the greatest challenges confronting the international community. Unlike refugees, whom IDPs greatly outnumber, there exists no single agency to assume responsibility for the promotion and protection of the rights of IDPs.

A Representative on IDPs was appointed by the Secretary-General at the request of the Commission on Human Rights in 1992, his mandate supported by OHCHR. The Representative's mandate is concentrated on three main areas:

— developing an appropriate normative framework for meeting the protection, assistance, reintegration and development needs of IDPs: significant progress has been made in this direction over the past few months with the formulation by the RSG of Guiding Principles on Internal Displacement. The Guiding Principles consolidate in one document the rights and guarantees relevant to the protection of persons from forced displacement and to their protection and assistance during displacement as well as during return or resettlement and reintegration. They are intended to provide practical guidance not only to the RSG but also to States and other authorities, intergovernmental organizations, NGOs and all other groups and persons with a role to play in addressing the needs of IDPs.

Ensuring the rights of IDPs worldwide to protection and assistance presents the international community with one of the most daunting challenges of our time. Under its technical cooperation programme, OHCHR's global project for IDPs, relying on effective institutional arrangements, will be implemented jointly with the Representative of the Secretary-General (RSG) on IDPs, with the objective of making the rights of some 25 million IDPs a reality.

The broad scope of priority activities to be put in place will guarantee the widest possible distribution of the Guiding Principles on Internal Displacement as well as other related materials—a Training Manual and Fact Sheets are examples—in the official UN languages and, as appropriate, local languages; field offices will rely on the Guiding Principles for the technical guidance essential in their monitoring and reporting functions. Educational and training activities will be provided primarily at the national level, in response to requests from Member States. Workshops on IDP-related issues will be attended by the RSG and his support staff. Interagency needs assessment missions will utilize staff seconded for that purpose. The project will also ensure a focus on IDP activities by the treaty bodies and the mechanisms of the Commission on Human Rights in Geneva.

- fostering effective institutional arrangements for addressing these needs; and
- focusing attention on specific situations of internal

displacement with the aim of ensuring that they are effectively addressed. The Secretary-General recognizes that addressing the plight of IDPs is a priority for the international community. Over the past few years OHCHR, in addition to supporting the work of the Representative, has become increasingly involved with IDPs in its own right.

OHCHR is developing a global project for internally displaced persons (IDPs) in the context of its technical cooperation programme. The aim of the project is to meet the growing operational requirements of the Representative, particularly in the areas of promotion, education, training, and strengthening of national capacities. The objective is to provide the necessary resource requirements to meet the commitments undertaken by OHCHR on behalf of IDPs.

The project also identifies possible future activities of OHCHR which could be initiated on behalf of IDPs, on condition that sufficient institutional capacity for mandated tasks and other commitments is first ensured. It will provide a framework for action by OHCHR and the Representative of the Secretary-General on the basis of individual requests from member states for activities at the national level or occasionally in a regional or sub-regional context.

As long as crimes of torture, rape and murder go unpunished, we cannot hope to prevent their recurrence. Those who contemplate indiscriminately attacking civilians, or forcing them out of their homes simply on account of their ethnicity or religion, must know that there is a price to pay for such actions. This justifies the pertinence of UN efforts to date to demand accountability—the establishment of the ad hoc criminal tribunals for former Yugoslavia and Rwanda is a case in point. Mary Robinson, High Commissioner for Human Rights, addressed the Diplomatic Conference in Rome concerning the finalization and adoption of the statute for a permanent ICC.

We look forward to cooperating closely and developing an effective modus operandi with the ICC in due course.

Indeed, the relationship of the ICC and UN human rights and humanitarian actors and institutions is a subject which elicits considerable interest. Discussion and analysis will complement OHCHR's ongoing efforts to facilitate access to the information available from treaty bodies and mechanisms of the Commission on Human Rights, to quantify and measure human rights progress (or lack of it) so that benchmarking becomes possible and readily available within the UN. There is a broad space for forging effective linkages between humanitarian assistance and human rights programmes.

3

A Long Journey

The concept of Human Rights is not an age-old one. International concern with human rights is a phenomenon of comparatively recent origin. Although it is possible to point to a number of treaties or international agreements affecting humanitarian issues before the Second World War, it is only with the entry into force of the United Nations Charter in 1945, that it is possible to speak of the advent of systematic human rights protection within the international system. None the less, it is clear that the international protection of human rights has its antecedents in domestic efforts to secure legal and dignified history, and are intimately connected with revolutionary activity directed towards the establishment of constitutional systems based on democratic legitimacy and the rule of law.

Even today, the protection of human rights at both the national and international level are intimately connected, if not symbiotic. All international instruments require states' domestic constitutional systems to provide adequate redress for those whose rights have been violated. It is only when those state's own internal protective systems falter or where in extreme cases, they are non-existent, that international mechanisms for securing human rights come into play. In a sense, therefore, international mechanisms operate to reinforce protection of human rights and to provide redress when the domestic system fails or is found wanting.

The Base

Although some scholars have been be able to trace a rudimentary concept of human rights back to the Stoic philosophy of classical times via the natural law jurisprudence of Grotious and the *ius naturale* of Roman law, it seems evident that the origins of the modern concept are to be found in the English, American and French revolutions of the seventeenth and eighteenth centuries.

The Origin

While Magna Carta (1215) is often erroneously seen as the origins of the liberties of English citizens (it was, in reality, simply a compromise on the distribution of powers between King John and his nobles, the language of which only later assumed the wider significance which is attributed to it today), it was not until the Bill of Rights (1689) that rules directed towards the protection of individual rights or liberties emerged. But even this development must be seen in context. The Bill of Rights, which is described in its long title as 'An Act Declaring the Rights and Liberties of the Subject and Setting the Succession of the Crown', was the outcome of the seventeenth-century struggle of Parliament against the arbitrary rule of the Stuart monarchs.

Passed after the enforced abdication of James II and the accession to the throne of William III and May II following the 'Glorious Revolution' of 1688, the Bill, which expressed itself to be declaratory of existing law and not creative of new law, subjected the monarchy to the power of Parliament by declaring illegal the claimed suspending and dispensing powers of the Crown. It also forbade the levying of taxes or the maintenance of standing army in peacetime by Crown without Parliamentary consent.

In Marxist analysis, the Glorious Revolution of 1688 and the

Bill of Rights which institutionalized it, was a bourgeois revolution: it simply confirmed the ascendancy of the gentry and merchant class over the monarchy. For the most part, therefore, the Bill represented a constitutional settlement which protected the sectional interests of one group. Whig historians, however, saw the Bill as the triumph of liberty over despotism and the protection of Englishmen (women had little say in the matter) from absolutist and arbitrary government.

There is merit in both these views, for the Bill of Rights not only secured the interests of the bourgeoisie, but it also dealt with certain matters having the characteristics of 'human rights', although they were not referred to as such at the time. In particular, the Bill provided the excessive bail ought not to be required, nor excessive fines imposed, nor cruel and unusual punishment inflicted'. It further provided the 'jurors ought to be duly empanelled and returned' and that all grants and promises of fines and forfeitures of particular persons before conviction are illegal and void'. While the 'human rights' elements of the Bill of Rights might appear to be slight and biased in favour of a particular class of citizens, nevertheless the whole context of the instrument was of fundamental importance, since it sought to replace the vagaries and excesses of arbitrary monarchical absolutism with parliamentary constitutional legitimacy.

The Glorious Revolution was also significant because it provided a precedent that rulers could be removed by popular will if they failed to observe the requirements of constitutional legitimacy. In the view of the eighteenth century English political philosopher John Locke, who sought to discover a theoretical basis for the constitutional revolutions of the seventeenth and eighteenth centuries, bad government violated the social contract which rulers enjoyed with the governed and empowered the latter to rid themselves of the former.

The experience of the English Revolution and the various philosophical and theoretical attempts to justify it were; not lost on the leaders of Britain's rebellious North American colonies in the latter part of the eighteenth century. Seeking to disengage the colonies from British rule following dissatisfaction over the levels of taxation and lack of representation in the British Parliament, the American Founding Fathers sought justification in the social contract; and natural rights theories of Locke and the French philosophes. In the American Declaration of Independence (1776), drafted by Thomas Jefferson, these ideas find particularly clear and felicitous expression:

> We hold these truths to be self-evident, that all men are created equal, that they are endowed by their creator with certain rights, that among these are Life, Liberty and the pursuit of Happiness - That to secure these rights, Governments are instituted among Men, deriving their just powers from the consent of the governed. That whenever any form of government becomes destructive of these ends, it is the right of the People to alter or abolish it.

While the high sounding ideals of the protection of life, liberty and the pursuit of happiness were sufficient for a declaration of independence, they were clearly inadequate as a catalogue of individual rights, which the state was obliged to protect. The Virginia Declaration of Rights, which was drafted by George Mason and which pre-dated the Declaration of independence by a month, included specific liberties that were to be protected from state interference. These included freedom of the press, the free exercise of religion and the obligation that no person should be deprived of their liberty except by the law of the land of the judgment of their peers.

The drafters of the US Constitution, influenced by Mason's Virginia Declaration, included the protection of these minimum rights. It was not until 1791, however, that the US adopted a Bill of Rights containing a list of guaranteed individual rights. This was effected by a number of amendments to the constitution. Among the more well-known amendments are the First, which protects freedom of religion, freedom of the press, freedom of expression and the right of assembly; the Fourth, which protects individuals against unreasonable search and seizure; and the Fifth, establishing the rule against self-incrimination and the right to due process of law. Subsequent amendments of the Constitution have extended the Bill of Rights, (for example, the Thirteenth adopted after the Civil War forbade the practice of slavery), but no rights have ever been removed or abridged by Congress.

In many ways, the eighteenth-century post independence constitutional settlement of the US established the model to be used in subsequent revolutionary struggles. Nowhere was this more apparent than France, where the US experience directly influenced the revolution against the ancient regime.

Although the French Revolution and the American struggle for independence had many common features, they differed in one crucial aspect. Whereas the rebellious colonies had simply sought to establish themselves as an independent sovereign nation, the French revolutionaries were concerned with the demolition of an old, absolutist system of government and the establishment of a new democratic order. This, of course, posed the same question of legitimacy which had been raised by the English Revolution a century earlier when the English had rid themselves of their monarch by enforced abdication. The theoretical solution to this problem identified by the French, taking the lead from American notions of popular legitimacy, was that of self-determination. The central proposition of this concept was therefore to be by the people of a nation lay with its people. Government was therefore to be—by the people, for the people, and any government which was not responsive to its citizens' demands could be changed by expression of the popular will.

The settlement following the French Revolution also reflects the social contract and natural rights theory of Locke and the French philosophes, Montesquieu and Rousseau. The Declaration of the Rights of Man and the Citizen (1789) made it perfectly apparent that government is a necessary evil, and that as little of it as possible is desirable. According to the Declaration, true happiness is to be found in individual liberty which is the product of the 'natural, unalienable and sacred rights of man'. Thus, while the Declaration states that certain individual rights are protected-the right to due process, the presumption of innocence, the freedom to hold opinions and religious beliefs, and the freedom to communicate ideas and opinions-it prefaces these with a clear libertarian philosophy. Article 2 of the Declaration provides that 'the aim of every political association is the preservation of the natural and imprescriptible rights of man. These rights are Liberty, Property, Safety and Resistance to Oppression'. Article 4 goes on to say:

> Liberty consists in being able to do anything that does not harm others: thus the exercise of the natural rights of every man has no bounds other than those that ensure to the other members of society the enjoyment of these same rights. These bounds may be determined only by Law.

A number of recurring themes and concepts in human rights law originate from the American and French Revolutions. Foremost among these is that rights are by nature inherent, universal and inalienable: they belong to individuals simply because they are human beings and not because they are the subjects of a state's law. Second, that the protection of rights is best afforded within a democratic framework. The concept of political self-determination formulated by the drafters of the French Declaration made it clear that the effective protection of rights was to be found only within the bounds of democratic legitimacy.

Third, that the limits to the exercise of rights could be determined or abrogated only by law. This might be seen as part of the concept of the rule of law which requires that rights should be protected by law, and that in abrogating or diminishing individual rights a government is obliged to conform to constitutional legal requirements. It also requires governments to act according to law, and that the law upon which the government seeks to act should be neither oppressive, arbitrary or discriminatory. Of course, one should not forget that the revolution which gave birth to these high sounding ideals and principles also gave birth to the Terror and the guillotine. Indeed, it was for these very reasons that the political philosophers Burke, Hume, Mill, Bentham and Austin rejected the notion of natural rights as being nothing more than unverifiable metaphysical phenomena.

Whatever the theoretical or doctrinal debates over the bases for the English, American and French Revolutions, it is clear that each, in its own way, contributed towards the developments of forms of liberal democracy in which certain rights were regarded as paramount in protecting individuals from the state's in-built tendency to authoritarianism. What was significant about the protected rights was that they were individualistic and libertarian in character, they were predominantly 'freedoms from' rather than 'rights to'. In modern parlance, these would be called civil and political rights, since they dealt primarily with an individual's relationship to the organs of the state. Such was the power of these revolutionary ideas, that there are few modern written constitutions which do not claim to protect these individual rights.

New Concept

Civil and political rights are not, however, the only rights which are protected by modern constitutions and contemporary international law. A variety of economic, social, cultural and other rights are also the subjects of various forms of protection. Karel Vasak has sought to classify the historical development of human rights according to the French revolutionary slogan 'Liberty, Equality and Fratenity'. Each of these, he argues, corresponds, more or less, to the development of distinct categories or generations of rights. Liberty, or first-generation rights, are represented by civil and political rights; the right of individuals to be free from arbitrary interference by the state. Equality, or second-generation rights, correspond to the protection of economic, social and cultural rights; the right to the creation of the conditions by the state which will allow every individual to develop their maximum potential. These second-generation 'rights to' require the state to put in place programmes for the full realization of the rights.

Economic, social and cultural rights are some times seen as a socialist legacy or as derivative rights not worthy of the name, but such rights were protected in the domestic constitutions of the Soviet Union, Mexico and Germany in the early part of the twentieth century and since then have been included in a number of other domestic constitutions and explicitly recognized by international law. Fraternity, third-generation rights or rights of solidarity, are the newest and most controversial category of rights. These are asserted by developing states which wish to see the creation of an international legal and economic order that will guarantee the right to development, to disaster relief assistance, to peace and to a good environment. Clearly, the implementation of such rights—if rights they be—depends upon international cooperation and not simply internal constitutional measures.

From this brief historical exposition, it will be apparent that the notion of human rights has made a transition from exclusive with the protection of the individual from state absolutism to the creation of social and economic conditions calculated to allow the individual to develop to the maximum of his or her potential. As Szabo puts it, the purpose of human rights is to 'defend by institutionalized means the rights of human beings against abuses of power committed by the organs of the State and, at the same time, to promote the multidimensional development of the human personality'.

It will also be apparent that the notion of the human rights is not static but dynamic, and that there may well be considerable debate about whether certain interests are worthy to be classified as rights in the proper sense—whatever that might be. The dialectic process by which it is determined that some claims or interests are predictable and others are not, is of crucial importance if it is believed that rights have a quality that is fundamentally different to other rules of law. This is an issue which will be addressed in detail in the next chapter.

Stature of Individual

Although the origins of human rights can be traced back to the revolutionary constitutionalism of the seventeenth and eighteenth centuries, it was not until the end of the Second World War that the international community began to manifest an interest in the promotion and protection of such rights through the medium of international law. In addition to the absence of the necessary political will to undertake the appropriate action, the structure of international law itself was one of the main impediments to progress in the field. At that time, international law was simply a law which regulated relations between states. States were the sole subjects of the international legal system; other entities, including individuals, were merely objects of the system. States might adopt rules for the benefit of individuals, but such rules conferred neither substantive rights on those individuals nor were they enforceable by any procedural mechanisms. Individuals, as citizens of the state, were subject to the complete authority of their government, and other states, in general, had no legal right to intervene to protect them should they be maltreated.

The position of aliens in a foreign state, was, however, slightly different. The state of which an alien was a national might, under certain conditions, be entitled to bring a claim under international law against a delinquent host state. This would usually occur where an alien had suffered arbitrary treatment at the hands of state agents, such as the police, and had not been afforded an appropriate remedy in the state in question. Western states also argued that there should be an international minimum standard to treatment applicable to all aliens travelling abroad against which state conduct could be judged. Developing states, however, rejected this notion, claiming that an alien in a foreign country could not expect a better standard of treatment than that which a state meted out to its own nationals. It is arguable, however, that the minimum standard and equality of treatment dispute has been overtaken by developments in international human rights law. The main purpose of such state claims was not necessarily to seek redress for the injured citizen; rather, it was to vindicate the rights to the state which had been indirectly injured through the mistreatment of its own national.

Human Dignity

Notwithstanding the position of aliens in international law, the general proposition remains that before the entry into force of the UN Charter, individuals remained essentially at the disposal of their rulers. An alleged exception to this was the so-called right of humanitarian intervention. Under this 'right', states could intervene militarily in order to protect the population or a portion of the population in another state if the ruler of that state treated his or her people in such a way to 'deny their fundamental human rights and to shock the conscience of mankind'.

It is doubtful whether such a right existed—although it has been asserted recently by the US and Vietnam as a justification for military incursions into foreign states—but even if it had, it was largely abused by powerful states seeking to expand their political influence. None the less, a claimed right of humanitarian intervention was invoked by a number of the Great Powers during the nineteenth century to prevent the Ottoman Empire from persecuting minorities in the Middle East and the Balkans.

Nuisance Ended

There were, however, certain humanitarian developments which occurred in international law during the nineteenth and early centuries. Foremost among these was, perhaps, the abolition of the slave trade. Although the economics of slavery in the late eighteenth and early nineteenth centuries made the practice commercially less attractive to European states than it had been previously, its abolition was also motivated by humanitarian concerns. The practice of slavery was first condemned in the Paris Peace Treaty (1814), between Britain and France, but within the space of 50 years the General Act of the Berlin Conference providing for the European colonization of Africa declared that 'trading in slaves is forbidden in conformity with the principles of international law'.

International action against slavery and the slave trade has continued throughout the twentieth century. The League of Nations adopted the Convention to Suppress the Slave Trade and Slavery in 1926 and prohibited the practice of slavery within the former German and Turkish colonies under the League's mandate system at the end of the First World War. The 1926 Convention still remains the basic international document prohibiting the practice of slavery, although it was amended by a protocol (an addendum to the treaty) in 1953 and supplemented in 1956 to deal with problems of defining the acts which constitute slavery in the modern world.

Labourers' Crusade

The other major achievement in international humanitarian law in the second half of the nineteenth century was the formation of the International Committee of the Red Cross (1863) and that organization's sponsorship of two international conventions to protect the victims of war and the treatment of prisoners of war. The work of the Red Cross has continued throughout two world wars and beyond, and it has sponsored a number of conventions dealing not simply with the status and treatment of combatants, but also with the treatment of civilian populations during times of war and limiting the methods by which wars may be waged.

Although of considerable importance, consideration of humanitarian law in time of military conflicts falls outside the scope of this work, which is concerned solely with human rights in time of peace.

Historic Summits

Early twentieth-century efforts in the humanitarian field are largely associated with the post-First World War international settlement. The International Labour Organization, created by the Treaty of Versailles (1919), was a response to the Allied Powers' concerns about social justice and standards of treatment of industrial workers which had largely been prompted by the Bolshevik Revolution of 1917.

The ILO, which became a specialized agency of the UN in 1946, may be seen as the precursor of systems for the protection of economic, social and cultural rights. The ILO has sponsored over 150 conventions dealing with, inter alia, conditions of work, remuneration, child and forced labour, the provision of holidays and social security, discrimination and trade union rights. Its work continues today and the organization ranks among the more important human rights institutions, although its work seldom attracts the attention it deserves.

The League of Nations, an international organization established after the First World War to provide a system for ensuring peace and security, and facilitating international cooperation, made no provision for the protection of human rights. Nevertheless, the League's founding document, the Covenant, committed the member states to work towards certain humanitarian objectives such as establishing human working conditions for individuals, the prohibition of traffic in women and children, the prevention and control of disease and the just treatment of native and colonial peoples. The creation of the mandate system under the League, by which the former colonies of the defeated Axis Powers of Germany and Turkey were placed under the tutelage of the victorious powers, was, perhaps, one of the major humanitarian achievements of the organization. Under this system, 'a sacred trust of civilization' was placed upon the administering states to bring the mandated territories to self-government. While the paternalistic language of the Covenant might be viewed with distaste today, nevertheless the administering powers were required to ensure the absence of racial or religious discrimination in the territories under their guidance. In fact, few of the mandates achieved independence before the Second World War, and two of the territories—Palestine and Namibia-created international problems of considerable longevity. The mandates which had not achieved independence before the Second World War were subsequently transferred to the Trusteeship system under the UN Charter.

Measures for Protection

Mention should also be made here of various treaties concluded after the First World War, since many of these contained provisions for the protection of minorities. While the post-war peace settlement attempted to respect the principle of self-determination based on the concept of national cohesion, it became clear that the re-establishment of Poland and the creation of successor states to the old Austro-Hungarian Empire meant that state boundaries would inevitably create divisions among certain peoples and consign them to live as ethnic, linguistic or religious minorities in the new states. A number of treaties were therefore concluded between the Allied Powers and these states in order to secure the protection of the civil and political rights of the minorities. Specific minority protection treaties were concluded with Poland, Czechoslovakia, Romania and Greece, while provisions on the protection of minorities were included in the peace treaties with Austria, Hungary and Turkey.

In addition to those treaties, certain states made declarations concerning the protection of minorities within their states as a condition of becoming members of the League of Nations; these were Finland, Albania, Latavia, Lithuania, Estonia and Iraq. The League of Nations also exercised a supervisory function in respect of these 'obligations of international concern'. A procedure was established whereby minority groups which considered that rights were being violated could bring the matter to the attention of the

Council of the League. The Council could then refer the matter to an ad-hoc Minorities Committee for conciliation and to attempt a friendly settlement between the parties. If a settlement was not forthcoming, the full Council could determine the matter itself or remit it to the Permanent Court of International Justice for determination.

It is clear that the minorities protection treaties were not concerned with the question of individual rights but rather with the rights of groups. The main purpose of the treaties was to ensure the equal treatment of the ethnic, religious or linguistic minorities in the states in question and to allow the peoples constituting these group to preserve and develop their own distinct identities within the framework of the nation state. It will also be apparent from the states with which treaties were concluded that the existence of minorities within them has proved fertile ground for dispute throughout the twentieth century. While the minority protection treaties did not amount to human rights treaties in the classic individualistic and libertarian mould, none the less they were of substantial significance in that they provide a basis within the context of the League of Nations of a right of petition under international law by a group of private individuals. It is possible to discern here the germ of the right to individual petition to a supervisory and protective international institution under international law.

Role of UN

Despite the advances made in the sphere of humanitarian law and in the protection of economic, social and cultural rights during the nineteenth and early twentieth centuries, it was not until after the cataclysmic events of the Second World War that international human rights law began to develop in a coherent and recognizable way. The atrocities of the Nazis against their own people in Germany and against those conquered territories created such revulsion that, even before the conclusion of the war, the Allies determined that the post-war settlement should include a commitment to the protection of human rights. This they saw as a necessary prerequisite to the creation of a just and stable international order under the auspices of the planned United Nations Organizations.

No longer should a state be able to argue that the way in which it treated its own citizens is simply a matter of exclusive domestic concern, but the treatment of those individuals, should, where appropriate national protection of rights was deficient, become the concern of the international community. The irony here was that while the Soviet Union denounced the Nazi genocide, Stalin himself had, before the war, systematically violated the rights of his own people, disposing of an estimated five million political opponents and enforcing collectivization on large number of peasants. The Soviet Union could also legitimately argue here that the matter was entirely within its domestic jurisdiction. None the less, the Charter of the International Military Tribunal at Nuremberg, which had been created by the Allied Powers, including the Soviet Union, to try Nazi war criminals on the basis of international law existing at the outset of the Second World War, declared the crimes against humanity were crimes under international law. While the tribunal's judgement may have been flawed in that assertion, it nevertheless established the basic principle that how a state treated its own citizens was now a legitimate matter of international concern.

Charter of Human Rights

Although Article 2(7) of the UN Charter reaffirmed the principle of non-intervention by the Organization in matters essentially within the domestic jurisdiction of the member states, thus appearing to preclude international intervention in the human rights field, it also contained several specific references to human rights. The Preamble to the Charter reaffirmed the faith of the 'peoples of the United Nations' in fundamental human rights, in the dignity and worth of the human person and in 'the equal rights of men and women'. The language of reaffirmation is interesting, since it appears to presuppose the existence of human rights prior to the entry into force of the Charter which, at least in the sense of positive law, would have seemed at that time to be a dubious claim. The Charter also included as one of its purposes in Article 1 'promoting respect for human rights and fundamental freedoms for all'. The promotion of human rights by the UN was also reinforced, by Article 55, and under Article 56 the member states pledged themselves to take joint and separate action in cooperation with the UN for the achievement of this and other objectives under Article 55. A number of other provisions in the Charter concerning various institutional competencies also referred to human rights as a general category. Although the UN Charter therefore appeared to acknowledge the prior existence of phenomena known as human rights, it contained no list of such rights, nor did it refer to a source for discovering exactly what the rights were. There had been a proposal to incorporate a list of rights in the Charter during its drafting, but this had been defeated. The absence of a catalogue of human rights was nevertheless viewed as a defect and a move to draft, in the words to US President Truman, 'an international bill of rights' was undertaken within one year of the entry into force of the Charter.

The work of drafting the 'international bill of rights' was assigned to the Commission of Human Rights (CHR), a subsidiary organ of the UN's Economic and Social Council (ECOSOC). The Commission, which was composed of government representatives, decided that the catalogue of human rights should take the form of a resolution of the UN General Assembly, since it was unlikely that any consensus could be achieved on incorporation of the rights into the Charter or that support for a legally binding human rights treaty would be forthcoming. The major advantage of a declaration in the form of resolution was that it would not be legally binding but would, in the words of Eleanor Roosevelt, the chairman of the CHR, proclaim 'a common standard of achievement for all peoples and all nation's. The Universal Declaration in its final form contained a list of civil and political rights and economic, social and cultural rights to which all persons were entitled without discrimination. Significantly, however, the Declaration did not contain any institution or mechanism for ensuring that the rights were observed. Although the Declaration was originally adopted in a non-legally binding form, subsequent practice has transformed it into an instrument of considerable juridical potency, although its precise legal status is still the subject of some debate.

Agreements in Operation

As it was recognized by the UN General Assembly at the outset that the Universal Declaration was not intended to create legally binding obligations on the member states, it mandated the CHR to complete the drafting of an internationally binding treaty which would not only transform the rights referred to in the Declaration into positive law, but would also provide institutions and mechanisms for supervision and enforcement. Unfortunately, this task proved to be more difficult than originally envisaged, since a dispute arose between members of the Commission about the relationship between civil and political rights, on the one hand and economic and social rights, on the other, and also over the appropriate means of implementation, supervision and protection. It was finally decided that instead of a single treaty or covenant being drafted to protect both categories of rights, two covenants would be prepared, each devoted to the different groups of rights. The two separate covenants, the International Covenant on Civil and Political Rights (ICCPR) and the International Covenant on Economic and Social Rights (ICESCR), were opened for signature in 1966, but did not enter into force—that is become effective—until a full decade later in 1976. The salient difference between the covenants is that while Article 2 of the ICCPR provides that the protected rights will be respected and ensured immediately, Article 2 of the ICESCR simply provides that states should 'recognize' the rights contained in the Covenant and should implement them progressively in accordance with specific programmes. It is also of particular significance that while the ICCPR establishes the Human Rights Committee (HRC) to supervise implementation of the Covenant and to provide by means of an optional protocol a mechanism by which individuals may petition the HRC, the ICESCR simply consigns the function of supervision to a political body of the UN, i.e. ECOSOC.

Important Conventions

Notwithstanding the difficulties of establishing the 'universal' system for promoting and protecting human rights, the UN also undertook programmes to draft legally binding instruments to deal with specific aspects of human rights. These have included treaties on the prevention and punishment of genocide. The prohibition of sexual and religious discrimination, the suppression and punishment of apartheid, the prohibition of the practice of torture, international cooperation on matters relating to refugees and statelessness and, most recently, a specific convention on the rights of the child. Brief mention should also be made here of a number of institutional measures and initiatives taken by UN in order to promote and protect human rights.. ECOSOC in particular has established procedures under Resolutions 1235 and 1503 by which gross and consistent violations of human rights by particular states may be investigated.

End of Exploitation

Of fundamental importance in the overall development of the UN's concern with human rights has been its practice in the field of decolonization. As indicated earlier, a number of the mandates created the League of Nations after the First World War had not proceeded to self-government before the outbreaks of the Second World War. The UN Charter therefore provided for the transfer of the mandates to a trusteeship systems under which the territories would be administered and prepared for independence. One of the basic objectives of the trusteeship system was stated in Article 76(1)(c) of the Charter to be encouragement of respect for human rights and fundamental freedoms for all. This is supervised by the UN through the medium of the Trusteeship Council. There is now only one trust territory left in the world—the Pacific Islands Territory—which is administered by the USA.

It was not only the former mandates which became subject to UN supervision under of the Charter. States with colonies or non-self governing territories (NSGTs) were placed under an obligation to have paramount regard for the well-being of the peoples within the territories and to facilitate their development. Administering states were placed under an obligation to report to the Secretary General of the UN of the advances made in their colonies. While Chapter XI did not place an obligation on administering states to grant independence to their colonies, none the less subsequent developments in the 1960s greatly increased the momentum of decolonization.

General Assembly Resolution 1541(XV), clarifying the reporting obligations of administering states, was adopted together with Resolution 1514(XV), the Declaration on the Granting of Independence to Colonial Countries and Peoples. This resolution called for the immediate decolonization of all NSGTs through the exercise by the people in such territories of the right of self-determination. No pretext, such as lack of economic or educational preparedness, was to be permitted to retard the process. Although the UN Charter referred to the principle of self-determination, it certainly did not refer to a right of self-determination. It is, however, now generally accepted that such a right exists in international law, and that view is reinforced by General Assembly Resolution 2625, the Declaration on Principles of International Law Concerning Friendly Relations and Cooperation Among States in Accordance with the Charter of the United Nations, which is regarded as a convenient statement of customary international law, and a common Article 1 to both international covenants which provide that all peoples have the right to self-determination. The underlying rational for inclusion of this right, which is clearly a collective right, is that a people which is under alien dominating through the institution of colonialism is not free, thus any notion of the enjoyment of individual or other rights within that context is meaningless.

Whether the right to self-determination extends beyond a right to decolonization or to the right to minority secession is an open question, although a reading of Resolution 2625 would seem to support this where the minority in question is subject to discriminatory treatment by the government of the state. Certainly, the effects of large-scale decolonization by the former colonial powers has had a massive impact on the structure of international society. New states, largely in the developing world, have transformed the context of international political and legal debate by an insistence on the restructuring of the international system to respond to their needs. It is largely from these developing states that third-generation rights have emerged.

An international development that occurred during the period of *detente* between the West and Communist blocs during the early 1970s, and which deserves mention, was the Conference on Security and Cooperation in Europe, otherwise, known as the Helsinki Process, since the Conference was convened in the Finnish capital of that name in 1973. Although the primary function of the Helsinki Process was to establish a framework for the development of peace and security in Europe, it also resulted in formal consideration of human rights issues. While the Soviet Union was concerned to have its western borders recognized, the West sought to exact human rights commitments from the Eastern bloc in exchange.

The Final Act of the Conference, which, significantly, was stated to be non-binding, declared the participating governments determination to respect and put into practice respect for human rights and fundamental freedoms including the freedom of thought, conscience, religion or belief. They also resolved that they would respect the rights of peoples and their right to self-determination.

Although the Final Act was clearly not a legally binding instrument, it did contribute in a significant way to state practice in the field of human rights, since it was declaratory of accepted human rights norms. In this way, it might be said to have contributed to customary international law in the human rights field.

Of considerable importance in the Helsinki Process was the fact that the Final Act of the Conference provided for assessment of the commitments established by a series of review conferences. This created the institutional structure whereby the declared intentions of the parties, including observance of respect for human rights, could be measured. The Helsinki Process continued in Madrid and more recently Paris (1990). At the latter meeting, the 'Charter of Paris for a New Europe' was adopted in which it was declared by the 34 participating states that:

> Human rights and fundamental freedoms are the birthright of all human beings, are inalienable and guaranteed by law. Their protection and promotion is the first responsibility of government. Respect for them is an essential safeguard against an over-mighty state.

There then followed a commitment to democratic government and political, pluralism and a list of individual civil and political rights to which all are entitled without discrimination. Although the Paris Charter is, again, not legally binding, it nevertheless reaffirms the juridical significance of the state rights under international law. It also marks the fact that the former Communist bloc states have demonstrated their commitment to the liberal-democratic ideal.

Different Systems

There are at present three regional human rights systems. These are the European human rights system, the inter-American human rights system and the Organization of African Unity's Charter of Human and Peoples' Rights. There have been proposals for the establishment of an Islamic human rights treaty, the most recent being the Cairo Declaration in 1990 by the Organization of the Islamic Conference, but as yet no concrete results have occurred. A regional human rights treaty for South-East Asia and the Pacific has also been proposed, but this emanated from LAWASIA, a private lawyers' group and has, as yet, had no discernible impact on the governments of the region.

Of the three systems currently in existence, the European Convention on Human Rights and Fundamental Freedoms (1950) is the most developed in terms of its longevity and the quantity of its jurisprudence. Created by the Council of Europe (an international institution designed to facilitate European cooperation; which should not be confused with the European Community), the European Convention was designed to fulfil a three-fold purpose; first, to strengthen democracy and commitment to the rule of law by the member states, second, to sound an alarm against incipient totalitarianism; and, third, to act as a bulwark against the perceived threat of encroaching communism. While the Convention has performed these functions tolerably well, the experience of the Greek Coup and its aftermath in 1967 demonstrated the limits of the Convention's effectiveness. Here, a military coup by a *junta* of army colonels resulted in totalitarian government and the large-scale denial of human rights. In particular, political opponents of the junta were arbitrarily imprisoned and subjected to torture. Despite its denunciation of the Convention and its withdrawal from the Council of Europe, Greece remained responsible under the Convention for its actions. Although this caused difficulty and considerable embarrassment for Greece in the conduct of its international relations, it provided little protection for those whose rights had been violated. None the less, in the 1970s, the newly democratized states of Greece, Spain and Portugal ratified the European Convention as a means of strengthening their democratic processes.

The main achievement of the European Convention, however, has been to provide a mechanism by which individuals who believe that their rights have been violated by their states can petition the European Commission in an attempt to secure redress. As will be seen subsequently, the Commission's main function is to secure a friendly settlement between the individual and his or her state, but if this is not forthcoming the matter may be remitted to the European Court of Human Rights, whose rulings and awards of damages are, binding on the state. Through this mechanism, substantial numbers of individuals have secured redress for both major and comparatively minor violations of their rights.

The European Convention and its ten protocols are concerned primarily with the protection of civil and political rights, although Protocol 1 does seek to protect the right to private property. Protection of economic and social rights in Europe is sought to be achieved by the procedures established by the European Social Charter (1961). This instrument, which was also adopted by the Council of Europe, is intended to be complementary to the European Convention.

Like ICESCR, it is drafted in a way that makes it clear that the realization of economic and social rights is to be achieved progressively. Supervision under the Social Charter is to be achieved simply by a state reporting system to the Council of Europe by a Committee of Independent Experts. While it might have been reasonable to expect that Europe would have been much dynamic than other regions of the world in implementing fully economic, social, and cultural rights, this has not proved to be so, and the Charter has been something of a disappointment.

The inter-American human rights system is distinctive since it is formed by two separate but clearly interrelated mechanisms of protection. First, all member states of the Organization of American States (OAS), a regional organization whose objectives are similar to those of the UN, are committed to human rights obligations under the OAS Charter. Like the UN Charter, the OAS Charter, which was adopted in 1948, does not contain a list of protectable rights. Nevertheless, through the processes of amendment of the

OAS Charter and institutional adaptation, the American Declaration of the Rights and Duties of Man (1948), which may be regarded as the analogue of the Universal Declaration, has been recognized by the Inter-American Court of Human Rights in an advisory ruling as an authoritative interpretation of the OAS Charter which is binding on all OAS member states. Furthermore, the Inter-American Commission on Human Rights is obliged by its Statute to apply the American Declaration when dealing with human rights issues under its country report, on site investigation or individual petition procedures.

The second pillar to the inter-American human rights system is the American Convention of Human Rights, otherwise known as the Pact to San Jose (1969). This is modelled on the European Convention, but since it was drafted at a later date, its framers were able to take account of some of the defects of the European Convention and correct; them. The American Convention, like its European counterpart, is concerned almost exclusively with civil and political rights, although a protocol, the Pact of San Salvador (1989), has added a list of economic, social and cultural rights which are to be implemented progressively by the states parties. A novel feature of the Protocol is that it creates a right of individual petition to the Inter-American Commission in cases where the right to join a trade union or the right to education is denied.

As with the European Convention, supervision of the rights protected by the American Convention is to be achieved through a commission and a court. The Commission screens all individual applications to ensure they comply with the Convention's admissibility requirements and, in the case of admissibility, attempts to secure a friendly settlement between the parties. If no friendly settlement is achieved, the case is remitted to the Court, which has the power to make binding rulings; and award compensatory damages against a delinquent state. Under the Convention, the Inter-American Court is given a very wide power to render advisory opinions or judgements relating not just to the Convention itself, but also to the OAS Charter and 'other treaties concerning the protection of human rights in the America States'. While this power of the Court has been utilized considerably by the Commission and member states of the OAS, it is significant that the contentious procedure; of the Court, that is, its procedure where individual violations of human rights have been alleged, has hardly been employed. There are, perhaps, a number of reasons for this, which will be considered in a later chapter.

The third and most recent of the regional system for the protection of human rights is the African Charter on Human and people's Rights (1981), which is sometimes known as the Banjul Charter after the Gambian capital where it was drafted. The Charter, which like the human rights instruments takes the form of multilateral treaty, was adopted by the Organization of African Unity in Nairobi in 1981 and it entered into force in 1986. While it enumerates the traditional list of civil and political rights, it differs from the other regional treaties by including within it economic, social and cultural rights and, more controversially, third-generation rights or rights of solidarity.

Thus, the right to self-determination, the right to peace and the right to a good environment are included in the text. Implementation of these rights is to be achieved solely through the functioning of the African Commission on Human Rights, since there is no provision for the creation of an African human rights court. The African Commission has now been in existence for some four years and it has received a number of state reports on the implementation of the protected rights and a small number of individual communications. As yet, no decisions have been reached on these communications.

Role of NGOs

Much of the foregoing text has been devoted to action taken in the sphere of human rights at a governmental level. Discussion of human rights would be incomplete, however, without some reference to the role played by NGOs or groups of private individuals concerned with such issues.

The earliest of these NGOs might be said to have been the International Committee of the Red Cross, founded in 1863 following a private initiative by Swiss physician Henri Dunant who was appalled by the suffering of the wounded following the battle of Solferino in which 70,000 men were killed or wounded. In the twentieth century, however, the number of NGOs concerned with human rights has proliferated, as the directory of Human Rights Internet (itself an NGO) will testify. Among the more well-known are the International Commission of Jurists, Amnesty International, the Anti-Slavery Society, Article 19 and the World Council of Churches. Some of these NGOs have been granted a degree of recognition by international organizations. ECOSOC, for example, is empowered by Article 71 of the UN Charter to make suitable arrangements for consultation with NGOs interested in its spheres of activity, and ECOSOC has conferred 'consultative status' on a number of such groups. Perhaps the most important work of NGOs is however, their actions in exposing to public view violations of human rights within states.

In many cases, adverse publicity about their human rights record is what states fear most. It should also be noted that NGOs are able to make communications to competent international institutions on behalf of victims of human rights abuses where those victims themselves are incapable of engaging the appropriate procedures because, for example, they are being held incommunicado.

Regular Process

From this brief historical excursus, it is perhaps apparent that both instruments and institutions for the protection of human rights on a universal and regional basis have developed exponentially since the end of the Second World War. There now exists a confusing plethora of treaties, conventions, covenants, charters and declarations dealing with human rights and related humanitarian issues. The proliferation of competent institutions under these instruments is no less confusing. Furthermore, a great many activities in the human rights field take place at a bureaucratic level, largely through the modification of existing institutions and institutional procedures, which are hardly apparent to the majority of casual observers. Much of the remainder of this book will therefore be devoted to a systematic analysis of the existing instruments and institutions concerned with human rights protection, and it will also attempt to illuminate the less accessible areas of international bureaucratic activity in the field.

Before this task; can be undertaken, there are two important preliminary matters which must be considered. First, considerable reference has been made so far to various groups of rights, especially the two major categories of civil and political rights and economic, social and cultural rights, without any attempt to define what they are.

4

Cultivation of Human Rights

Dignity in living is basic entitlement of every individual. The principles of human rights were drawn up by human beings as a way of ensuring that the dignity of everyone is properly and equally respected, that is, to ensure that a human being will be able to fully develop and use human qualities such as intelligence, talent and conscience and satisfy his or her spiritual and other needs.

Dignity gives an individual a sense of value and worth. The existence of human rights demonstrates that human beings are aware of each other's worth. Human dignity is not an individual, exclusive and isolated sense. It is a part of our common humanity.

Human rights enable us to respect each other and live with each other. In other words, they are not only rights to be requested or demanded but rights to be respected and be responsible for. The rights that apply to you also apply to others.

The denial of human rights and fundamental freedoms not only is an individual and personal tragedy, but also creates conditions of social and political unrest, sowing the seeds of violence and conflict within and between societies and nations.

Basically, human rights are the claims of the individual for such conditions as are essential for the fullest realization of the innate characteristics which nature has bestowed him/ her with as a human being. It implies that there are inherent and inalienable rights which are due to an individual by virtue of his/her being a human being and that they are necessary to ensure the dignity of every person as a human being irrespective of one's race, religion, nationality language, sex, or any other factor.

All "claims" of the individual, for example, freedom to live as one wishes to or to do whatever one wants to do, cannot be treated as human rights. Only those claims which are essential for the development of one's personality and recognized as such by the "society" constitute rights. But one has to recognize the fact that this idea is not the reality and that what is conceptually recognized as rights, is often not legally enforced or enforceable. So one must distinguish between what is morally and universally accepted as rights and what constitute 'legal rights' established according to the law-creating process and judicially enforceable in a given society.

The nature has bestowed man with two related characteristics first as an individual and then as a social being. Living in a group organized community is natural to him. To understand human rights, one must look through their history, which will take us back to the day when man first started living in groups. It was natural that in many instances might prevailed over what was right; those who held power dominated the weak.

With the passage of time, these rights or established customs or understandings including the relationship between the ruler and the ruled were brought together in different forms in various parts of the world.

They found expression in the concept of natural law and

became the symbol of peoples movement against absolute despotism, and the corner stone of constitutional democracy every where. The Magna Carta in England, the American Declaration of Independence, the French Declarations on the Rights of Man, the Bolschevik Revolution in Russia could be cited as important landmarks in the development of the concept of human rights.

Magna Carta yielded certain concessions only to the feudal lords, though it did set limitations to arbitrary rule and laid the foundation for the Rule of law. The American Declaration followed by constitutional amendments contained fairly exhaustive guarantees for the rights of man. While the American and French declarations set the seal on the basic principles of equality before the law, freedom of thought, human dignity and democratic government, the countries undergoing rapid industrialization were experiencing the need more for social justice and economic security. The Bolschevik Revolution in Russia (1917), went a step further. It emphasized that economic and social rights were as important as the civil and political rights.

In Europe and North America, the concept of natural right was secularized, rationalized and democratized. By the end of the 18th century there emerged a concept what was called "the Rights of Man". This concept covered substantially what is now known as civil and political rights. Beginning in the mid-nineteenth century, the developments that followed, sometime accompanied by violence within the industrial-capital economy of Europe and North America took a new direction.

While countries in Europe and North America, with rapid industrialization, were moving towards larger freedoms both political and economic, the people of the rest of the world were more or less experiencing the sufferings and humiliations of colonialism and imperialism. It was natural that interaction and comparison between peoples of the two groups generate wider awareness and demand for human rights among the peoples under colonial rule. For them, a declaration of great historical significance was the clarion call made at the turn of the century in India, by Bal Gangadhar Tilak: "Swaraj is my birth right and I shall have it". (Swaraj means complete self government and independence).

Universalization Process

As a result of convergence of several historical factors, a concept of human rights was emerged by the middle of the present century. This development found expression in the Charter of the United Nations-which proclaimed "universal respect for, and observance of, human rights and Fundamental freedom for all without distinctions as to race, sex, language or religion." The Charter made promotion of these rights as one of its basic purposes and obligated member states "to take joint and separate action in cooperation with the United Nations for the achievement of this purpose". Thus human rights were being universalized and internationalized. UN charter has laid down principles of a general nature. Human rights are not defined or specified in this Charter.

There arise necessity to define human rights and fundamental freedoms so that the objectives of the Charter could be pursued and an international system, for promotion and protection of human rights could be instituted.

Hence in December 1948, the UN General Assembly proclaimed the Universal Declaration of Human Rights. It defines specific rights-civil and political as well as economic, social and cultural-with equality and freedom from discrimination as a principal and recurrent theme. The Universal Declaration was not conceived as law but as a "common standard of achievement" for all people and all nations.

The Declaration carries no legal sanction to compel states to meet the obligation of ensuring observance and implementation of human rights enshrined in the Declaration. To seek such a legal framework and to convert the norms set in the Declaration into legally binding obligations, efforts were directed, beginning 1947. After 20 years of preparatory work the General Assembly promulgated International Covenants in December 1966, comprising three instruments as follows:

(i) International Covenants on Economic, Social an Cultural Rights,

(ii) International Covenants on Civil and Political Rights, and

(iii) Optional Protocol (on individual petition) to the Covenants on Civil and Political Rights.

The covenants have assumed a prime place in international law as the instruments that influence and at the same time judge the disregard of States and by which the conditions of individual rights in particular countries are to be assessed.

Rights and Obligations in Society

Man is a social animal. An individual can achieve full development of his personality by proper association with all other human beings. So his rights are not coterminous with his free desires, but can only exist insofar as they do not impinge upon the rights of the rest of the community. Thus, rights implies duties. In other words, duties can be described as the "rights" of the community against the individual.

Many civilizations have sought to bring about and promote social order and harmony not by setting forth the rights of the members of the community but by framing rules of social behaviour in terms of duties. But today, the growth of modern state system has changed the lives of human beings almost everywhere. Therefore, an approach to realization of rights through emphasis on duties could prove to be counterproductive. A person cannot enjoy one's rights if one is not performing one's duties towards others.

Base of Ideology

The study of human rights occupies a very important place, in the discussion of politics and political theory. Internationally human rights occupy a very high place among the theorists. The most outstanding theories of human rights are given below:

1. The Theory of Natural Rights;
2. The Legal Theory of Rights;
3. The Social Welfare Theory of Rights;
4. The Idealist Theory of Rights;
5. The Historical Theory of Rights.

Natural Rights

The theory was advocated by the authors of the Social Contract Theory like Hobbes, Locke and Rousseau. They say that man had natural rights even before society and state were born. According to Locke, nature has made all men free and rational, and has given him rights like right to life and liberty. Herbert Spencer, who also thinks along the same lines believes that the process of evolution shows that all men have the fundamental right to equal freedom, which enables them to do what they will. Such a right comes from nature, and not from any human agency like state.

The theory was in the limelight in the seventeenth and eighteenth centuries; its basis was essentially non-juristic. Rights are natural. Every human being enjoys them and finds them indispensable for his very existence.

The theory can be back to ancient Greece and Rome. The stoic philosophers of Greece spoke about natural rights and their writings influenced Rome. The Romans believed that all human beings were subject to certain common principles of life as created by nature, and hence, these principles, which Roman thinkers called natural law, were applicable to people living within the Roman empire. This natural law bound people of all races together in Rome.

The concept of natural law, suffered a set-back in the middle ages, as the Church thinkers spoke on terms of the law of God and of the Church. The English political thinker John Locke in the seventeenth century took up the concept again and made it important. While dealing with his social contract, Locke spoke of natural rights. The declarations made by the American and the French revolutionaries echoed the ideas of Locke.

The Americans proclaimed that "all men are by nature equally free and independent and have certain inherent rights." Similarly, the French National Assembly breathed the same spirit pertaining to natural rights as given by the great American leaders like Jefferson. The French Assembly spoke in terms of "the natural, inalienable and sacred rights of man." Rousseau also spoke of natural rights. He said that though man surrendered some of his natural rights, he continued to enjoy the remaining rights.

In England, Thomas Paine spoke of the principle of natural rights without connecting it with the Social Contract Theory. According to Paine, the rights to "liberty, property, security and resistance to oppression" are based on natural rights.

It is proper to interpret that natural rights stand for those rights which work for man's good and create opportunities for his development. As far as theory says that natural rights are necessary for man's ethical and moral development, it is very valuable.

Legal Rights

According to the Legal Theory of Rights, the state is the source of rights. Rights have not been gifted by nature, and are not in man's nature itself. They are created by the state whose membership brings rights to man. So, rights can be regarded as artificial creations, Rights emerge from the state, and are maintained by the state. The state makes laws, and laws create rights. The, individual owes every right to the state, and he has no right against the state. Thus, the legal theory is against the theory of natural rights.

According to the theory, Rights spring from the state. The state defines what rights are and what are not rights and the state provides the list of basic or fundamental rights. The State makes laws to uphold rights, and also sets up a machinery to enforce law and uphold rights. The state can change rights and their contents as it can change laws.

Pluralists strongly criticised the theory. They give great importance to various associations, and say that the membership of the state alone does not confer rights on the individual. According to them, the individual owes much to the various social groups for enjoying different rights, and it is incorrect to regard the state alone as the source of all rights.

Welfare Rights

According to the Social Welfare Theory, rights are created by society, and are aimed at realising social welfare. Conditions which make the individual and society happy are rights, and these should have precedence over customs, usages, traditions and natural rights. This theory looks at rights solely through the angle of social welfare. The theory has the great merit of upholding the principle of social welfare. Utilitarians, who supported the theory made a practical approach to rights, and advocate legislation in different fields to uphold rights.

Idealistic Approach

The Idealist or Personality Theory of Rights says that the human being needs congenial external conditions for the development of his personality. Green, the idealist thinker of England says that rights are powers necessary to the fulfilment of man's vocation as a moral being. Krause, Henrici and Wilde said that without rights man cannot become his best self.

It is implied that rights arise in a society, and the rights of the individual should be in harmony with those of others. Rights are to be linked with the individual good and the common good of all. The theory links with moral development of man, and looks rights essentially from the ethical point of view. The opportunities or rights are to be enjoyed by the individual and society. Hence they are to be understood in a social context. As the individual wants to develop his personality, others in society also have a similar aim. According to the idealists like Kant and Green, conditions for the individual's ethical and moral development are created by the state. But, extreme idealists like Hegel subordinate the individual to the state, and expect the individual to surrender himself completely to the state.

Historical Approach

As per the Historical Theory of Rights, rights are the result of historical evolution. In ancient times, rights were based on customs and usages. But in the modern state, rights are recognised and supported by law. In the course of ages, human beings in society evolved certain usages, traditions and customs for the common good, and these unwritten form became the basis of law, which gave rights to the individuals in actual written form. To the primitive man, custom was unwritten law. A custom which people go on following generation after generation becomes a customary right, and this provides a basis for law. The theory says that several rights rose as a result of historical evolution. When the state was evolved, human beings must have had certain customs and traditions hardened by time and these provided an evolution. Certain rights are created by law, and they do not have history as the source of their origin.

All products of history or custom cannot be regarded as rights or continued as rights. For example, in some countries in ancient times, buying and selling slaves was a custom or right of the slave-dealer. So we can see that long-standing customs can come in the way of rights instead of becoming rights themselves.

General Observation

The Contract Theory : It would be a grave mistake to attempt to trace back the origins of human rights to social systems which were not familiar with its basic condition governing the existence of human rights, namely, the idea of freedom and equality. It is not possible to project a new institution upon social relation which have been superseded, and to which it does not correspond. In order for human rights to appear as the general rule in society, and for them to be felt both as a need and as a reality. It was indispensable for there to be basic social changes in the relations of production (more precisely, in the relations of ownership) within the previous social system-feudalism. Everyone's rights had to be recognised as being, in principle, equal with regard to ownership and the acquisition and enjoyment of property.

The right to property had previously been regarded as a natural right or in other words as a fundamental and inalienable right of man, first by Aquinas, then later more explicitly by Grotius, who set this right outside the universe of natural rights Grotius had asserted that the right to property had been "introduced by human will" and so that we should not be offended. He invited us to understand and to consider our property as corresponding to natural law.

Two major ideas emerged from this line of reasoning, but both subsequently splintered off from this origin were: the ideas of freedom and equality. The idea of freedom was that of free ownership, of the free possession of property and to this was later added the idea of free enterprise, with all other corollaries of freedom.

As for the idea of equality, it too owes its origin, to the appearance of a new type of ownership. It signified equality for all as regards the right to acquire property. But considering more closely its true origin turns out to be connected with the political idea of the state in the modern sense of the term. It also concerned equality in respect of participation in political life. Consequently, equality was, a political idea and a political right, whereas freedom possessed an economic character, at least so far as its origins were concerned.

According to modern political philosophy, every individual should possess equal rights in the life of the State. Subsequently the notion of equality was made to apply to the whole of man, to ' all of man's abilities and all of his rights. However, an important difference was to remain between freedom and equality-bound up with ownership, freedom was considered to be a right which the State would not restrict because it was an absolute right. This was not true of equality as it was regarded as a political right and, as such, it could be restricted by the State.

Origins at the Level of Positive Law : The origins of human rights, in respect of positive law, are traced back to documents which appeared in recent centuries. According to this point of view human rights are contracts concluded by the State with the population and, first of all, with the mobility. These contracts are seen as preserving certain rights for men while preventing the State from interferring in the exercise of those rights. The legal force of these rights is seen as being founded (contrary to the conception of the theory of the contract founded on natural law) on the will of the State, or better still, in the circumstances of the period, on their recognition by the King.

The fact that human rights or agreements with a similar objective in view have been given the form of Charters, Bills or Petitions and, where appropriate, Declarations, has led to these documents being placed on the same theoretical footing, although they were produced at different periods and for different purposes. In particular, in the specialized literature, a whole discussion is to be found on the common or different nature of the Magna Carta, the Petition of Rights and the Bill of Rights, as well as of the Declaration of Virginia and the Bills which followed it, and the French Declaration of 1789.

In Central Europe, George Jellinek's book on the declaration of human rights (1904) caused a turmoil by subscribing to the view that the documents-i.e., Magna Carta, the Petition of Rights and the Bills of Rights as well as the Declaration of Virginia and the Bills which followed it and the French Declaration of 1789– followed on from each other and were consequently directly related to each other. Moreover, he was not the only one who expressed that opinion.

Jellinek found it necessary to observe, in the second edition of his book, that in United States the Bill of Rights has represented the culminating point, whereas the French Declaration was the starting point, which in itself constitutes a radical difference. Jellinek indirectly acknowledges, at the level of the history of civilization and of philosophy, as well as from the social point of view, the importance of the Declaration adopted by the Constituent Assembly of 1789. The starting point of human rights in the modern sense of the term is clearly to be found both in the 'Declaration of the Rights of Man and of the Citizen', voted during the French Revolution, and in the social conditions underlying it.

Conceptions Based on "Natural Law": According to the most traditional conception of human rights, at the time that men passed from the primitive state to the social state they concluded a contract between themselves, and by this contract they renounced part of their natural rights, which they hid enjoyed in their free state, while preserving certain basic rights : the right to life, freedom and equality. The rights thus preserved constituted eternal and inalienable rights that every social and State system was obliged to respect.

As for the origin of these rights, there are various differences to be found in the way in which the conception founded on natural law is set forth. The theory of the social contract is the product of the school of natural law, which made its appearance in the 15th and 16th centuries. According to this school, human rights are bound up with man's basic nature from which they derive, and for which reason they constitute human rights.

According to another conception, which goes back to Locke, the starting point was tolerance in respect of their religions or, in other words, right to profess any religion. Again, what is involved is a conception referring to natural law. Furthermore, this idea set the scene for the creation of the United States of America, considering that freedom of religion played an important role in this connection.

There exists other conceptions of human rights, for instance that according to which human rights originated in human understanding. Conceptions of this kind were already subscribed to the Middle Ages. Virtually all the feudal varieties of the natural law theory belong to this type of thinking, and the same is true of the Kantian theory of law, founded on reason. This theory, like all others is forced to start off from certain promises established *a priori* and from which it is possible to deduce human rights.

The Rights of Man and of the Citizen : The French Declaration of the Rights of Man and of the Citizen of 1789 and other documents which appeared subsequently, made a distinction between the rights of man and, on the other, rights of the citizen. Man in these texts appears as a being who is imagined to exist outside society, who is assumed to exist prior to society. As for the citizen, he is subject to the State's authority. On this account, the rights of man are natural and inalienable rights, while the rights of the citizen are positive rights, rights granted by the positive law.

In the course of social, political and ideological development, this hierarchy in respect of the appearance and existence of the rights of man and of the citizen has, to certain extent, become blurred. As the distinctions between the rights of man and the rights of the citizen has disappeared, the two categories have merged. Insofar as certain traces of this distinction have remained, it has assumed new forms and has come to appear as a criterion for differentiating between branches of law. All rights as a whole which are recognized by constitutions are thus considered as belonging to the category of the rights of the citizen, wherever the rights of man are those covered by international law.

Like this, the problem of human rights has been entirely reduced to the question of the simple relationship between two branches of law, a relationship in which constitutional law seems to be subordinate to international law.

Constitutional Law : In national systems human rights re-appear in the form of citizen's rights in constitutional law. It is in the constitutions that human rights are established. For example, the French Constitution of 1791, the text of which is preceded by the Declaration of the Rights of man and of the citizen of 1789. The constitutions which followed no longer provide a general formulation of these rights in their preambles but integrate them unto the actual text as basic rights upon which the State is founded. These rights determine the relations between the State and the citizen and define the domain in which the State does not intercede.

At the same time, human rights become affected by a specific bias in constitutional law in that they acquire a particular character, linked up with the State's internal structure. The various constitutions, strange to say, omit-to define the effect of the rights listed. They do not explicitly State which of these rights have a direct effect on the basic of Constitutional law, and which ones necessitates special laws in order for them to be put into effect. Consequently, fundamental rights are provisions binding solely upon the legislature and are of no benefit to citizens except by this indirect channel.

In the socialist countries, there are different views as to the place that the citizen's fundamental rights should occupy in the constitution, whether they should be formulated ahead of constitutional law or, on the contrary, be included in the actual text of the constitution.

In constitution law, there is a mixture of human rights and citizen's rights. It falls to theory to re-establish the notion of human rights and to set them back in their place. In practice, constitutions contain a hierarchical system of citizen's rights which constitutes the starting point of the system of human rights as international law outlines it.

Human Rights have ushered in a new era. Fukuyama's conceit (I mean it in both senses) that the triumph of Western liberalism has stopped the clock of change—has put an end to history—is already waning. We may reflect that human rights themselves have played a sacrificial role in this process, for the demise of the regimes of Eastern Europe was accelerated by a megaphone rhetoric of human rights from States, including our own, with an embarrassing capacity for overlooking human rights abuses among their own allies and clients and even within their own frontiers. The message between the lines has been that human rights are a commodity like any other, capable of being traded for political or economic advantage, and the rhetoric little more than the conduct of politics by other means.

This is not, however, a complaint about the politicisation of human rights. They are by nature political, for they seek to condition how States treat individuals. The reason why it is we who feel able to lecture others about them is that human rights are historically and ideologically the property of the liberal democracies of the West. In their received and accepted form, whether one takes the European Convention or the Universal Declaration as the example, they enshrine values which are universal neither in time nor in place. They are in essence the enlightenment's values of possessive individualism, derived from the historic paradigm, which has shaped our world, of the conscious human actor whose natural enemy is the State—a necessary evil—and in whose maximum personal liberty lies the maximum benefit for society. To accept, as we can and should, that this view is rooted in time and place is not to consign it to the bin of relativism, for the same has been and will continue to be true of all historic proclamations of self-evident and universal truths. (The two most self-evident truths of life on this planet are after all that the earth is flat and that the sun goes round it.) The truth that all men are created equal was far from self-evident to the slaves owned by some of the men who proclaimed it at the dawn of American republicanism. That free speech or family life is today a fundamental individual right is by no means self-evident in a good number of the contemporary world's States, where history and conditions have made it apparent that they are primarily the State's business; and it is entirely conceivable that the States of Western Europe may during the coming century recast their thinking about family life and the right of the incurably or expensively ill to life itself as social and economic pressures be are down on ethics and theology. Who will then be right: our grandchildren or us?

State of Affairs

It is perfectly possible to recognise the localisation of ideas in time and place and to assert that they are none the worse for it; indeed, that ideas which pretend to universality are historical delusions. To do so, however, carries two corollaries. One is that as times change our premises and assumptions about the content of fundamental rights will change. Secondly, what is made of currently accepted rights in each country and each generation by its courts and adjudicators is itself a function of time and place. (Law spends its life stretched on the rack between certainty and adaptability, sometimes groaning audibly but mostly maintaining the stoical appearance of steady uniformity which public confidence demands.) But lest the mask become the face, it is important that new generations of lawyers should become actively curious about why the certainties of the law themselves change constantly.

How and why is it that the same American Constitution in 1896 legitimated racial segregation in public services and then in 1954 forbade it? How does it come about that not dissimilar abortion laws have in recent years been struck down by Canada's Supreme Court as too restrictive and by Germany's Constitutional Court as too permissive? On our own patch, how did it come to be self-evident to the Court of Appeal in 1925 that it was perfectly all right for an education authority to sack married women teachers on the ground that their duties lay at home or, in 1948, that it was perfectly all right for Wednesbury Corporation to use its cinema licensing powers to stop young people going to the pictures on Sunday?

Not one of these decisions, each of them affecting what we

would recognise now as fundamental human rights, is intelligible today except by situating the reasoning of the deciding court in its peculiar time and place; and the same will, I hope, be true of the decisions handed down by this judicial generation—for it would be only in an ossified and retrograde society that the laws of one generation were good enough for the next.

Precedent, far from becoming redundant, takes on an organic role in this scheme of things—not perhaps in the grand Tennysonian image of freedom slowly broadening down in a kind of Fabian long march to happiness, but a centuries-long culture of reasoning and principle which ebbs and flows, so that, for example, the charge of contempt of court made on behalf of a Zairian asylum-seeker against the holder of one of the three great offices of State, the Home Secretary, could found upon Sir Edward Coke's assertion of the sovereignty of the courts in the face of the Crown's prerogatives and upon Wilkes's recovery of punitive damages from an earlier Home Secretary, Lord Halifax, for the unlawful issue of a general warrant. A former jobbing electrician who became a distinguished teacher of law once told me that in both jobs he had found the most useful part of his equipment to be a well-filled box of junk; and while I would not put the great cases I have been referring to in that class, an eclectic mind is not a bad asset in a modern lawyer.

The ministerial contempt case illustrates, too, the way in which modern public law has carried forward a culture of judicial assertiveness to compensate for, and in places repair, dysfunctions in the democratic process. It is a remarkable fact that a judiciary which has taken a public battering in recent years over miscarriages of criminal justice has in the same period earned large public approbation for its willingness to prevent and correct abuses of governmental power. When the history of modern judicial review is written, it will recount how the coming of the adult franchise through the two great nineteenth century Reform Acts was matched by the introduction of the Northgate Trevelyan civil service. This replaced ministers' placement with an intellectual and administrative elite from the same schools, universities and clubs as the judges themselves, and encouraged the judiciary to retreat from its prickly Victorian invigoration of the executive into a passivity.

This passivity by the 1950s, had allowed executive and local government an unprecedented measure of unchallenged power, to the extent that even the administrative tribunals set up to adjudicate between citizen and State were treated as instruments of departmental policy. It will also, I hope, observe how the subsequent reassertion of judicial oversight of government which has been the achievement of the 1970s and 1980s in this country has been replicated all over the common law world as judiciaries have moved to fill lacunae of legitimacy in the functioning of democratic polities—a process of which the Pergau Dam decision can stand as a sharp recent illustration. The historian's conclusion may well be that the last three decades of the twentieth century have seen a judicial refashioning, with popular support sufficient to mute political opposition to it, of our organic constitution. If so, its consequence is that we have today both in this country and in those with which it shares aspects of its political and judicial culture a new and still emerging constitutional paradigm. This is no longer of Dicey's supreme parliament to whose will the rule of law must finally bend, but of a bi-polar sovereignty of the Crown in Parliament and the Crown in its courts, to each of which the Crown's ministers are answerable—politically to Parliament, legally to the courts. That the government of the day has no separate sovereignty in this paradigm is both axiomatic and a reminder of the sharpest of all the lessons of eastern Europe: that it is when State is collapsed into party that democracy flounders.

Opinion of People

To assume a jurisdiction of this kind is of course to assume, without having argued it, the primacy of democracy. It is therefore worth remembering how temporary and vulnerable the desirable sense of democracy is. A term of abuse synonymous with mob rule in Burke's vocabulary, its contemporary feel-good usage finds its origin in America, where from its first known modern use in the Rhode Island Constitution of 1641 it became a vehicle of challenge to the colonial power in the hands of Hamilton and his contemporaries and in due course a vehicle of challenge in this country in the hands of the Chartists and their successors to the rotten boroughs and aristocratic oligarchies which electoral reform was eventually to sweep away. But although the power of the world has become such that there is barely a regime anywhere in the world which has not sought during the twentieth century to characterise itself as democratic, there is nothing which determines that the notion of democracy as the higher-order law beneath which constitutions must operate is there for all time. If anything, history should lead us to expect the converse; but apart from watching phlegmatically as the great oxymoron of the nineteenth century, the nation States, fissiparate and super States now arm the world's poor nations to kill each other, we cannot peer very far into that darkness.

For these and other reasons one sees trouble with the concept of a higher-order of law as the basis of human rights adjudication. To postulate such a law is to attract all the theological problems which attend any argument from a first cause and which can ultimately only be answered by an act of faith. (It may be in the end that a society's consensus about its basic values is an act of faith, but my own preference is to reason, as Hobbes or Bentham might have done, that it is society itself which is given and which poses certain overriding needs for its own existence.) While shared perceptions of what those needs are change as societies change, there are moral and practical continuities—of which the democratic principle is one—which can be powerfully represented as fundamental values, at least within the temporal and social horizons of each society. This relatively modest foundation for the legitimacy of human rights has perhaps the virtue that, without reducing all discourse to incoherent subjectivity, it recognises that a single 'right' outcome to every issue is attainable, if at all, only locally and temporarily, and that just as the only universal truth is that there are no universal truths, true objectivity may well consist in recognising the reality of history and of change. When the future Chief Justice Hughes of the US said eighty years ago, "The Constitution is what the judges say it is", he was speaking of all rights instruments at all times, and to a realist concerned with human rights he was offering not despair but hope.

This will be thought perverse by many whose views I respect and who point to what happens when the judges are put in the driving seat in order to show the that way constitutional madness lies. They point, among many other examples, to the record of the Privy Council as a constitutional court composed chiefly of English judges, veering between indefensible interference with democratic decisions (for example with the legislation by which Canada was trying to replicate Roosevelt's New Deal, and which the Privy Council actually wrecked because Canada could deploy no equivalent of Roosevelt's threat to pack the Supreme Court), and indefensible abstention in the face of illiberal and oppressive conduct by Commonwealth regimes.

They point too, to the outcomes of a series of cases from Northern Ireland decided in the House of Lords and in the European Commission and Court of Human Rights, in which principle seems to have taken second place to expediency and the lesson of Liverside v. Anderson to have been forgotten. These critics are opposed, however, by a respected school of rights discourse which holds that once fundamental human rights are articulated and set down, to attack them for their outcomes is to substitute venality for principle and to drag rights adjudication in the political mud.

Base of Ideology

For reasons elaborated, there should be little sympathy with this critique: it not only makes historical assumptions about the primacy and universality of currently accepted principles of political and social conduct, but assumes the neutrality of adjudication and at worst ascribes rogue decisions to rogue judges. It is equally plain, nevertheless, as the end of the century approaches that the argument for a bill of rights for the United Kingdom is being won by its proponents, and that the off-the-shelf solution of incorporation of the European Convention heads the list of possible measures if only on the practical ground that adherence to a set of standards enforceable on the State by an international tribunal but not by its own citizens in its own courts makes no sense at all. Moreover, the House of Lords has now recognised that our constitution knows such a thing as a fundamental law—the European Communities Act 1972—capable of overriding subsequent primary legislation if the courts find the two to be in conflict; so self-evident in fact was the doctrine that the House in Factortame (No. 2) found it unnecessary to articulate it before giving it effect.

As to the shape of a UK bill of rights I shall have a little more to say; but my present argument is that our agenda for the twenty-first century is not necessarily confined to a choice between a rights instrument interpreted for better or for worse by a judiciary with a long record of illiberal adjudication, and rejection of any rights instrument in favour of parliamentary government. Certainly, the better government becomes, the less scope there will be before judicial review of it: it is not mere piety to say that the aim of the nominated judges is to work themselves out of a job. But for the foreseeable future we have a problem, shared in large part with other developed democracies: how to ensure that as a docility we are governed within a law which has internalised the notion of fundamental human rights. If posing it this way means adopting the rule of law, like democracy, as a higher-order principle, we likewise have the social consensus, which alone—and without the need of a leap of faith— can accord it that primacy. And if in our own society the rule of law is to mean much, it must at least mean that it is the obligation of the courts to articulate and uphold the ground rules of ethical social existence which we dignify as fundamental human rights, temporary and local though they are in the grand scheme of things.

The Achievements

The largely unexplored avenue to this end, and the one I want to explore, is what I will perversely call the principle of outcomes. In common with the critics of a bill of rights I believe that in a democracy people have every right to scrutinise and appraise not merely the integrity of the judicial process but what it actually delivers. It is one thing, however difficult, to explain to the public that a directed acquittal because of an improperly extracted confession seeks to preserve the integrity of legal process as a greater good than the conviction of a possibly guilty individual without due process; it is another to try to justify, by reference to the legal principles which undoubtedly explain them, the kinds of award made in major libel actions. There is nothing wrong with the argument that if this is the due result there is something wrong with the principles or the processes that have produced it.

Refusing to accept the objectionable outcome alongside the welcome one is not simply allowing predilection to triumph over principle: it is to recognise that outcome—the result we want—is symbiotic with principle, because it is only for their concrete effect that we reconsider principles worth having and fighting over. If I thought there were any self-evident truths I would rank this high among them. Take the right to life, qualified as it ordinarily is in favour of limited inroads made into it by law. No rights instrument I know of tells you whether capital punishment is compatible with this fundamental right, but nobody suggests that for this reason the right is not worth articulating or that courts cannot adjudicate on it. It is simply that argument about the content of the right cannot be conducted in purely overrun principally legal terms, and the answers given by constitutional courts are inevitably and rightly a function of that large debate.

The new transitional Constitution of South Africa, a country which till recently led the world in the rate of judicial executions, accords the right to life and permits derogation to any extent which is reasonable and justifiable in an open and democratic society, but not so as to negate the essential content of the right in question: The first case in the list of the new Constitutional Court has been a challenge to the constitutionality of the death penalty. Its judgement, whichever way it goes, will resolve an issue which politicians had consciously decided was better left to the courts, even if (as one suspects) the prohibition on derogations which negate the essential content of the right makes the outcome fairly certain.

The Canadian Charter of Rights and Freedoms puts it very differently: "Everyone has the right to life . . . and the right not to be deprived thereof except in accordance with the principles of fundamental justice", but the words are capable of giving rise to much the same debate. In tomorrow's world the role which courts have had to accept as society's arbiter and conscience is a role capable of embracing issues of this kind without forfeiting the epithet judicial. It is not a new role; it was the English courts which, however reluctantly, grasped the nettle that legislators would not touch and declared slavery—at least on these shores—illegal; although it is a fine irony that the famous phrase of Lord Stowell in the case of the Slave Grace in 1827, that the air of England was too pure for a slave to breathe, appears to have originated in a sixteenth-century decision of the Court of Star Chamber, which had used the same metaphor in depriving an Englishman of his imported slave. But to say that the courts are likely to continue to discharge this role, whether under the name of public policy or of human right adjudication, tells us little about how and by what standards they will do it.

Protection by Law

Until recently it was to Canada that we could most usefully look from this country for a prognostication of how a common law judiciary might be expected to interpret and apply a modern rights instrument. These messages have been mixed: it has become apparent that the big battalions are getting an unfair share of Canadian rights adjudications; but there have been many decisions to cheer up liberal thinkers. But it is in Australia that the real problem has recently been highlighted: its High Court has reached into the bowels of the country's now elderly Constitution and extracted certain modern human rights—a process that outcome watchers might applaud; but it has proceeded in one case to apply them to an effect which, seen from this side of the globe, looks so partial as to justify every fear the outcome watchers have expressed.

In the first of two cases decided on the same day in 1992, a statute which criminalised criticism, justified or not, of members of the Industrial Relations Commission was struck down as creating a fetter on free speech out of all proportion to the permissible objective. In the second, the court struck down a statutory provision which, in order to stop the loading of the dice in elections in favour of candidates or parties with wealthy supporters who bought television advertising time and used it to promote them, provided for free airtime for all parties and allowed full and free journalistic coverage, but banned other broadcast political advertising in the run-up to elections. The reasoning in the second case went like this: the Australian Constitution of 1900 contains no bill of rights and gives the courts no express power to review primary legislation; but it is predicated on the primacy of representative government, which in turn depends on the full and free communication of ideas; so that any legislation which obstructs the fullest desired flow of opinion in the electoral process is unconstitutional. In Australia too the Constitution appears to be what the judges say it is, and these two decisions and their more recent successors have serious implications.

First, they illustrate vividly the trend in the free-market democracies for the courts, with a great measure of popular support, to keep government within the law by—if necessary—strong and innovative measures. In the UK we are already some way down the road of legislative review, and legislation may well carry us the rest of the way by the end of the century. Whether it does so by entrenchment, giving a power to strike down legislation on human rights grounds as well as European Union ones, or by infiltration along the lines of the New Zealand Bill of Rights Act 1990, may not matter very much—at least if we can expect in the latter event to emulate the approach to outcomes adopted by Sir Robin Cooke in a recent leading case. He said: "It is necessary to be alert in New Zealand to the danger that both the courts and parliament at times may, or at least be asked to give, lip service to human rights in high-sounding language, but little or no real service in terms of actual decision." And he went on to hold that there was now a cause of action for breach of the Bill of Rights Act, basing himself—to be fair—on a 1979 decision of the Privy Council.

Secondly, however, the cases illustrate the fickleness of outcomes. Speaking for myself as a citizen I applaud the first and deplore the second. The first cuts down an indefensible protection of public figures from civilised criticism. But the second adopts, it seems to me, a very particular and partisan view of what free speech is: because it demands a free flow of ideas, the court holds that to accord a hearing to ideas in proportion to the wealth of those who hold them is not only a democratic course but the only democratic course; and in doing so it assumes a symmetry which simply does not exist between freedom of speech and freedom of information.

In Britain where we have lived all our lives with Representation of the People Acts predicated (despite judicial inroads) on a financially limited and level playing field for all contenders, and with a complete prohibition on political advertising on television, the fallacy is more readily seen. In the United States, by contrast, the Australian decision is prefigured by a long history of legislative attempts to stop wealth buying seats, frustrated every time by a Supreme Court with both eyes fixed mesmerically on the First Amendment, and with results that are well known in terms of the wealth needed to run for office. The Australian decision certainly makes it harder to defend the fitness of the courts to undertake constitutional adjudication on human rights issues, for the High

Court of Australia has taken to be self-evident and universal views which many would regard as partial and highly contentious in a democracy.

What then is to be done? The answer, whether we like it or not, is in large part being determined for us. The courts of these and other countries—India prominent among them—are by now engaged on a broad highway of constitutional adjudication along which issues of fundamental rights relentlessly present themselves. In this country, as I have outlined, the modern growth of public law and the internationalisation of our jurisprudence have moved adjudication towards a new catholicity of subject-matter and a greater preparedness to intervene to right wrongs in the polity. The only choice in this situation—and it is a choice which the judiciary can make for itself but which Parliament can no longer realistically make for 'it—is to retreat from rights adjudication into the long sleep of Wednesbury and before, or to develop the role with which we are now becoming familiar and to continue to move in the direction of a rights culture compatible with constitutional adjudication in a democracy. With all its pitfalls, the latter looks to be the only worthwhile choice.

There is no means of standing still, but neither is there any virtue in proceeding down the path of constitutional and human rights adjudication without taking very careful stock indeed of where it might lead us. This is why it is to outcomes as much as to principles that we need to look for the future, recognising that even then the future will one day be the past and its decision be seen, like ours, to be creatures of a dialectic of time, place and principle. It is also why there is nothing unprincipled in arguing from outcomes.

The first and most important lesson that experience is teaching us is that human rights can be treated as commodities and, like commodities, appropriated by those who have the means to do so. I began by mentioning this on the international plane, but it is equally true domestically, and the free speech issue provides perhaps the sharpest illustration of how and why. The splendour of American First Amendment jurisprudence sets a standard, which nobody can ignore: the marketplace of ideas, the heresy that grows into orthodoxy.

It is between the glories of the First Amendment and the horrors of a Ministry of Truth that the region of debate lies, for all societies place a restraint at some point on who can say what. Time and again in recent years it has been the free speech issue which has come banging at the court's door, asking it to open up, in the name of fundamental human rights— in this country from the Sunday Times thalidomide case to the Sinn Fein broadcasting ban, in Australia in the television broadcasting case and a number which have followed it. I do not for a moment contest the right of any of them to do so, nor the vast importance of the Miltonic freedom, and I might privately applaud what each plaintiff or applicant was setting out to achieve. But if I ask myself: why of all the human rights issues there are, should it be the issue of free speech which is constantly at the head of the queue for rights adjudication? The answer is very clear: it is because for the mass media free speech is a valuable commodity and litigation a worthwhile investment in it.

This in itself in no way negates the importance of the issue, for there is no law against doing well in the process of doing good; but it throws up a series of further issues which either a future rights instrument or the courts are going to have to address. For example, freedom to speak includes freedom to keep silent. In relation to the State, this is one thing—though not a thing beyond the reach of our law if we are prepared to take freedom of information seriously. For a transitional corporation on which hundreds of millions of people depend for their information about the world, it is another: the power to suppress information, of which we should firmly deny the State control, is a power possessed by the media corporations. Does human rights theory then have anything to say about a transitional media corporation which, in order to secure satellite TV rights for China, agrees not to transmit BBC broadcasts because they have a standard of objectivity which the Chinese government dislikes?

Is it perhaps a corollary of the right to speak freely that others have a right to listen freely, and not merely to hear what those who control the media think they should hear? If so, who is to articulate it and on whose behalf? Are human rights there for corporations or for people? Are they a form of property or a constraint on power? If freedom to speak is a right, does it carry correlative obligations towards those who wish to hear? Above all, by what possible test of democracy or of equality before the law is it possible to pose a State, which maintains a high standard of public service broadcasting, as the unique natural enemy of individual liberty, and a media corporation possessing far greater communication resources than any State, as a disempowered candidate for freedom from State interference with its right of free expression? And where in this grand contest does the intended human beneficiary of the dialogue sit?

However the problem is posed, it is as impossible to discuss principles divorced from outcomes as it is outcomes divorced from principles: if the reception of news and information at large is a principle which matters, the operative matrix in which the principle is to be cast cannot matter less.

If then, without abandoning principle, we are to escape the cold wind of history, which blows, sooner or later on higher-order laws and self-evident truths, it is to our present epoch's consensus about society's ground rules that we have to turn. To admit this is to admit, as perhaps we should, that different societies will agree on different ground rules, and to accept accordingly that we have both a right to review and recast our standards and an obligation to make the case for the adoption of them by others rather than continue to assert loftily that ours, being self-evident, are the only acceptable ones. It certainly denies us any moral right to preach to others what we do not practise ourselves.

Position of Command

One of the keynotes of our epoch was struck by the Civil War radical John Warn who, writing in 1649, looked for 'a spirit of understanding big with freedom and having a single respect to people's rights' (a phrase 150 years ahead of its time). Wan contended that justice was anterior to law and postulated as the prime function of law 'the protection of the poor against the might'.

One of the principles we have derived from the upheavals of the seventeenth and eighteenth centuries is the primacy of democracy, but it is a principle which carries with it a baggage of inchoate assumptions—free speech according to means is only one of them—which are capable of subverting the principle itself. Both in enacting our own rights instruments for the future and in applying them by adjudication it is important to understand that such principles are not self-implementing and that in their application they can readily be hijacked by those who already possess the greatest power in society. It is only by being rigorous, as Warr was, about a second such ground rule or principle, substantive equality before the law, that it becomes feasible to set about fireproofing the juridical elements of life in a democracy and to be serious about preventing the appropriation of legal rights and democratic processes for private or partial ends. There is a potential tension, in other words, between the principle of democratic government and the principle of equality before the law. If human rights theory has an urgent job in the coming years it is to turn this tension from its present destructive motion towards a creative balance between the individual whom democracy offers to empower and the sources and the repositories of power, both within and outside the apparatus of State, which a democracy has both to licence and to control.

This is why a rights instrument for the new century needs to address in its terms the imbalances and appropriations of power which threaten the values—possibly even the meaning:—of democracy; and it is equally why a judiciary charged with upholding the rule of law in a democracy has in making its adjudications to address the same questions.

To take a modest example, in the US an enacted right of reply has been struck down as an unconstitutional interference with freedom of expression—conceiving the freedom, therefore, as a form of property—and an informal right of reply is resisted here for the same reason. In an attempt to meet this problem, an ANC draft of South Africa's transitional constitution proposed to provide: There shall be freedom of thought, speech, expression and opinion, including a free press, which shall respect the right to reply.

The last clause of the formulation was omitted from the final document, but the issue remains a real one and the Constitutional court may one day be asked to decide, since the legislature has declined to do so, what responsibilities are bound up with this and other human rights.

New Approach

If then we are to anticipate a continuing debate about outcomes, these too can and should be debated in terms of principle, focused now by experience on the more complicated subtext, which every rights instrument silently carries. To say that the courts are not fit to absorb and respond acceptably to such a debate is to assume both too much and too little; too much because our judicial culture has historically pretended to be insulated from public debate and so has always had to disguise its social and ethical judgements as value-free adjudications; and too little because our capacity for open and intelligent response to the wider issues of human rights is as a consequence largely unexplored: it is a language in which we are not entirely illiterate but are certainly dyslexic, and in which with remedial help we can probably do a great deal better.

The tale told in Canada that a Supreme Court judge, debating an early Charter case (Canada, Charter of Rights and Freedoms) and told by his clerk that Dworkin has written something on the point, said 'Who's Dworkin?', while apocryphal, can stand as a parable of the expansion of a common law universe under the impulse of rights adjudication—for many of today's Charter decisions have a degree of legal literacy and an intellectual catholicity which our courts have so far been able (I am thinking principally of the Tony Bland case) to touch only briefly.

I hope that in constitutional adjudication, which is what our public law cases are, we shall be moving in the not too distant future toward the reception of Amicus and Brandeis briefs—the kind that were desperately lacking in the Gillick case. To do so will help us to escape the pincers which at the moment are closing on us: the pressures, which cannot be wholly resisted, towards omnicompetent adjudication, and the want of any corresponding expansion in the data and culture with and within which we carry it out. There are no guarantees that better educated the courts will get everything right, but to be sent as history is sending us on a voyage without modern navigational aids and supplies is to experience the worst of both worlds, the old and the new. My argument is that we should assemble the equipment and go on.

If, as is almost inevitable, this voyage is going increasingly to take us into the deep water of fundamental rights, this is a culture which English lawyers are going to have to acquire and absorb. To rest, as our courts sometimes do, on the laurels of having been the first to articulate a number of the freedoms the world now takes for granted is not really enough, not least because the content of these rights has at present to be subordinated giving the courts a currently watertight defence for illiberal decisions. But where, in John Mortimer's metaphor, we have so far survived by 'clinging to the wreckage', rights adjudication under a fundamental law of some description is going to mean that we have to learn to swim. This much is uncontentious. What may be more contentious is the proposition that the waters in which we shall be swimming are shark-infested and that our human rights armoury at present gives us little protection against the predators.

The notion that the prime function of human rights and indeed the rule of law is to protect the weak against the strong is not mere sentimentality. It is the child of an era of history in which equality of treatment and opportunity has become perceived—as it is not perceived in societies based on status—as an unqualified good, and of a significant recognition that you do not achieve equality by proclaiming it but only by levelling up from the inherited or systemic inequalities which make some social actors too weak to make use of their rights and others strong enough to stifle their aspirations.

The deconstruction of the State as provider as well as entrepreneur is now a world-wide phenomenon; but because power in every society on this planet is and perhaps always will be unequally distributed, every society today has a problem not just with Leviathan, against whom contemporary rights instruments continue to be directed, but with Jaws. It is going to be the task of those who write and those who implement the human rights instruments of the next generation to build on the jurisprudence of substantive race and gender equality which has been one of the real achievements of this generation, so as to distinguish between the strong and the weak as claimants of fundamental rights and to avoid what one writer has characterised as a culture in which self-respect and human dignity depend upon being in a position to make strident, querulous and adversarial claims.

I have not embarked on the vexed questions of group rights as against individual rights or of social and economic rights as fundamental human rights. As to the first, it seems to me that the dichotomy of individual and group involves at least in part a false antithesis, for as individuals we are defined by our relationships with others, and which social cadre is to be the context of an individual's rights is itself a function of the rights debate; so that the Inuit women comes by political choice to have rights as a Canadian citizen which deny the relationships of an aboriginal culture recognised but not entrenched by the Charter of Rights and Freedoms.

Nor have I entered the debate about whether the right to shelter or to work can or should rank as a human right, for these are in my view questions to be answered by social consensus from time to time, not by definition *a priori* and certainly not by derivation from some higher law. Simply observe that the right not to suffer racial or sexual discrimination, which we now take as axiomatic, was entirely foreign—except perhaps as an aspiration—to the thinking of our grandparents' generation; that rights to education or to justice could only have been treated as self-evident in their time—which is our time—by societies that could afford to provide them; that the right to an unpolluted environment which the Indian High Court has in recent years extracted from the constitutional right to life depends less on what a society can afford than on what it cannot afford; and that it is not easy to see how in any humane society a right to shelter and food deserves any less regard than the right to life.

5

Women's Status in Society

Relevant Articles as included in the Draft Commission:

(I) The State shall not discriminate against any citizen on grounds only of religion, race, caste, sex or any of them.

In particular, no citizen shall, on grounds only of religion, race, caste, sex or any of them, be subject to any disability, liability, restriction or condition with regard to:—

(a) access to shops, public restaurants, hotels and places of public entertainment, or

(b) the use of wells, tanks, roads and places of public resort maintained wholly or partly out of the revenues of the State or dedicated to the use of the general public.

(II) "Untouchability" is abolished and its practice in any form is forbidden. The enforcement of any disability arising out of "Untouchability" shall be an offence punishable in accordance with law.

Fundamental Rights

(a) Nothing in this article shall affect the operation of any existing law or preclude the State from making any law;

(b) for social welfare and reform or for throwing open Hindu religious institutions of a public character to any class or section of Hindus.

These were introduced for the first time before the Constituents Assembly through the Report of the Sub-Committee on Fundamental Rights and were discussed then.

Mr. Promatha Ranjan Thakur (Bengal: General)

Moreover, this list of fundamental rights should have been considered in the light of the reports of the Minorities Sub-Committee. The Minorities Sub-Committee sat only for two days and they could not go into details as regard safeguards required for minority communities. You know that Minority Sub-Committee's Report is very much connected with the list of fundamental rights.

Another point to which I wish to refer is in relation to clause 6—regarding untouchability where it is said that:

> "Untouchability in any form is abolished and the implementation of any disability and that account shall be an offence."

I do not understand how you can abolish untouchability without abolishing the very caste system. Untouchability is nothing but the symptom of the disease, namely, the caste system. It exists as a matter of caste system. I do not understand how this, in its present form, can be allowed to stand in the list of fundamental rights. I think the House should consider this point seriously. Unless we can do away with the caste system altogether, there is no use tinkering with the problem of untouchability superficially.

Mr. President

We now proceed to consider the Report clause by clause:

Rights of Equality

Srijut Rohini Kumar Chaudhury (Assam: General)

The second part of my amendment is for defining untouchability. It may be clearly stated that:

"Untouchability means any act committed in exercise of discrimination on ground of religion, caste or lawful vocation of life mentioned in clause 4."

In the fundamental rights, it has been laid down that untouchability in any form should be an offence punishable by law. That being so, it is necessary that the offence should be properly defined. As it stands, the word 'untouchability' is very vague. It should be defined in the manner in which I have put it, or in some other better form which may be decided upon by the House.

Dr. S.C. Banerjee (Bengal: General)

The word "untouchability" actually requires clarification. We have been accustomed to this word for the last 25 years, still there is a lot of confusion as to what it cannotes. Sometimes it means merely taking a glass of water and sometimes it has been used in the sense of admission of 'Dalits' into temples, sometimes it means inter-caste dinner, sometimes inter-caste marriage. Mahatma Gandhi, who is the main exponent of 'untouchability' has used it in various ways and on different occasions with different meanings. So when we are going to use the word 'untouchability' we should be very clear in our mind as to what it really means by it. What is the real implication of this word ? I think we should make no distinction between untouchability and caste distinction, as Mr. Thakur has said, untouchability is merely a symptom, the root cause is caste distinction and unless and until the root cause that is caste distinction is removed, untouchability in some form or other is bound to exist. and when we are going to have an independence India, we should expect every one to be enjoying equal social conditions. It is incumbent on us that we should be very clear as to make explicitly that in the future independent India, there shall be no distinction between man and man in the social field. In other words, caste distinction must be abolished. Of course there is difficulty as to whether we can make it justiciable or not. I have thought over it for a long time. I do really believe that in place of untouchability, some other word, such as 'caste distinction' should be used or the word 'untouchability' should be clearly defined so as to leave least doubt in the mind of any one as to what we really mean by it.

Mr. K.M. Munshi

I oppose this amendment. The definition is to worded that if it is accepted, it will make any discrimination even on the basis of place of birth or caste or even sex untouchability. What does the definition say?

"'Untouchability' means any act committed in exercise of discrimination on grounds of religion, caste or lawful vocation of life mentioned in clause 4."

Now clause 4 does not deal with untouchability at all. It deals with discrimination regarding services and various other things. It may mean discrimination even between touchables and touchables, between people of one province and another. The word 'untouchability' is put purposely within inverted commas in order to indicate that the Union legislature when it defines 'untouchability' will be able to deal with it in the sense in which it is normally understood. The present amendment will be extending the scope of the definition of untouchability. I oppose the amendment.

Mr. Dhirendra Nath Datta (Bengal: General)

It seems to me that whether the definition suggested by Mr. Rohini Kumar Chaudhury is accepted or not, it is necessary that there should be some definition put it. Here it is said that 'untouchability' in any form is an offence. A magistrate or a judge dealing with offences shall have to look to the definition. One magistrate will consider a particular thing to be untouchability while another magistrate may hold a different thing to be untouchability, with the result there will be no uniformity on the part of the magistracy in dealing with offences.

It will be very difficult for the judge to decide cases. Moreover, untouchability means different things in different areas. In Bengal, untouchability means one thing, while in other provinces, it means an entirely differnt thing. So, unless a definition is put in, it would be impossible for the judiciary to deal with offences coming under untouchability. Whether you accept the amendment of Mr. Rohini Kumar Chaudhury or not, some definition must be these. This question may be left to the Drafting Committee to find out some suitable definition of the word 'untouchability'. I strongly feel that unless there is a definition, it cannot be dealt with as an offence. We all feel that untouchability should be made an offence and it should be done away with.

I also feel with my friend Mr. Thakur that the root cause of untouchability, namely the caste system, in Hindu society should be abolished altogether. Unless the caste system is abolished, untouchability will persist at in some form or other. It has been said time and again by our leaders that unless Hindu society is drastically reformed by abolishing the caste system, it is bound to perish. Caste system should be abolished. So, if we are to deal with 'untouchability' as an offence, there should be some definition and I hope it would be left to the Drafting Committee to frame suitable definition so that it will be placed before the House for discussion. With these words I support the amendment.

Mr. President

I should like to draw the attention of the House to clause 24 which says:

> "The Union Legislature shall make laws to give effect to those provisions of this part which require such

> legislation and to prescribe punishment for those acts which are declared to be offences in this part and are not already punishable."

I take it that the Union Legislature will define the word 'untouchability' so that the courts might prescribe proper punishment.

Sardar Vallabhbhai Patel (Bombay: General)

I beg to move clause 4 which runs as follows:

(1) The State shall make no discrimination against any citizen on grounds of religion, race, caste or sex.

(2) There shall be no discrimination against any citizen on any grounds of religion, race, caste or sex in regard to:

   (a) access to trading establishments including public restaurants and hotels;

   (b) the use of wells, tanks, roads and places of public resorts maintained wholly or partly out of public funds or dedicated to the use of the general public:

   Provided that nothing contained in this clause shall prevent separate provision being made for women and children.

This is a non-discriminatory clause which is provided in almost all constitutions and adjustments have been made here to suit the special conditions of our country.

Mr. R.K. Sidhwa

The word, 'Hotels and public restaurants' have been mentioned for special reasons and specific purposes. They are used by the public and even at present licence from the local bodies is necessary before they are allowed to function. It is very necessary that these public places of entertainment—hotels, and restaurants should be specifically mentioned, so that the owners may not say that A shall be allowed and B shall not be allowed. These words have a definite and special meaning, and they are absolutely necessary. I, therefore, strongly suggest that the words be retained as the Hon'ble Sardar Patel has moved.

Mr. P.S. Deshmukh (C.P. and Bihar: General)

May I say a word as a matter of general observation on this clause? In drafting such a long clause we are throwing a shadow of untouchability over the whole Constitution of India. In this particular clause, I submit to the House, if we merely say that—

> "the State shall not permit any discrimination against any citizen on grounds only of religion, race, caste, or sex."

It should be quite sufficient, and it will leave ample opportunity to the Union Government to make specific provisions with regard to hotels, restaurants, parks, theatres, etc. I think, therefore, that the whole of the second part should be omitted. We should not forget that we have to confine ourselves to the rights which are and must be fundamental.

This is not the place to enumerate all the various rights a citizen should have. We are here concerned with only justiciable fundamental rights and it would be improper to burden the clauses with a detailed list of places which should be accessible to all. I, therefore, suggest that it will serve our purpose if we merely substitute the place of the whole clause the following:

> "That the State shall not make nor permit any discrimination against any citizen, on mere ground of religion, race, caste or sex."

Shri D. Govinda Dass (Madras: General) (Spoke in Telugu)

I move:

> "That in sub-clause 2(b) of clause 4, after the word 'roads' the words 'schools, temples or places of worship' be inserted."

Shri V.C. Kesava Rao (Madras: General)

I move:

> "That in sub-clause 2(b) of clause 4, after the word 'roads' the words 'schools, temples or places of worship' be inserted."

I want to say that though some schools are thrown open to the Dalits in the villages, they are not allowed to sit along with the caste Hindu students. They are asked to sit on the floor or at distance. I would like to say in this connection that education is the birth-right of every citizen. So a Dalit or an untouchable should be given the same right as every other citizen. As regards temples, I may submit that untouchables are made to worship God only from a distance and not before God. Even though the untouchables are saying that they are Hindus for the last so many centuries, they are being denied this right and they are made to worship God only from a distance and not within the temple itself. I think that untouchables into temples. I request that these things may be taken into consideration.

Srijut Rohini Kumar Chaudhury

I beg to move:

> "That the following explanation be added at the end of clause 4:

Explanation: A place of public resort includes a yard or house attached to any temple where musical and dramatic performances, cinema shows or other entertainments are held for entertainment of general public."

There are many temples which have got attached to them houses called Nat Mandirs. During festivals and on other occasions also dramatic performances and cinema shows are held there. The performances are sometimes given by people belonging to what you call the Dalits, but the Dalits themselves are not allowed to go. This is very galling to the people. Therefore, whenever any show or any dramatic performance takes place in any place attached to the temple, all members of the public must have access to it.

Shri M. Ananthasayanam Ayyangar (Madras: General)

I would like to submit that there are sources of water supply other than wells, tanks, etc. such as channels, and I think these also should be covered by clause No. 4. Therefore, I think it necessary to add the words 'and other sources of water supply' after the word "tank". Otherwise, there will be a lacuna.

Then again, there may be discrimination in giving medical relief, on grounds of religion, etc. That will be a dangerous thing. Therefore, if you do not think want of notice a serious objection against it, I would request you to permit me to add the words "and medical institutions" after the words "public resort". It would then read:

> "the use of wells, tanks, roads and places of public resort and medical institutions maintained wholly or partly out of public funds or dedicated to the use of the general public."

Sardar Vallabhbhai Patel

.......I am glad that on the whole the House is of opinion that this clause is aptly drafted.......

The motion was adopted.

Sardar Vallabhhai Patel

I may be allowed to move clause 6 which runs thus:

> "6. 'untouchability' in any form is abolished and the imposition of any disability on that account shall be an offence."

There can be no difference of opinion on this question. This is now an accepted proposition all over and should be provided for in the fundamental rights, and any one who suffers a disability on this account should have the right to go to a court of law and have redress. I hope there will be no amendment on this.

Mr. H.V. Kamath

I move that in clause 6, after the word 'Untouchability' the word 'unapproachability' be inserted, and after the word "any" the word "and every" be inserted.

By this amendment I want to make the clause more comprehensive because in some parts of India the practice of unapproachability besides untouchability used to obtain some years ago, to my own knowledge. I thought that if you include the word "unapproachability" it would make the clause more comprehensive. The other small amendment that I propose is purely verbal. It does not change the meaning but only emphasises the clause.

Shri S. Nagappa (Madras: General)

I move that in clause 6, for the words, "imposition of any disability", the words "observance of any disability" be substituted. My reason is that imposition implies that one party that imposes it on another is guilty but I suggest that if the untouchability is observed by any person it must be an offence. Unless this amendment is made I do not think the provision made here is enough to punish a person. So I request the House to see that by accepting my amendment observance of untouchability is made a punishable offence.

Shri P. Kunhiraman (Madras: General)

I move that in clause 6 after the word "offence" the following words be inserted:

"punishable by law"

The original clause makes it an offence and implies that it will be punishable; I want to make it more explicit. It is just a verbal amendment and I commend it for acceptance. Moreover, if we only say that it is an offence it may be interpreted later on in the sense that it is not a legal offence. So it is necessary that it should be made explicit.

Mr. President

The motion and the amendments are now under discussion.

The Hon'ble Sardar Vallabhbhai Patel

The first amendment is by Mr. Kamath. He wants the addition of the word 'unapproachability'. If untouchability is provided for in the fundamental rights as an offence, all necessary adjustment will be made in the law that may be passed by the Legislature. I do not think it is right or wise to provide for such necessary corollaries and, therefore, I do not accept this amendment.

The other amendment is by Mr. Nagappa who has suggested that for the words 'imposition of any disability' the words 'observance of any disability' may be substituted. I cannot understand his point. I can observe one man imposing a disability on another, and I will be guilty. I have observed it. I do not think such extreme things should be provided for. The removal of untouchability is the main idea, and if untouchability is made illegal or an offence, it is quite enough.

The next amendment was moved by Mr. Kunhiraman. He has suggested the insertion of 'punishable by law'. We have provided that imposition of untouchability shall be an offence. Perhaps his idea is that an offence could be excusable, or sometimes an offence may be rewarded. Offence is an offence; it is not necessary to provide that offence should be punishable by law. I do not accept this amendment either.

Then it was proposed that for the words 'any form' the words 'all forms' be substituted. Untouchability in any form is a legal phraseology, and no more addition is necessary. The motion was adopted.

Faith's Role

Mr. K.M. Munshi

I move an amendment to the effect that, after the last Explanation, the following words be added:

> "and for throwing open Hindu religious institutions of a public character to any class of section of Hindus."

After the Explanation, above was drafted. It was thought that the practice of religion referred to should not be of such a character as will interfere with the right of the Legislature to legislate on social questions. The question arose with regard to the throwing open of all temples to all classes of Hindus, whether it would be religious practice. In order to prevent any such construction of the clause, it was decided that the throwing open of Hindu religious institutions shall not be held to contravene the practice of Hindu religion.

In case Mr. Munshi's amendment to this clause is accepted, it may be necessary to have a definition for 'places of public worship'. Unless this is done it may be difficult for people to know which is a place of public worship. Even where admission to people of all classes is given, depressed classes are not allowed. Even when there is a written record that a certain temple is open to worship by depressed classes, the Pujaris obstruct and say that temple is a private one and, therefore, not open to depressed classes. So, if there is definition of 'places of public worship' there will be no difficulty. I suggest, therefore, that there should be a definition for "places of public worship" ...I want a definition for "religious institutions of a public character".

Sardar Vallabhbhai Patel

I accept Mr. Munshi's amendment and I congratulate the House on agreeing to pass this very controversial matter which has taken several days in the Committees and gone through several Committees. There might be differences of opinion, but on the whole we have tried our best to accommodate all sections of the people.

Clause 13, as amended was adopted.

Special Rights for Dalits

K.M. Munshi (Bombay: General)

Another reason is this, and I might mention that reason is based on the decisions which have already been taken by this House. The distinction between Hindu community other than Scheduled Castes and the Scheduled Castes is the barrier of untouchability. Now, by the Fundamental Rights which we have accepted, untouchability is prohibited by law and its practice is made a criminal offence under the law of the Federation. We have also accepted in the Fundamental Rights that no public place should be prohibited to anyone by reason of his birth. So far as the Federation is concerned, we have removed the artificial barrier between one section of the Hindu community and the other.

V.I. Muniswamy Pillai (Madras: General)

Going through the various sections, one has to note whether the underdog, the common man, the communities that have been neglected in the past, have been well protected, and facilities for citizenship have been afforded. Reading this constitution, one finds that there are two noval things that are not obtaining in any of the constitution of the world; first of all, the eradication of untouchability. As a member of the so-called Dalit community, I welcome it. Untouchability has eaten into the vitals of the nation, and with all pride and privilege of the Hindu community the outside world have been looking at India with a doubtful eye. I welcome this provision because it shows the greatness of the majority community that they found out that there is a fungus that eating into nation's pride and they have come forward to remove this curse of untouchability. There are people in India today who say that enough propaganda has been made to eradicate untouchability and there is no need for further propaganda. But I honestly feel if you go to the village parts, untouchability is rampant still and a provision of this sort in the Constitution is a welcome thing. The second feature is the abolition of forced labour (begar). If there is any labour required for common purposes in the villages, this most unfortunate fellow, the Dalit is always caught hold of to do all menial and inferior service... I am glad that the Drafting Committee have made provisions to eradicate untouchability and forced labour on this unfortunate community. In the Draft Constitution, they have stated that the eradication of untouchability can be made by laws. I plead that mere laws are not enough. Special laws have to be made. In my own province the legislature was good enough to pass an Act to remove the civil disabilities, but in putting the Act into operation, it was not possible even for the Government to enforce the facilities that were sought to be conferred by the Act. Therefore, I plead that there ought to be special laws if you really want to do away with untouchability and forced labour.

S. Nagappa (Madras: General)

I am glad that social problems have also been touched. In the Constitution it has been made an offence to practise untouchability in any form. I am glad that the Drafting Committee has taken care to see that this is incorporated in the Constitution.

V.I. Muniswamy Pillai (Madras: General)

The great thing that this Constitution brings to notice, not only to this country but to the whole world is the abolition of untouchability. The fain name of India was a slur and a blot by having untouchability. Great avatars and great saints tried their level best to abolish untouchability but it is given to this august Assembly and the new Constitution to say in loud terms that no more untouchability shall stay in our country.

Again, article 29 gives power to the would be Government throwing open all Hindu religious institutions to all classes and sections of Hindus. At one time dogs and swine might enter the sacred precincts of temples but the shadow of an untouchable was considered a great abomination. I feel proud that by this article that slur has been removed away. Due to this discrimination of not allowing a certain section of Hindus, my people have been converted to various faiths and thereby our population has dwindled as also their merit, but today I am proud that under article 29 not only all Hindu religious institutions have been thrown open to all classes and sections of Hindus but all educational institutions maintained by the State or are receiving aids from Government will be thrown open to all the sections of the people....

B.G. Kher (Bombay: General)

...We have abolished untouchability the curse of an public life...

Arun Chandra Guha (West Bengal: General)

.......Yet this Constitution has embodied some very significant achievements of the National Government during the last two years. First, I should mention the abolition of untouchability. Untouchability was the greatest blot, the greatest slur on the Indian civilisation and culture. That has been made a thing of the past at least according to the statute of this Constitution.....

Shankerrao Deo (Bombay: General)

.......The Scheduled Castes, have insisted on having at least some kind of reservation. We have allowed it to continue for ten years. But if we all work and try to remove this blot of untouchability, not from the Constitution but from our hearts, if we destroy it not in law but in spirit, then I am sure this last blot on the sign of it will also go.

H.J. Khandekar (C.P. and Berar: General)

......No section of the Indian people will welcome this Constitution more enthusiastically than the members of the Scheduled Castes of this country for the reason that this Constitution has made a provision for the abolition of untouchability and thereby enabled the Dalits to live like human beings in the country. I being a member of Scheduled Castes welcome this Constitution whole heartedly. You also know that untouchability is a curse on the Hindu society, and seven crores of people of this country have been treated or are being treated like dogs and cats by their caste Hindu brethren.

They have been segregated for the last so many centuries. When the agitation for India's independence intensified, leaders found that there can be no freedom for India without removing untouchability from the Hindu society. When India became formally independent on the 15th August, 1947, I remember that Sardar Vallabbhai Patel said on some occasion that India's hard-won independence cannot be preserved if untouchability is continued. So also I remember that our veteran leader Pandit Jawaharlal Nehru, the Prime Minister of India, said on an important occasion that the foreign countries blamed India only because it observes untouchability. The social workers and the religious worked and even the political workers of this country worked very hard for removing this untouchability but they could not succeed. So also the social and political workers, leaders amongst the Scheduled Castes and many others in the country worked hard for years together to get rid of untouchability, but it is not removed. But we could only succeed to the extent to make the Dalits feel that they too are human beings.

This country was being governed for ages together by the law of Manu and you know what are the effects of this law on this country. Varnas were created, caste within castes were formed and even one caste could not see the face of other caste. The untouchables according to the law of Manu were to go and settle outside a village or a town and that too in the east. Even today, if you minutely see the situation of villages and towns the houses of the untouchables will be found in the east. What of that? We untouchables, at that time called Sudras, were not allowed to name our children according to our wishes. In Manu Smriti there is a sloka: "Mangalam Brahmanasya syat Kshatriasya Balanvitam vaishyasya Dhansaiyukte shudrasya Too jugupsitam." If we Sudras, today's Dalits, were to name our children according to our wishes we were not allowed to name like Jawaharlal, Brahmadatta and so on but we could use only names that are jugupsitam which means Nanda Janak and this was the law of Manu.

Now today, we are enacting a law of Independent India under the genius of Dr. Ambedkar, the President of the Drafting Committee. If I may do so, I call this Constitution the Mahar law because Dr. Ambedkar is a Mahar and now when we inaugurate this constitution on the 26th January, 1950 we shall have the law of Manu replaced by the law of Mahar and I hope that unlike the law of Manu under which there was never a prosperity in the country the Mahar law will make India virtually a paradise. Well, even the social, political and religious reformers in the country found it very difficult to get rid of this ghost of untouchability. They agitated in the country but they did not succeed. Now, we have embodied an article No. 17 in this Constitution to remove untouchability and I am sure that untouchability will be removed, but I have seen Acts for removing untouchability in the Provinces, the Temple Entry Act and the Removal of Disabilities Acts passed by the different Provinces in this country. What is the effect of these laws? Not an inch of untouchability has been removed by these laws and, therefore, if this law of removing untouchability remains in the bank of Constitution itself, I do not think that untouchability will be removed.

If at all the ghost of untouchability or the stigma of untouchability from India should go the minds of these crores and crores of Hindu folks should be changed and unless their hearts are changed, I do not hope, that untouchability will be removed. It is now upto the Hindu society not to observe untouchability in any shape or form. My honourable Friend, Mr. Ranga in his speech the other day said that no is an optimist and he is sure that untouchability and even the name of Scheduled Caste will be removed from India within ten years' time. Well, he may be an optimist, I am not. But I am a practical man. Being an untouchable I know the difficulties of untouchables. I am an untouchable; I have got the practical knowledge of untouchability and I can say that it cannot be removed within ten years if the Hindu community is not sincere. It will take, in my opinion, very many years because the hearts of the Hindu society are not changed.

I have got so many instances, but I have very little time at my disposal and therefore, I do not want to go into details but I can only say to my honourable Friend, Prof. Ranga that making speeches in the Assembly will not remove untouchability. He should go in the country from corner to corner and reach to the Hindu society and change the minds of that society to his views and then only untouchability has a change to be removed... The other thing is the Government of India, the Provincial Governments, the Congress and other political bodies will also have to do their best to remove untouchability. For this untouchability the civilized countries in the world were looking upon India with contempt so far and now I would ask those countries to judge us by the Constitution that we are now passing.

No wise Dalit or reasonable Dalit would like to be an untouchable or a Scheduled Caste for ever. We all wish that we should be merged immediately into the Hindu society because we also being the children of this country want that India's head should be high in the whole world.

Sardar Hukam Singh (E. Punjab: Sikhs)

......Mr. Khandelkar today referred that there was no untouchability among the Sikhs, and that seats had been taken out of the Scheduled Castes seats. I may briefly refer to these observations of his. Certainly according to Sikh religion, there is no untouchability. But does it stand to reason that if there are two sons of one father and they are untouchables and one embraces the Sikh religion he should be neglected simply because he professes that religion different from the one which he originally professed? Would that not have been discrimination on account of religion? I think that injustice has been removed and the Scheduled Castes should have no complaint about it.....

S. Nagappa (Madras: General)

.......Unfortunately we were not only lagging behind in all these respects but there was also a stigma attached to us namely the untouchability. I am thankful to the majority community for having recognised what wrong they have done to use all these centuries. They have now been good enough to abolish this untouchability by a statutory provision. We are abolishing untouchability today, but I would request the framers of this Constitution and those who are going to work this Constitution from the 26th January, 1950 to see that in every bit of it, every letter and work and work and spirit this untouchability lies more on your shoulders, as you have taken the pledge that you should bring us upto your level within 10 years time. I hope with this goodwill, with your generosity, we will be able to come to that level. We will also endeavour on our part to come to that level at the earliest opportunity that is possible.

Jaspat Roy Kapoor (Uttar Pradesh: General)

.......One of the criticisms against this Constitution is that it is not inspired by Gandhism, as Shri Sampurnanand has said and some other friends have also said it, though their number is small. But nothing is farther from truth than this. The chapter on Fundamental Rights and that on Directive Principles give a direct lie to such criticism. What is that Mahatma Gandhi stood for? The thing nearest to his heart was the removal of untouchability. Have we not laid down in definite and specific terms in this Constitution that hereafter there shall be no untouchability and if it is practised it shall be an offence punishable under the law?

Amiya Kumar Ghosh (Bihar: General)

.......There are also very good articles in the Constitution and some of them require special mention. The removal of untouchability has removed a strong barrier to our social and economic progress and I think the future Government will try to implement this with a strong hand.......

Jadubans Sahay (Bihar: General)

.......I think that no amount of guarantees in the Constitution or the filling up of the omissions mentioned will carry us to the goal. It depends upon those who work the Constitution. It depends on how we develop the spirit of tolerance and not on the Constitution or the letter of the law. It depends on the spirit of love towards those that are downtrodden and those who call themselves minorities. We may enact in the Constitution that untouchability is abolished in every hearth and home but that carries us nowhere. You should have love and sympathy for what we call the 'have-nots'. It does not depend on the Constitution or its articles. It depends upon our own character, our own vitality as a nation......

Ajit Prasad Jain (Uttar Pradesh: General)

......Untouchability, which has disfigured the entire history of thousands of years of this country, has been abolished and its practice in any form has been forbidden. It has been declared a penal offence. Everybody has been guaranteed equal rights of access to tanks, bathing ghats, and places of public resort. We have already achieved reasonable success in removing untouchability under the inspiring leadership of the Father of the Nation and these provisions in the Fundamental Rights will accelerate that process. But untouchability is essentially an economic disease.

Kamlapati Tripathi (Uttar Pradesh: General)

......I shall now take up the other speciality of the Constitution which has been constantly referred to and for which we have resorted to self-praise and mutual congratulations. It is the abolition of untouchability. We very proudly say that through this Constitution we have totally effaced untouchability. It is a surprise to me that we take pride on the abolition of untouchability and that we consider it a great success. I want to ask whether we have abolished untouchability only today? By declaring untouchability as illegal in the Constitution have we done anything as can bring great credit to us? Have we done any great and novel thing? Untouchability was abolished long ago when Bapu raised his voice against it and revolted against untouchability and said that it was a blot on India and that it should be removed. That powerful and explicit voice ended untouchability years ago. Today we say that we have abolished untouchability through this Constitution. I ask had we not done what Bapu had asked us to do and what had met general approval, how would we have kept face with our people? Therefore, it does not appear proper to me to say that we have done a great and unique thing. I think that it is altogether unnecessary for us to take pride in the abolition of untouchability....

K.M. Jedhe (Bombay; General)

......I stand here to congratulate Dr. Ambedkar and his colleagues for having taken great pains in framing India's new Constitution. We have spent nearly three years and now we are completing our great work. Some Members while congratulating Dr. Ambedkar have called him the present Manu. I am certain that he would not like this appellation. I know he hates Manu who has created four castes, the lowest of which is the untouchable class. I remember that he has publicly burnt *Manu Smrithi* in the huge meeting of the untouchables at Mohad in 1929. He is the great leader of the Dalits and is greatly extolled by them as their champion and is worshipped as an idol. They are very proud of him. They call him Bhim and make it known to the public that he has framed Bhim Smrithi. I also call it Bhim Smrithi though

I belong to the Sprasya Class. Dr. Ambedkar is a great lawyer and a man of great ability and intellect; nobody will doubt that. Untouchability has been removed by law and while framing the Constitution, Dr. Ambedkar was very keen and earnest in safeguarding the interests of the Dalits. All Dalits must be grateful to him. At the same time, we must also be grateful to our country's Father, Mahatma Gandhi, who gave us independence. He was a great soul who make great efforts during his life-time to remove untouchability. His great wish was to bring the Dalits to the levels of touchables. He is not amongst us to see his great wish fulfilled and bless us......

L.S. Bhatkar (C.P. and Berar: General)

......But many shortcomings still remain in it. The rights granted to the people under article 19 of the Fundamental Rights are a farce, because whatever has been given under this article has been taken away by the proviso of that article. Article 17 provides for the abolition of untouchability for which I congratulate the Drafting Committee. Every Province has passed legislation for the abolition of untouchability, but that is only on paper, it is not followed anywhere. Only a few people are trying to eradicate untouchability which has entered if I may say so, the blood and bones of caste Hindus on account of its existence for thousands of years. But before any law can be of any help, the caste Hindus should effect a change of heart. Untouchability can be abolished only in this way, it is your responsibility to study the lesson taught by the Father of the Nation, Mahatma Gandhi in this respect and to come out successful in the test......

B. Pattabhi Sitaramayya (Madras: General)

......And next, you have also been able to remove untouchability which had divided one section of Hindus from the rest. Mahatmaji began his fast unto death on the 20th September, 1932 and worked a miracle in the space of six days. Now we have removed untouchability not merely in name, not merely in word and spirit, but also in law, so that nobody can hereafter say that so-and-so is an untouchable, for he would be punished with fine and imprisonment.

Rights for Society

Historical Backdrop : When the Constitution of India was framed, a provision was made in the form of Article 17 which provides as below:

> Article 17 which makes the practice of untouchability an offence must be read with Act 35 (a) (ii) which confers upon Parliament the exclusive power to make laws prescribing punishment for those acts, which are declared to be offences under part III including Section 17. In the exercise of the powers, conferred by Article 35, Parliament has enacted the Untouchability (Offences) Act, 1955.

Broadly, it prohibited enforcement of any kind of religious disability in any religious places like temples, and social disabilities in public places like shops, restaurants, etc. It gave the untouchables the same rights as any other person in the enjoyment and use of wells, water tap, public conveniences and cremation grounds, educational institutions, hotels and hospitals. Any act which prevents an untouchables from availing these rights is made punishable. The present Act came into force on June 1, 1955. The Act had no doubt some statutory effect, but the evil of untouchability was not completely eradicated.

Ever since the Untouchability (Offences) Act, 1955 came into being, there has been criticism both inside and outside the Parliament that the Act is not serving the purpose for which it was enacted. It was observed that punishments awarded under the Act were too few and inadequate. Because of these criticisms, the Government of India appointed a committee under the chairmanship of R. Elayaperumal to analyse, amongst other things, the problem of untouchability with reference to the working of the

Untouchability (Offences) Act, 1955 and to make suitable recommendations to the Government for its amendment. A Bill to amend the Untouchability (Offences) Amendment and Miscellaneous Provision Bill 1972, was introduced in the Lok Sabha in April 1972. Subsequently the Bill was referred to a joint committee of both the Houses of Parliament which submitted its report in February 1974. It was passed by Parliament in the monsoon session of 1976 and assented to by the President on September 13, 1976. The crucial issues concerning offences connected to untouchability were discussed via the aforesaid Bill and portions of the debates are reproduced below.

Prof. S. Nurul Hasan: I have already moved that the Bill to amend the Untouchability (Offences) Act, 1955 and further to amend the Representation of the People Act, 1951, be taken into consideration.

This is a very simple but important Bill. The House would recall that in 1955, the Untouchability Offences Act was passed to give effect to the solemn declaration contained in the Constitution in Article 17, according to which untouchability stood abolished. But inadequacies were felt in the existing Act and many Hon. Members, in Parliament as well as others pointed out those inadequacies. The government, therefore, decided to refer this matter as well as other matters to the Committee on Untouchability, Educational and Economic Development of Scheduled Castes, set up under the chairmanship of Shri Elayaperumal in 1965. The Elayaperumal Committee studied the problem of untouchability as well as the functioning or the working of the Untouchability Act, 1955 in detail, and made a number of recommendations. The purpose of those recommendations was to plug some of the existing loopholes and to make the penal provisions more stringent. Most of these recommendations have been accepted by government.

There has been only one modification and I shall explain each of the major provisions of the Bill.

First of all is the question of amendment relating to the raising of the quantum of punishment under the Act. The second is making offences under the Act non-compoundable. Thirdly, bringing within the definition of 'place of public worship' privately-owned temples used as places of public worship and disqualifying persons convicted under the Act from contesting elections to the Central and State legislatures. Lastly, the utterances of public personalities justifying untouchability whether on historical or philosophical grounds are also proposed to be brought within the purview of the law.

I am placing for the consideration of the House a small change government have made in the Bill from the recommendations of the Elayaperumal Committee. The Committee had recommended that in the case of the first offence, it should be punished by imprisonment of not less than 3 months but upto 6 months and also fine of not less than Rs. 50 but upto Rs. 200. While government naturally agree that the punishment must be deterrent, it has been felt that if the punishment for the first offence is quite so deterrent, there may be a tendency on the part of court to acquit the accused on the basis of some doubt or the other.

Therefore, government have proposed that in the case of the first offence the punishment may not be less than one month but upto six months—the maximum remains the same and the fine must be not less than Rs. 50, as was also recommended by the Committee, but upto Rs. 200, also in accordance with the Committee's recommendation. Hence the only difference is that in the case of the first offence, the minimum punishment recommended by the Committee as 3 months has been changed to 1 month in the Bill. I would like however to make it clear at the very beginning that government do not wish to adopt any very rigid attitude in the matter and if it is the general feeling of the House that we should accept the Elayaperumal Committee's recommendation *in toto*, I would be prepared to do so.

I would request the House to give this matter expeditious

consideration because the whole matter has been gone into in great detail by the Elayaperumal Committee. The report of the Committee was submitted in 1969 and for reason best known to the House, it has not been possible for government to bring forward legislation amending this very important Act. I move.

Mr. Speaker: Motion moved:

> "That the Bill to amend the Untouchability (Offences) Act 1955 and further to amend the Representation of the People Act, 1951, be taken into consideration."

Krishna Chandra Hader (Ausgram): Mr. Speaker, Sir, I would like to speak in Bengali.

I, on behalf, of my party rise to support this Bill. Sir, we are going to celebrate the silver jubilee of our independence but the cases of offences of untouchability are very much prevalent even today. Untouchability has been proclaimed an offence in Article 17 of the Constitution. In pursuance of the provisions of Article 35 of the Constitution, the Untouchability (Offences) Act, 1955 was passed in this House. The Elayaperumal Committee was formed to study the offences committed under untouchability and to review the working of the Act. A discussion also had taken place in this House in 1970.

We speak of democracy, equality etc. but even today we find that about 8 crores of downtrodden people in our country are deprived of real freedom and equality. Even today we find that members of the Scheduled Castes and Scheduled Tribes and the Adivasis are living as untouchables and like second class citizens and at many places they are treated worse than animals. It has been stated in this House many times that the members of the Scheduled Castes, Scheduled Tribes, the Harijans etc., are deprived of the fundamental rights that are available to other Indian citizens. In villages members of these communities are prohibited to draw water from the common ponds or wells. In many places like Kerala, etc.they are prohibited to worship in temples or places of public worship. It is not enough that the problem is left to be tackled by the Ministry of Education and Social Welfare alone. We will have to review this from different angles, i.e., social, economic and political.

All departments like Planning, Finance, etc. should be alive to this problem and then only there can be some betterment in the lot of these backward classes of people. Major portion of these 8 crores of downtrodden people are either landless labourers or share croppers or they work as industrial labour in the urban industrial areas. We have discussed in this House the sad incident where 30 Adivasis were burnt alive in Purnea district of Bihar because they were involved in disputes over possession of land. This is the way how people of higher classes are committing atrocities on them. We have also discussed in this House the sale of Adivasi girls and women in Orissa who are our sisters. This is regrettable condition of the so-called untouchables in our country. For this purpose mere legislation is not enough. We had already passed legislation against such offences as far back as 1955. But even today after 25 years of freedom and in spite of all these legislations, untouchability is prevalent.

The Elayaperumal Committee says, I quote. "The problem of untouchability is, therefore, inseparably linked up with the question of caste system and the social set up based on that. It is an indisputable fact that the caste system is the dominating social force in this country. Hence any attempt to remove untouchability without striking at the root of the caste system is simply to treat the outward symptoms of a disease or to draw a line on the surface of water. Untouchability can not be abolished in this country unless the social order is changed by establishing new values, and for this purpose the values based on the Hindu religion must be changed first."

It further says: "A clear realisation of this fact on the part of the people is the pre-condition for any steps towards a social reconstruction resulting in the removal of untouchability for

Scheduled Castes in this country". Therefore, Sir, today we will have to go to the roots of this malady to solve this problem. Because we have not yet been able to eradicate the malady of untouchability in our country. Our prestige in the eyes of the outside world has suffered a blow. In the *Patriot* newspaper of 11th September, 1971 it was published how the Harijans were treated in Hodal town in Gurgaon.The news item says, "The caste Hindus of Hodal town in Gurgaon district have been blocking all roads and streets leading to a Harijan locality in the town thus immobilising the residents completely for the last one month and have not been allowed to lodge a complaint with the authorities."

Sir, the aggrieved people were not even allowed to lodge a complaint with the authorities. The Registrar General of India has carried out a survey to some extent but the Committee has gone to the extent of saying: at page 46 they say: "However, the general impression which we gathered during our tours is that the figures, cannot be truly representative, which promoted the Committee to conduct a plot survey in one of the districts of UP." Therefore, Sir, this act should be given wide publicity to inform the people that practice of untouchability is an offence punishable under the law. Not only that, many officials in our police departments also are either ignorant or indifferent to this piece of legislation due to lack of sympathy and feelings for the backward classes of people. In that very report of the Committee it has been said, I quote, "As regards the provisions of the Act, the figures are unsatisfactory. It is a matter of great regret that out of 30 only 2 police officials could tell something about the provisions of the Act (the Untouchability Offences Act.)" This is the situation in which we find ourselves. We will have to examine the problem from economic, social and political points of view. The ruling party speak about ideals of Mahatma Gandhi but in his birth place, Gujarat, at places like Porbandar, Rajkot etc., untouchability is prevalent and people of lower castes are looked down upon. This evil is in existence in Gujarat, Rajasthan, Uttar Pradesh, Tamil Nadu and various other States. I feel Sir, that more enactment of legislations is not adequate to counter and eradicate this evil. The people of higher castes should come forward to help its removal from the roots. There is need to create social consciousness among members of higher castes to tackle the problem. They should change their outlook otherwise this problem is not likely to be solved.

I would also like to recall, Sir, what Dr. Ambedkar, the author of our Constitution and a prominent leader of the people belonging to the Scheduled Castes and other backward classes, said in 1936. He said, "Democracy is not merely a form of government. It is primarily a mode of associated living of conjoint communicated experience. It is essentially an attitude of respect and reverence towards fellowmen. Any objection to liberty ? Few object to liberty in the sense of a right to face movement in the sense of a right to life and limb... Why not allow liberty to benefit by an effective and competent use of a person's power...? To object this kind of liberty is to perpetuate slavery. For slavery does not merely mean a legalised form of subjection. It means a state of society in which some men are forced to accept from others the purposes which control their conduct".

Sir, even while supporting this Bill, I would like to refer to a news item that appeared in the Madras edition of the *Hindu* dated 22.4.1972. It says, Mr. O.P.D. Salappa complained that private educational institutions were not entertaining Scheduled Castes students."

Sir, I only want to point out that Scheduled Castes students are prevented even from getting admission to schools in many parts of the country. Not only that Sir, an IAS Scheduled Caste Officer at Jaipur was allotted a quarter in an area habited by high caste people but he was not allowed to live there and was forced to shift to another residence in the Bhangi colony. This is the condition in which we are living. Sir, on the 16th February this year a news item appeared in the *Hindu* (Madras edition). It says "There are ten temples in Kasargot area in Cannanore district which are barred to Harijans." Therefore, we see, Sir, that even now Harijans are debarred from entering and worshipping in temples in many places. It has also been seen at certain places that Harijan teachers though appointed by authorities were not allowed to conduct classes just because they were Harijans. They were relieved of their duties and were told not to come to the school but collect their pay when due. Sir, in section 7 of this amendment Bill it has been stated that "In section 8 of the Representation of the People Act, 1951, sub-section (1) after the words "The Indian Penal Code' the words, brackets and figures 'Or under the Untouchability Offences Act, 1956', shall be inserted."

Krishna Chandra Halder: Sir, here mention have been made about the disqualifications of candidate for election to the legislatures either of the Centre or the State. I will suggest Sir, that if a person is found guilty of offence under the Untouchability Act, he should be debarred from voting rights for a period of six years. His name should be removed from the voters list for a period of six years. Our poet Tagore has said that "he, whom you have left behind, is pulling you back and retarding your progress." If such a big section of our population remained downtrodden and backward, the entire nation will remain backward. It can never progress. It has been said that "Man is the supreme and ultimate truth, there is nothing beyond Man." In this spirit Sir, I will appeal to all sections of people to come forward with open mind and help the cause of uplift of these downtrodden people. Those who have been denied human values and basic rights so long, should be welcomed in our folds and all their rights should be restored to them. With these words, Sir, I conclude my speech.

P. Venkatasubbaiah: Sir, the Hon. Minister of Education has brought forward this Untouchability (Offences) Amendment and Miscellaneous Provisions Bill, 1972. When we discuss the subject pertaining to untouchability, we have to understand that there is a history behind this problem and that the future of Millions of destitute peoples who have for ages been neglected by society and are outside the pale of society. For the emancipation of these unfortunate peoples the Father of the Nation devoted his life and energies and formulated many schemes. Instead of being called the low caste people or the cobblers or scavengers, they have been christened as Harijans, children of God. Our history is replete with the heroic struggle launched on behalf of these people by various social welfare organisations and social workers. We cannot easily forget the historic Poona Fast undertaken by the Mahatma for securing to these unfortunate people social and economic justice. And we all know the memorable role played by Dr. Ambedkar in this struggle. But what is tragic is that in spite of twenty-five years of our independence and in spite of the work of these great leaders in this behalf, this social inequality and injustice is still in our midst.

We have heard with shame of the incidents in Kanchikacherla in Andhra Pradesh and in other places like Gujarat and Maharashtra. Only a few cases come to our notice through the newspapers but there will be many more which are not reported about the atrocities committed against these poor unfortunate people. These incidents go to show how deep-seated is the prejudice against these so-called untouchables in our body politic. So the question we should ask ourselves is whether through legislation we can eradicate this deep-rooted malady. We assume that this prejudice is got evident in the cities. But as I said earlier this prejudice is in our blood. This is evident in our neglect of these people in the matter of allotment of house sites or even in the fundamental need of providing drinking water to them. On paper we have grandiose schemes for the betterment of their lot but for some reason we have so far not been able to translate these plans into tangible action. We have provided that adequate representation should be given to them on the Panchayati bodies, Zilla Parishads. But in point of fact, what is happening? The tenants of rich landlords or their stooges get elected to these bodies defeating the very purpose for which such reservations have been made for these backward classes. Because of the policy of the government there is a suspicion in the minds of the people whether instead of eradicating this social evil we are perpetuating it. For instance, you are allotting them house sites on the outskirts of the villages or towns leading to segregation of these low-caste people from the so-called high caste people. By confining them to these specified areas, you are shutting out the human and other channels of communication between these classes and the high caste people. Until you try to integrate these people socially with the other communities you will not wipe out the feeling of distinction between these two classes. And social justice will not be done by these unfortunate people. Till this integration takes place and till you secure to them a better status than now, untouchability does not stand the ghost of a chance of being eradicated and your plans and programmes will not succeed.

In the matter of providing them educational opportunities and in the matter of their marriage also, the social consciousness should be aroused. There should, in fact, come about a social revolution. Encourage intercaste marriages with these people. Incentives like increased job opportunities for the persons contracting such marriages and for the offspring of such union should be liberally offered. Sir, as matters stand now these people are discontented and disheartened. Even though reservation of jobs is there for them, people belonging to these classes are not appointed to these reserved posts on the plea that suitable and deserving persons of these communities are not forthcoming. Thus, they are denied even the small percentage of opportunities provided to them. This is the bare fact. This is happening every day everywhere—be it in the Railways or other government departments. If this is how we are going to accept them as our social partners we can know how far we have progressed in our society.

There are so many social welfare organisations and *Harijan Sevak Sanghs*. Government should encourage such social organisations. Not only in the public field but more so in the social field, the increasing need of non-official organisations is being felt and they should be encouraged by government.

Sir, ninety-nine per cent of our agricultural labour or landless labour are Harijans. So government has to consider how best to improve the economic conditions of these people. They depend on the land they cultivate and in justice they should get all the surplus land that would be available after the ceilings of land are imposed. Otherwise, there is the possibility of such lands being cornered by rich landlords. These landless Harijans will then be deprived of their rights and cheated out of their rights and due.

You may make the punishment for practising untouchability more and more stringent. But I would like to remind that this social scourge cannot be wished away by legislation only. Great leaders like Mahatma Gandhi and Dr. Ambedkar have given their lives for the eradication of this social evil a stigma on the fair name of our country. If social justice is to be done by these people, there should be a sea-change not only socially but even in the attitude of the government. In the matter of jobs, the Harijans should be posted as high officials like District Collectors. They should be provided jobs much more than the reserved quota for them. Then only there will be social transformation. Otherwise they would be deprived even of the rights guaranteed to them.

Sir, the progress of the plans and programmes meant for these backward classes has so far not been upto our expectations. Therefore, I request that a special committee should be appointed to go into the question of the implementation of these programmes and to identify the areas where there has been a shortfall in the targets. They should be empowered to evaluate the progress of these activities in each and every State.

With the problems of Harijans are closely connected those of the Adivasis in various parts of our country. These innocent people have also been neglected by us so far. As a result of this neglect, they have fallen a pray to the philosophy of violence. Whenever the neglected find that through democratic processes and constitutional methods they cannot enforce their rights, they enforce them through violent means, government should, therefore, see that these people are weaned away from the path of violence by restoring to them their rights and opportunities.

In conclusion I would reiterate that if we want to integrate these Harijans into the mainstream of our society, if we want to provide them social, political and economic equality, all of us, the government and social welfare organisations should work for them and towards this end. At least then we would have in part atoned for our past neglect of these Harijans, the children of God.

"The judge should study the character and age of the offender, his early breeding, his education and environment, the circumstances under which he committed the offence, the object with which he committed it and other factors. The object of doing so is to acquaint the judge with the exact nature of the circumstances so that he may give a punishment which suits the circumstances".

Mr. Speaker: Nine or ten minutes for each at the most. Sometimes Members grab some time and the next Member has to suffer because of that.

J.M. Gowder (Nilgiris): Hon. Mr. Speaker, Sir I am thankful to you for giving me an opportunity to say a few words on the Untouchability (Offences) Amendment and Miscellaneous Provision Bill, 1972 on behalf of my party, the Dravida Munnetra Kazhagam.

Sir, the provisions of the Untouchability (Offences) Act, 1955 are sought to be amended through this Bill. In spite of the fact that this amending Bill has been brought before this House after a lapse of so many years, still there are many lacunae and loopholes in the statute that are to be removed and plugged. In the legislation formulated by the Government which swear solemnly by the establishment of a secular state in the country you find the word 'religion'. Is this in consonance with the professions of the ruling party? This is what you come across in the original Act:

> "Whoever on the ground of "untouchability" prevents any person:
>
> from entering any place or public worship which is open

> to other persons professing the same religion or belonging to the same religious denomination or any section thereof...

If untouchability is practised in respect of a person professing the same religion, then there is a penal provision under this Act. I am sure, Sir, you will agree with me that in a secular State the people belonging to different religions should have the freedom to worship wherever they want. For example, if a section of Hindu religious faith prevents another section from entering a place of public worship on the ground that that section belongs to Scheduled Castes, then the penal provision is attracted, as the practice of untouchability is an offence. If you extend this a little further, what happens if non-Christians or non-Muslims are prevented from entering the place of public worship of Christians and Muslims? This is not an offence. Only when such discrimination is practised with the express sanction of laws, the efficacious penal provisions for eradication of untouchability lose their intrinsic value. I have advanced this argument to show that if the government are keen to have the word 'religion' in such a legislation, then naturally there cannot be any possibility of having a secular state in the country. You will agree with me that religion is the bedrock of casteism and bigotry that are bedevilling the entire country. Unless 'religion' is deprived of its legal backing, you cannot successfully implement any legislation for the removal of untouchability.

I have no hesitation in saying that the government are to be blamed for the perpetuation of untouchability in the country because they do not seem to plug the loopholes in the Act. These loopholes are the breeding ground for the practice of untouchability in the country. To whichever religious faith a place of public worship may belong, there should not be any practice of untouchability and here there is no need for mentioning 'religion', in the Act.

[Mr. Deputy Speaker in the Chair]

I am proud to say that the Tamil Nadu Government are occupying a premier place in the country so far as removal of untouchability is concerned. That is because the Government of Tamil Nadu have taken certain pioneering steps in this direction. For centuries the people belonging to a particular community could alone become the priests in the temples.

This profession had been the exclusive perogative of a certain section of the society. Now, the DMK Government has passed an Act under which anyone can become the *archaka* (priest) in a temple. Even a Harijan can hope to become an *archaka* in a temple. You will agree with me, Sir, that this laudable legislation is worthy of emulation by other States and in fact the Central Government should give a lead in this direction. During the five-year period of administration the DMK Government have enacted such progressive measures. Now the Congress Party is in power at the Centre and also in most of the States. I do not think it will be impossible for the ruling party to enact such meaningful and progressive measures throughout the country. Similarly, in the matter of inter-caste marriages to which a reference was made by the speakers who preceded me, the Government of Tamil Nadu are awarding Gold Medals. The people contracting inter-caste marriages with Harijan community are given incentives and encouragement. I wonder why other State Government should not take the cue from the Tamil Nadu Government for the removal of untouchability.

The Central Government seems to be concentrating all their energies in political manipulations and in political expediencies. The ruling party is more interested in winning elections and in toppling the Opposition Governments in the States than in implementing the Acts for the removal of untouchability and in encouraging inter-caste marriages with Harijan community. I would like to ask which of the Central Minister is giving serious thought to remove untouchability and to provide ways and means for the upliftment of Scheduled Castes.

During 1968 the number of untouchability offences was 203. There were only 203 offences when the number of Scheduled

Castes people is about 11 crores. Out of this, in 35 cases there was conviction and there was acquittal in 52 cases. In 39 cases, reconciliation was reached outside the court. 77 cases were reported to be pending. From this it is clear as to how many cases of offences are brought to the notice of the authorities. Firstly, the Harijan against whom this offence has been committed has no courage to approach a court. Secondly, he has no money to spend on such a case.

Thirdly, after contesting a case against a caste Hindu, how is he going to live in the midst of a community predominated by caste-Hindus after the case is disposed of in his favour? The very fact that the Scheduled Castes are economically at the lowest rung of our society is resulting in the perpetuation of untouchability in our country. Even if a Central Minister belongs to the Scheduled Castes, he is not known by that factor. The power that is vested in him makes him known better throughout the country. Only when the economic status of the Harijans and the Scheduled Castes is improved, these people will gain respect in the society, I would like to know what concrete steps have been taken for their economic upliftment. The father of our nation, Mahatma Gandhi, two and half decades ago, gave the clarion call to the nation that untouchability should be done with immediately. What has been done by the government to translate his vision into action? I am sorry to repeat that the energies of the government are getting dissipated in other directions, but not in the removal of untouchability.

I commend this amending Bill which seeks to enhance the punishment. But what steps have been taken to give free legal aid to the Harijans who are the target of such offences? It is common knowledge that these people have no resources to fight in a court of a law. Unless they are given free legal aid, how are they going to take advantage of the provisions of this Act? If the government want to implement this Act vigorously; there must be a provision in this very Act, giving free legal aid to the Harijans and the Scheduled Castes, who are the harassed victims of other sections of our society. The Elayaperumal Committee has made many valuable suggestions. The Hon. Minister himself stated that though this committee had recommended three months of imprisonment the government have brought it down to one month in this amending Bill, as if the practice of untouchability is coming to an end in our country.

I regret to point out that this Act has not yet been made available in regional languages. The police, the magistrates and the revenue officers are not fully acquainted with the provisions of this Act. They are the people to implement this Act: I would like to suggest that in the syllabus of the training schools for Police, for Magistrates and for Revenue Officers, the Untouchability Offences Act should get a prominent place so that the concerned people get an intimate knowledge about the provisions.

You know, Sir, that it is impossible for the Harijans to go to a First Class Magistrate's court situated far away from their place. They have neither conveyance facility nor they have money to spend on such visits. I would suggest that mobile courts should be established throughout the country for the purpose of implementing this Act vigorously. I would also like to point out that adequate protection should be given to the people belonging to Scheduled Castes and Harijan community, who take courage in their hands to report such offences committed by caste Hindus. I would also stress the need for raising the standard of living of these people, which will ensure them a place of honour in our society and not the place of exploitation. The government cannot eradicate untouchability solely with the assistance of this Act providing punishment.

I came across a report that in Chandigarh there are separate dharamshalas and cremation grounds for Scheduled Castes people. While they live they are ill-treated, harassed and victimised. But after their death also, they should be burnt or buried in a separate cremation ground. I would like to know why this kind of a thing should not be made an offence under this Act. I would ask of the Minister as to what action has been taken by the government against the people like Puri Shankaracharya who want to perpetuate untouchability in the country.

Mr. Deputy-Speaker : This is provided for in the Bill by which such things will be taken care of.

J.M. Gowder : What happened to the case against Puri Shankaracharya? Before I conclude, I would appeal to the Hon. Minister that the lacunae and the loopholes in the legislation meant for the removal of untouchability are removed. This kind of amending Bill should not be taken advantage of by the ruling party to get the votes of Scheduled Castes people. The provisions of the Bill should be implemented mainly in the interest of removing untouchability and in the interest of uplifting the economic interests of people belonging to Scheduled Castes.

Mr. Deputy-Speaker : Have you read the Bill?

Shivnath Singh : Yes, Sir, I have read it, I have gone through it thoroughly.

Mr. Deputy-Speaker : You are talking of inter-caste marriage and things like that.

Shivnath Singh : I am going to the root cause.

Mr. Deputy-Speaker : What you say is something different from what is provided in the Bill.

Mr. Deputy-Speaker : He is yet to make a speech.

Atal Bihari Vajpayee : The Hon. Minister did make a speech while moving the Bill for consideration. He could have said many things. I will wait for his speech.

Mr. Deputy-Speaker : Would you like these as amendments to the Bill?

R.S. Pandey : I wanted to enlighten the House how the society is to be adjusted.

K.S. Chavda (Patan) : I raise to support the amending Bill before the House. The Elayaperumal Committee submitted its report in January, 1969. The Minister has come forward before the House today with this amending Bill. That shows that government is not serious in case of removal of untouchability. Otherwise government would have come much earlier because 4 years have passed. When the preaching of any reform fails, the law takes the place of preaching. In case of removal of untouchability, when the preachings of saints and great men like Mahatma Gandhi and Dr. Babasaheb Ambedkar did not remove untouchability to a considerable extent, then, Sir, Article 17 was provided in the Constitution and our Indian Parliament has passed the Untouchability Offences Act of 1955. But, Sir, I am sorry to say that there is wide gap between the legislation and the implementation.

Today the Scheduled Castes people in the villages are not allowed to fetch water from the same common well in the village. In the same way they are not allowed to worship God together with caste Hindus in the same village. Even the barbers and the washermen do not serve them in the villages. This is the position, Sir, even after twenty-five years of our independence. Now the circumstances are more favourable than they were when Mahatma Gandhi and Dr. Ambedkar tried their level best to remove untouchability.

Still, Sir, the Government of India and the State Governments are not serious to remove untouchability lock stock and barrel. Otherwise it would have been removed by now. The figure of murders of Schedule Castes people during the years 1967, 1968 and 1969 were 1112 for the whole country.

Out of them, nearly 556 murders were from Madhya Pradesh and U.P. A Harijan girl was burnt in 1970 in Madhya Pradesh. When the question was raised by me on the floor of the Rajya Sabha, the Prime Minister promised to make a statement regarding that case. But she never made a statement though she was and till now is the Minister of Home Affairs and if this is the position regarding the Prime Minister, naturally, Sir, the State Chief Ministers will follow the same thing and do nothing to improve the condition of the Scheduled Castes and Scheduled Tribes. This portfolio of the removal of untouchability and amelioration of the condition of the Scheduled Castes should be in the hands of the Chief Ministers in the States and in the case of the Centre it should be with the Prime Minister. Then only something can be done with regard to the removal of untouchability.

If she takes keen interest, then things can be improved. The Prime Minister held about a month back a meeting for the development of her constituency, namely Rae Bareli and all the Ministers were invited for that meeting, but only the Minister for Social Welfare was not invited. For the development of her own district, she has taken so much interest....

Mr. Deputy-Speaker : The Hon. Member has made a reference to it. That should be enough. Let him not divert his attention from the Bill.

K.S. Chavda : I am not diverting my attention. The whole thing is only the Minister for Social Welfare...

Deputy-Speaker : Untouchables are being bypassed by many other matters. Let him now come to the main thing.

K.S. Chavda : The main thing is that if the head of the whole nation takes the initiative, then something can be done.

Mr. Deputy-Speaker : Let him not go off the main subject to Rae Bareli.

K.S. Chavda : At that meeting she said that she wanted to make Rae Bareli a model district. That is why I say that she should take this up first, namely the removal of untouchability.

Mr. Deputy-Speaker : That is relevant...

K.S. Chavda : Here is the press report which mentions the names of all the Ministers who were present...

Mr. Deputy-Speaker : Let him not go into the details of all that. He is going away very far from the main subject. He has made a reference to that and that should be enough.

K.S. Chavda : The main subject is the removal of untouchability, and I am coming to that also. If she takes the initiative, then something could be done. All the Ministers, Central and State were present there, but only the Minister for Social Welfare was not present...

The Deputy Minister in the Ministry of Irrigation and Power (Shri B.N. Kureel) : No Minister was invited. The Ministers went on their own.

K.S. Chavda : Shri Om Mehta, Shri H.N. Bahuguna...

Mr. Deputy-Speaker : Then Hon. Member has already made the suggestion that it will be most effective if the Prime Minister herself takes over the responsibility. That is very relevant and very pertinent and I have allowed it. But beyond that, if he goes off and goes into the details of what happened in Rae Bareli, then he will be going very far away from the subject, and the poor untouchables whom he is trying to defend would be the sufferers.

K.S. Chavda : She wants to make Rae Bareli a model district. I was submitting that in the case of removal of untouchability also she should take up that responsibility. My point was that....

Mr. Deputy-Speaker : I have allowed that and that is quite relevant...

K.S. Chavda : But the Deputy Minister says that no Minister was invited to that meeting. I should say something in reply to it and say that all the Ministers were invited....

Mr. Deputy-Speaker : I do not allow it.

K.S. Chavda : That is quite relevant.

Mr. Deputy-Speaker : The Hon. Member has made the point. If he wants to go into the details and deflect the entire discussion into something else....

K.S. Chavda : But the Deputy Minister says that I am wrong. Should I not say something in reply and save my position?

Mr. Deputy-Speaker : Rae Bareli is not untouchability. Now, the Hon. Member should conclude. I am calling the next Member.

K.S. Chavda : This is unfair. She says that Rae Bareli should be made a model for the whole nation. Should I not refer to that and say that untouchability should be removed?....

Mr. Deputy-Speaker : He has made that point and I have allowed him.

K.S. Chavda : The Deputy Minister said that no Minister had been invited. That is why I am quoting from the report...

Shashi Bhushan (South Delhi) : The Hon. Member should be made a model Member of Parliament.

K.S. Chavda : If I would have been in charge, there would not have been any untouchability at all.

Mr. Deputy-Speaker : I have a feeling, and I do not know how really concerned Members are for those whom some people consider untouchables...

K.S. Chavda : If even you, Sir, fail to understand what I say, I do not know what to do.

Mr. Deputy-Speaker : The Hon.Member has made his point and it is a pertinent point and I think he should be satisfied with that.

Now, the Hon. Member should conclude, Shri B.R. Shukla.

B.R. Shukla (Bahraich) : The real point of the controversy has been missed by many Members who have participated in the debate. The question is not whether untouchability is a course and whether it should be abolished or not. When we adopted the Constitution, we made a provision that untouchability in any shape or form shall not be tolerated or practised in this country.

In pursuance of the constitutional directive, the Untouchability Offences Act, 1955 was passed. The question which this Bill raises for discussion is whether the punishment already provided for under the Parent Act should be enhanced so as to meet the situation. The question is whether when we bring an amendment for enhancement of the punishment or for providing a minimum rigorous imprisonment for an act which amounts to an offence under the Act we have made out any case or not. Only if the existing penal provisions in the Act are inadequate amendment becomes necessary. The real point to consider is whether the punishment of fine or imprisonment upto six months has been inadequate to remove untouchability. For that we have to see how many cases have gone to courts and how many persons have been really prosecuted and convicted, and in spite of the conviction and light punishment under the Parent Act, those very persons have persisted in repetition of the offence. Only then it would be necessary to make a change. But if the implementation of the provisions of the Parent Act has been insufficient, there is no question of bringing an amendment Bill.

The principle of punishment is based on three grounds, retributive, reformative and deterrent. As for retributive punishment, if a person has beaten another person, instead of the person who has been beaten taking to private vengeance against the wrong doer, he seeks the assistance of the court which awards the punishment. This should be settled through the agency of the court of law. Then there is reformative punishment and deterrent punishment. Deterrent punishment is punishment of such a nature as to strike terror in the hearts of potential wrong doers and prevent them from committing the offence. I would submit that the punishment provided under the Untouchability (Offences) Act is neither the retributive type nor of the deterrent type but by its very nature it is of the reformative type. A very distinguished jurist, Mr. Salmonds in his famous book on Jurisprudence has said that law lags behind public opinion, as public opinion lags behind truth.

Mr. Deputy-Speaker : How does he define this Bill?

B.R. Shukla : I am saying there is no case made out by government for bringing a bill of this type for making the punishment which should be minimum of one month imprisonment in the case of first offence, then adding another term for the second offence and adding a further term for the third offence. It means we are encroaching upon the discretion of judges because after a judge has come to the conclusion that a certain person has committed an offence for which he should be punished, what should be the quantum of punishment should be left to the discretion of the judge who decides it taking into account a variety of reasons. Therefore, my submission is that Bill is uncalled for. The punishment is already there; to amend it is now uncalled for. The Bill says in the case of first offence under the Act, there should be a punishment of rigorous imprisonment of not less than one month. Such type of provisions do not improve the matter. I will give an illustration.

There are two other enactments in this country where the minimum imprisonment has been provided for. One is the Prevention of Food Adulteration Act where the compulsory punishment is not less than six months imprisonment and a fine of about Rs.1,000. The very fact that the minimum punishment of six months has been provided has gone a long way for the wrong-doers to defeat the provisions of the law by adopting corrupt methods, because they know that once they are convicted, no mercy would be shown and therefore, they must go to the police officer and the food inspector and see that that is not allowed. Under the Gambling Act also, the minimum punishment is six months rigorous imprisonment if a certain place or a certain house is used for gambling. That provision has not been very successful.

So, my submission is that this amendment should not be allowed to be passed, although being a Member of the party which is ruling, I shall only support it, but because it is a radical and social measure, I have ventured to put forth my point of view.

B.S. Murthy (Amalapuram) : I am unable to understand why this Bill has been brought forward in this way. Earlier, the provision was that punishment might extend upto six months. Now it says; one month onwards and the fine is Rs. 550. Is this an indication that untouchability is almost abolished in India? Is it true? It is not true. Why should we misguide ourselves and our people and the world? Every speaker here today was at pains to show how untouchability was on the increase. Just now Mr. Vajpayee said that in one of the central offices in Delhi the Scheduled Castes were not allowed to take water from the common pot. Scheduled Castes officers coming to Delhi are not given houses. I need not say how many persons have been murdered.

Mr. Deputy-Speaker : You were yourself in charge of this matter when you were a Minister.

Shashi Bhushan (South Delhi) : How many houses did you give them when you were in charge of that portfolio?

B.S. Murthy : Generally speakers do not inconvenience other speakers. You have taken the liberty and I shall take the same liberty. When I was the Minister in charge of housing, I saw to it that at least five per cent of the houses were reserved for Scheduled Castes.

Mr. Deputy-Speaker : I wanted this to come from you.

B.S. Murthy : I was able to manage to do that and the government accepted that suggestion. I am not speak-about what I did or did not.

It is not a fact that untouchability is on the decline; on the other hand it is on the ascendancy. In Andhra Pradesh a youngman was burnt alive in daylight. In Rajasthan....

P.K. Deo (Kalahandi) : In your party's government, in Kanchikarla.

B.S. Murthy : Is the Swatantra Party better? Are you supporting it?

P.K. Deo : I am not supporting it.

B.S. Murthy : It is a serious matter. Nearly eighty per cent of the Members in this House are absent. I am requesting those who are present to look upon the Harijans as human beings. It is very bad. He quoted the Kanchikarla case. What difference does it make if it was under the Congress Government, or the Communist Government or the Swatantra Government? Crime is a crime. Even if he is a Maharaja, I do not bother.

P.K. Deo : He should have resigned from the party.

B.S. Murthy : He does not understand how it touches the chords of our hearts. After 25 years of independence, these are happening. He is talking of Kanchikarla happening under the Congress Government. What has he done? What have you done in the Swatantra Government in Orissa? Have you not been encouraging Scheduled Tribes girls to be sold? Shame on you.

Atal Behari Vajpayee : What is happening?

B.S. Murthy : Nothing is happening. We go to philosophy and say *karma*. I am glad Mr. Vajpayee is supporting urgent measures to remove untouchability lock, stock and barrel.

This is a Bill which will beguile the world. I do not know why Prof. Nurul Hasan has brought it. Untouchability is not on the decline. Has any trouble been taken to see how far the legislation so far available has benefited the Scheduled Castes? No. We have been requesting several times that a high level commission may be appointed to go into the whole matter as to what legislation is available at the Centre and what legislation is available at the States to improve the conditions of Scheduled Castes and Scheduled Tribes and find out what reforms are necessary to be made.

In the statement of objects and reasons, it is said that the Elayaperumal Committee made certain recommendations and based on that, this Bill has been brought. I am afraid there are a number of very important suggestions of the Elayaperumal

Committee and all of them have been forgotten. I am not for any enhancement punishment but when you are bringing a legislation, do not beguile the people. We had said, six months; but today it is only one month. Originally we said, Rs. 500; but today it is only Rs. 50 to begin with. Whom are you deceiving? This is very bad. Sometimes State Governments come and tell the Centre. "We do not have money." When the Department of the Welfare of Scheduled Castes and Scheduled Tribes was under the Home Ministry and when Mr. Pant was there as Home Minister, he always appealed to the State Ministers that this is a very important thing. Is not removal of untouchability a nation-building process? Can all the other people have their own way without the willing consent and cooperation of 10 crores of Harijans? We have seen how 7½ crores of people in Bangladesh have revolted and broken off the chains from their hands and formed an independent and sovereign State of Bangladesh. Do you think Scheduled Castes numbering 8 or 10 crores will always remain like this? Is it not because of this ill-treatment by caste Hindus that the movement of Bangladesh was originally started? Who were these Bangladesh people? Were they not 200 years ago Hindus? What is not because of the ill-treatment and harassment by the Calcutta *babus* that they embraced Islam? Do you want the Scheduled Castes in India to follow the same thing? Beware! I am giving you a warning. During the last 25 years, you had spent crores and crores on others. Did you not spend crores of money on Bangladesh? I want more money to be given to more Bangladesh, because they were originally my cousins.

But don't try to deceive the country by bringing in a legislation like this.

Mr. Deputy-Speaker : What shall we do with the Bill now?

B.S. Murthy : You have asked me that. I will also give a reply.

If the government wants to pass it because it has brought in, I shall give my vote. But my heart will not be there; the heart of the millions of people will not be there. Because nothing adequate has been done. You come out and say that untouchability is on the decline and, therefore, not six months, you make it one month, and not Rs. 500, you make it Rs. 50. Any person who violates the law can give Rs. 50 every time.

I am anxious to say that the question will not be ended with this legislation. The question is much more serious, much more difficult. I appeal to the Prime Minister to bring to bear her dynamism in solving this problem. She has solved many problems. She is going to solve many other problems. But of all these problems of the removal of untouchability lock, stock and barrel, is the one which will benefit India for ever and ever.

I am sorry I did not want to say anything against the Maharaja of Kalahandi. With these words, I commend this legislation to be accepted by the House. I would also request the Minister in-charge to bring forward another legislation which will be more beneficial to the sufferers, to the victims of religious oppression.

B.V. Naik (Kanara) : Mr. Deputy-Speaker, Sir, I welcome the Bill without any reservations unlike my esteemed previous speaker. But in the process, I would like to find out and take a sort of balance-sheet about what has been done regarding the existing provisions in the Removal of Untouchability Act.

There is a previous provision, trying to remove untouchability from access to shops, public restaurants, etc. I think, that has been a part success and a part failure. Coming to the use of utensils, it is a total failure. Then, about occupation, trade or business, legally, it may not come into question but still it is a failure. The use or access to rivers, streams, wells, tanks, water taps, etc.— it is a major failure. As regards the enjoyment of benefit under the charitable trusts. I have no information as to how far it has been successful. Coming to the use or access to public conveyance, I would not say it is a failure. The public conveyance is always permitted. Then about the use of dharamshalas, of course, the dharamshalas, in these days, are principally occupied by the under-privileged sections of society. Then I come to the question of access to religious premises. I myself feel that we are not trying to bring in anything in this section of our society which is God-fearing, by giving it such a high sort of pedestal, by making an access to the temples, as though it is the biggest thing in life. I do not think going to a temple or a church or a mosque is a very important thing at all. I think the less we have of this godlines or religious superstition, particularly among the weaker sections of the society and the underprivileged, the better for this section of society, if we want to improve them.

Then I come to the hierarchical nature of the Hindu society, even though it may hurt the sentiments of some of the people in the Hindu society.The first jolt that was given to the hierarchical system of Hindu society, or the negative system of society, was really given by the assault of Islam and the Mohammedans about a thousand years ago. After the recovery, because of the protected existence under the British, the Hindu system never had a challenge to its life.

Unless we want to see that this system, this hierarchical system, this exploited system is going to be given another rude jolt we will have to take adequate steps. I hope it will not be a jolt by communism or a jolt by Mao. In spite of the effort of Mahatma Gandhi, we have not been able to do anything substantial about the removal of untouchability or the ill-treatment of Harijans. So, unless you want Mao's thoughts to come, you should better take adequate steps to see that the existing system is removed lock, stock and barrel, root and branch.

An Hon. Member : How is Mao relevant here?

B.V. Naik : Mao will come if we do not take care of the society ourselves. At least, his thoughts will come. But there is time for us to change before that.

In regard to this emancipation, instead of letting these people to enter into conventional temples, I would urge upon the Minister of Education....

Mr. Deputy-Speaker : Say something about the Bill.

B.V. Naik : I will do that at the very fag end.

Mr. Deputy-Speaker : There is not much time.

B.V. Naik : We have a Harijan culture. We have a sort of super-imposed culture. In my constituency there is the cock fight and fowl sacrifice. In the course of years we have not found it possible to give stimulation to this sort of culture which is there. If we are in a position to make these people worship their own type of god, I think we will be able to make them understand.

I am not speaking in the DMK terms, but in regard to the emancipated Harijans I would like to put in a word of caution. The emancipation of our downtrodden or weaker section of society invariably leads to the limitation of those sections which does not really liberate them. In the circumstances, if we have to make a frontal attack on the Harijan problem, or for that sake take the entire two-thirds or half of the population, social emancipation will have to be there.

Mr. Deputy-Speaker : I always thought of you as one of these new intellectually gifted Members of Parliament. Why not give some examples of relevance also?

B.V. Naik : I was coming to that. Social emancipation depends on economic emancipation. As far as the details of this Bill are concerned, they are perfectly all right.

Mr. Deputy-Speaker : So, you support the Bill.

B.V. Naik : Economic emancipation will mean for the next five to ten years actual reduction, if not *status quo*, in regard to the real income of the organised section of society. I would, therefore, suggest that we have to do a certain amount of basic thinking in regard to the welfare of the weaker sections of our society, call them by any other name, and that will mean something deeper much more radical than what has been given in this Bill, which I welcome for the time being.

Mr. Deputy-Speaker : We started this debate at 12.28 and four hours have been allotted. So, we should conclude by 4.28 p.m. and take up the discussion on the drought situation in West Bengal at 4.30 p.m. How much time would the Hon. Minister take?

Prof. S. Nurul Hasan : About twenty minutes.

Mr. Deputy-Speaker : So, I will call him at 4 o'clock. I have got with me some names from the Congress Party. I think I will be able to accommodate all of them if they try to be brief.

R.D. Bhandare (Bombay Central) : I rise to support this measure on a single ground. I draw your attention and the attention of the House including my Hon. friend, Shri B.S. Murthy, to Explanation II. It says:

"A person shall be deemed to incite or encourage another person to practise 'untouchability' if he justifies, whether on historical, philosophical or religious grounds, the practice by such other person of 'untoucha-bility'."

The measure which has been incorporated in Explanation II is a welcome measure. But I don't know to what extent in India, either the Police or the Magistracy or the Judges would interpret the meaning of this Explanation II.

B.S. Murthy : And the past experience.

R.D. Bhandare : Experience—we have gone through these processes. I need not repeat our experience.

I am, therefore, drawing the attention to the speech made by my great friend and my admirer, Shri Vajpayee....

Mr. Deputy-Speaker : He is admiring you.

R.D. Bhandare : Even if he does not, at least as a social hypocrisy I must say that he admires me as I do. He says, unwittingly perhaps, that the *Chaturvarna* had no origin either in the Shastras or in the Vedas. Forgetting that he is a Brahmin, as he is, there is *Purusha Sukta* in the Vedas which is the origin of *Chaturvarna* followed by *Panchavarna*. Now, if the word is uttered and justified on the ground whether of historical, philosophical or religious grounds then it is made an offence under this piece of legislation. I do not know what the meaning will be, what the connotation will be, what the interpretation will be, of this explanation.

Atal Behari Vajpayee : To justify untouchability on any historical ground—that is made an offence, but history cannot be made an offence.

R.D. Bhandare : I hope you are not a lawyer....

Atal Behari Vajpayee : I have studied law.

R.V. Bade (Khargone) : It is not in *Purushasuktha*, it is in *Manusmruthi* only.

Mr. Deputy-Speaker : Let us leave it to the courts of law for interpretation.

R.D. Bhandare : I wonder when my learned friends show their ignorance.

R.V. Bade : It is not in *Purushasukta; panchama varna* is not there.

R.D. Bhandare : I need not go to the extent of saying more. You are a great *pandit*, but ignorant of these simple matters.

Atal Behari Vajpayee : I am not a great *pandit*.

R.D. Bhandare : That much I know.

Therefore, Sir, reading of the explanation raises a number of questions. A number of questions arise in my mind.

Mr. Deputy-Speaker : In support or in opposition?

R.D. Bhandare : As I told you, this is a new innovation; I welcome it. I welcome it because this is a new innovation for the first time to be found in a piece of legislation.

My children are taking their education in the schools. I

happened to read their books. The books to be taught to them say, Dr. Ambedkar is a Chamar. They never mention that he was the Constitution-maker. Now, writing of these things does what? Does it encourage or discourage?

Prof. Madhu Dandavate (Rajapur) : Burn the books.

R.D. Bhandare : Professor Dandavate, it is not a new thing that you are suggesting: we have been saying so for ages together.

Prof. Madhu Dandavate : I also suggest, burn the scriptures which stand for inequality.

R.D. Bhandare : I hope that courts of law, the political parties, the leaders, etc. will try to understand the meaning and the significance to carry on propaganda, to prepare for change of mind of the Indian people, so that they may change their attitude. I hope on the basis of this Explanation. Two, we shall recast our educational system so that the educational system will be the instrument of reconstruction of the Indian society. I hope this aspect of social changes will be emphasised duly and made a part and parcel of the programme of every party and every public man. We have to see whether power is shared by the classes for whose benefit this explanation is there. I do not know what interpretation will be given to this explanation.....

Mr. Deputy-Speaker : Let them interpret it. We are not here to interpret it.

R.D. Bhandare : We are making a legislation, and I am quite aware of the consequences of the legislation. If an occasion arises to put an interpretation on the pieces of the legislation....

Mr. Deputy-Speaker : Let the occasion arise.

R.D. Bhandare : When I am a legislator, why should I allow that occasion to arise? At the time of the legislation, I must foresee the danger which is lurking...

Mr. Deputy-Speaker : If he were opposing the Bill, I would have understood it. But when he is supporting it, why should he go into all those things?

R.D. Bhandare : I wonder, when we are trying to understand the clause, the meaning and the connotation and when doubts are raised and questions and problems are raised, you interpret that either I must oppose the Bill *in toto* or I must accept it as it is and sit quite. We have to benefit from the experience cited by a number of friends.

We suffer in experience and we become wiser by experience, and we never take any word at its own face value because we know that hypocrisy of the best form has been used in the choice of words for ages together in this country. Therefore, the question of interpretation arises. But, as I said, Shri Atal Behari Vajpayee will certainly carry on the propaganda in view of what I have said and instruct his own people to try to give the correct interpretation...

Mr. Deputy-Speaker : There are other Members also to speak. Now, the Hon. Member should conclude.

R.D. Bhandare : What is your suggestion, Sir?

Mr. Deputy-Speaker : I think he has supported the Bill with eyes and mind open. Let the Hon. Member now conclude.

R.D. Bhandare : I doubt whether a proper interpretation....

Atal Behari Vajpayee : What about the Hon. Member's own party?

R.D. Bhandare : I have joined the Congress Party and I shall try to emphasis and try to persuade...

Mr. Deputy-Speaker : I would request the Hon. Member that if he wants to enlighten Shri Atal Behari Vajpayee, he can do so outside. He can fix up some time and give him proper tuition.

R.D. Bhandare : I can quite understand if you say that my time is up.

Mr. Deputy-Speaker : Yes.

R.D. Bhandare : You should have said that first.

Mr. Deputy-Speaker : I have rung the bell so many times.

R.D. Bhandare : No, you have always been telling me....

Mr. Deputy-Speaker : I have been ringing the bell so many times.

R.D. Bhandare : I beg your pardon, if I appear to be rude to you.You have always been telling me to instruct these people, and therefore, I wanted to give the interpretation. You should have told me earlier if my time was up.

Mr. Deputy-Speaker : His time is up. Now, let the Hon. Member sit down. Shri M. Ram Gopal Reddy.

Mr. Deputy-Speaker : Shri C.M. Stephen.

C.M. Stephen (Muvattupuzha) : Mr. Deputy-Speaker, Sir, I rise to support this Bill. But even while supporting that, there are certain questions occurring to my mind which I would like to spell out for the consideration of the House and of the Hon. Minister who is piloting this Bill. This amending Bill has got two novel features; one is that the imprisonment is made compulsory and the other is, Explanation 2 to sub-section (2) of Section 7. This Explanation 2, I am afraid, may not cover the field which, probably, my friend Mr. Bhandare was having in view. Explanation 2 can apply only to a case in which a particular person is hauled up for an offence and it is shown that with respect to that particular person an abetment is proved, in the sense that he has justified the offence on historical or religious or whatever grounds. But there is an other clause which the Hon. Minister should have thought about bringing within the ambit of this legislation. That is what my friend from the DMK benches mentioned during his speech. Propaganda is going on unrelated to any particular offence from high places justifying untouchability on the grounds mentioned out in Explanation 2. No particular offence is committed, but campaign is going on, that untouchability is good for historical reasons, religious reasons and so many other reasons, whether that is not an offence and whether that could not be counted as an abetment deserves to be considered. Explanation 2 as framed, would not cover that case and I feel, Sir, in view of certain campaigns taking place in the name of Shankaracharya or some other high dignitaries, these amendments should have provided for bringing that too under punitive coverage. This is a lacuna which should have been filled up and unless that is filled up, Sir, in fighting a social malady like this, we will not be making any headway. Ban that campaign to create an impression that the nation treats untouchability as a great crime. Even as a treasonable speech is treated as something condemnable, so also the campaign in this direction should be treated as heinous and penal. That is the point I wanted to make.

With regard to enhancement of punishment, there are two-three questions arising.

The first question is, why has this enhancement become necessary? After all, the statistics spelt out by the report of the Commission show that in 1968, the total cases challenged was 203, convicted 35, acquitted 39 and compromised 52. If in a large country like India the aberrations amount to only 203 cases, is there a case for enhancement of punishment and bring in special legislation or is it that the cases have not been adequately dealt with? Certainly the latter, i.e. the reason. All cases have not been picked up and prosecutions have not been launched. Severe punishment has not been given. Therefore, society or administrative machinery has not been geared up to face the challenge with regard to this social malady. As an Indian, I feel like bowing my head in shame that in the 25th year of our independence, this Parliament has got to consider a legislation suggesting enhancement of punishment for untouchability, i.e. for treating a human being as untouchable.

When the Constitution was passed, it was contemplated that

reservation will be necessary only for ten years. But it was further extended. Now we say enhancement of punishment is necessary. That is to say, in this vital respect, we have not made any advance at all. The Schedule to the Parent Act contains a number of Acts which have been repealed under the repealing provision of that Act. This covers a long period, from 1946. Nevertheless, this malady remains. Are you going to fight it by enhancing punishment? I am all out to support enhancement of punishment, but what made this legislation necessary? Have you got statistics to show that although the cases were proved, the judiciary has not been awarding the punishment? That is the case here.

That is the case with respect to labour legislation or any legislation seeking to protect the weak and unprotected. The judiciary gives a punishment which is only formal, although the law says imprisonment or fine or both. Whereas with respect to Section 323 of the IPC although law says this or that and yet the magistracy does impose a punishment of imprisonment, when it comes to untouchability, the most heinous thing you can have which has been specifically spelt out as such by incorporation in the Constitution, the judiciary refuses to give the punishment of imprisonment. Is that not the statistics? If that is so, what is to be our concept about our judiciary? Are they keeping pace with the revolution we want to accomplish? I am pinpointing the source. The internal infrastructure of society has not been recast in such a manner as to face this malady. For that, a real change in the infrastructure is necessary.

During the period of Mahatma Gandhi, much more, work was done in terms of Harijan welfare than in all these 25 years after independence. He did not have any law or government to support him. He had the entire religion against him. But nevertheless, by a process of social revolution which he carried out like a hurricane from one end of the country to the other, this problems was tackled and the Harijan felt more secure during Mahatma Gandhi's time under his benign protection than now. But with this legislation, that revolutionary urge has gone. No political party is taking it up in that spirit. Nobody is approaching the problem in the spirit of explanation of the sins our forefathers committed against these masses of people. Unless that spirit comes in, this problem cannot be solved. Certainly, so far as this legislation is concerned; its value is that of a symbolic declaration that the whole country is behind anybody who attempts to carry it out.

This can be done, as has been suggested by the Commission, only by self-assertion and self-realisation on the part of the people of the Scheduled Castes themselves. I am saying this from my experience. Wherever the agricultural labourers; mostly of the Scheduled Castes, are organized and are coming forward to fight for their rights, nobody dreams of untouchability so far as they are concerned because they have got the strength and they go ahead. I say this from my experience in my State. Wherever agricultural labour is organized, it is not under any complex and nobody else is under any complex because he is aware of his rights. If these persons are to be rehabilitated, let there be enhancement of the punishment. I am not questioning that but unless you give him the place of power in the governmental machinery, in your secretariat, in your judiciary, in your first class cadre, unless you give him the place of power, he will not come to his own.. Where you attempt to give him the place of power, so many obstacles are coming: Chapter 10 of the Commission's report is revealing enough about the gulf between your promises and what they are getting. Not that the Scheduled Castes people are not qualified to get, but so many things are coming up to keep them away. Scheduled Castes graduates float about without employment.

But it is said that qualified persons are not available. Let them organize themselves, and that will be the solution.

I view this legislation as a welcome measure only in one respect, that this is a re-avowal, re-pledging of the Indian nation on the 25th Anniversary of Indian Freedom, declaring to the whole world that we are pledge to the end that we are to achieve, nothing more than that. And it will have a salutary effect if the Scheduled Castes people themselves and the political parties who are behind them take up the challenge and go ahead in a revolutionary spirit in which Mahatma Gandhi addressed him to the task. Otherwise, socialism will be a far cry; and we will be deluding ourselves and deluding the people.

With these words, I support this legislation.

T. Lakshmikanthamma (Khammam) : In this country from time immemorial, Harijans and women have been the worst sufferers at the hands of the society...

Mr. Deputy-Speaker : There is no provision for women in this Bill..

Smt. T. Lakshmikanthamma : We are also untouchables.

Puri Sankaracharya does not allow women to touch his feet.

There was a time when Harijans were not allowed to go with chappals in the streets where Brahmins lived and they were also not allowed to use umbrella. Also the woman, when the husband died, was to have her head shaven, and she was not allowed to eat more than once. Even now, so many things are happening. (*Interruptions*). The same conditions still exist. I am bringing this to the notice of the House because the House should be aware of the social conditions of Harijans, and along with Harijans also of women...

Vasant Sathe (Akola) : You want them also to be added in the Bill.

Smt. T. Lakshmikanthamma : I am saying this, so that at a later date another Bill like this for women may also be brought forward.

S.M. Banerjee : The country is headed by a woman.

Smt. T. Lakshmikanthamma : Once she heads the country, she is not a woman, she is a man. In fact, she is the only man.

That is what has been said. It has been said that in this country there has been only one man.

S.M. Banerjee : If she calls herself a man, who is woman? (*Interruptions*)

Smt. T. Lakshmikanthamma : All of us are women.

Some Hon. Members were reminding the House about what had happened in Kacherla and other places. At Kanchi Kacherla, a Harijan boy was burnt, and the then Minister went to the length of supporting the incident.

I am glad to inform the House that the Minister is no more a Minister and he is no more in our party. I think such a person who has such views, does not deserve to be in our party. I am glad he is outside our party.

There was also an instance, which I know, where a Harijan boy went to a hotel because he was feeling hungry. It is not something which we see in some cinemas or read in some stories. But these things do happen in our society. The boy went to the hotel and ate something and since he was not able to pay the money, he was tied and his hands were burnt. There was also another instance where a child, just because she sat on a mat, in U.P., that child was taken and thrown into a well. These are not old stories, these are recent things, that had happened. I am glad that our government intend taking some stringent measures through this Bill.

So many people mentioned about socialism and more socialism. I am one with Mr. Shashi Bhushan and other Members that mere removal of economic disparities will not solve the problem. Socialism and more socialism is the only panacea for these economic ills. Yes, we got and touch the feet of Babu Jagjivan Ram. On the other day when Mr. Sanjivayya died....

Mr. Deputy-Speaker : Is touching the feet socialism?

Smt. T. Lakshmikanthamma : It depends on the status

you give to a woman or a Harijan or to the backward classes, whoever it is.

I am glad at least in our Andhra Cabinet, there are four Harijans in the Ministry and a number of backward class people also. There was a time when giving a Ministership to a Harijan was considered as though it was a favour being done to the community. But now, the country has started moving in a different direction. Now, we want to give them importance so that they will take their place in their own right.

They are a force now. There is a story that the great Hanuman did not know his strength unless somebody reminded him that he was so powerful. So also, these sections. We know what a great force women are because of the equal vote they have along with men and they could now shape the destinies of a country. So also the Harijans and to her poorer sections. When we talk of backward classes, it is not that all are backward. There may be a few—one or two rich people among the backward classes. But, there are only two classes now, the rich and the poor.

There was a discussion about Vedas and Upanishads. According to the Shastras, a Brahmin is one who has the knowledge of Brahman. Brahman is the supreme origin. According to me, Avadutram who is a Harijan is Brahmin and Puri Sankaracharya is an Achut. A person is a Brahmin by attainment and not by birth. The great Viswamitra had to struggle to attain that Brahminhood.

I will give one more suggestion and I will conclude my speech. This is about the inter-caste marriages. There should be a provision wherein you give priority or preference to a person who marries a Harijan girl or Harijan boy.

K.S. Chavda : In government jobs?

Smt. T. Lakshmikanthamma : Government can do this much. (*Interruptions*) There are only a few classes of people who believe in this. The general upsurge among the masses is against all these social evils.

I will now give an example and I will conclude. In Tirupati, as an experiment, we gave a seat to a Harijan, who was a Christian student leader. All orthodox people came and said 'How did you give a seat?' Big people came and complained to the Prime Minister. But ultimately, that boy won by a 15,000 majority. That means the country is not thinking on these lines. The people also are not thinking on these lines. It is only a few classes, and among those few classes, only a few individuals who are thinking like this. They are getting extinct, I am sure. There is a peaceful revolution coming up and these forces that are coming in the way, will be wiped out. [Shri K.N. Tiwari: *In the Chair*].

Prof. S. Nurul Hassan : I am extremely grateful to the Hon. Members for having given their whole-hearted support to this Bill.

S.M. Banerjee (Kanpur) : The Speaker said that he is going to call the Minister at 4 p.m. I am not seeking to speak. I have only a suggestion. Because the second reading of the Bill may come up tomorrow at 4.30 we have another discussion, what I am suggesting is that many good amendments were suggested by Hon. Members but they could not send them because abruptly this Bill came. So....

Mr. Chairman : No please.

S.M. Banerjee : Are you going to pass this Bill today?

Mr. Chairman : Yes, Sir.

S.M. Banerjee : After all, there are so many Members who have spoken...

Dr. Kalias (Bombay South) : It would be better if it is sent to the Select Committee.

S.M. Banerjee : We may have the second reading of the Bill tomorrow.

K.S. Chavda : The Deputy-Speaker said that the Minister will reply at 4 p.m.

K.S. Chavda : The time was fixed by the Deputy Speaker for his reply.

Mr. Chairman : I know what the Deputy-Speaker said and what he has told me and how I should conduct the House. Now, please take your seat.

The Minister of Education, Social Welfare and Culture (Prof. S. Nurul Hasan) : So far as this particular measure is concerned, it is limited in character. It is not a measure which would by itself lead to eradication of untouchability. Hon. Members from all sections of the House have rightly pointed out that to eradicate the real malady something else is needed. We need a social revolution. We need a basic change in our outlook. It is necessary that social and political workers should mobilise the masses of our people to arouse their conscience against this canker of untouchability. I think there cannot be any difference of opinion on this. The way all sections of the House have expressed themselves on this issue of untouchability is a proof (if any proof is needed at this stage) that the people of India will not tolerate untouchability. Even though it may be practised to our utter shame and disgust, the people of the nation as a whole will not tolerate and if the people as a whole will not tolerate it, then, it becomes the duty of all of us, particularly of the government to take all such measures which are necessary for the eradication of untouchability.

Sir, various measures have been proposed; many measures have already been undertaken; many more are likely to be undertaken in the future the net effect of all of which would be to undermine the whole ideological, social and economic basis of the society which tolerates and engenders untouchability. I will not go into the details of all those measures.

I would only make one very brief reference to education. I am deeply conscious of my responsibility in the sphere of education, to ensure that the education system does not contribute in any way to the concept of untouchability, but on the other hand, to see that effective measures are taken to see that those who have had the benefit of education reject outright the concept of untouchability and the social and ideological basis of this particular attitude.

Smt. Sahodra Bai Rai then left the House

Prof. S. Nurul Hasan : I am only too painfully conscious also of the various incidents that have taken place against the Harijans. I am also conscious of the fact that as land legislation is going to be enacted in various States and changes of land relationships are in the offing, social tensions have increased and as a result of these social tensions attempts have been made to use violence against the Harijans. It is the duty of all political parties and all social organisations to ensure that Harijans are protected but the duty of the government is even more than that of the social workers and of the political leaders. It is with this aim in view that the government considered it necessary to bring forward this long-delayed measure before the House, a measure, which as I said before, is based on the well-considered recommendations of the very high-powered committee, namely, the Elayaperumal Committee. It would have been easy for me to say that let us refer it to yet another committee. Then, the Fifth Lok Sabha's term would be over and again a measure would come, and again the society would undergo a change, and again there would be a Bill and again there would be a demand and yet another Select Committee. I feel that even if we find that there are certain gaps or certain loopholes, we should point out those things; I heard with rapt attention all the arguments that were advanced in the House, and on the basis of the arguments, I am seeking your indulgence to move some amendments myself. But I would beg of Hon. Members not to postpone this further, because a postponement at this stage when these tensions are increasing is likely to create more complications than it would solve.

A reference was made quite rightly by almost all Hon. Members to the machinery for implementation. I am conscious again of the fact that our machinery is not what all of us would like it to be. But governments have been conscious—I am referring to the State Governments—of the need to enforce properly and adequately this Act. I myself addressed a letter in February to all the State Governments in which I made a special plea that the Collectors and District Superintendents of Police be held personally responsible to ensure adequate protection to Harijans against any kind of discrimination arising out of untouchability and that they should take prompt action *suo moto* in all instances where the practice of untouchability comes to their notice.

The State Governments should take a note of the work done by the Collectors and the District Superintendents of Police in connection with the protection and welfare of Harijans, Adivasis and other backward classes and that special notice should be taken in connection with their annual confidential reports. A further request was made that the presidents of district panchayats be asked to take prompt action against taluk and village panchayats which were found to be discriminating against the Harijans in their jurisdiction.

K.S. Chavda : What is the response from the State Governments?

Prof. S. Nurul Hasan : Some State Governments have started taking energetic action. The Government of the State from which the Hon. Members comes, has taken very important decisions in this respect, and I am happy to state that.

I would like to draw the attention of the House to another measure which the Government of India have taken. We have requested the Chief Secretaries to the State Governments and drawn their attention to this particular Bill and we have also said that the State Governments may consider the need to make provisions similar to the provisions that is sought to be made here in the Representation of the People Act, that is to say, debarring anyone from seeking election to zila parishad or village panchayat, who has been convicted of the offence of untouchability.

I am also extremely gratified that Hon. Members have made a special reference to this very significant Explanation No. 2 which has been inserted here, that is to say, any person who justifies whether or historical, philosophical or religious grounds the practice of untouchability will be deemed to have incited or encouraged another person to practise untouchability. This is a very important point added. After this, I would only submit that we should not go in for banning of books. As a teacher, I am a little worried when books are sought to be banned. I want ideology to be met with ideology. Books written in a given set of historical circumstances may have a totality of values which may be valid for the time, but parts of those books may not be valid today. Therefore, if every historical work is to be subjected to censorship by each subsequent generation, perhaps it would not be possible for us even to understand the proper development of society in any given age. Hence by evaluating a historical work, let us see what was the total contribution of that work in a given society at a given moment of time.

B.S. Murthy : Are you prescribing them as textbooks?

Prof. S. Nurul Hasan : At the same time, it will be very difficult for us to ignore the feeling reflected in this House that in the matter of textbooks meant for schools, we have to be very careful about what sense of values we wish to inculcate. That was why I started my very speech by saying that in the educational system we will have to take measures to ensure that the values we inculcate in the new generation are not values which will tolerate this canker of untouchability.

Reference was made to the number of cases registered with the police and actual convictions obtained. I have with me the figures right from the beginning. I am particularly happy at the decline in the number of cases registered with the police. I am told these figures are incomplete, but even so, I think they do reflect a trend that the number of cases registered by the police, even though these are cognisable offences, is not on the increase, even though reports are that these offences are being committed on a fairly wide scale. In 1968, 214 cases were registered; 184 were challaned; 19 were convicted; 28 were acquitted; 53 were compounded, and 84 were pending.

C.M. Stephen : Any information about the nature of convictions?

Prof. S. Nurul Hasan : If you just bear with me for a few seconds, I will be coming to it. In 1969, the cases registered with the police were 251; challaned 207; convicted 28; acquitted 13; compounded 46; pending 120. In 1970, cases registered 203; challaned 168; convincted 15; acquitted 14; compounded 83; pending 56. You will see from the percentage of cases compounded why it has been necessary for us to come forward with this Bill.

Another point which has been raised and quite correctly raised is that what has been the attitude of the presiding magistrates when convictions were done. Sir, the Elayaperumal Committee studied 70 cases, of which 23 ended in conviction; out of these 23 cases, 17 cases resulted in fine only. The amount of fine ranged up to Rs. 25 in 12 cases and between Rs. 25 and Rs. 100 in five cases, and of the two cases which ended in imprisonment, in one case the imprisonment was for only one week and in another case only up to the rising of the court. Therefore, it was necessary for the government to take due note of the very valuable recommendations of the Elayaperumal Committee and to bring forward this particular piece of legislation.

Sir, in my introductory speech, I had made a reference to the fact that the government had deviated in one respect from the recommendations of the Elayaperumal Committee, and that was that we should take the view that if for the first offence the minimum punishment is one month instead of three months, then perhaps there would not be so many acquittals, but as I had thought from the speeches that I heard here, I gathered that Hon. Members would prefer that the minimum punishment which has been prescribed should not be lowered. I am, therefore, going to crave your indulgence that the minimum punishment recommended by the Elayaperumal Committee, of three months plus Rs. 50 as fine should be incorporated in this Bill.

S.M. Banerjee : Are you going to move an amendment?

Prof. S. Nurul Hasan : Yes.

S.M. Banerjee : When are you going to move it? The Bill is going to be passed today. (*Interruptions*) If the government are moving an amendment, who not allow us also to move amendments?

Mr. Chairman : Let the Minister finish his speech.

Prof. S. Nurul Hasan : There have been many other suggestions which I am sure the government will benefit from by accepting them. For example, one suggestion was that the provisions of the Bill should be properly publicised and brought to the notice of the various authorities.

Prof. S. Nurul Hasan : Then the question about free legal aid to the Harijans was raised.

This is a cognizable offence and Harijans do not have to fight the case themselves; it is for the police to take up the case and fight it. My Hon. friend Shri Vajpayee made a specific reference to an incident about separate *surahi* being kept in the Central Secretariat. It is a serious matter and I would beg of him to let me know further details. We must take up this matter seriously and take strong action... (*Interruptions*). My Hon. friend was having some discussion and did not probably hear what I said; otherwise he would not have raised this matter. I have already said that it should be our special responsibility to fight against the concept of untouchability through educational institutions. I commend the Bill to the House.

Mr. Chairman : The question is:

"That the Bill to amend the Untouchability (Offences)

Act, 1955 and further to amend the Representation of the People Act, 1951, be taken into consideration."

Raj Bahadur : I move.

"That the debate on the Bill be adjourned".

Atal Behari Vajpayee : Honourable Chairman, what is the motion? Is the motion to stop the debate? If so, why? Have not all the members participated in this debate? Is the Honourable Minister agreeing to referring this Amendment Bill to a Joint Committee? If yes, then there can be agreement on it. But why is the debate being adjourned at this point of time.

Raj Bahadur : Even for the consideration of the motion to refer the Bill to a Joint Committee, time is needed....(*Interruptions*)

Mr. Chairman : First let me dispose of Mr. Vajpayee's point. According to rule 109 at any stage of a Bill under discussion in the House, a motion that the debate on the Bill be adjourned may be moved with the consent of the Speaker.

I am giving my consent.

Raj Bahadur : I mentioned rule 109 myself and I have formally moved.

Raj Bahadur : It is a matter which deeply affects the psychological satisfaction and actual satisfaction of our friends belonging to the Scheduled Castes and Scheduled Tribes. We must not do anything in a hurry which leaves a feeling in their mind that we are rushing with the Bill. I am not really happy with the adjournment, but I would rather like to take an uncomfortable step for us but I would not like that they should go with the impression that we are rushing with it without giving them the fullest opportunity to discuss it. You are quite right in saying that it was circulated on 13.4.72.

Mr. Chairman : As Mr. Vajpayee pertinently asked, what is the purpose for which the adjournment is being sought?

Raj Bahadur : The purpose is to consider whether this Bill could not be referred to a Joint Select Committee.

Mr. Chairman : I think this is the opinion of the House also. The question is:

"That the debate on the Bill be adjourned".

The motion was adopted.

S.M. Banerjee : I am extremely happy that it has been adjourned. I have given a motion which I sent to you saying that it should be referred to a Select Committee, the names of which are to be announced by the Minister of Parliamentary Affairs. It is already with you. As you know, Sir, amendments are moved upto 3 p.m. Now it is 4.20. I would request you to allow us a special case to move amendments upto 5.30 or 6 p.m.

Mr. Chairman : You can give amendments till 5 p.m.

Jyotirmoy Bosu (Diamond Harbour) : On a point of order, Sir, You have not only been misled the Table but you have been equally misled by the Minister of Parliamentary Affairs. His actions are unparliamentary. The rules are very clear on the subject. Rule 74 clearly says that when a Bill is introduced, the motion can be moved that it be referred to a Joint Committee. Now, has anybody under Rule 74 formally moved a motion with the intention of sending the Bill to a Joint Committee?

S.M. Banerjee : I have moved it.

Mr. Chairman : Before my friend Mr. Banerjee, my friend from this side, Shri Shambunath, also made that request.

S.M. Banerjee : He mentioned it, but I moved.

Mr. Chairman : Your motion is not in order.

Raj Bahadur : When a Bill is introduced, at any subsequent occasion the member in charge may make one of the following motions in regard to the Bill, and one of them is reference to the Select Committee of the House. I can move it even now.

Atal Behari Vajpayee : But he is not in charge of the Bill.

Raj Bahadur : I do not know whether Shri Jyotirmoy Bosu is more parliamentary or the chair is more parliamentary.

Jyotirmoy Bosu : As far as the chair is concerned, the powers are quite well-defined. Rule 89 says that the Speaker may, if he thinks fit, postpone the consideration of the clause, not the Bill. As far as Rule 74 is concerned....

Mr. Chairman : Kindly read Rule 109.

Jyotirmoy Bosu : I am referring to the rule relating to reference to Select Committee, and that is Rule 74.

Mr. Chairman : Rule 75 (2) (b) says:

> "If the member in charge moves that the Bill be referred to a Select Committee of the House, or a Joint Committee of the Houses with the concurrence of the Council, any member may move as an amendment that the Bill be referred to a Joint Committee of the Houses with the concurrence of the Council or a Select Committee, as the case may be, or that the Bill be circulated for the purpose of eliciting opinion thereon by a date to be specified in the motion".

The Minister of State in the Ministry of Home Affairs, Department of Personnel and Administrative Reforms and Department of Parliamentary Affairs (Shri Om Mehta). Sir, I beg to move:

"That the Bill to amend the Untouchability (Offences) Act, 1955 and further to amend the Representation of the People Act, 1951, as passed by the Lok Sabha, be taken into consideration."

Sir, the Untouchability (Offences) Act, 1955 was passed in pursuance of Article 17 of the Constitution which has abolished 'untouchability' and has made its practice in any form punishable by law. The Act has been in force more than 20 years. A Committee was appointed under the Chairmanship of Shri Elayaperumal to go into the working of the Act and on the basis of the recommendations of that Committee, a Bill was introduced in the Lok Sabha in April, 1972.

The Bill was referred to a Joint Committee of the two Houses. The Joint Committee went thoroughly into the various aspects and made many far-reaching changes. The Bill as reported by the Joint Committee has been passed by the Lok Sabha with a few amendments.

The name of the principal Act is being changed to 'the Protection of Civil Rights Act'. So, in future, the name of the Act will be the Protection of Civil Rights Act instead of the Untouchability (Offences) Act.

The present amending Bill considerably tightens the provisions relating to the removal of untouchability. Privately owned places of worship along with lands and subsidiary shrines appurtenant to such privately owned places of worship which are allowed by the owner to be used as places of public worship are being brought within the purview of the Act. The direct or indirect preaching of untouchability or its justification on historical, philosophical or religious ground is being made an offence. The compelling of any person to do any scavenging, sweeping, removing of carcasses, flaying of animals or removing the umbilical cord is also being made punishable. The State Governments are being empowered to impose collective fines on the inhabitants of any area who are concerned in or abetting the commission of untouchability offences. All untouchability offences are cognizable. They will now become non-compoundable and in cases where the punishment does not exceed three months, they can be tried summarily. The punishment of untouchability offences is being considerably enhanced and now both fine and imprisonment will be awarded for untouchability offences. For the first offence the minimum punishment will be one months' imprisonment and a fine of Rs. 100 and the maximum six months' imprisonment and a fine of Rs. 500. For the second offence, the minimum punishment is six months' imprisonment and a fine of Rs. 200 and the maximum, one years' imprisonment and Rs. 500 fine. For the third and subsequent offences, the punishment can range from one years' imprisonment with Rs. 500 fine to two years' imprisonment with Rs. 1000 fine.

The significant characteristic of the present Bill is that public servants who wilfully neglect in the investigation of any offence punishable under this Act shall be deemed to have abetted an offence punishable under this Act. Persons convicted of untouchability offences shall be disqualified from contesting elections to Central and State Legislatures. The Proba-tion of Offenders Act will not supply to untouchability offenders unless they are below the age of fourteen years.

Thus the Bill will have a deterrent effect in curbing the commission of untouchability offences. The Bill also contemplates surveys and studies for determining the areas where untouchability is practised, the setting up of Committees for implementing the Act and the grant of adequate facilities to persons subjected to disabilities arising out of untouchability to enable them to avail of their rights.

Government is making every endeavour to uplift the Scheduled Castes and to ensure that the last vestiges of untouchability are completely eradicated from the country within the shortest possible time. Under the 20-point programme of the Prime Minister, various measures are being taken for the economic uplift of these downtrodden sections of the society. Most of them are agricultural labourers and petty artisans and for them, special measures for the grant of house-sites, agricultural lands, loans for settlement in trades, fixation of minimum wages and abolition of bonded labour are being undertaken so that their economic and social conditions improve and they are better able to assert their rights. The massive education programme for the Scheduled Castes both at the school stage as well as at the post-matric stage also helps them in improving their social and educational standards. The great strides achieved in filling posts in the country's public services at various levels have also contributed to raising the status of this community and also to give them adequate strength to assert their rights. All these, together with the legal protection provided under the present Bill, will help in the complete eradication of this evil practice.

With these words, Sir, I commend the Bill for the consideration of the House.

The question was proposed.

The Vice-Chairman (Loknath Misra) : Now, there are 12 speakers in all. Therefore, under compulsion the Chair will have to restrict each speaker to 10 minutes and not a minute beyond ten. So, in all we will take two hours for the speakers and 15 minutes for the reply of the Hon. Minister so that by 5-15 punctually we finish this Bill and take up the other Bill. We must go according to the schedule. There will not be the slightest departure from the schedule. Mr. Bhola Prasad.

Yogendra Makwana (Gujarat) : Mr. Vice-Chairman, Sir....

The Vice-Chairman (Loknath Misra) : Kindly be brief.

Yogendra Makwana : Sir, I will confine myself only to the Bill, I will not go into all the other details.

Mr. Vice-Chairman, Sir, I rise to support and welcome this Bill introduced by the Home Minister. I congratulate the Home Minister for introducing such a revolutionary Bill. As I described it, it is really a revolutionary Bill in a way, because it has so many provisions which enable an untouchable to get those persons prosecuted who observe untouchability and it also enables him to protect himself against the possibilities arising out of untouchability.

Sir, first of all, I will like to refer to the title of the Bill. The title is changed and instead of "practising of untouchability", the words "preaching and practising of untouchability" have been used. Sir, those words look very simple, but they have a great effect. The word "preaching" is inserted before the word "practising".

The practice of untouchability was an offence in the principal Act. Now, preaching of untouchability also becomes an offence under this Bill. In the previous session and before that also, I have often remarked in this House against the religious heads of this country. Sometimes they make derogatory remarks against the Scheduled Castes. Sometimes they have preached untouchability. With the insertion of these words, Shankracharya of Puri and Doongri Maharaj or any other religious heads who were preaching untouchability will not be able to do it.

They can be prosecuted under the present law. Sir, in sub-section (1) of section 1, the words "the Untouchability (Offences) Act" have been substituted by the words "the Protection of Civil Rights Act". This is also an important change in the principal Act because the civil rights of the so-called untouchables were not honoured by some of the people of this country. I do not mean all the people of this country. But some people who are orthodox and reactionary have been always attacking the untouchables.

Sir, another salient feature of the Bill is to be found in section 3 (iii) of the Bill. Whereas the minimum punishment was fixed for one month or fine under the principal Act, the word "or" has been substituted by the words "and also" in the new Bill. This is a very significant change because fine has also to be paid over and above the punishment of imprisonment. It will become a sort of deterrent to those who are observing untouchability. As I have said in the beginning, mostly the religious heads are responsible for untouchability. As the change in the title is an important thing, so also Explanation II after Explanation I in section 7 is a very important explanation. It reads like this:

> "***Explanation II :*** For the purposes of clause (c), a person shall be deemed to incite or encourage the practice of "untouchability"—

(i) if he, directly or indirectly, preaches untouchability or its practice in any form; or

(ii) if he justifies, whether on historical, philosophical or religious grounds or on the ground of any tradition of the caste system or on any other ground, the practice of "untouchability" in any form."

Sir, these words are very important because all the religious heads have been describing untouchability as a part of religion as it is given in the religious books and sometimes they give some historical background to it. In the present day and in the present society, that background has been lost. Nowadays, the accepted principle is that every human being is equal. It has become an accepted universal principal. Therefore, such outdated discourses by the religious leaders should be banned.

Sir, there is also a provision under section 7(a) which gives an opportunity for untouchables to perform other occupations. In small villages, even the educated persons were asked to take the night soil on their head and to scavenge the streets, Sir, with this insertion of section 7(a), there is a ban on it. So, it will be a very good provision in the principal Act. Then, Sir, there is an insertion of an explanation at the end of Section 10. This is a most important explanation which is now inserted in the principal Act. It reads out like this: "A public servant who wilfully neglects the investigation of any offence punishable under this Act shall be deemed to have abetted an offence punishable under this Act."

Sir, in most of the cases of atrocities we have seen that the public servants have neglected their duty at the time of investigation. Even the FIRs are changed at many places, and the public servants, specifically the police officers, instead of investigating and prosecuting the offender, help the criminals. And the history shows that even one person was not punished during these 25 years. Now, Sir, with the addition of this explanation to the principal Act, I hope, there will be a good check on the police officers who will try to play mischief and evade their responsibility. (*Time bell rings*)

I will complete within a few minutes. Sir, Sir, I described this Bill as revolutionary and I must justify why I called it a revolutionary Bill, and I congratulate the Home Minister. He should also recommend to give me some more minutes.

The Vice-Chairman (Shri Loknath Misra) : All of us should be precise and concise also.

Shri Yogendra Makwana : Sir, this Bill is really a very good Bill. Sir, so many provisions are included here and I cannot go into details. As you say, Sir, the time is limited I will throw some light on some of the general aspects of the Bill. There was a very good provision suggested by the Joint Select Committee under Explanation 2, after Section 10, which is now deleted. I do not know why it is deleted.

The Explanation reads like this: "Any appointing authority, in relation to any service or post in connection with the affairs of, (a) the Union or any State Government (b) the corporation or undertaking, owned or controlled by the Central Government or the State Government or by both, (c) any authority or body established by any Central, State or Provincial Act, (d) any local authority, who show any negligence in giving effect to the orders of the appropriate authority relating to the reservation of posts for the employment of the members of the Scheduled Castes shall be deemed to have abetted an offence punishable under this Act." Sir, I would request the Hon. Minister to accept this Explanation even now at this stage. I would like to invite his attention and the attention of the House to the report of the Commissioner for Scheduled Castes and Scheduled Tribes. This is the latest report for the year 1973-74 in which he has mentioned about recruitment to the Central Government services and other services in different States. I will not read the figures because they are very negligible. But I will read the remarks of the Commissioner. He says: 'The figures in this Table reveal that the representation of Scheduled Castes in these services is still far from satisfactory. The position regarding Scheduled Tribes is much worse.' Sir, these are the remarks made by the Commissioner for the Scheduled Castes and Scheduled Tribes. Why are these remarks there? It is only because the bureaucrats, the government officers, who are the recruiting officers who sit in the committees do not like and do not observe the provisions relating to reservations. Recently, Sir, we had an occasion to examine the Delhi authority where some rules are framed. But they have recruited their sons and daughters and their relatives only and the percentage of recruitment of the Scheduled Castes and the Scheduled Tribes is not maintained. It is not only negligible but in some cases it is not at all there. No Scheduled Castes man is taken in the Delhi Administration authority.

Sir, I appreciate this Bill very much because I have also had occasions, as a political leader of my district, to suffer so many attacks by high caste Hindus in the course of elections and at several other times too. In the course of elections the Harijans became the victims particularly because they favour the government or some party, especially the Congress Party which works for the upliftment of the Harijans and downtrodden people. That is why the Harijans who support the Congress Party in the interior parts are attacked. Several times in this House also. Sir, if you remember the Prime Minister herself has given two examples of my own State and of my own district. In the course of the last elections, in a Christian locality in village in Kaira District the houses of workers of the Congress, were put on fire and several families were burnt.

In the case of election of my wife we were attacked at so many places and we were not allowed to enter five villages and we lost the election only because of these things. Therefore, I say that this Bill is a revolutionary Bill and heartily congratulate the Home Minister and the Prime Minister for introducing this Bill. It will be a red letter day in the History of India when it becomes an Act. With these words, I end my speech.

Shri S.K. Vaishampayen (Maharashtra) : Mr. Vice-Chairman, Sir, I wish to extend my wholehearted support to this Bill. The Bill has been brought forward after a very careful consideration by the Joint Committee of the two Houses. At the same time, I consider that this Bill is a little belated. But it is a step in the right direction to end the scourge of untouchability. The Bill removes all the vagueness that was there in the earlier Act. The clauses have been so framed that there is some definiteness in regard to the action to be taken.

It also lays a firm hand on those who would act against the spirit of the Constitution. I support the provision made in this Bill particularly for imposing collective fines. As I see it, untouchability has assumed a very acute from during the last three to four years. There are social boycotts, burning of huts of Harijans and even murders. So, this provision of collective fines is really a provision which will to a long way to see that this certainly very stringent but there should also be other measures which must be taken by the government as such. I should say that the Hon. Home Minister should issue directives to all the State Governments to have a special cell in their respective Home Departments.

Secondly, there should be vigilance committees at district level and they should have Member of Parliament as Chairman and the Collector as the Secretary of that committee. It is because I have the experience of such a vigilance committee. We have tried to see that offences of this nature which come under untouchability have become less.

Thirdly, I would like to say that this social evil is still much deep-rooted. According to whatever information I have, I would like to point out that the extent of atrocities committed during these years has increased. I would like to give figures of atrocities committed during the years 1972, 1973 and 1974 and this information has been given by the Home Ministry in a reply given in the Rajya Sabha on 27th February, 1975. I will only quote a few figures from two or three States. I will take my State first. In Maharashtra during 1972, 124 atrocities have been committed. In 1973 the number was 223 and in 1974 it was 277. This shows that the number has gone up year by year. Similarly, in Gujarat the number in 1972 was 246, in 1973 it was 248 and in 1974 it was 352. In Uttar Pradesh the figure is still rising high. The number in 1972 was 567, in 1973 it was 1179 and in 1974 it was 1178. So, this is still a deep-rooted malady and we will have to take other measures along with these stringent provisions to combat the menace. We shall have to undertake intensive promotional activity also. I will suggest that incentives must be given to those villages who have freed themselves of this particular malady of untouchability.

There are a number of villages who have declared that there is no untouchability in their villages. All the communities have come together in gram sabhas and declared so. We should give some incentives to such workers, not of the Scheduled Castes and Scheduled Tribes, who are working in the field for the welfare of Harijans, for ending untouchability. They must also be given some special awards by the State Governments. Then, there are provisions made in our State. We have Zila Parishads. There are provisions for the welfare of the Scheduled Castes and Scheduled Tribes. But our experience is that these provisions are not spent. Not only they are not spent but the provisions are transferred to some other measures which do not help the Scheduled Castes and Scheduled Tribes.

I have figures from Maharashtra which go to show that 10 Zila Parishads, despite the provision being there for the welfare of the Scheduled Castes and Scheduled Tribes, have spent zero per cent. Seven Zila Parishads have spent one per cent, four have spent one to five per cent and three have spent five to ten per cent of the provisions that were made in the Zila Parishad budgets. So, this aspect also should be gone into in each State and a directive should be issued by the Home Ministry that whatever provisions are made for the welfare of the Scheduled Castes and Scheduled Tribes should be spent on their welfare. Rather I would suggest, Sir, that these provisions should be earmarked and the allocations should not be transferred to any other department as such.

Then the question of untouchability has taken a new dimension and that dimension has an economic aspect also. Under the 20-point economic programme we are now helping the economically weaker sections, and amongst the economically weaker sections the percentage of the Scheduled Castes and Scheduled Tribes is as high as 50 per cent at some places and even 70 per cent at some other places because they are all landless labourers. Naturally because of the measures which are there under the 20-point economic programme, those who are going to benefit under them are coming into clash with the landed, vested interests in the rural areas.

The question of untouchability has taken a new dimension and, therefore, it is necessary that the Scheduled Castes and Scheduled Tribes be organized into a movement by forming a united front with the other economically weaker sections so that all the economic injustices that are being done to these poorer sections in the rural areas ended.

And if all these measures succeed—the measures under this Bill, other promotional measures and also a movement by the Scheduled Castes and Scheduled Tribes and their leaders with a common united front with the other economically weaker sections in the rural areas—the day of deliverance is not far off. Thank you, Sir.

K.K. Madhavan (Kerala) : Sir, it was long ago that the Constitution of India abolished untouchability. But even before that, there was a movement for the annihilation of untouchability, right from the days, when Dr. Ambedkar had to fight the social evil through his book, which was originally meant for a presidential speech at a meeting which did not take place. Later on it was published as a book. The meeting did not take place and he said many things in that which were very unpalatable to the would be audience. This book is well known under the title *Annihilation of Caste*. I for one say that abolition of untouchability alone cannot deliver the goods. We have to abolish the caste system also. Untouchability is a consequence of the caste system, and the caste system, in its turn, is a consequence of the "Chathur Varnjya" system. I do not want to deal with the theoretical aspect of this question.

Whatever we have gained in India against untouchability is because of three factors: (i) by the resistance of the weaker sections of the society, the so-called untouchables; (ii) by governmental help; and (iii) the most important of all, by the efforts of an enlightened section of the society in India. Of the three factors, the third factors for which Mahatma Gandhi is largely responsible, is gradually going down, now I do not know what the reason is. I have my own explanation. In the present context, in free India, the erstwhile untouchables have a sense of right, an awareness of their rights, and they have begun to assert. It is only natural that when the weaker sections of the people become aware of their rights and they begin to strike back or when they begin to assert themselves, certainly, the exploiters will have with redoubled vigour, a new programme for suppressing the underdog. That is exactly what happens. In many States, the cases of atrocities on the Scheduled Castes and Scheduled Tribes are on the increase. It is admitted even by the official quarters. Why does this happen? This happens simply because the casteist monopolists who look down upon these weaker sections of people as their slaves, cannot to erate the later coming up. This is not untouchability, Sir. This is something worse than untouchability. This is an inhuman attitude which cannot be tolerated in any civilised society. This unsocial attitude is known under the nomenclature 'casteism'. Why does this casteism occur? This casteism occurs, I would say, because of untouchability, which has been declared, treated and punished as a crime. The basic law now being against it, it has now gone underground. It has gone underground into the minds of men and there it reigns raising its ugly head in the form of a war of nerves the Scheduled Castes and the Scheduled Tribes. I say, it is a perpetual war of nerves. This war of nerves cannot be defeated very easily. A war can be won only by a stronger force. In the case of a war of nerves also it can be won by a superior force combating the evil. That is what is happening in India. Some of our friends in this Hon.

House were saying that certain social service organisations like the Ramakrishna Mission, the Arya Samaj and some other Samajams, that they should take up the work, that the Scheduled Castes leaders should themselves take up the work. We are prepared Sir. We are actually doing that work. No body need advice us on that account. But I would ask, is it enough for Hon. Members to sit in their armchairs and exhort people to do the job for them? I would say, Sir, that it is the duty of these people, the leaders of this country, to take up the cause and fight it to extinction as the Father of Nation has done.

Now, Sir, though I admit that this is a progressive Bill and it provides for so many good things, still I have a feeling that there is a section which ought not to have found a place in this Bill. What is that section?

That is clause 2 of section 17 of the Bill which seeks to amend section 15 of the principal Act. Now, clause (2) of section 17 of the Bill says : "Notwithstanding anything contained in the Code of Criminal Procedure, 1973, when any public servant is alleged to have committed the offence of abetment of an offence punishable under this Act, while acting or purporting to act in the discharge of his official duty, no court shall take cognisance of such offence of abetment except with the previous sanction (a) of the Central Government in the case of a person employed in connection with the affairs of the Union, and (b) of the State Government, in the case of a person employed in connection with the affairs of a State". Sir, why this exemption? Sir, this protection aggravates the caste mentality of the officers. My complaint is : "Why do you provide this section?" I am getting hundreds of complaints against casteism being practised in government offices in the matter of appointments as well as administration at all stages in public sector undertakings are much worse.

N.H. Kumbhare : This amendment is made at the instance of the government. This is a government amendment, otherwise there was no such provision.

K.K. Madhavan : Casteism largely is the cause of our disability whereas untouchability is under control. The disease has assumed the new form of casteism in government offices and in farms and factories. In the farms where the workers refuse to be dictated by others, we find that by the substitution of the new provision in section 15 government servants will be protected and only the government will have the power to sanction prosecution against them. Sir, it is the right of a private citizen to complain if he is discriminated against. Why should the aggrieved Scheduled Castes citizen be denied of that right to take the matter to a court of law. If the wrongdoer is an officer of the Central Government it is only the Central Government which has the powers to take legal proceedings against him. If he happens to be a public servant of a State Government it is only the State Government which is competent to institute proceedings against him. Why should these public servants be given this exemption, this protection?

[The Vice-Chairman (Shri Ranbir Singh) *in the Chair*]

It is unwarranted, Sir, I should say that clause (2) of section 17 of the Bill should be taken away from the Bill for the simple reason that it places the victims of the wrong at a disadvantage when he files a complaint. This clause (2) of section 17 of the Bill is a black spot on this legislation. It is not consistent with the spirit of our democracy; it is not consistent with the spirit of the 20-point programme which has been hailed from all quarters. So, I would suggest that better wisdom should prevail against this clause.

Sir, I was referring to casteism entertained in government offices and at other public places. Such public places are not mentioned in this Bill or in the Principal Act. That is the deficiency. This deficiency has to be made good. How should it be made good? I would suggest that the amplitude of this Act should be made wider so as to include anti-Harijan, anti-tribal, attitude and discriminatory actions of government officers punishable within the Act. Unless that is done, the administration would not improve, would not become free from casteism.

The Vice-Chairman (Shri Ranbir Singh) : Try to wind up now.

K.K. Madhavan : Sir, unless this is done our social system and our democracy will not progress. Thank you, Sir.

Abu Abraham (Nominated) : Mr. Vice-Chairman, Sir, every year, a few times we, in Parliament discuss the subject of untouchability of Harijans and we have done this for many years now. But since independence, it seems that the condition of Harijans has not changed very much. We still read in the newspapers everyday of open discrimination against Harijans, violence against them, their living conditions also remaining the same. We have cases of landlords attacking Harijan villages and the police doing nothing about it.

The Harijans get arrested very often and the landlords get away with it. We have to consider why the situation is like this. Why, after so many years and after trying to do so much, have we made so little progress? I think it is because we have an attitude of doing charity to the Harijans like the salvation army used to do the poor in the old days. And this had got to change. What we have to do is to improve the political and economic power of the Harijans. Unless we do that, it will be very hard for any legislation to improve their condition.

Sir, this Bill is a progressive Bill, a radical Bill and its provisions, I am sure, will give to untouchables the legal right that they deserve and should have. But this is not enough. I think we have to attempt to make radical changes in the social structure, the basic structure of our society. Unless that is done, we cannot expect the conditions of the Harijans to improve very much.

The important point to be considered here is that Harijans

themselves should have the means to defend themselves and to look after their interests. They will have to organise themselves. They will have to educate themselves. They will have to take a greater part in the democratic processes in this country. It is these things that matter and the government should try to help them, enable them to assert themselves and to organise themselves. But so long as the Harijans remain largely illiterate, they will neither be able to defend themselves nor make any economic progresss. I know that the recent measures of land distribution to the landless has helped Harijan communities in many parts of the country but a great deal more needs be done.

There has to be a massive attempt to educate the Harijans, to give them literacy, to give them the basic tools with which they can improve their conditions. Sir, for example, Kerala's work in this matter is worthnoting. A hundred years ago, when Swami Vivekananda visited Kerala, he said that this was the most reactionary State that he had ever been to: In those days, there was not only untouchability, but there was also unapproachability and unseeability. Today, if you go to Kerala, you can see the differences. This is not necessarily because of legislation, not even by propaganda or by charitable acts, but by organising the rural labour and the industrial labour and by giving them the tools and the means by which they could fight for their rights. This is what should have been done in other States also.

This has been done in Kerala. Kerala has a very high level of education and this has made a tremendous impact in destroying the caste system. I do not say that it is completely destroyed. But it is very negligible now. Privately, people may have prejudices. But in most parts of Kerala, it is very difficult to see any open discrimination against the Harijans. The Kerala Government have built houses for the poor people. In these houses, the Harijans live side by side with the other people who belong to the higher castes. It is not so in other States. In the other States, separate housing schemes are there for the Harijans.

K.K. Madhavan : For the information of the Hon. Member, I would like to state that in Kerala the Harijan population is not segregated generally.

Abu Abraham : This is what I am saying. But in the old days, there were segregated areas where the Harijans lived. Therefore, our most important task should be desegregation of the Harijan population. When we build hostels for students, they should be for every one. Why should there be Harijan hostels? If such is the case, why not we have buses and trains exclusively for the Harijans? It has been said that the Railways have made a great contribution in changing the social pattern in this country because in our trains, the Harijans and other people travel together. In the same way, I think we should have common hostels, we should have hostels where the Harijan boys can stay along with the boys belonging to the higher castes. In any case, it has been proved to be a racket where these people have been exploited and people have been making money. This is a well known fact.

Sir, we say all the time that we are a secular State and we are getting more and more secular as years pass by. But the interesting thing is that while we say that we are becoming more secular, it seems to me that we are getting more and more religious. I do not see any attempt being made in this country to break the hold of religious orthodoxy on our society. Now, many distinguished people, political leaders, and high dignitaries seen to be encouraging orthodoxy. In this connection, I would like to give the example of the revival of the cow protection campaign. May I ask why the ban on cow slaughter has so suddenly been introduced in Tamil Nadu, Andhra Pradesh and Maharashtra? This has directly affected the poor people in this country.

This has directly affected the Harijans in this country. I can only say this is a way of encouraging religious orthodoxy. The other day Shri Vinoba Bhave made an extraordinary remark that vegetarianism is the answer to removal of untouchability. Now this is a direct insult to all people who eat meat. The implication of that remark is that people who eat meat automatically go down the social ladder. On the contrary, I say that people must all be encouraged to eat meat so that they can all achieve equality. This should be the aim of the government and they should not give in to Vinoba Bhave. Any agricultural scientist will say that we have too many cattle in this country and it is necessary to have a certain amount of slaughter and meat-eating.

Sir, the new duties of citizens include "the cultivation of a scientific temper" and is it too much to ask the government itself to show a scientific temper in this matter?

Om Mehta : Sir, I am very grateful to the Honourable Members for the unanimous support that they have given to this Bill and I am grateful particularly to Shri Prakash Veer Shastri, Pandeje's arguments I heard at my residence as unfortunately, I was not present here. But it was a good speech, I must say—and then to Mr. Vaishampayen, Mr. Kumbhare—I think, Sir, Mr. Kumbhare has not spoken.

N.H. Kumbhare : I had no opportunity to speak.

Om Mehta : Sir, he has given an amendment and so, I thought that he must have spoken. I am grateful to Mr. Kalp Nath Rai, Rani Sahiban, Mr. Makwana and many others. I am really thankful to all of them.

Sir, this is a very significant Bill. This was before the Lok Sabha for the last two years. Unfortunately, for one reason or the other, it could not be passed. It is good that it is being passed today and it is a very significant achievement so far as eradication of untouchability is concerned which, Sir, is a malady of our times. Sir, the word "untouchability" has been removed from our Constitution and this word is not there now. But untouchability is still practised in some parts of the country and it is a matter of shame for this country and for the people of this country who still practise it and I think it is high time that we took stringent action against those who still practised untouchability and to meet this need, Sir, we have brought forward this Bill.

Even before this Act came into being, we were not obvious of this fact. Our beloved Prime Minister wrote to the Chief Ministers of all the States to set up special cells under their personal supervision to look into the grievances of the Scheduled Castes and Scheduled Tribes people and other minorities. Such cells have been set up in a number of States. Not only this, Sir, the Home Minister has been issuing instructions from time to time to the States to look into the grievances of these down-trodden people, these exploited people, and we have issued instructions to them to the effect that in each and every State, the district officers must be requested to obtain relevant information about all incidents involving the Harijans, irrespective of whether such incidents have arisen due to any caste consideration or not and send it to the State and Central Governments since communication of such information to the State and Central Governments would help them in placing these matters in proper perspective.

Sir, we have said that investigation of all offences involving Harijans, whereas any caste considerations are suspected, should be promptly, efficiently and adequately supervised. Investigation serious offences involving the Harijans, where caste considerations are suspected, should be treated as special report cases and entrusted to selected investigation officers. A suggestion made that such investigation should be conducted by an officer not below the rank of Deputy Superintendent of Police or Inspector of Police, was adopted wherever possible. Any failure to undertake prompt and efficient investigation or to exercise adequate supervision should be regarded as grave dereliction of duty on the part of the officers concerned.

Sir, it can now be confidently said that a new orientation has been imported into the official approach—a steady improvement has also been made in regard to the administrative response to the needs of the situation.

Sir, my friend, Mr. Vaishampayen has quoted some figures also to show that in Gujarat and Maharashtra the number of atrocities is increasing. He gave figures for 1972, 1973, 1974, 1975. Sir, there is no doubt that previously whenever atrocities were committed they were not being reported. The Harijans were thinking that there would be retaliation from the higher castes and they were reluctant to report these atrocities to the *thana* or to the government. Now, as the consciousness is growing, education is growing more and more such incidents are being reported. Sir, as politically, also they are becoming more and more conscious of their rights and privileges they are bringing more and more such incidents to the notice of the authorities.

Some points have been raised here that against these officers who are negligent or who do not register the cases whenever these poor people go to the police station, action should be taken. The present Bill is only to meet that situation. Where we find that there is a wilful negligence on the part of any officer to take any action against those who commit atrocities or to write the reports, action would be taken against that officer also.

Sir, not only that. We have said that in the case of those officers who do not go to the rescue of the Scheduled Castes and Scheduled Tribes, the offence will be a cognizable offence and there also action will be taken against him.

Shri Makwana raised a point about the services. Sir, as I said in the other House, in this Bill we could not bring a provision for the services. But the government is trying that whatever quota is fixed, it should be filled completely. Sir,. I have been saying repeatedly in this House that full quota of Scheduled Castes and Scheduled Tribes has been filled in the all-India services, that is IAS, IPS, IFS, in the past.

Wherever their representation is less, not only in Class IV services, but in Class I, Class II and Class III services also, in recent years we have tried to see to it that their number is increased. I should say that the number of Scheduled Castes Officers is 35,061 in Class I, 54,129 in Class II, 16,32,397 in Class III and 12,38,818 in Class IV. In recent years, we have taken certain more steps. Reservation in promotion quota now applied to all the grades and classes where the element of direct recruitment does not exist. It is 66.33 per cent. Earlier this limit was 50 per cent. From 1974, recruitment to posts filled by selection has been extended to promotions from Class III to Class II, within Class II and from Class II to the lowest rung of Class I. Before 1974, such reservations were confined to Class III and Class IV posts. Carry forward provisions have been liberalised in favour of the Scheduled Castes and the Scheduled Tribes with effect from June 1975. Scientific and technical posts for research up to the lowest grade of Class I have been brought within the purview of reservation orders. Earlier, no reservation existed for such posts. The UPSC an other competent authorities have been authorised to lessen qualifications relating to experience if otherwise suitably qualified Scheduled Castes and Scheduled Tribes candidates are available. The position has also improved in the public sector undertaking where the representation of Scheduled Castes has risen by 26.5 per cent in Class IV and 14 per cent in Class III. In the case of Scheduled Tribes, the representation has risen to 12 per cent and 6 per cent respectively.

Sir, a High-Power Committee under the Chairmanship of the Prime Minister meet regularly to review the progress relating to matters concerning Scheduled Castes and Scheduled Tribes including their representation in services. Instructions have also been issued that reservation orders will apply to staff recruited by voluntary agencies which receive substantial grants-in-aid from the Government under certain conditions. We have seen to it that whatever orders are being issued by the Government of India, Department of Personnel, are implemented. It is not only the Commissioner for Scheduled Castes and Scheduled Tribes who keeps an eye on this. Also, a High-Power Committee of both the Houses of Parliament, which is there, looks to it whether the orders issued by us are implemented or not. The report of the Commissioner for Scheduled Castes and Scheduled Tribes who keeps an eye on this. Also, High-Power Committee of both the

Houses of Parliament, which is there, looks to it whether the orders issued by us are implemented or not. The report of the Commissioner for Scheduled Castes and Scheduled Tribes and, also the report of the High-Power Committee of both the Houses of Parliament are placed on the Table of the House.

A point has been raised here by Mr. Wajd. He said lakhs and lakhs of Harijans and other backward class people are still houseless.

Sikander Ali Wajd : I said about nomads.

Om Mehta : Nomads are those who have got no lands and no houses. When I talk of houseless people, that means nomads also. It does not mean that we are excluding them. We are proud of what we have done during the last two or three years under the leadership of our honourable Prime Minister. There are lakhs and lakhs of houseless people. (*Interruptions*) No, I am not yielding. He has said whatever he wanted to say. Sir, apart from whatever Mr. Wajd has said, I have high regards for his ability, for his experience, for his poetry and also other things.

I think, Sir, he has seen the figures of what has been achieved after the launching of the 20-point programme. The first priority which we are giving in this is to giving houses to the houseless. That is agricultural labour and those who are without houses. Sir, up to this time, seventy lakh people have been provided with house sites. Not only that. We are seeing to it that actually their possession is given to those people who never had any house-sites up to this time and they should be able to build the houses there. When we talk of houses, I must say, in Delhi, when I was in the Housing Ministry, it was for the first time that we made a reservation of 20 per cent for the Scheduled Castes and Scheduled Tribes in all the flats which were being built by the DDA. We started separate reservations for the Harijans. Previously, a common list was being kept and, unfortunately, from the Janata houses and other houses, the Scheduled Castes and Scheduled Tribes were not getting any houses. So, we made it a special thing that 20 per cent of the houses built by the DDA would be reserved for the Scheduled Castes and Scheduled Tribes and they would get priority in that. Not only that, Sir, the money which was to be paid by them as first instalment or as registration fee was also reduced considerably. And there is no discrimination. For persons who are without houses, whatever possible is being done to give them houses so that they can also live a happy and contented life.

Sir, some other points have been made by the Hon. Members, Shastriji made a point that there are separate schools for the Harijans. Sir, I should inform Shastriji that there are no separate schools. We allow other boys also to come to the Ashram school and schools which are opened for Harijans. But generally what happens is this. Mostly the schools which are opened for Harijans are in areas where their population is predominent. And as Mr. Makwana says in many of the schools, they have got ten per cent reservation but many student do not come there. When we talk of untouchability, we do not want that. But still we should take certain steps by which this untouchability is not perpetuated. In schools and other places, we want that Harijan boys should be allowed to sit with other boys so that from the very beginning this idea that they are untouchables is not there in their minds.

Abu Abraham : What about the reservation of twenty per cent? You were saying that 20 per cent of the housing is reserved for Harijans. Could you please tell us whether these houses will be separated for Harijans or will they be mixed houses?

Om Mehta : They will be mixed houses. This is only reservation. But it is not that we will fix certain blocks only for Harijans where the Harijan live. They will live with other communities in any colonies and wherever the houses are there.

The motion was adopted.

The Vice-Chairman (Shri Ranbir Singh) : The question is:

"That the Bill to amend the Untouchability (Offences),

> Act, 1955 and further to amend the Representation of the People Act, 1951, as passed by the Lok Sabha, be taken into consideration".

The Vice-Chairman (Shri Ranbir Singh) : We shall now take up clause by clause consideration of the Bill.

Clauses 2 to 16 were added to the Bill.

Clauses 17—Substitution of Section 15.

The Vice-Chairman (Shri Ranbir Singh) : There is one amendment by Shri Kumbhare.

N.H. Kumbhare : Sir, I did not any opportunity to speak on the Bill. I am an entire agreement with the Hon. Minister when he says that it is a really radical measure. The Bill is, no doubt, comprehensive and it is also more purposeful; I say the scope of the Bill is also enlarged.

The Vice-Chairman (Shri Ranbir Singh) : Are you moving the amendment?

N.H. Kumbhare : I am just coming to the amendment. I am just making the opening remarks.

The Vice-Chairman (Shri Ranbir Singh) : May I know whether you are moving the amendment?

Would you like to speak on the clause?

N.H. Kumbhare : Sir, I want to point out the relevant clauses.

"That at page 8, after line 7, the following be inserted namely:

> A survey of the district will be conducted by Assistant Director of Civil Rights for locating the area of social disability in such manner as prescribed and shall submit a report as to the nature of untouchability being practiced and the extent of social disability to which the Scheduled Castes people are subjected.'

Explanations : 'Area of social disability is a place or places where members of Scheduled Castes, on account of their subjection could not exercise their right, accrued to them, by reason of the abolition of untouchability under Articles 17 of the Constitution.'

(1) On receipt of the report from the Assistant Director and after making an enquiry as may deem appropriate and on being satisfied as to the situation existing at the place, the Director of Civil Rights will make a declaration specifying the area of social disability and other particulars as may be prescribed.

(2) The area of social disability having been so declared the Assistant Director shall proceed to take such steps and in such manner as may be prescribed to deal with the situation, and shall endeavour to persuade the dominant class through conciliation and seek to create condition so that the members of the Scheduled Castes do not suffer from any social disability provided the said area will be kept observation for such period as may deem necessary. Provided further the period of observation will not be for a period exceeding six months.

(3) The Assistant Director of Civil Rights after having succeeded in his efforts in creating favourable conditions submit a report to the Director who will make a declaration accordingly, in the manner as may be prescribed.

(4) The Assistant Director of Civil Rights having satisfied that he has failed in his efforts to create favourable conditions to facilitate enforcement of rights by members of the Scheduled Castes, submit a failure report to the Director of Civil Rights. This report shall contain the particulars as may be prescribed including the names of the persons who are likely to commit or attempt to commit or abets the commission of an offence.

(5) (A)The Sub-Divisional Magistrate having jurisdiction and specially empowered by the State Government in this

behalf may be given information of the names referred to in the failure report of the Assistant Director of Civil Rights and the S.D.M. may require such persons to show cause why they should not be ordered to execute bond with surety for their good behaviour for such period not exceeding three years as the Magistrate may direct.

(B) The Provision of the Code of Criminal Procedure, 1973, shall in so far as they are applicable apply to any proceedings under sub-section (1) as if the bond referred to therein were a bond required to be executed under section 110 of the said Code."

The question was proposed.

N.H. Kumbhare : Sir, formerly only practice of untouchability was forbidden but now not only practice but preaching of untouchability is also forbidden. If anybody preaches or practises now he will be dealt with and will come under the clutches of the Law. Therefore, I say that the scope of the Bill has been enlarged. It has been made more deterrent because these offences have now been made cognizable. It is also non-bailable. If anybody is found guilty the magistrate has no discretion except to send him to jail because the minimum jail sentence is one month.

Sir, I would be failing in my duty if I do not say a word about the good work of the Joint Select Committee which was presided over by Mr. S.M. Siddiah, Mr. Mirdha was the Minister in charge of the Bill. But for their co-operation it would not have been possible to give such a good shape to it. I may however point out that it could have been made more comprehensive we could have been incorporated a scheme by which we could locate the areas of untouchability and deal with those areas. It is essentially a matter which comes within the purview of the Central Government and we desire that the Central Government should set up a machinery to enforce these provisions. As has been pointed out by my friends, laws are there. But laws become dead letters if we do not set up an administrative machinery to enforce those laws and therefore we want them to take the entire responsibility in this behalf and government should set up a machinery to enforce these provisions. Unfortunately that suggestion has not been accepted and the entire responsibility has been transferred to the State Governments. Of course, under the Act itself the Central Government will make the rules whereby a duty will be cast on the State Governments to set up a machinery. I have stated that government must make the entire provisions more explicit and, therefore, in regard to my amendment, I only want to cite an example. Even today if you go to a village there will be a well. If that well is located in a high caste locality, the Scheduled Castes people will not be allowed to fetch water from that well. So, according to me, it is an area of disability. Such areas have to be identified and located. Let the government play a more positive role. I have suggested that an officer should be appointed under the Act. A duty will be cast on the officer to have a survey made to find out how many places are there where the Scheduled Castes people, even though they have got a right given under the Constitution, are denied those rights. The reasons are obvious. They know that they have got a right but they cannot muster courage to assert that right because they are in a minority, because they have to depend upon them. In such a case the officer will go and find out himself how the position is. He will make an enquiry and if he comes to the conclusion that even though on the face of it there appears to be no discrimination, the caste Hindus are dominating and practising untouchability and preventing these people from taking water, suitable action should be taken.

So, in that case, under the survey, that area will be identified as an area of social disability. The Government will notify it and then there will be a stage of conciliation. As I said, the officer will go and try to bring about a conciliation and tell those elements that these are the provisions in the Act and that they must allow the Scheduled Castes otherwise they will have to suffer and go to jail. In that way, I think, people in the village will not be opposed to it. But, if there are certain elements still, the officer will make a note of those bad elements who are opposed to it and then he will make a report to the Director and the Director will file proceedings in the court. The court will then issue summons to them and tell them that they must create conditions whereby the Scheduled Castes people would have full freedom to go and fetch water. That is the scheme which is incorporated and I think it should be acceptable to government.

Unfortunately, Sir one of the important recommendations has not been accepted by the Government. It reads like this:

> "A public servant who shows any negligence in the investigation of any offence punishable under the Act shall be deemed to have abetted the offence punishable under this Act."

I know the reasons and that way I am convinced that if the Government is going in for a separate legislation providing for reservations for the Scheduled Castes and the Scheduled Tribes, then such a provision could find a place. So, we would like to know from the Hon. Minister whether such a legislation is under contemplation. And if so, when are we going to have it?

Om Mehta : Sir, I have already replied to points raised by the Hon. Member. Whatever he has said with regard to recruitments and other things, I have already given an assurance that we are trying to see whether orders issued by our Ministry are being implemented or not. Still, if he finds that they are not being implemented, we will have to codify these orders and find out how a suitable legislation can be brought in. We can consider it only after taking stock of the whole thing.

Sir, I must tell Mr. Kumbhare that by article 17 of the Constitution, untouchability has been abolished and disability arising out of untouchability has been declared to be an offence. Under article 35(a), sub-section (ii), Parliament has the exclusive legislative competence to provide for punishment for enforcement of the disability arising out of untouchability. The Act in question is, therefore, restricted to the above mentioned constitutional provision.

Sir, in this particular Bill, we also have got some provisions for the machinery for the enforcement of this Act. Under that provision, some officers will certainly be appointed who will be going to find out if there are certain places where the Harijans who are very poor or in minority, are not able to take the shelter of the law or are not able to go to those whom they can go for protection. These officers will report about those areas and, as you know, Sir, we have got a provision of collective fines from those villages and that action will be enforced. That provision has also been kept.

Sir, with these words, I oppose this amendment.

The Vice-Chairman (Shri Ranbir Singh) : Mr. Kumbhare, do you want to withdraw the amendment?

N.H. Kumbhare : Yes, Sir.

The Vice-Chairman (Shri Ranbir Singh) : The question is:

> "That leave be granted to the mover to withdraw the amendment."

The motion was adopted.

The amendment was, by leave, withdrawn.

Does he mean to say that the Scheduled Castes and the Scheduled Tribes should not have some share in the industry? Does he mean to say that there should not be proper roads where there are concentrations of people belonging to the Scheduled Castes and Scheduled Tribes? I do not know what he means. But all that he says is that there is only one need and that is giving scholarships and providing schools and colleges near their homes. I think this is a stupid scheme. With all respect to the learned friend, I should say that it is a stupid proposal, because he does not see reality.

U.K. Lakshmana Gowda (Karnataka) : It is very harsh.

K.K. Madhavan : When harsh things are said, hard replies are needed. He does not see what the problems of the Scheduled Castes and the Scheduled Tribes are. I do not deny the necessity of education. Due emphasis should be laid on education. At the same time, one cannot close one's eyes to the other problems that face them. My Hon. friend himself was admitting that one of the main problems is economic backwardness. I say he had not understood the problem. It is not economic backwardness only. If economic backwardness is the only problem, then certainly there are other people also who are backward. But, fortunately, the framers of our Constitution and the moulders of our administrative system, however, imperfect they may be now, have rightly analysed the problem.

The problem of the Scheduled Castes and Scheduled Tribes has different facets. That is why they have earmarked funds for housing, for industry, for co-operative institutions, for education, for drinking water facilities and for so many other things. My learned friend thinks that only by giving education to a few students and by establishing a few new schools and colleges in the vicinity of their homes all these problems will be solved. As a matter which needs a multi-faceted programme. In India both the Central Government and the State Government are alive to the situation and they have evolved a working programme, a comprehensive working programme for ameliorating the conditions of these backward people. I do not know what prompted out my friend to bring forward a Resolution like this. My only inference is that he has not seen the Scheduled Castes and the Scheduled Tribes in the right perspective.

He has not lived among them. He does not know the sentiments of these people. He does not know the emotions of these people. He does not know the aspirations of these people. His is not the perspective of a social reformer. Evidently he is not a social reformer, as is patent from the words and tone of his speech. Had he been social reformer he would certainly have come to the proper solution to this problem. I am not interested in his pedigree. I am not interested in his background of education. I am not interested in his birth and other things. This is a personal matter and I do not want to go into that. By whatever standards I measure him, seeing the contents of the Resolution which he has placed before us.

I have reason to think that he has not cared to see the conditions and such surroundings of these unfortunate people, the Scheduled Castes and the Scheduled Tribes. I can understand his saying that the administration is top-heavy. In that case it was his duty to give proper suggestions, healthy suggestions, positive suggestions as to how the administration could be streamlined instead of recommending outright the abolition of all the institutions, departments and organisations. It is equally surprising, Sir, that from the other side also a sympathetic response has come in favour of the Resolution. Strangely, Sir, this is a matter where the reactionaries and the revolutionaries agree as against the Scheduled Castes and the Scheduled Tribes. If there is any inadequacy in an administration, it ought to be improved.

My learned friends here do not say that certain other departments which are notorious for their imperfections and malpractices should be abolished. But they are very happy at that. But there is extra unanimity when there is a proposal to abolish all these institutions, departments and organisations which are positively meant for the welfare of the Scheduled Caste and the Scheduled Tribes. I do not understand this humanity in spite of their political differences. All that I can infer is that the cultural background of these people is the same old one. In spite of the political differences, that they profess, they have the same feelings and they have the same psychological response to the problems of the Scheduled Castes and Scheduled Tribes. Sir, it is time that this type of defective approach to the problem is put an end to. What is required is a positive programme the basis for which has been laid by the Father of the Nation by Pandit Jawaharlal Nehru and by all our great leaders who knew the problem and who organized this welfare programme—both official as well as non-official. Sir, I am not very happy; I am not satisfied that we have done all the things for them. I am not satisfied. I am dissatisfied because these are, as I said the other day, problems which have been created during centuries and ages and they cannot be wiped off in a day or two. It requires patience; it requires determination; it requires self-sacrifice. It was for this that Mahatma Gandhi said that everybody, every enlightened citizen in this country should be prepared to do something for these unfortunate people. He ended the fast only on the promise by leaders of this country that they would take up the responsibility of removing the unfortunate condition of these people. The leaders gave an undertaking and it was only after the Mahatma Gandhi gave up his epic fast.

My learned friends I wish to stress the importance, the human emotions behind, this huge problem. There may be differences between the leaders. But fortunately, with the exception of a few handful of people, the large majority of the thinking people in this country are agreed on the problem and the approach, that the problems of the Scheduled Castes and Scheduled Tribes are very big, multitudinous and complicated and that they ought to be solved by effective means. Unfortunately this attitude is wanting among some of our latest political leaders.

They profess revolution, but their course is that of reaction. That is the paradox. The main requirement for approaching this problem is to have enlightened type of people organised in such a way that we can show to the world that we are dedicated to the cause of these people. The Resolution, I think, reminds me of Judas. A poor woman, Mary of Magdalene came to see Jesus. She brought ointment which she applied to his feet. But Judas came forward and said: "What a foolish woman! If she had instead of purchasing this ointment distributed this money to the poor people, hundreds of poor people could have been served and saved." From the Resolution, and from the tone of the move of the Resolution and of the persons who supported the Resolution,

I feel that 'Judasism' has not totally disappeared from this country. Sir, I oppose this Resolution. The Act came into force from November 19, 1976. The intention of the legislation is to protect the civil rights of the untouchables. The title of the Act has been changed to Protection of Civil rights Act. This Act aimed at abolishing untouchability in totality.

Under the new Act, punishment has been considerably increased and there is a provision for both, fine and imprisonment. For the first offence, the minimum punishment is one month imprisonment and a fine of Rs.100/- and maximum six months imprisonment and a fine of Rs. 500/-. If the offence is committed a second time, the punishment will be six months imprisonment and a fine of Rs. 200/- the maximum being six months imprisonment and a fine of Rs. 500/-. For the third and subsequent offence, the punishment may range from one year imprisonment and a fine of Rs. 500/- to two year imprisonment and a fine of Rs. 1000/-.

Until now, untouchability offences though cognizable, could be compounded but they become non-compoundable under this Act. The Act also provides that persons convicted of untouchability offences shall be disqualified from contesting elections to the Central or State legislatures.

The new Act also imparts greater powers to the State Governments to deal with the offenders. The State Governments have been empowered to impose collective fines on the inhabitants of any area if they commit or abet the commission of an untouchability offence. They are further needed to provide sufficient facilities including legal aid to persons subjected to any disability on account of untouchability. The Act also requires of the State Governments to appoint officers for initiating supervision over prosecutions to set up special courts, to constitute committees at appropriate levels, to conduct periodic surveys and identify areas where untouchability is practised and take suitable remedial measures for enforcement of the provisions of this Act. This Act has brought the law in favour of the Dalits.

The Results

1. This Act may be called the Protection of Civil Rights Act, 1955.
2. It extends to the whole of India.
3. It shall come into force on such date the Central Government may, by notification in the Official Gazette, appoint.

Definitions

In this Act, unless the context otherwise requires,

(a) "Civil Right" means any right accruing to a person by reason of the abolition of "Untouchability" by Article 17 of the Constitution.

(aa) "Hotel" includes a refreshment room, a boarding house, a lodging house, a coffee house and cafe;

(b) "Place" includes a house, building and other structure and premises, and also includes a tent, vehicle and vessel;

(c) "Place of Public entertainment" includes any place to which the public are admitted and in which an entertainment is provided or held.

"Entertainment" includes exhibition, performance, game, sport and any other forms of amusement;

(d) "Place of public worship" means a place, by whatever name known, which is used as a place of public religious worship or which is dedicated generally to, or is used generally by persons professing any religion or, belonging to any religious denomination or any section thereof, for the performance of any religious service, or for offering prayers therein and includes.

(i) all lands and subsidiary shrines appurtenant or attached to any such place;

(ii) a privately owned place of worship which is, in fact,

allowed by the owner thereof to be used as a place of public worship, and

(iii) land or subsidiary shrine pertaining to such privately owned place of worship as is allowed by the owner thereof to be used as a place of public religious worship.

(da) "Prescribed" means prescribed by rules made under this Act;

(db) "Scheduled Castes" has the meaning assigned to it in clause (24) of Article 366 of the Constitution.

(e) "Shop" means any premises where goods are sold either wholesale or by retail or both wholesale and by retail (and includes),

(i) any place from where goods are sold by a hawker or vendor or from a mobile van or cart;

(ii) a laundry and a hair cutting saloon;

(iii) any other place where services are rendered to customers.

6

Protection for Women

Recognition of women's rights as human rights is a revolutionary notion. This radical reclamation of humanity and the corollary insistence that women's rights are human rights have profound transformative potential. The incorporation of women's perspectives and lives into human rights standards and practice forces recognition of the dismal failure of countries worldwide to accord women the human dignity and respect that they deserve simply as human beings. A woman's human rights framework equips women with a way to define, analyse, and articulate their experiences of violence, degradation, and marginality.

During the UN Decade for Women (1976-1985), women from many geographical, racial, religious, cultural, and class backgrounds took up organising to improve the status of women. The United Nations-sponsored women's conferences, which took place in Mexico City in 1975, Copenhagen in 1980, and Nairobi in 1985, were convened to evaluate the status of women and to formulate strategies for women's advancement. These conferences were critical venues at which women came together, debated their differences and discovered their commonalties, and gradually began learning to bridge differences to create a global movement.

In the late eighties and early nineties, women in diverse countries took up the human rights framework and began developing the analytic and political tools that together constitute the ideas and practices of women's human rights. Taking up the human rights framework has involved a double shift in thinking about human rights and talking about women's lives. Put quite simply, it has entailed examining the human rights framework through a gender lens, and describing women's lives through a human rights framework.

In looking at the human rights framework from women's perspectives, women have shown how current human rights definitions and practices fail to account for the ways in which already recognised human rights abuses often affect women differently because of their gender. This approach acknowledges the importance of the existing concepts and activities, but also points out that there are dimensions within these received definitions that are gender-specific and that need to be addressed if the mechanisms, programmes, and the human rights framework itself are to include and reflect the experiences of the female half of the world's population. When people utilise the human rights framework to articulate the vast array of human rights abuses that women face, they bring clarifying analyses and powerful tools to bear on womens experiences.

This strategy has been pivotal in efforts to draw attention to human rights that are specific to women that heretofore have been seen as women's rights but not recognised as human rights. Take, for example, the issue of violence against women. The Universal Declaration states: "No one shall be subject to torture or to cruel, inhuman or degrading treatment or punishment". This formulation provides a vocabulary for women to define and articulate experiences of violence such as rape, sexual terrorism and domestic violence as violations of the human right not to be subject to torture or to cruel, inhuman or degrading treatment or punishment.

The concept of women's human rights has opened the way

for women around the world to ask hard questions about the official inattention and general indifference to the widespread discrimination and violence that women experience everyday. Whether used in political lobbying, in legal cases, in grassroots mobilisation, or in broad-based educational efforts, the idea of women's human rights has been a rallying point for women across many boundaries and has facilitated the creation of collaborative strategies for promoting and protecting the human rights of women. While women have raised questions for a long time about why their rights are seen as ancillary to human rights, a coordinated effort to change this attitude using a human rights framework gained particular momentum in the early part of the 1990s.

The opening of space for new debates afforded by the end of the Cold War facilitated the exchange of ideas and experiences among women around the world that led to strategising about how to make women's human rights perspectives more visible. As women's activities developed globally during and following the United Nations' Decade for Women, more and more women raised the question of why women's rights and women's lives have been deemed secondary to the human rights and lives of men.

Over the past decade, a movement around women's human rights has emerged to challenge limited notions of human rights, and it has focused particularly on violence against women as a prime example of the bias against women in human rights practice and theory. The United Nations World Conference on Human Rights held in Vienna in 1993 was the first such meeting since 1968, and it became a natural vehicle to highlight the new visions of human rights thinking and practice being developed by women.

Since the conference represented a historic reassessment of the status of human rights, it became the unifying public focus of a worldwide Global Campaign for Women's Human Rights-a broad and loose international collaborative effort to advance women's human rights. The campaign launched a petition calling upon the World Conference to comprehensively address women's human rights at every level of its proceedings and to recognise gender violence, a universal phenomenon which takes many forms across culture, race, and class as a violation of human rights requiring immediate action.

The petition was eventually translated into 23 languages, and was used by over 1,000 sponsoring groups who gathered a half million signatures from 124 countries. The petition and its demands instigated discussions about why women's rights, and gender-based violence in particular, were left out of human rights considerations, and served to mobilise women around the World Conference. Women acted to inject issues of women's human rights into the entire pre-conference preparatory process: Women from all regions demanded that women's human rights be discussed at the preparatory meetings held in Tunis, San Jose, and Bangkok, as well as at other non-governmental and national preparatory events.

The idea of women's human rights was a framework for women to articulate and collaborate around broad and similar concerns about the status of women; it also provided women with a way to elaborate on the most pressing human rights issues specific to particular political, geographic, economic, and cultural contexts. By the time the World Conference convened, the idea that women's rights are human rights had become the rallying call of thousands of people all over the world and one of the most discussed new human rights debates.

The Vienna Declaration and Programme of Action, which is the product of the conference and is meant to signal the agreement of the international community on the status of human rights, states unequivocally that:

> The human rights of women and of the girl-child are an inalienable, integral and indivisible part of universal human rights. Vienna Declaration (1, 18,1993).

At subsequent United Nations Conferences, women continued to lobby for and gain wider recognition of women's human rights.

So, for example, at the International Conference on Population and Development in Cairo in 1994, women's reproductive rights were explicitly recognised as human rights. A particularly significant development was the way in which the Platform for Action at the IV World Conference on Women in Beijing in 1995 became virtually an agenda about the human rights of women. This signalled the successful mainstreaming of women's rights as human rights. The agreements that are produced by such conferences are not legally binding; however, they do have ethical and political weight and can be used to pursue regional, national, or local objectives.

Conference documents can also be used to reinforce and interpret international treaties such as the Covenant on Civil and Political Rights, or the Covenant of Social, Economic and Cultural Rights. These covenants, when signed by a country, do have the status of international law and have been used in courts by lawyers seeking redress for human rights violations. The most important international treaty specifically addressing women's human rights is the Convention on the Elimination of All Forms of Discrimination Against Women (CEDAW) which was initiated during the UN Decade for Women and has been ratified by over 130 countries.

Women's human rights not only teach women about the range of rights that their governments must honour; it also functions as a kind of gestalt by which to organise analyses of their experiences and plan action for change. The human rights framework creates a space in which the possibility for a different account of women's lives can be developed. What is so useful about this framework is that it provides women with principles by which to develop alternative visions of their lives without suggesting the substance of those visions. The fundamental principles of human rights that accord to each and every person the entitlement to human dignity give women a vocabulary for describing both violations and impediments to the exercise of their human rights. The large body of international covenants, agreements and commitments about human rights gives women political leverage and a tenable point of reference.

In the Fourth World Conference on Women in Beijing in September 1995, the then United Nations Secretary-General, Boutros Boutros Ghali, said that violence against women is a universal problem that must be universally condemned. But he said that the problem continues to grow. The Secretary General noted that domestic violence alone is on the increase. Studies in 10 countries, he said, have found that between 17 per cent and 38 per cent of women have suffered physical assaults by a partner. In the Platform for Action, the core document of the Beijing Conference, Governments declared that violence against women constitutes a violation of basic human rights and is an obstacle to the achievement of the objectives of equality, development and peace.

Advancement of women's rights has concerned the United Nations since the Organisation's founding, Yet the alarming global dimensions of female-targeted violence were not explicitly acknowledged by the international community until December 1993, when the United Nations General Assembly adopted the Declaration on the Elimination of Violence against Women. Until that point, most governments tended to regard violence against women largely as private matter between individuals, and not as a pervasive human rights problem requiring state intervention. In view of the alarming growth in the number of cases of violence against women throughout the world, the Commission on Human Rights adopted resolution 1994/45 of 4 March 1994, in which it decided to appoint the Special Rapporteur on violence against women, including its causes and consequences. As a result of these steps, the problem of violence against women has been drawing increasing political attention.

Females fall prey to violence before they are born, when expectant parents abort their unborn daughters, hoping for sons instead. In other societies, girls are subjected to such traditional practices as circumcision, which leave them maimed and traumatised. In others, they are compelled to marry at an early age, before they are physically, mentally or emotionally mature. Women are victims of incest, rape and domestic violence that often lead to trauma, physical handicap or death. And rape is still being used as a weapon of war, a strategy used to subjugate and terrify entire communities.

The Platform for Action adopted at the Fourth World Conference on Women declared that rape in armed conflict is a war crime and could, under certain circumstances, be considered genocide. Secretary-General Boutros-Ghali told the Beijing Conference that more women today were suffering directly from the effects of war and conflict than ever before in history.

The Declaration on the Elimination of Violence against Women is the first international human rights instrument to exclusively and explicitly address the issue of violence against women. It affirms that the phenomenon violates, impairs or nullifies women's human rights and their exercise of fundamental freedoms. The Declaration provides a definition of gender-based abuse, calling it "any act of gender-based violence that results in, or is likely to result in, physical, sexual or psychological harm or suffering to women, including threats of such acts, coercion or arbitrary deprivation of liberty, whether occurring in public or in private life". The definition is amplified in Article 2 of the Declaration, which identifies three areas in which violence commonly takes place:

(i) Physical, sexual and psychological violence that occurs in the family, including battering; sexual abuse of female children in the household; dowry-related violence; marital rape; female genital mutilation and other traditional practices harmful to women; non-spousal violence; and violence related to exploitation;

(ii) Physical, sexual and psychological violence that occurs within the general community, including rape; sexual abuse-sexual harassment and intimidation at work, in educational institutions and elsewhere; trafficking in women; and forced prostitution; and

(iii) Physical, sexual and psychological violence perpetrated or condoned by the state, wherever it occurs.

The importance of the question of violence against women was emphasised over the last decade through the holding of several expert group meetings sponsored by the United Nations to draw attention to the extent and severity of the problem. In September 1992, the United Nations Commission on the Status of Women established a Special Working Group and gave it a mandate to draw up a draft declaration on violence against women. The following year, the United Nations Commission for Human Rights, in resolution 1993/46 of 3 March, condemned all forms of violence and violations of human rights directed specifically against women.

The Vienna World Conference on Human Rights laid extensive groundwork for eliminating violence against women. In the Vienna Declaration and Programme of Action, governments declared that the United Nations system and member states should work towards the elimination of violence against women in public and private life; of all forms of sexual harassment, exploitation and trafficking in women; of gender bias in the administration of justice; and of any conflicts arising between the rights of women and the harmful effects of certain traditional or customary practices, cultural prejudices and religious extremism.

The Safeguards

Violence against women takes a dismaying variety of forms, from domestic abuse and rape to child marriages and female circumcision. All are violations of the most fundamental human rights.

Oppression at Home

Domestic violence against women occurs in developed and

developing countries alike. It has long been considered a private matter by bystanders-including neighbours, the community and government, But such private matters have a tendency to become public tragedies. In the United States, a woman is beaten every 18 minutes. Indeed, domestic violence is the leading cause of injury among women of reproductive age in the United States.

Despite governments' promises to guarantee women's equality and full rights under the constitutions of their countries, governments denied women legal freedom to achieve such rights. In many countries statutory restrictions curtailed, among other things, women's ability to inherit property, contract marriage, and seek divorce.

In South Africa, women married under customary law were still considered minors and could not enter into any legal contract without the consent of their husbands or guardians. In India, Syria, and Pakistan women were discriminated against in divorce and inheritance laws.

The Zimbabwe's highest court ruled in February 1999 in Magaya vs. Magaya that women were perpetual minors without the legal capacity to inherit property and that it was not contrary to 'the anti-discrimination clause of the Zimbabwean Constitution to give preference to male heirs in inheritance rights. The Zimbabwean Constitution's anti-discrimination clause did not apply to customary law. This constitutional limitation effectively undercut women's rights and status in the family, especially in instances where customary law governed cases of marriage, divorce, inheritance, and other personal matters. The Magaya case was met with outrage by women's groups in Zimbabwe, who considered it a major setback in their efforts to achieve equal status for women under the law.

Many governments now recognise the importance of protecting victims of domestic abuse and taking action to punish perpetrators. The establishment of structures allowing officials to deal with cases of domestic violence and its consequences is a significant stop towards the elimination of violence against women in the family. The Special Rapporteur's report highlights the importance of adopting legislation that provides for prosecution of the offender. It also stresses the importance of specialised training for law enforcement authorities as well as medical and legal professionals, and of the establishment of community support services for victims.

In many countries, women fall victim to traditional practices that violate their human rights. The persistence of the problem has much to do with the fact that most of these physically and psychologically harmful customs are deeply rooted in the tradition and culture of society.

The World Health Organisation (WHO) have reported that 85 million to 115 million girls and women in the population have undergone some form of female genital mutilation and suffer from its adverse health effects. Every year an estimated two million young girls undergo this procedure. Most live in Africa and Asia, but an increasing number can be found among immigrant and refugee families in Western Europe and North America. Indeed, the practice has been outlawed in some European countries. In France, a Malian was convicted in a criminal court after his baby girl died of a female circumcision-related infection. The procedure had been performed on the infant at home. There is a growing consensus that the best way to eliminate these practices is through educational campaigns that emphasise their dangerous health consequences.

The consequences of son preference can be anything from foetal or female infanticide to neglect of the girl-child over her brother in terms of such essential needs as nutrition, basic health care and education. In China and India, some women choose to terminate their pregnancies when expecting daughters but carry their pregnancies to term when expecting sons. According to reports from India, genetic testing for sex selection has become a booming business, especially in the country's northern regions. Indian gender-detection clinics drew protests from women's groups after the appearance of advertisements suggesting that it was better to spend $38 now to terminate a female foetus than $3,800 later on her dowry.

Misbehaviour after Marriage

In many countries, weddings are preceded by the payment of an agreed-upon dowry by the bride's family. Failure to pay the dowry can lead to violence. In India, an average of five women a day are burned in dowry-related disputes.

Not Mature Relationship

Early marriage, especially without the consent of the girl, is another form of human rights violation. Early marriage followed by multiple pregnancies can affect the health of women for life. The report of the Special Rapporteur has documented the destructive effects of marriage of female children under 18 and has urged governments to adopt relevant legislation.

Assault and Exploitation

Rape occurs in the community, where a woman can fall prey to any abuser. It also occurs in situations of armed conflict and in refugee camps. In the United States, national statistics indicate that a woman is raped every six minutes. In 1995, the case of a Brazilian jogger raped and murdered in New York City's Central Park drew international attention once again to the problem. The incident occurred only a few years after an earlier sensational jogger-assault case in which the victim- an American assaulted in the same general area of the park -barely survived after her assailants left her for dead.

Relations between residents of the Japanese island of Okinawa and American GIs were thrown into turmoil in 1995 after two marines and a sailor allegedly kidnapped and raped a 12-year-old girl. The Special Rapporteur's report underlines the importance of education to sensitise the public about the special horrors of rape, and of sensitivity training for the police and hospital staff who work with victims.

In many countries sexual assault by a husband on his wife is not considered to be a crime: a wife is expected to submit. It is thus very difficult in practice for a woman to prove that sexual assault has occurred unless she can demonstrate serious injury. The report of the Special Rapporteur noted that light sentences in sexual assault cases send the wrong message to perpetrators and to the public at large: that female sexual victimisation is unimportant.

Sexual harassment in the workplace is a growing concern for women. Employers abuse their authority to seek sexual favours from their female co-workers or subordinates, some times promising promotions or other forms of career advancement or simply creating an untenable and hostile work environment. Women who refuse to give in to such unwanted sexual advances often run the risk of anything from demotion to dismissal. But in recent years more women have been coming forward to report such practices.

Many women are forced into prostitution either by their parents, husbands or boyfriends or as a result of the difficult economic and social conditions in which they find themselves. They are also lured into prostitution, sometimes by mail-order bride agencies that promise to find them a husband or a job in a foreign country. As a result, they very often find themselves illegally confined in brothels in slavery-like conditions where they are physically abused and their passports withheld. Most women initially victimised by sexual traffickers have little inkling of what awaits them. They generally get a very small percentage of what the customer pays to the pimp or the brothel owner. Once they are caught up in the system there is practically no way out, and they find themselves in a very vulnerable situation.

Since prostitution is illegal in many countries, it is difficult for prostitutes to come forward and ask for protection if they become victims of rape or want to escape from brothels. Customers, on the other hand, are rarely the object of penal laws. In Thailand, prostitutes who complain to the police are often arrested and sent back to the brothels upon payment of a fine.

The extent of trafficking in women and girl children has reached alarming proportions, especially in Asian countries. Many women and girl children are trafficked across borders, often with the complicity of border guards. In one incident, five young prostitutes were burned to death in a brothel fire because they had been chained to their beds. At the same time, sex tours of developing countries are a well-organised industry in several European and other industrialised countries. The Special Rapporteur has called on governments to take action to protect young girls from being recruited as prostitutes and to closely monitor recruiting agencies.

According to the International Labour Organisation's (ILOs) estimates in ten years 80 per cent of all women in industrialised countries and 70 per cent globally would work outside the home. Human rights violations continued for women trapped in forced labour throughout the world. As the numbers of women in the labour market swelled, their disproportionate responsibility for uncompensated domestic labour did not diminish. On an average, in a review of the issue in selected developing countries, the United Nations Development Programme (UNDP) reported that women's work burden was 113 per cent that of men. In industrialised countries, women's share was 105 per cent that of men.

The US government reported that murder continued to be the leading cause of women's death in the workplace. In Mexico, the government side-stepped its duty to protect women in the export-processing sector from corporate discrimination. Human Rights Watch's research in 1998 and 1999 demonstrated that corporations operating in this sector subjected virtually all women applicants to pregnancy exams or other methods of determining pregnancy status as a condition of work; denied employment to those who were pregnant; and put those who became pregnant after being hired at the risk of being fired. These problems continued despite local, national, and international efforts to improve conditions in the *maquiladoras.*

As a part of a Human Rights Watch-initiated review under the labour rights side agreement of the North American Free Trade Agreement (NAFTA), the United States engaged Mexico in ministerial-level consultations on the issue of pregnancy based sex discrimination against women. One component of the ministerial consultation agreement was a trilateral conference in Merida, Yucatan, in March 1999. At that conference, Mexico continued to vacillate on the issue of women's right to equality in the labour force. Mexican officials avoided the issues under consideration, disseminated misinformation, and denied their labour law obligations. In one such episode, the Mexican government at long last admitted that pre-hire pregnancy testing violated its labour law, but then undermined the significance of its admission by justifying pregnancy testing as long as it was intended to protect the woman's reproductive health or the health of her foetus.

Despite excellent organisation and planning by local womens NGOs, the NAFTA process in this case produced only slim results in 1999. In contrast to the slow progress of the NAFTA process, two days after being sworn in as Mexico City's first female mayor at the end of September 1999, Rosario Robles signed into force a new law that would punish Mexico City businesses that required women to take a pregnancy test before being hired.

Through coercion, deception, and debt bondage, traffickers held women in involuntary servitude and slavery-like conditions. Trafficking of women from Thailand to Japan remained a large-scale problem in 1999, as thousands of women from Thailand travelled to Japan to work. Although their initial decisions to migrate were voluntary, the vast majority found themselves trapped in debt bondage and forced into prostitution by the agents who facilitated their travel. Recruiters and agents regularly deceived women about the nature of the work, wages, debt amounts, and/or working conditions.

Once in Japan, women were given no choice over their occupation or terms of employment. While in debt, women could not refuse clients or clients' demands and received no compensation for their labour. Agents and traffickers enforced the repayment of debts through abusive tactics such as passport deprivation, illegal confinement, physical violence, and threats of resale into renewed levels of debt. The government of Japan, as in many other destination countries, approached trafficking as an immigration problem, summarily deporting women found working illegally. In rare cases, the Japanese government prosecuted abusive traffickers and agents for employing illegal aliens. But victims of trafficking did not have access to justice or compensation for the severe human rights violations they had suffered while in Japan.

US federal law enforcement officials brought indictments against thirteen ringleaders of a nationwide trafficking network. Federal prosecutors alleged that the traffickers had brought hundreds of young women and girls from Asia to work in forced prostitution in cities throughout the United States. According to press accounts, traffickers held the women in debt bondage, forcing them to perform approximately 600 sex acts without salary before their debt was cleared. In many trafficking cases in the United States, women were arrested, detained, and deported without any opportunity to file charges or demand compensation from employers.

Hundreds of women from the former Soviet Union and Eastern Europe, some of them promised lucrative employment opportunities in West European countries, found themselves sold into slavery-like conditions and held as virtual prisoners in cafe-bars throughout the Federation. The women had no legal redress; instead, local law enforcement officials in Bosnia and Herzegovina often forced the women to stand trial, fined them, and deported them across country lines, allowing traffickers to pick them up and sell them to another bar owner.

Women migrant workers themselves fare badly, and sometimes tragically. Many become virtual slaves, subject to abuse and rape by their employers. They typically leave their countries for better living conditions and better pay-but the real benefits accrue to both the host countries and the countries of origin. For home countries, money sent home by migrant workers is an important source of hard currency, while receiving countries are able to find workers for low-paying jobs that might otherwise go unfilled.

In regions of Middle East and Persian Gulf, there are an estimated 1.2 million women, mainly Asians, who are employed as domestic servants. According to the independent human rights group Middle East Watch, female migrant workers in Kuwait often suffer beatings and sexual assaults at the hands of their employers. The police are often of little help. In many cases, women who report being raped by their employers are sent back to the employer or are even assaulted at the police station. Working conditions are often appalling, and employers prevent women from escaping by seizing their passports or identity papers. There are many international instruments that can be used to prevent abuse against migrant women and suggests some measures to protect the human rights of migrant women.

Case of Women Refugees

Women and children form the great majority of refugee populations all over the world and are especially vulnerable to violence and exploitation. In refugee camps, they are raped and abused by military and immigration personnel, bandit groups, male refugees and rival ethnic groups. They are also forced into prostitution. The number of refugees and internally displaced persons assisted by United Nations High Commissioner for Refugees (UNHCR) in 1998 exceeded 21 million people. The populations of refugees and displaced persons around the world remained predominantly made up of women and their dependent children.

Women refugees had limited or no legal recourse for sexual and domestic violence, partly as a result of their unfamiliarity with and wariness of local police and judicial authorities and partly because of the lack of proactive, systematic, and sensitive responses by the relevant international and local authorities. In many situations women faced particular protection and security risks in refugee camps, as well as the challenges of heading households while suffering from their disadvantaged status as women.

Refugee women were subjected to rape, sexual assault, and other forms of sexual violence. Levels of domestic violence were also reported to be very high in many refugee communities, perhaps because in the refugee setting, pressures regarding housing, food, security, and resources further strained domestic situations and erupted in violence. Moreover, extended networks of family, neighbours, and community leaders that may have acted as a deterrent to abuse no longer existed in the unfamiliar territory of refugee camps.

Problem of Discrimination

Despite assurances made in 1995 at the UN Conference on Women in Beijing, many governments continued to discriminate against women directly or to allow others to do so unimpeded. When the opportunity arose to remedy this discrimination, particularly during post-conflict reconstruction and development periods, the international community passed it by, choosing instead to reinforce previously existing patterns of discrimination. As a consequence, women faced many barriers in their access to justice, services, and resources, with many governments refusing to recognise, let alone remedy, the laws and practices perpetuating women's inequality. While some countries took positive steps toward ensuring women's equality, patterns of discrimination against women surfaced in the laws, policies, and practices of governments and non-governmental bodies around the world.

The Taliban militia in Afghanistan, having gained territorial control of 90 per cent of the country, continued to enforce official gender-based discrimination unparalleled in its harshness. The discriminatory measures imposed by the Taliban not only completely marginalised Afghan women from the mainstream of political life, they placed women's very survival, and that of their families, at risk.

The enforcement of the Taliban's strictures on women varied to some extent in different areas of the country, but this geographical variation in enforcement was largely a matter of degree rather than substance. The restrictions had a severely detrimental effect on women's health, security, and personal freedoms in all areas under Taliban control.

In most parts of Afghanistan, the education of girls and the employment of women outside the health sector remained banned or severely restricted. In some areas, however, home or mosque-based education for girls was reportedly permitted. In most areas, women could not appear in public without a *burqa*, a garment that cloaks the head, face, and body. Women's freedom of movement was severely curtailed as they were generally required to appear in public escorted by a male relative or *mahram*. Punishments for violations of these edicts were extremely harsh.

During times of armed conflict, women's rights were in particular jeopardy. During these periods, judicial structures that should both prevent violence against women and respond to it were in disarray, could not be relied on and, in some cases, were controlled by the very people who were instigating or participating in rapes. In every civil conflict in recent memory including East Timor, Afghanistan, Angola, Indonesia, Sierra Leone, Kosovo, the Mexican state of Chiapas, Algeria, Bosnia, the Democratic Republic of Congo-women were targeted for sexual violence.

One of the most promising developments of 1999 was that important international actors such as the United Nations successfully identified gender-specific abuses committed against women at the start of conflicts, rather than not at all or only once those conflict were long over, as had been the pattern in the past. This early recognition, however, was still not matched by vigorous investigation and prosecution of perpetrators of rape, tasks that were often left to post-conflict national authorities.

The international community was able to do very little to prevent sexual violence in conflict. In fact, combatants defied international standards prohibiting rape and, in some cases, made sexual assault a deliberate weapon. As a consequence, in 1999 many women were treated as reward for soldiers, targeted for forced marriage and domestic labour, and attacked as substitutes for their male relatives or as symbols of communities' honour and reproductive capacity.

Women of Sierra Leone faced severe sexual abuse in the country's eight-year civil war, mainly at the hands of Revolutionary United Front (RUF) rebel forces. In January 1999, RUF rebels launched an offensive against the capital, Freetown, temporarily capturing it from government troops and the soldiers of the Nigerian-led peacekeeping force. During this attack, RUF rebels detained women at base camps, raped them daily for weeks, and forced them to cook and clean for rebel leaders. The fragile July peace agreement crafted between the government of Sierra Leone and the RUF merely recognised the violence that women suffered and called for special attention to integrating women into post-conflict reconstruction and development, while, at the same time, granting a blanket amnesty to combatants.

During Serbian-Kosovo war, Serbian paramilitaries entered the homes of ethnic Albanians and raped women and girls in front of their families or outside in their gardens. An unknown number of women and girls died after these attacks. In other instances, Serbian paramilitaries, many of them volunteer irregular soldiers bussed in from Serbia, demanded money from fleeing Kosovar Albanians, threatening to rape, kill, or torture those who did not comply.

Serb paramilitaries subjected an unknown number of women to gang rapes in forests, in trucks, or along the road. They held women captive for periods ranging from twenty minutes to several days. In some cases, paramilitaries forced women to undress and subjected them to physical searches and interrogations. Many women found these searches terrifying, fearing that they were a precursor to rape.

Violence against women in conflict situations remained so persistent that governments consistently failed to hold perpetrators accountable post-conflict. Women raped in conflict had to contend not only with post-conflict impunity for what happened to them, but also with the dire health consequences of rape. In addition to psychological trauma, physical injuries, and sexually transmitted diseases, sexually abused women faced HIV infection, a potential death sentence, especially in countries in which health care and medicine were scant.

Atrocities by Police

Custodial violence against women is widespread. Women are physically or verbally abused; they also suffer sexual and physical torture. According to Amnesty International, thousands of women held in custody are routinely raped in police detention centres worldwide. States should prosecute those accused of abusing women while in detention and to hold them accountable for their illegal actions.

Role of Government

Despite some positive efforts by state and non-state actors, abuses against women were carried out frequently and with virtual impunity, as states largely failed to fulfil their obligations to prevent and provide redress for such crimes. States were particularly negligent in addressing violence in the family. This problem received widespread international attention in recent years, but concrete action was slow in coming. Japan, for example, only began to consider specific legislation and support services to combat domestic violence in mid- 1999.

The United Nations International Children's Emergency Fund

(UNICEF) reported in 1999 that violence against women was rising in post-communist countries as economic crises increased women's financial dependence upon men. In many of these states, domestic violence was not prohibited by law and marital rape was not recognised as a crime. Speaking on a more global level, in her 1999 report to the UN Commission on Human Rights, the special rapporteur on violence against women noted the growing prevalence of violence against women generally and domestic violence specifically.

Russian attempts to pass national legislation on women violence against women, the topic failed, and little was done to improve the state response to the abuse. The federal government did not make financial ' resources available for combating violence against women. Activists, expressing frustration with the lack of progress nationally, focused their attention on local level initiatives, establishing cooperative links with local law enforcement, city officials, and journalists. The number of non-governmental crisis centres grew across the country, while the few existing government-sponsored centres and shelters closed due to budget cuts. Crisis centre leaders travelled throughout Russia, training judges, police, and activists on rape and domestic violence issues. The Russian Association of Crisis Centres for Women officially registered in 1999 and held a national meeting in September to coordinate its activities.

According to current estimates in Pakistan eight women were raped every twenty-four hours and 70 to 95 per cent of women had experienced domestic or familial violence. Extreme forms of familial violence included the so-called honour killings and bride burnings, with both practices claiming the lives of hundreds of women every year. Women victims of violence who turned to the criminal justice system confronted a discriminatory legal regime, venal and abusive police, untrained doctors, incompetent prosecutors, and sceptical judges. As a result, few women reported crimes of violence, and fewer still saw their attackers punished.

The Mexicoan government revised its rape law in several important ways. A provision was eliminated that allowed a man who raped a minor to avoid prosecution if he agreed to marry her. Now judaes are required to hand down a decision regarding access to an abortion within five working days.

The government of Canada announced a new four-year Family Violence Initiative intended to mobilise community action, strengthen Canada's legal framework, establish services on Indian communities, develop resources to help victims and stop offenders, and provide housing for abused women and children.

A Ministry of State for Women was established in Turkey, whose main goals are, among others, to promote women's rights and strengthen their role in economic, social, political and cultural life. Legal measures are being adopted towards the elimination of violence against women. The establishment of special courts to deal with violence is envisaged. Psychological treatment for abused women is also planned, along with the establishment of women's shelters around the country. Specially trained female police officers could provide assistance to victims of violence.

Many governments have introduced police units specially trained for dealing with spousal assault. It is a well known fact that states have tended to adopt a passive attitude when confronted by cases of violations of women's rights by private actors. Most laws fail to protect victims or to punish perpetrators. Passing laws to criminalise violence against women is an important way to redefine the limits of acceptable behaviour. States should ensure that national legislation, once adopted, does not go unenforced.

State responsibility is clearly underlined in Article 4 of the Declaration on the Elimination of Violence against Women, which stipulates that "States should exercise due diligence to prevent, investigate and, in accordance with national legislation, punish acts of violence against women, whether those acts are perpetrated by the State or by private persons". Any approach designed to combat violence must be twofold, addressing the root causes of the problem and treating its manifestations. Society at large, including judges and police officers, must be educated to change the social attitudes and beliefs that encourage male violence.

Combating violence against women requires challenging the way that gender roles and power relations are articulated in society. In many countries women have a low status. They are considered as inferior and there is a strong belief that men are superior to them and even own them. Changing people's attitude and mentality towards women will take a long time at least a generation, many believe, and perhaps longer. Nevertheless, raising awareness of the issue of violence against women, and educating boys and men to view women as valuable partners in life, in the development of a society and in the attainment of peace are just as important as taking legal steps to protect women's human rights. It is also important in order to prevent violence that non-violent means be used to resolve conflict between all members of society.

Universal Concerns

The international community is confronting the challenges of protecting and promoting women's human rights in conflict and post-conflict situations. Although some significant steps were taken toward greater protection of women's rights, the conflict in Kosovo reminded human rights defenders yet again how sexual violence against women paradoxically can be used to rally support for military intervention and yet risk being ignored when holding perpetrators of human rights violations accountable.

On the twentieth anniversary of the Convention on the Elimination of All Forms of Discrimination against Women (CEDAW), Deputy Secretary-General Louise Frechette recognised how violence and discrimination against women pushes them to society's margins: Women are more commonly found in part-time work in the informal sector, among the unemployed and the underemployed. Women's work in subsistence farming and in family enterprises is ignored and there are no social security, health or old age benefits attached to such work.

Aware of its role in ending the human rights violations that reduce women's status, the United Nations and its various programmes and agencies continued their slow progress in integrating protection of women's rights into their work. For example, the UN Food and Agricultural Organisation (FAO) conducted an analysis of the impact of education of women on food production and determined that increasing women's primary schooling alone could increase agricultural output worldwide by 24 per cent.

After determining that information provided by agricultural extension agents to male heads of households is rarely conveyed to women in the same households, FAO implemented programmes to ensure that women, particularly those cultivating subsistence crops, received information and services. In addition, UNESCO organised in partnership with governmental and non- governmental groups, a Pan African Women's Conference on a Culture of Peace in Zanzibar in May to design ways for women to influence the making of policy, particularly as the policies pertain to conflict prevention, conflict resolution, and peace building.

The final Zanzibar Declaration and Women's Agenda for a Culture of Peace was to be submitted to the United Nations, the Organisation for African Unity (OAU), and the World Bank for approval and financial support. At the same time, diminishing voluntary contributions from governments threatened to close the International Research and Training Institute for the Advancement of Women (INSTRAW), the only UN institute focusing exclusively on women.

The UN's ability to galvanise successfully government funding to save INSTRAW has to be a measure of its commitment to programmes supporting women's rights. The Commission on the Status of Women took a significant step toward protecting women from human rights violations by adopting, after four years of negotiations, an optional protocol to CEDAW. The protocol, which was to enter into force after ratification by ten states, would enable women to submit claims of rights violations to the Committee on the Elimination of Discrimination against women, and would create an inquiry procedure enabling the committee to initiate investigations into situations of grave or systematic violations of women's rights. On October 6, 1999, the UN General Assembly adopted without vote the optional protocol to CEDAW.

The International Criminal Tribunal for the former Yugoslavia (ICTY) appeared to have increased its credibility among women reporting conflict-related violations. Women meeting at a July conference in Vienna on rape in the Kosovo conflict expressed hope that perpetrators of sexual violence in Kosovo would be brought before the ICTY. However, all participants agreed that the women victims and witnesses needed to be represented by their own counsel to protect their interests.

The ICTY still had not created a witness protection and assistance unit which women trusted. Bosnian women scheduled to testify before the ICTY on rape charges told Human Rights Watch that they had no luck seeking help with immigration claims and relocation issues. With the threat of forced repatriation hanging over their heads, witnesses temporarily residing in Germany and other third world countries feared what they perceived as the potentially deadly consequences of testifying without a guarantee that they would not be forcibly returned to Bosnia.

UNHCR was inundated with funds to provide for the refugees, and the media tracked it's every move. This contrasted sharply with the inattention of the international community and media to ongoing and larger refugee crises in Africa. Yet UNHCR demonstrated in Kosovo that, if adequately resourced, it could respond better to these crises and the specific protection needs of women refugees.

UNHCR largely ignored sexual and domestic violence in the emergency phase of the camps and later responded to the problems in an *ad hoc* manner. Only in the first half of 1999 did UNHCR adopt a more comprehensive and coordinated response to violence against women in the camps. In February 1999, Human Rights Watch met with UNHCR staff in Geneva to discuss UNHCR's response to sexual and domestic violence in the Tanzanian camps and to underscore the need to better implement UNHCR's policies on protecting refugee women in all refugee settings and to adopt policies addressing domestic violence.

New protection initiatives of UNHCR included providing firewood to vulnerable refugees, i.e., unaccompanied minors living alone, unaccompanied elderly men and women, elderly couples, handicapped and terminally ill persons, trauma victims, and some single female and male heads of household. UNHCR provided some victims of domestic violence with alternative shelter on a short-term basis, and strengthened ongoing community education on gender violence and counselling services to victims of sexual attacks.

The European Union (EU) has declared a campaign against violence against women in Western Europe. As part of the campaign, the European Commission supported a comprehensive study on the prevalence of domestic violence in the region. The Commission also funded a meeting on rape as a war crime in Kosovo, which brought together activists and experts from the Balkans, other parts of Europe, and the United States. The Balkan Stability Pact Summit for South Eastern Europe, held in July in Sarajevo and attended by President Clinton and fifty other world leaders, was designed to develop a comprehensive strategy for political stability and economic reform in the Balkans.

The Organisation for Security and Cooperation in Europe (OSCE) made some moves to integrate women's human rights into its efforts to monitor human rights violations and develop policies to curtail such abuses. But women's groups in the region, and even in the Sarajevo office of the OSCE, protested that planners had left women off the agenda and excluded them from the meeting. An appeal signed by women's human rights activists throughout the region demanded an equal and active role for women in the development and implementation of the Pact.

In December 1998, the Permanent Council allocated funds for gender issues and activities, such as women in politics trainings in Kazakhstan and Poland, and called on member states to provide voluntary contributions for staffing. The British and Swiss governments each seconded a staff member to serve as gender advisors to the OSCE, one in Warsaw and one in Vienna.

A gender focal point person continued to work in the secretariat in Vienna. To some extent, human rights reporting and field activities increased their attention to women's human rights. In Tajikistan, a local OSCE staff member initiated a project working with traumatised women survivors of the civil war.

During the crisis in Kosovo, female OSCE human rights officers successfully documented cases of rape and other violations against women. Their achievement was all the more noteworthy given that none of the OSCE monitors received instruction in the challenges of interviewing female rape victims and only three per cent of the OSCE staff in Kosovo was female.

The OSCE's public commitment to women's rights did result in several positive developments. The OSCE held a supplementary Human Dimension Meeting on gender issues, where non-governmental organisations were allowed to participate actively in creating recommendations for the institutions of the OSCE.

The US government's commitment to women's rights around the world was jeopardised by two competing foreign policy concerns: the desire to promote advantageous economic and strategic relations with other governments regardless of human rights considerations, and the desire to protect US practices at home and abroad from scrutiny and criticism on human rights grounds. The US government demonstrated leadership in the area of trafficking, an activity that traps hundreds of thousands of women in exploitative working conditions and debt bondage with little legal recourse.

In 1999, the United States played a critical role in crafting a new, markedly improved international protocol on trafficking of persons. The protocol, proposed in the process of negotiating a new Convention against Transnational Organised Crime, would create a new international standard on trafficking to afford trafficked people greater rights and protections. During the negotiations, the US advocated a broad, inclusive definition of trafficking. Despite this positive step, the US stopped short of further advancing trafficked people's rights by failing to provide sufficient support for protocol provisions that would offer greater protections to victims of trafficking.

Preoccupied with keeping US citizens outside the court's jurisdiction, the US played an obstructionist role at the February and August Preparatory Committee meetings for drafting the rules of evidence and procedure and elements of crime for the ICC; it seemed intent on either undermining the power of the court or negotiating a blanket agreement that would exempt any US national from being tried before it. Moreover, the US delegation remained a reactionary force in areas that directly affected women's rights.

The commitment of US government to protect women's rights in the refugee context was evidenced by its attention to Kosovar women refugees. In July 1999, the US government pledged $10 million for the Kosovar Women's Initiative (KWI), which was being implemented by UNHCR. This initiative, which will continue through September 2000, addressed the immediate survival needs of Kosovar women refugees affected by rape and other gender violence by, among other things, providing psychosocial support and counselling, programmes to re-establish women into their communities.

The US government avoided addressing the substantive findings of the report of the UN special rapporteur on violence against women that detailed human rights violations of women in detention in the US, including extensive sexual misconduct and systematic violations of women's right to privacy. The US delegation to the UN Commission on Human Rights insisted that women incarcerated in the US have protection from and recourse against human rights violations, even though passage of the Prison Litigation Reform Act of 1995 made it extremely difficult for women to bring legal claims against corrections departments, especially in cases of sexual assault and abuse.

The CEDAW languished in the Senate Foreign Relations Committee. While the Clinton Administration stepped up its efforts to promote ratification of this treaty, which included attempts to cultivate Senate leadership on this issue and the unveiling of a White House ratification strategy, those efforts were minimal, and had not yet resulted in the treaty being offered for a vote. The Clinton administration was a steadfast critic of women's rights violations in areas where the sheer scale and severity of the physical violence could not be ignored.

However, the US government was much less critical about blatant sex discrimination practised in places like Mexico, its second largest trading partner.

The global commitment to equal human rights for women has progressed rapidly during the last half a century. This has necessitated a radical departure from the previous practice, embodied in national and international law, of taking lesser rights for women for granted. Suffice to recall the following examples: when the United Nations was established, political rights of women were an exception rather than a rule; when the Universal Declaration of Human Rights was being drafted, it was proposed that its first article should read 'All men are brothers'; and protection of maternity in international labour law implicitly discriminated against women by protecting their child-bearing role at the expense of their equal right to work and equal rights in work. With the benefit of hindsight, it is all too easy to criticize such examples, and many more could easily be added. This, however, tells us how much progress has been achieved during the past half-century.

Evolving human rights norms were only recently merged with the parallel process of 'advancement of women', improvement of the 'status of women', or 'women-in-development'. The series of United Nations awareness-raising activities in the 1970s was a catalyst for introducing gender into international and national policy making by giving women visibility in all areas: political, economic, social, cultural, environmental and humanitarian. Gender has today become an integral part of global policies, not only in human rights, but also in development, environment and housing, or with regard to combating violence or refugee protection. Towards the end of the 1980s, human rights were integrated into evolving global policies, and thus opened the way towards merging the previously dissociated 'women's' and 'human rights' approaches. No global conference is nowadays likely just to mention women, as was customary during past decades, when women were added somewhere at the bottom of the agenda, along with children and the disabled.

The series of global conferences in the early 1990s included the Fourth World Conference on Women, which was 'the largest international meeting ever convened under United Nations auspices'. From the human rights viewpoint, the Beijing conference, as it is commonly called, opened questions which were deemed to have already been settled, perhaps wrongly so. Most importantly, the final document of the conference devotes one section to Human rights of women, thus creating an impression that education for the girl child falls outside the realm of human rights, or that human rights have no contribution to make relating to the elimination of poverty. Moreover, that final document reflects how much dissent accompanied its adoption, because 65 participating states submitted reservations. The preparations of the Beijing conference also revealed misunderstandings relating to the term 'gender'. In human rights, that term denotes the fact that discrimination on the ground of sex can victimize both men and women, while gender discrimination victimizes women on a range of grounds alongside sex. This is discussed in detail below.

Activity against Discrimination

The United Nations Charter affirmed explicitly 'the equal rights of men and women" in its Preamble, and included sex among the prohibited grounds of discrimination, alongside race, language and religion. The explicitness of the Charter regarding equal rights for women was thereafter reaffirmed and strengthened in a multitude of international human rights treaties. This process has had to overcome many different obstacles; it was neither rapid nor easy.

The Universal Declaration of Human Rights in its final text reaffirmed and reinforced the Charter's postulate of equal rights for women. An early draft of the Universal Declaration, as mentioned above, had proposed that its first article should begin by stating: 'All men are brothers.' This was indicative of the relative lack of gender sensitivity at the time within the Commission on Human Rights, which was drafting the Declaration, although it was chaired by Eleanor Roosevelt, and despite the efforts made by some of its members. The exclusion of the female part of humanity in the wording of a future Declaration was effectively opposed by the Commission on the Status of Women. As a result, the Universal Declaration was in its final text genuinely universal. Keeping in mind that it was drafted in the late 1940s, the careful use of the terms 'everyone' and 'no one' throughout its text appears even more impressive.

The progress in tackling many different obstacles to equal human rights of women during the past five decades can be illustrated by pointing to the principal issues which were singled out by the Commission on the Status of Women. Political rights of women had been recognized in few countries 50 years ago and were therefore tackled first. The World's Women reported that, in 1987-88, women had no ministerial positions in 93 countries of the world, while their representation in national parliaments exceeded 20 per cent only in the former Eastern Europe and USSR. This situation has deteriorated since: 'From an average 33 per cent representation in pre-1989 state socialist parliaments, women now hold an average 10 per cent of parliamentary seats.' Such data show the enormity of the task once equality in political representation of women is accepted as a yardstick. The availability of such data, however, has resulted from the initial commitment to equal political rights of women: the fact that inequality has become an object of monitoring in itself indicates commitment.

The initial focus on political rights was followed by a focus on gender discrimination in the private sphere, within the family, neighbourhood and community which necessitated refocusing human rights standards from the conventionally dominant public sphere, namely relations between the government and the individual, to the private sphere.

Perhaps the most important accomplishment of the past decades has been the realization that women are not discriminated against because of their sex alone, and hence the change from 'sex' to 'gender' in standard-setting instruments aimed at the eradication of discrimination against women. Six different grounds of discrimination may deprive women of the recognition or exercise of their equal human rights: (1) sex, (2) pregnancy and child bearing, (3) maternity, (4) marital status, (5) family status, and (6) family and/or household duties and responsibilities.

Women can be denied property rights, or equal access to citizenship, because they are female. An unregulated labour market can, however, lead to discrimination against pregnant women and mothers with dependent children, not affecting all women, but institutionalizing inequality between men (who cannot bear children) and women (who can), based on the inability of women to compete with men on the labour market, owing to pregnancy and child bearing. Looking further at the role of maternity, one can easily see that legal protections assumed that the parental role pertained to women alone. Women's marital status constitutes an illustrative example of a loss of rights which marriage may entail: single women may have a wider scope of rights than those who are married, such as freedom of movement and residence, access to bank loans or to employment, or even access to health care and/or family planning services. Law has for centuries embodied the notion of the 'head of family' or 'breadwinner' and this role still pertains to men. Women's marital and family status thus determines the scope of rights and freedoms. Their traditional role within the family and/or household further limits their ability to exercise rights and freedoms, even if they are formally granted to them. The evolving human rights standards have had to address each of these different forms of discrimination in turn.

Evolving global policies and standards do not automatically translate into effective measures for the elimination of gender discrimination. Even in the part of the world which calls itself 'developed' , the translation of norms against gender discrimination into enforceable equal rights for women remains a task for the future. It is no coincidence that the motto of the UN activities was— and remains— Equality, Development and Peace. It is the first term, equality, which defines the approach to every and any pertinent issue.

Global Standards

The Convention on the Elimination of All Forms of Discrimination against Women (the Women's Convention), as much as any other human rights treaty, lays down human rights norms which are necessarily worded in abstract terms. Human rights treaties are negotiated during protracted and sometimes conflictual intergovernmental meetings. In the case of the Women's Convention, the drafters 'had to face the difficult task of preparing a text applicable to societies of different cultural characteristics and traditions. The ways in which discrimination against women manifested itself varied from one culture to another. The Convention therefore represents a constructive compromise. Specificity and clarity are thus attained through the interpretation and application of the Convention. It is through the reporting process that the Convention is translated from abstract requirements into a yardstick to monitor the realization of the human rights of women. At least, this should be so in theory. The Committee on the Elimination of Discrimination against Women (CEDAW) has been established on the basis of the Convention, with the main task of monitoring progress made in its implementation,

Governmental reports are rarely self-critical. In most cases, they reproduce the existing constitutional and legal provisions relating to non-discrimination, and do not venture into analysing their application, or, indeed, obstacles to the enjoyment of equal rights by all women. Not only is there often a wide gap between formal legal status and reality, but the Convention itself also requires the eradication of defacto discrimination. Without data on the actual position of women regarding all their human rights and fundamental freedoms, *de facto* discrimination remains invisible, and policies for its eradication are difficult to elaborate. CEDAW has adopted, following the practice of other human rights treaty bodies, a 'constructive dialogue' for the examination of reports by States Parties.

These reports are discussed during public sessions in the presence of representatives of the State Party who introduce the report prepared by their government and respond to questions and comments by the members of CEDAW. Quite often these questions relate to issues which have not been addressed in the report, but they frequently venture into examining whether a specific law, policy or practice is consistent with the requirements of the Convention. CEDAW has been criticized for failing to move one step further and declare when and where a national law, governmental policy or country's practice constitutes a breach of the Convention: CEDAW has never formally pronounced a State Party to be in violation of the Convention, even though the members have clearly felt that some states have failed to carry out their obligations.

The definition of the nature and scope of governmental obligations under the Convention, however, cannot be assumed but requires an assessment of the impact which many reservations have made, both for the human rights of women in the countries concerned, and also for the entire Women's Convention. The problem of reservations to the Women's Convention was brought to the attention of the World Conference by CEDAW and numerous other bodies. CEDAW noted that this problem was global and therefore should be placed on the agenda, added that the Women's Convention had the highest number of reservations of all human rights treaties, and stressed that 'most reservations were worded so generally' and therefore necessitate the determination of 'the impact the reservations have on the obligation to eliminate discrimination against women'." The following table lists the reservations to the Women's Convention.

Significance of Convention

Substantive Provision	***Country***
Definition of discrimination (Article 1)	United Kingdom
Commitment to eradicate discrimination (Article 2)	Bangladesh, Cook Islands, Egypt, Iraq, [Libya], Malawi, Tunisia, United Kingdom
Measures to accelerate *de facto* equality (Article 4)	[Malawi]
Measures to eliminate prejudices and stereotyping (Article 5)	Cook Islands, France, [India]
Elimination of discrimination in political and public life (Article 7)	Austria, Belgium, Germany, Luxembourg, Spain, Thailand
Equal citizenship rights (Article 9)	Cyprus, Egypt, France, Iraq, Jamaica, Jordan, Korea, Thailand, Tunisia, [Turkey], United Kingdom
Elimination of discrimination in education (Article 10)	Thailand, United Kingdom
Elimination of discrimination in employment (Article 11)	Malta, Mauritius, New Zealand, Thailand, United Kingdom
Equal labour rights (Article 11)	Australia, Austria, Ireland, New Zealand, Thailand, United Kingdom

Equal access to financial credits (Article 13)	Bangladesh, Ireland, Malta, United Kingdom
Full legal capacity (Article 15)	Austria, Brazil, Ireland, [Libya], Jordan, Malta, Thailand, Tunisia, Turkey, United Kingdom
Elimination of discrimination in marriage	Bangladesh, Brazil, Egypt, France, [India], Iraq,
and family (Article 16)	Ireland, Jordan, [Libya], Luxem-bourg, Malta, Mauritius, Korea, Thailand, Tunisia, Turkey, United Kingdom

Note: Countries in brackets submitted their reservations upon signature.

Source: Discrimination against Women: The Convention and the Committee, Human Rights Fact Sheet No. 22, United Nations, November 1994, pp.63-72.

In order to facilitate the process of undertaking human rights obligations, governments can reserve the right not to apply a specific part of a treaty and have to declare so when ratifying a treaty by submitting a reservation. This procedure, in the area of human rights, is designed to enhance the realization of human rights by providing for exceptions to those guarantees which governments cannot immediately and fully undertake at the time of ratification. It is not intended to enable governments to behave in a self-contradictory manner: to ratify a human rights treaty and thus express their commitment to it, but to reserve their right not to apply the crucial human rights safeguards which such a treaty requires. Much controversy has been created regarding the Women's Convention, because reservations in many cases appear to be contrary to the very aim of the Convention.

Reservations are presented in this table as they relate to specific provisions of the Convention, starting from the general principle of non-discrimination. These are important because they indicate the unwillingness of governments to undertake a commitment to eradicate discrimination against women in all its forms, which is the aim of the Convention. The purpose of the table is to review the contents of the Convention in order to show the degree of agreement and disagreement with respect to specific provisions. As can be seen, most reservations have been entered with respect to non-discrimination in family law and citizenship, and with respect to the legal capacity of women. Countries which apply Shari'a law submitted reservations concerning the very obligation to eliminate gender discrimination. To illustrate how farreaching some reservations are, that of Libya states that accession 'is subject to the general reservation that such accession cannot conflict with the laws on personal status derived from the Islamic Sharia'. The reservation of Malawi, subsequently withdrawn, said: 'Owing to the deep-rooted nature of some traditional customs and practices of Malawians, the Government of the Republic of Malawi shall not, for the time being, consider itself bound by such of the provisions of the Convention as require immediate eradication of such traditional customs and practices'.

Some reservations reflect the exclusively male heritage in the exercise of royal powers (Belgium, Luxembourg, Spain), others exclude women from employment in the armed forces or from access to combat duties (Germany, New Zealand, Thailand); yet others restrict employment of women in nightwork or at jobs deemed hazardous to their health (Malta, United Kingdom). Most, however, retain restrictions on equal rights regarding personal status: as to marriage, family, citizenship and legal capacity of women.

The practical implications of reservations can be described by taking Bangladesh as an example. In 1984, at the time of ratification, the government submitted its reservations on a number of articles of the Convention, including the key article on the obligation to eliminate gender discrimination, and also equal rights of spouses and equal rights and responsibilities of parents with regard to their children 'as they conflict with Shari'a law based on Holy Koran and Sunna'. Numerous objections were raised to this reservation, both by other States Parties to the Convention and by CEDAW. Mexico and Germany objected to Bangladeshi reservations, alleging their incompatibility with the object and purpose of the Convention.

Sweden explained its objections at greater length. It said that the reservations in question, if put into practice, would inevitably result in discrimination against women on the basis of their sex, which was against everything the Convention stood for. It concluded by saying that, if tolerated, such reservations would make human rights obligations meaningless. During the consideration of the initial report of Bangladesh on the implementation of the Convention, CEDAW raised the issue of reservations as a problem and hoped that the government would soon withdraw its reservations.

While reservations made possible the ratification of the Womens Convention by virtually all countries because they can opt out of some of its requirements, they also jeopardized the integral and effective application of the Convention as a whole. In other words, the problem is that formal adherence to the Women's Convention is not accompanied by full commitment to the Convention. This problem led to repeated calls upon the United Nations to secure an authoritative determination of the permissibility of reservations which apparently undermine the commitment to the core human rights obligations towards women. The UN Sub-Commission for Prevention of Discrimination and Protection of Minorities noted in 1993 its concern:

> that certain reservations to the Convention, in particular those in relation to the adoption of policies and institutional measures to implement the terms of the Convention (Article 2), political and public life (Article 7), discrimination in the field of employment (Article 11), equality of men and women before the law (Article 15), and marriage and family relations (Article 16), might diminish the international legal norm and legitimize its violation.

State Liability

The multitude of human rights standard-setting efforts which the United Nations have undertaken has led to the realization that human rights standards relating to women have to encompass three levels:

1. formal affirmation that human rights and fundamental freedoms apply to women as they do to men;
2. prohibition of discrimination based on sex; that is, safeguards for equal treatment and equal opportunities for women;
3. identification and elimination of obstacles to equal exercise of human rights and freedoms by women, which are gender-specific and derive from child bearing and child rearing or woman's marital or family status.

It is obvious that elimination of gender discrimination necessitates unequal rather than equal treatment: obstacles to equality cannot be eliminated unless they are recognized and, because they hinder women's (but not men's) exercise of human rights, special measures in favour of women are necessary so as to enable them to overcome such obstacles. Because such measures are structural and accord preferential treatment to women as a category, they often appear to be discriminating against individual men, and remain controversial. Governmental obligations aimed at eliminating discrimination, which were useful as a precedent in the drafting of the Women's Convention, had first been laid down for racial discrimination. It was realized that a formal prohibition of discrimination is an indispensable first step, but insufficient to eliminate racial or gender discrimination: it does not provide sufficient grounds for redressing the inherited consequences of decades, even centuries, of discrimination. Categories victimized by discrimination have to be assisted in order to attain a status comparable to that of the rest of the population so as to exercise their nominally equal rights on equal terms with others.

Human rights entail two types of governmental obligations: to prevent abuses of power and to create conditions for the realization of human rights and fundamental freedoms. Prohibitions have been defined quite well, but norms which require governments to undertake specific measures, rather than to refrain from a prohibited action, were and are more difficult to elaborate and monitor. Elimination of gender discrimination involves both types of obligations. The challenge to inequality is inherent in the very notion of human rights; thus the core principle is that all human beings have equal rights, which are properties inherent to human beings. Thus, not only should women be accorded rights equal to those of men, but they should be equally able to enjoy all these formally accorded rights. This requires that other than legal obstacles be identified and eliminated. Eliminating *de facto* discrimination is much more difficult than enacting laws which recognize equal rights for all.

The move beyond a formal recognition of equal rights to the identification of problems which specific categories of women face in trying to exercise their rights is evidenced in changed global policies; they evolved towards recognizing that 'women' do not constitute a homogeneous group. Some categories are often deprived of their basic rights (for example, rural women or refugee women) and others are particularly susceptible to human rights violations (for example, imprisoned women or prostitutes). Others may be able, in theory, to enjoy all human rights and freedoms, but their family and household duties prevent them from even knowing about their rights; yet others may be legally denied specific rights, and freedoms because they are daughters and wives (rather than husbands and fathers), and whatever their family status may be in practice, in law they are not deemed to be 'heads of the family'. This is particularly important in access to land: many national laws, as well as land reforms, have prevented women from owning land. The UN Rapporteur on Property Rights found that 'the lack of appropriate information from States and other materials on the legal status of women in all geographical regions and their status in possessing property rights did not permit [him] to elucidate this question completely. This issue is still awaiting more profound and wider study'; and he added: 'The Committee on the Elimination of Discrimination against Women should consider adopting a concise statement or assessment concerning the discrimination faced by women in many countries concerning the exercise of their right to own property. Special attention should be paid to methods aimed at eradicating such discrimination.'

When women's concerns first became articulated in international development policy and practice, the prevalent approach was to identify specific 'women's issues' and design 'women's projects' to address them. The postulate of equality for women in development slowly moved to a formal recognition of equal rights and then beyond to the identification and elimination of multilayered gender discrimination: legal and factual, public and private, direct and indirect, visible and invisible, intentional and unintended. It also necessitates the understanding of the multiplication of the grounds for discrimination affecting women: a woman may be subjected to discrimination because she is an asylum seeker, disabled (and a woman), because she is imprisoned, black, a foreigner (and a woman); a woman migrant worker can be victimized as a migrant worker and, in addition, as a woman. Thus, the General Assembly adopted in December 1993 a resolution on violence against women migrant workers in addition to its Declaration on Violence against Women.

Untypical human rights issues, those emerging in the private rather than public sphere, have attained prominence in standard-setting with regard to women. While human rights are generally perceived as protection of the individual against abuses by public authorities, with regard to women marriage and family often represent the focal point for change because denials of equal rights to women and girls are the most noticeable, but also the most difficult to change at that level. A married woman, compared to an unmarried woman, can be discriminated against because of the inherited attitude that the man, the husband, is the head of the family, the breadwinner. The Human Rights Committee therefore affirmed in 1989 that governments are required to ensure equality of rights and responsibilities of spouses as to marriage, during marriage and at its dissolution, and added that 'it is a positive duty of States to make certain that spouses have equal rights'. Because gender discrimination jeopardizes all human rights, persistence of unequal rights in marriage are addressed as a breach of governmental human rights obligations.

Decisions on eliminating discrimination against married women, such as access to unemployment and social security benefits, were adopted under the International Covenant on Civil and Political Rights. These cases illustrated another facet of untypical human rights issues: although ,violations' are commonly perceived as abuses, equal rights of married women were violated by governments' failures to change their national legislation; although violations of economic and social rights generally remain outside the mandate of international human rights bodies, those denying equal rights to women have been accepted as breaches of the right to protection against discrimination.

A case concerning the national legislation of Peru illuminates typical obstacles which women may have to overcome to acquire equal rights in the private sphere. According to the Peruvian Civil Code, when a woman is married, only the husband is entitled to represent matrimonial property before the court. The Peruvian Supreme Court affirmed this approach in a case involving a married woman who sought access to justice so as to protect her own property rights. She submitted a communication to the Human Rights Committee, stating that she was denied access to courts because she was a woman, and Peru thus breached the principle of equal rights.

The Committee found Peru in breach of the International Covenant on Civil and Political Rights, stating that the application of the Peruvian Civil Code resulted in denying the woman equality before the courts and constituted discrimination, and urged the government to initiate necessary legislative changes.

This case illustrates persisting obstacles to equal rights for women embodied in national legislation which in many countries preclude women from exercising all rights which they should, but do not yet, have. Thus married women may still be required to have the permission of their husbands to enter employment in some countries. Married women are not considered independent or equal (either to men or even to unmarried women) in migration or citizenship. The concept of the 'head of the family' in land ownership, or in loans and credits, constitutes an obstacle for women, who may be responsible for the family in practice, but are considered dependent family members in law.

The cases which were brought before the Human Rights Committee show that women, whether in Africa or Latin America, are determined to seek redress - when they are given access to remedies and when they know both their rights and remedies for cases of their violation.

It may have come as a surprise that the denial of equal rights concerning citizenship figures prominently in national and international case law. One could assume, wrongly, that such basic issues as citizenship were solved for all a long time ago. Such false assumptions have to be dispelled to open the way for increased use by women of international complaints procedures.

The UN human rights bodies only addressed the human rights of women in the 1990s. An overview of violations of the human rights of women, however, still necessitates sifting through mountains of documents produced by various human rights bodies. There is no separate agenda item specifically on women which would make such an overview easy and comprehensive. Reasons for this are many. One, often voiced by women's organizations, is the traditional disregard of women in human rights as much as in other areas. Another reason is that it is often difficult to determine whether a specific human rights violation is gender-specific, or whether women are victimized for reasons unrelated to their sex. However, because such an analysis is rare, even those violations which are gender-specific are often not dealt with as human rights issues.

Act for Equality

Human rights norms do not treat people as if they were equal because they are not. They demand that people be recognized as having equal rights. Thus, disabled persons are accorded a specific set of rights to compensate for their disability and to prevent this from amounting to a handicap. Similarly, pregnant women and mothers with small children enjoy special protection, not because they are women, but because child bearing and child rearing necessitate social and economic support. The main aim of human rights is to accord everyone equal opportunities for free and full development, hence methods of eliminating discrimination include redressing factual inequalities in the enjoyment of human rights.

Human rights require that women do not have to earn societal recognition and protection through motherhood; that women are, as much as men, entitled to full protection of their rights and freedoms because they are human beings. The implications of motherhood for equal rights of women emanate from the biological fact that women bear children and men do not. Societal and legal protection aim to compensate for this biological difference. This protection derives from the acknowledgment that child bearing and child rearing are a societal function; hence compensation is earned by women who perform it: it is not granted them for the mere fact that they are women.

Women's biological role of child bearing, rather than being compensated by society as equal rights require, can be used to perpetuate inequality. Where women are considered to be the property of their husbands and instruments for child bearing (of sons), unequal rights for women remain sanctioned by law. In many countries, women remain minors throughout their lives; national law denies them a full legal personality. They are considered the property of their fathers, husbands and sons. Denial of their full legal personality entails the authorization or consent (of their father or husband) for their access to health services, including family planning. Women's access to family planning continues to be a criminal offence in some countries, while in others it may be conditional upon the husband's written authorization, which denies women full and equal legal personality. Significantly, the Earth Summit urged governments to strengthen the legal capacity of women through constitutional, legal and administrative procedures in order to enable women to enforce their equal rights.

Literature on the effectiveness of population policies regularly singles out the status of women as the principal obstacle to their effectiveness. Moreover, the mere availability of family planning services is often expected to produce significant effects in terms of decreased fertility, but may prove to have a limited effect on human reproductive behaviour:

> 'Family planning, as a health measure, is partly one of practical containment, and it can be defeated by more primary influences. These 'primary influences', particularly the status of women, require a broadening of population policies to factors which influence or even determine their reproductive behaviour. They regularly derive from discriminatory heritage. Much has been written about their manifestations, be it women's preference for large fan-Lilies or for sons. Such attitudes are, however, analysed as a cause of reproductive behaviour but not as a consequence of discriminatory heritage, namely a manifestation of gender discrimination.

The identification of causes is obviously crucial for designing remedies. This has yet to be introduced into international policies which originate from 'women's' or 'women-in-development' departments. For example, the 1990 SIDA Guidelines for Activities within the Area of Population include a pledge to ensure that 'an increased number of girls/women participate in primary education'. The low participation of girls in primary education is a consequence of a discriminatory heritage, thus its elimination, namely equalizing educational participation for girls, should be the aim and also a yardstick against which progress is measured. When the objective is equal, rather than increased but still unequal, educational participation, an increase of educational enrolment of girls from 10 to 20 per cent is not seen as success, but as persisting discrimination. When human rights standards replace those conventionally adopted to improve the status of women, a different yardstick for measuring progress - departures from the posited equality - sheds a different light on past accomplishments.

Neither legal norms nor development policies can provide more than just a starting point, a catalyst, for change. The emergence of gender discrimination on the human rights agenda broadened the reach of human rights from 'vertical' relations, between individuals and governments, to 'horizontal' relations, between private individuals, within families and communities, and ultimately within couples. The human rights argument is that women should not be left unprotected from abuses from which they may suffer, and that governments have to take the lead in eradicating such abuses even when they occur within families and may be justified by tradition and religion. Rights of individual women thus take precedence over respect for family autonomy.

Moreover, women's participation in decision making underlines the importance of the indivisibility of human rights: women may be denied access to decision making when population policies are being formulated and adopted. These policies affect women—many refer only to women—while decisions may be made by men. Research has shown that 'the most forceful opposition to family planning comes from older males, especially from the devout among them'. Because of their biological role of child bearing, women can be transformed into instruments for the attainment of fertility objectives if they are denied equal rights and fundamental freedoms.

International population policies therefore posit that women's empowerment represents the crucial, but most difficult, area for governmental intervention, and define education as the main path towards it: 'Education is one of the most important means of empowering women with the knowledge, skills and self-confidence necessary to participate fully in the development process.' The Social Summit has gone further and listed a whole range of requirements for women's empowerment, such as 'effective measures, including through the enactment and enforcement of laws, and implement policies to combat and eliminate all form of discrimination, exploitation, abuse and violence against women and children', and removing 'the remaining restrictions on women's rights to own land, inherit property or borrow money, and ensure women's equal right to work'.

International human rights law defines basic rights and freedoms and also their limitations. If limitations do not form part of analysis, human rights appear as a catalogue of rights which may be mutually conflicting, and whose conflicts jeopardize their consistent application. For example, public health is explicitly envisaged as grounds on which individual rights and freedoms may be limited. Another important limitation is embodied in the protection of the rights of others; nobody is allowed to abuse individual rights or freedoms if this negates the equal rights and freedoms of others.

Freedom of religion is often counterpoised to access to family planning, but also to the postulate of equal rights for women and girls, particularly within the family. Much controversy has been generated with regard to family planning. The fact that many countries have submitted reservations to the specific provisions of international human rights treaties on family planning, most recently also to the final document of the International Conference on Population and Development (ICPD), Cairo, September 1994, accepting internationally mandated or recommended policies only to the extent to which they conform to their domestic, religious or customary law, has created many objections and much criticism, but not as yet decisive action to uphold international human rights law. The 1993 World Conference on Human Rights, held in Vienna, called for the 'eradication of any conflicts which may arise between the rights of women and the harmful effects of certain traditional or customary practices, cultural prejudices and religious extremism, thus reinforcing demands for full application of international human rights law.

The human rights documents emanating from Islamic organizations illustrate an approach which indicates that human rights standards are not defined uniformly in all parts of the world. Thus the Cairo Declaration, adopted by the 1990 Islamic Conference of Foreign Ministers, postulates that 'the husband is responsible for the support and welfare of the family', expressing the Shari'a principle of men's guardianship over and superiority to women. A woman is deemed equal to a man in dignity, but does not have equal rights: a woman 'has rights to enjoy as well as duties to perform; she has her own civil entity and financial independence, and the right to retain her name and lineage'. The notion of the family is based on marriage and 'both the foetus and the mother must be protected and accorded special care'. Such approaches point to the fact that international human rights instruments were adopted during earlier decades with an assumption that all countries would be governed by secular rather than religious law. An important reason for difficulties in the application of human rights is therefore the fact that quite a few countries have adopted religious law to govern both the public and the private sphere.

This was not anticipated by the drafters of human rights instruments, who had assumed that freedom of religion would constitute one out of many human rights and that national laws would be secular rather than religious. Ensuring compatibility of religious and human rights law has become one of the main controversies today, when the geopolitical map of the world has changed. It is sufficient to recall that, at the time of the Universal Declaration of Human Rights, UN membership was less than one-third of today's. There are, however, two distinct visions of what human rights are: the focus on state sovereignty is increasingly being replaced by an emphasis on state responsibility. Regarding women, it has been stressed, for example, that 'in the Asia-Pacific region, women's rights are violated by increasingly militant assertions of religious and ethnic identity; the fact that these violations often take place through private actors is used by States as a pretext for failing to counter them as transgressions of human rights'.

Besides differences in the approach to the status of women within the family originating in religious or other societal norms, the role of the family as an entity has yet to be defined in international human rights law. The International Year of the Family (1994), proclaimed by the United Nations, drew international attention to the insufficient emphasis that the family had obtained in human rights, in development, or even in population policies. The focus of human rights on the individual vested each member of the family with a set of rights, while the rights of the family as a unit remain undefined. Moreover, the earlier tendency of governments to replace traditional family functions with social provision further undermined the rights of the family as a unit. The detrimental impact of this process has become obvious in many countries where the dominant development pattern has caused the disintegration of extended families, while their functions have not been taken over by public bodies. The International Year of the Family proposed the reversal of this orientation, and implicitly a departure from the excessive individualism typical of Western Europe and North America, suggesting that 'programmes should support families in the discharge of their functions, rather than provide substitutes for such functions'.

Extensive research has been carried out into factors influencing decision making on family size, and results have often pointed to old-age support in the motivation to have large families. It is significant that regional human rights instruments, those originating in Africa and in the Middle East for example, include the obligation of children to provide for their aged parents, thus incorporating into human rights family solidarity between generations. Such provisions seem alien to the Western notion of human rights, but are common in other regions. The obvious implication for the design of population policy is a broadening of the coverage of national social security systems as an indirect method of influencing decisions on family size. However, such indirect measures rarely form part of population policies, recently even less so, owing to financial stringency affecting the entire social sector in both developing and industrialized countries.

The human rights definition of an adequate living standard postulates the family, not the individual, as the bearer of this right and thus the 'unit of measurement' in defining the standard of living. The standard of living encompasses food, clothing, housing, medical care and social services. This right, as much as other economic and social rights, has been relatively disregarded in international human rights standards in terms of definitions of its nature and scope, and corresponding governmental obligations.

The right to social security is included in many international human rights instruments and, although formulations vary the essence of this right is to secure a minimum livelihood for everybody in circumstances beyond the person's control which jeopardize his or her survival. Old-age pensions are part of most social security schemes and thus eliminate, in theory at least, the necessity of parents to rely on their children to provide for their security in old age. In practice, particularly in Africa and Asia, the coverage of social security schemes is limited to the civil service, industry and commerce, thus leaving beyond their reach the bulk of the population. The gap between governmental willingness and ability to exercise traditional family functions constitutes an important factor in family planning; failure to recognize this leads easily to ineffective population policies, which necessarily affect women because of their reproductive role.

Females at Par

The low worth of the female child, evidenced in the extreme practice of 'femicide', has been made one of the principal targets in international efforts to overcome the continuing prejudice against the female part of humanity. Gender discrimination may start before birth. A girl child is considered a liability not an asset, to the family into which she is to be born. She becomes an asset to the family into which she is married if she can bear male children. The emergence of traditional practices on the human rights agenda in the 1970s, and the subsequent broadening and deepening of the understanding of what traditional practices are, and what effects they have on women, provide a significant contribution to the design of population policies. At first, traditional practices harmful to women's health and lives had been confined to genital mutilation, but it was soon realized that they reach much further and sometimes lead to death.

The preference given to sons is a reflection of patriarchal society and is worldwide. This constitutes a fact that many would not associate with human rights. Parents who prefer a son to a daughter are not breaching any law, nor could law ever attempt to outlaw people's wishes. The preference for sons becomes an important human rights issue when it results in discrimination against female children, ultimately in femicide. Perhaps the strongest incentive to address 'son' preference within population policies comes from the World Bank, which has argued that it jeopardizes the lowering of fertility rates:

> In China the one-child policy has been challenged by an apparent preference for sons. The same bias in favour of sons exists in Korea, and has been partly responsible for keeping the total fertility from declining to replacement level. To counteract this bias, governments need public information campaigns and legal reforms of inheritance, property rights, and employment, Incentives might also be offered to one-child families with girls, such as lower educational and medical costs.

The human rights movement in India placed 'son' preference in the human rights context. Indian human rights organizations addressed the use of amniocentesis (originally designed to detect genetic abnormalities of a foetus, but widely applied to determine its sex), "and prompted the adoption of legislation to outlaw this practice which, in fact, amounted to femicide: data revealed that female, not male, foetuses were aborted." Statistical evidence of gender discrimination was gathered and became a publicly debated issue. The 1991 Indian Census revealed the effects of gender discrimination: the sex ratio decreased from 934 women per 1000 men in 1981 to 929 in 1991. This relatively small decrease in the sex ratio, translated into absolute numbers, becomes alarming: estimates of 'vanished women have' reached one hundred million for Asia. A study into health implications of sex discrimination suggested that causes of 'son' preference be addressed:

> Long-term measures to deal with the phenomenon of 'son' preference would include enactment and implementation of legislation against discrimination on the grounds of sex; provision of adequate social security for older people so that a son is no longer a must for security in old age; abolition of practices such as dowry and bride price; and changing laws to enable women to maintain their maiden name and pass it on to their children so that continuation of the family name is not threatened by non-birth of a son.

Protection of girls from early marriage represents a good example of the need to counter a widespread and historically prevalent practice. The right of everyone to marry and to found a family is conditional upon free consent, while such consent cannot be validly given by children. Knowledge of the widespread practice of child marriages prompted the adoption of the 1962 Convention on Consent to Marriage, Minimum Age for Marriage and Registration of Marriages. This Convention has had a minuscule number of ratifications. The small number of countries bound by this Convention reflects the fact that marriages of young girls are not only widespread, but also all too rarely challenged as a human rights issue. Data reported to the United Nations, although incomplete and sometimes outdated, are illustrative of the problem: Gambia does not have any minimum age for marriage; in Kenya the minimum age is 9; eight countries keep the minimum age for girls at 12 (Chile, Ecuador, Ethiopia, Honduras, Lebanon, Sri Lanka, Trinidad and Tobago, and United Arab Emirates); in Iran it is 13; and 12 countries have the minimum age of 14 (Argentina, Bolivia, Colombia, El Salvador, Guatemala, Guyana, Madagascar, Malta, Mexico, Nicaragua, Peru and Spain). All these countries implicitly recognize that girls of compulsory school age can be married. It is indicative that Asian countries, such as China and Korea, have raised the minimum age for marriage to above 20 for girls.

Law generally prescribes younger ages for marriage for women than for men, for girls than for boys. Statistics on women's age at marriage, where these are available, tend to reflect officially registered marriages in urban centres and thus report the average age at marriage of 20, or even higher. Official statistics can therefore be misleading rather than revealing. Child marriages remain regularly unrecorded and unreported, even in those countries which have enacted laws prohibiting them. Such laws often remain unenforced. World's Women reported: 'In Mauritania, 39% of girls are married by age 15 and 15% have already given birth. In Bangladesh, 73% of girls are married by the age 15, and 21% have at least one child." In Nigeria, which has no statutory minimum age for marriage, the fertility survey of 1981/1982 found that 25 per cent of women were married by the age of 14, 50 per cent by the age of 16, and 75 per cent by the age of 18. The majority of girls thus married while they were still children according to the Convention on the Rights of the Child.

Protection of Rights

The World Conference on Human Rights (Vienna, June 1993) created a precedent by including equal rights of women in the main body of its final document(s), and thus created a platform for the translation of this commitment into holding governments accountable for safeguarding women's equal rights. The Vienna Declaration and Programme of Action achieved a veritable precedent by incorporating women's human rights into the mainstream of reaffirmed human rights principles and also into the agreed programme of action for their implementation.

This happened, much as with other improvements, following worldwide mobilization around equal rights for women. The sheer number of non-governmental organizations' initiatives and proposals aimed at placing women's human rights on the agenda of the 1993 World Conference was impressive. Specific proposals to redress the neglect of women's rights on the global human rights agenda came from all corners of the world. In the words of the NGO Forum which took place during the Conference: 'in all regions it has been found that the United Nations and Governments have by and large failed to promote and protect women's human rights, whether civil and political or economic, social and cultural'.

The many and varied proposals also testified to the fact that demands to respect and protect women's equal rights are universal. Proposals addressed all levels, from global to individual; all actors, governmental and non-governmental, public and private; all sectors, from education and health to employment or international development cooperation, and to international migration or environmental protection; all methods of action, from legislative reform to legal literacy; last but not least, they pertained to all areas of human activity. This also demonstrated the growing awareness that:

> any strategy aimed at raising the status of women by using or confronting the law should include not only formal legal remedies and methods, but also political ones as well. Effecting desired changes in legislation requires an organized, conscious constituency, able to articulate grievances and exert influence. Drafting new legislation and building persuasive arguments to justify it are technical tasks and require legal skills and

methods. Most strategies will require a combination of legal and political methods.

The fact that equal rights of women are not recognized in an country, and thus women remain victimized by de jure discrimination, not only unequal possibilities for the exercise of nominally equal rights, received an implicit mention in the final document of the Vienna Conference in one important aspect, namely the conflict between equal human rights and religious or customary laws which deny them. The general affirmation of the universality of human rights opened the way for its specification relating to equal rights of women in the Vienna Declaration and Programme of Action.

Nevertheless, the 'escape clause' that accompanied this general reaffirmation of universality of human rights - the need to bear in mind national and regional particularities - was repeated with respect to women in the Programme of Action. It calls on states to take measures to counter practices of discrimination against women, embodied in 'intolerance and related violence based on religion or belief and in compliance with their international obligations and with due regard to their respective legal systems'. This was followed by a reference to the rights of the child, where states were urged to 'repeal existing laws and regulations and remove customs and practices which discriminate against and cause harm to the girl-child' and also relating to violence against women, where the Programme of Action calls for the 'eradication of any conflicts which may arise between the rights of women and the harmful effects of certain traditional or customary practices, cultural prejudices and religious extremism'.

During the preparations for the Vienna Conference, the Commission on Human Rights adopted on 8 March 1993 its first resolution on 'integrating the rights of women into the human rights mechanisms of the United Nations', which stressed its wish 'to ensure that information concerning violations of the rights of women is integrated regularly and systematically into all United

Nations mechanisms for the promotion, protection and implementation of human rights'. The Commission reminded the UN Centre for Human Rights that it had been requested to utilize gender-disaggregated data in preparing studies for the World Conference and further instructed it 'to ensure that special rapporteurs, experts and working groups are fully apprised of the particular ways in which the rights of women are violated. The Sub-Commission on Prevention of Discrimination and Protection of Minorities recommended:

> that information on the equality and empowerment of women, and their access to equality in education, work, health and literacy, be included in States' reports to all human rights monitoring bodies and not only to the Committee on the Elimination of Discrimination against women.

Moreover, the conceptual abyss between 'women' and 'human rights' is being slowly overcome. Efforts to redress the damage caused by genderless development policies were hampered by the invisibility of gender distinctions in the data used in conventional development research and planning. Thus, women's participation in the labour force was under reported, women's work ignored, women's ownership of land or access to agricultural loans unknown and wage differentials by sex impossible to document. Genderless categories such as 'peasants'/the rural poor' or 'the landless' prevailed. Only after the gathering of gender-specific data have inequalities become visible and gender discrimination been documented. The 1989 World Survey on the Role of Women in Development noted 'a dramatic increase of research on economic variables taking the factor of sex into account'.

The search for causes of harm to women identified institutionalized discrimination against women in virtually every aspect of development: political, economic, social, cultural, and—last but not least legal. Gender inequalities are often reflected in, and strengthened by, discriminatory laws. These legalize the denial of equal rights to women. Law has not conventionally constituted an area of primary concern in development, which has recently been redressed through increasing insistence on the recognition and protection of human rights in development. Participation in development includes taking part in decision making, not only in carrying out development projects. The recognition of women's rights therefore encompasses all aspects and all levels of development. Moreover, it spans the full range of the rights of women: civil, cultural, economic, political and social. The Jakarta Declaration for the Advancement of Women in Asia and the Pacific is a good example. Its strategy towards participation and empowerment is based on full protection of all women's human rights as its necessary prerequisite.

Within the [Economic and Social Commission for Asia and the Pacific] region, gender inequality remains embedded in legislation on marriage and the family legislation that defines household obligations and the intra-household distribution of authority. Inequality also persists in matters pertaining to nationality, inheritance, land tenure, ownership and control of property, agricultural co-operatives, and access to credit.

The sequence of UN-organized global conferences in the 1990s makes possible a review of increasing difficulties in affirming adherence to universally applicable norms. The World Conference on Human Rights can be seen, with the benefit of hindsight, as having opened the way towards preference for regional and national standard setting. The International Conference on Population and Development (ICPD) in Cairo, affirmed universally recognized rights, but posited national sovereignty as the ultimate guide to the implementation of all recommendations. Moreover, the Cairo document was adopted with reservations.' It stated that:

> the implementation of the recommendations contained in the Programme of Action is the sovereign right of each country, consistent with national laws and development priorities, with full respect for the various

> religious and ethical values and cultural backgrounds of its people, and in conformity with universally recognized international human rights.

The Preamble noted that, 'while the International Conference on Population and Development does not create any new international human rights, it affirms the application of universally recognized human rights standards to all aspects of population programmes', but added immediately that 'the Programme of Action will require the establishment of common ground, with full respect for the various religious and ethical values and cultural backgrounds.'

The Beijing Conference conformed to the practice established at ICPD one year earlier, and included at the beginning of the Platform for Action a clause which emphasizes sovereignty in implementing recommended approaches and actions, which is accompanied by a list of potentially self-contradictory values which should guide states in translating words into deeds:

> The implementation of this Platform, including through national laws and the formulation of strategies, policies, programmes and development priorities, is the sovereign responsibility of each State, in conformity with all human rights and fundamental freedoms, and the significance of and full respect for various religious and ethical values, cultural backgrounds and philosophical convictions of individuals and their communities should contribute to the full enjoyment by women of their human rights in order to achieve equality, development and peace.

The fact that inter-governmental consensus seems more difficult to reach with every subsequent global conference should not overshadow the fact that much has been accomplished in international standard-setting. The progress in tackling human rights of women during the past four decades is noticeable. While the early efforts in standard-setting were aimed against the discriminatory heritage of humanity, the 1970s marked an orientation towards 'modernity'. It was realized that development might harm women rather than benefiting them: when introduced into an unequal society, development tended to reinforce the pre-existing inequalities. The particular feature of human rights is that respect for them does not occur spontaneously; improvements in human rights are not a necessary corollary of development. Therefore human rights constitute governmental obligations.

The Fourth World Conference on Women, held in Beijing in 1995, included as its first priority area 'increasing awareness among men and women of women's rights under international conventions and national law'. The range of important issues which have yet to be addressed include guarantees for equal political representation of women, attention to human rights of women in the administration of justice, and the need to abolish gender-specific criminal offences. They show how far standard-setting should go in the future so as to fully address all gender-specific issues throughout the global human rights agenda.

The Beijing Conference gave women's human rights less prominence than had been expected, or perhaps hoped for. The most important reason for this is that humman rights norms are set in treaties rather than by inter-governmental meetings, which are preceded by a lengthy process of agreeing and disagreeing, which is carried out within the framework of human rights law in existence.

Worldwide violence affects the lives of millions of women, in all socio-economic and educational classes. It cuts across cultural and religious barriers, impeding the right of women to participate fully in society. Violence against women takes a dismaying variety of forms, from domestic abuse and rape to child marriages and female circumcision. All are violations of the most fundamental human rights.

In a statement to the Fourth World Conference on Women in Beijing in September 1995, the then United Nations Secretary-

General, Boutros Boutros-Ghali, said that violence against women is a universal problem that must be universally condemned. But he said that the problem continues to grow.

The Secretary-General noted that domestic violence alone is on the increase. Studies in 10 countries, he said, have found that between 17 per cent and 38 per cent of women have suffered physical assaults by a partner.

In the Platform for Action, the core document of the Beijing Conference, Governments declared that "violence against women constitutes a violation of basic human rights and is an obstacle to the achievement of the objectives of equality, development and peace."

The issue of the advancement of women's rights has concerned the United Nations since the Organisation's founding. Yet the alarming global dimensions of female-targeted violence were not explicitly acknowledged by the international community until December 1993, when the United Nations General Assembly adopted the Declaration on the Elimination of Violence against Women.

Until that point, most governments tended to regard violence against women largely as a private matter between individuals, and not as a pervasive human rights problem requiring State intervention.

In view of the alarming growth in the number of cases of violence against women throughout the world, the Commission on Human Rights adopted resolution 1994/45 of 4 March 1994, in which it decided to appoint the Special Rapporteur on violence against women, including its causes and consequences.

As a result of these steps, the problem of violence against women has been drawing increasing political attention.

The Special Rapporteur has a mandate to collect and analyse comprehensive data and to recommend measures aimed at eliminating violence at the international, national and regional levels. The mandate is threefold :

— To collect information on violence against women and its causes and consequences from sources such as governments, treaty bodies, specialised agencies and inter-governmental and non-governmental organisations, and to respond effectively to such information;

— To recommend measures and ways and means, at the national, regional and international levels, to eliminate violence against women and its causes, and to remedy its consequences;

— To work closely with other special rapporteurs, special representatives, working groups and independent experts of the Commission on Human Rights.

Some females fall prey to violence before they are born, when expectant parents abort their unborn daughters, hoping for sons instead. In other societies, girls are subjected to such traditional practices as circumcision, which leave them maimed and traumatised. In others, they are compelled to marry at an early age, before they are physically, mentally or emotionally mature.

Women are victims of incest, rape and domestic violence that often lead to trauma, physical handicap or death.

And rape is still being used as a weapon of war, a strategy used to subjugate and terrify entire communities. Soldiers deliberately impregnate women of different ethnic groups and abandon them when it is too late to get an abortion.

The Platform for Action adopted at the Fourth World Conference on Women declared that rape in armed conflict is a war crime and could, under certain circumstances, be considered genocide.

Secretary-General Boutros-Ghali told the Beijing Conference that more women today were suffering directly from the effects of war and conflict than ever before in history.

"There is a deplorable trend towards the organised humiliation of women, including the crime of mass rape," the Secretary-General said. "We will press for international legal action against those who perpetrate organised violence against women in time of conflict."

A preliminary report in 1994 by the Special Rapporteur, Ms. Radhika Coomaraswamy, focused on three areas of concern where women are particularly vulnerable: in the family (including domestic violence, traditional practices, infanticide); in the community (including rape, sexual assault, commercialised violence such as trafficking in women, labour exploitation, female migrant workers, etc.); and by the State (including violence against women in detention as well as violence against women in situations of armed conflict and against refugee women). In the Platform for Action adopted at the Beijing Conference, violence against women and the human rights of women are two of the 12 critical areas of concern identified as the main obstacles to the advancement of women.

Governments agreed to adopt and implement national legislation to end violence against women and to work actively to ratify all international agreements that relate to violence against women. They agreed that there should be shelters, legal aid and other services for girls and women at risk, and counselling and rehabilitation for perpetrators. Governments also pledged to adopt appropriate measures in the field of education to modify the social and cultural patterns of conduct of men and women. And the Platform called on media professionals to develop self-regulatory guidelines to address violent, degrading and pornographic materials while encouraging non-stereotyped, balanced and diverse images of women.

Nuisance Identification

The Declaration on the Elimination of Violence against Women is the first international human rights instrument to exclusively and explicitly address the issue of violence against women. It affirms that the phenomenon violates, impairs or nullifies women's human rights and their exercise of fundamental freedoms.

The Declaration provides a definition of gender-based abuse, calling it "any act of gender-based violence that results in, or is likely to result in, physical, sexual or psychological harm or suffering to women, including threats of such acts, coercion or arbitrary deprivation of liberty, whether occurring in public or in private life."

The definition is amplified in Article 2 of the Declaration, which identifies three areas in which violence commonly takes place :

— Physical, sexual and psychological violence that occurs in the family, including battering; sexual abuse of female children in the household; dowry-related violence; marital rape; female genital mutilation and other traditional practices harmful to women; non-spousal violence; and violence related to exploitation;

— Physical, sexual and psychological violence that occurs within the general community, including rape; sexual abuse; sexual harassment and intimidation at work, in educational institutions and elsewhere; trafficking in women; and forced prostitution; and

— Physical, sexual and psychological violence perpetrated or condoned by the State, wherever it occurs.

The importance of the question of violence against women was emphasised over the last decade through the holding of several expert group meetings sponsored by the United Nations to draw attention to the extent and severity of the problem. In September 1992, the United Nations Commission on the Status of Women established a special Working Group and gave it a mandate to draw up a draft declaration on violence against women.

The following year, the United Nations Commission for Human

Rights, in resolution 1993/46 of 3 March, condemned all forms of violence and violations of human rights directed specifically against women.

The World Conference on Human Rights, held in Vienna in June 1993, laid extensive groundwork for eliminating violence against women. In the Vienna Declaration and Programme of Action, governments declared that the United Nations system and Member States should work towards the elimination of violence against women in public and private life; of all forms of sexual harassment, exploitation and trafficking in women; of gender bias in the administration of justice; and of any conflicts arising between the rights of women and the harmful effects of certain traditional or customary practices, cultural prejudices and religious extremism.

The document also declared that "violations of the human rights of women in situations of armed conflicts are violations of the fundamental principles of international human rights and humanitarian law," and that all violations of this kind—including murder, systematic rape, sexual slavery and forced pregnancy—require a particularly effective response."

Violence against women in the family occurs in developed and developing countries alike. It has long been considered a private matter by bystanders— including neighbours, the community and government. But such private matters have a tendency to become public tragedies.

In the United States, a woman is beaten every 18 minutes. Indeed, domestic violence is the leading cause of injury among women of reproductive age in the United States. Between 22 and 35 per cent of women who visit emergency rooms are there for that reason.

The highly publicised trial of O. J. Simpson, the retired United States football player acquitted of the murder of his former wife and a male friend of hers, helped focus international media attention on the issue of domestic violence and spousal abuse.

In Peru, 70 per cent of all crimes reported to the police involve women beaten by their husbands. In Pakistan, Prime Minister Benazir Bhutto strongly defended a 35-year-old mother of two who was severely burned by her husband; in a domestic dispute.

"There is no excuse for such a behaviour," the Prime Minister declared after visiting the hospitalised victim. "My presence here is to send a message to all those who violate Islamic teachings and defy laws of the land with their inhuman treatment of women. This will not be tolerated."

According to the Human Rights Commission of Pakistan, in the 400 cases of domestic violence reported in 1993 in the province of Punjab, nearly half ended with the death of the wife. According to the Special Rapporteur's report, many governments now recognise the importance of protecting victims of domestic abuse and taking action to punish perpetrators. The establishment of structures allowing officials to deal with cases of domestic violence and its consequences is a significant step towards the elimination of violence against women in the family.

The Special Rapporteur's report highlights the importance of adopting legislation that provides for prosecution of the offender. It also stresses the importance of specialised training for law enforcement authorities as well as medical and legal professionals, and of the establishment of community support services for victims, including access to information and shelters.

In many countries, women fall victim to traditional practices that violate their human rights. The persistence of the problem has much to do with the fact that most of these physically and psychologically harmful customs are deeply rooted in the tradition and culture of society.

According to the World Health Organisation, 85 million to 115 million girls and women in the population have undergone some form of female genital mutilation and suffer from its adverse health effects.

Every year an estimated two million young girls undergo this procedure. Most live in Africa and Asia, but an increasing number can be found among immigrant and refugee families in Western Europe and North America. Indeed, the practice has been outlawed in some European countries.

In France, a Malian was convicted in a criminal court after his baby girl died of a female circumcision-related infection. The procedure had been performed on the infant at home.

In Canada, fear of being forced to undergo circumcision can be grounds for asylum. A Nigerian woman was granted refugee status since she felt that she might be persecuted in her home country because of her refusal to inflict genital mutilation on her baby daughter.

There is a growing consensus that the best way to eliminate these practices is through educational campaigns that emphasise their dangerous health consequences. Several governments have been actively promoting such campaigns in their countries.

Son preference affects women in many countries, particularly in Asia. Its consequences can be anything from foetal or female infanticide to neglect of the girl-child over her brother in terms of such essential needs as nutrition, basic health care and education.

In China and India, some women choose to terminate their pregnancies when expecting daughters but carry their pregnancies to term when expecting sons.

According to reports from India, genetic testing for sex selection has become a booming business, especially in the country's northern regions. Indian gender-detection clinics drew protests from women's groups after the appearance of advertisements suggesting that it was better to spend $38 now to terminate a female foetus than $3,800 later on her dowry.

A study of amniocentesis procedures conducted in a large Bombay hospital found that 95.5 per cent of foetuses identified as female were aborted, compared with a far smaller percentage of male foetuses. The problem of son preference is present in many other countries as well. Asked how many children he had fathered, the former United States boxing champion Muhammad Ali told an interviewer: "One boy and seven mistakes."

Internal Atrocities

In some countries, weddings are preceded by the payment of an agreed-upon dowry by the bride's family. Failure to pay the dowry can lead to violence.

In Bangladesh, a bride whose dowry was deemed too small was disfigured after her husband threw acid on her face. In India, an average of five women a day are burned in dowry-related disputes—and many more cases are never reported.

Early marriage, especially without the consent of the girl, is another form of human rights violation. Early marriage followed by multiple pregnancies can affect the health of women for life.

The report of the Special Rapporteur has documented the destructive effects of marriage of female children under 18 and has urged governments to adopt relevant legislation.

Rape can occur anywhere, even in the family, where it can take the form of marital rape or incest. It occurs in the community, where a woman can fall prey to any abuser. It also occurs in situations of armed conflict and in refugee camps.

In the United States, national statistics indicate that a women is raped every six minutes. In 1995, the case of a Brazilian jogger raped and murdered in New York City's Central Park drew international attention once again to the problem. The incident occurred only a few years after an earlier sensational jogger-assault case in which the victim— an American assaulted in the same general area of the park —barely survived after her assailants left her for dead.

Relations between residents of the Japanese island of Okinawa and American GIs were thrown into turmoil in 1995 after two marines and a sailor allegedly kidnapped and raped a 12-year-old girl.

The Special Rapporteur's report underlines the importance of education to sensitise the public about the special horrors of rape, and of sensitivity training for the police and hospital staff who work with victims. In many countries sexual assault by a husband on his wife is not considered to be a crime: a wife is expected to submit. It is thus very difficult in practice for a woman to prove that sexual assault has occurred unless she can demonstrate serious injury. The report of the Special Rapporteur noted that light sentences in sexual assault cases send the wrong message to perpetrators and to the public at large: that female sexual victimisation is unimportant.

Sexual harassment in the workplace is a growing concern for women. Employers abuse their authority to seek sexual favours from their female co-workers or subordinates, sometimes promising promotions or other forms of career advancement or simply creating an untenable and hostile work environment. Women who refuse to give in to such unwanted sexual advances often run the risk of anything from demotion to dismissal.

But in recent years more women have been coming forward to report such practices—some taking their cases to court.

In her report, the Special Rapporteur stressed that sexual harassment constitutes a form of sex discrimination. "It not only degrades the woman," the report noted, "but reinforces and reflects the idea of non-professionalism on the part of women workers, who are consequently regarded as less able to perform their duties than their male colleagues."

Prostitution Problem

Many women are forced into prostitution either by their parents, husbands or boyfriends—or as a result of the difficult economic and social conditions in which they find themselves. They are also lured into prostitution, sometimes by 'mail-order bride' agencies that promise to find them a husband or a job in a foreign country. As a result, they very often find themselves illegally confined in brothels in slavery-like conditions where they are physically abused and their passports withheld.

Most women initially victimised by sexual traffickers have little inkling of what awaits them. They generally get a very small percentage of what the customer pays to the pimp or the brothel owner. Once they are caught up in the system there is practically no way out, and they find themselves in a very vulnerable situation.

Since prostitution is illegal in many countries, it is difficult for prostitutes to come forward and ask for protection if they become victims of rape or want to escape from brothels. Customers, on the other hand, are rarely the object of penal laws. In Thailand, prostitutes who complain to the police are often arrested and sent back to the brothels upon payment of a fine. The extent of trafficking in women and girl children has reached alarming proportions, especially in Asian countries. Many women and girl children are trafficked across borders, often with the complicity of border guards.' In one incident, five young prostitutes burned to death in a brothel fire because they had been chained to their beds. At the same time, sex tours of developing countries are a well-organised industry in several European and other industrialised countries.

The Special Rapporteur has called on governments to take action to protect young girls from being recruited as prostitutes and to closely monitor recruiting agencies.

Female migrant workers typically leave their countries for better living conditions and better pay— but the real benefits accrue to both the host countries and the countries of origin. For home countries, money sent home by migrant workers is an important source of hard currency, while receiving countries are able to find workers for low-paying jobs that might otherwise go unfilled.

But migrant workers themselves fare badly, and sometimes tragically. Many become virtual slaves, subject to abuse and rape by their employers. In the Middle East and Persian Gulf region, there are an estimated 1.2 million women, mainly Asians, who are employed as domestic servants. According to the independent human rights group 'Middle East Watch,' female migrant workers in Kuwait often suffer beatings and sexual assaults at the hands of their employers.

The police are often of little help. In many cases, women who report being raped by their employers are sent back to the employer—or are even assaulted at the police station. Working conditions are often appalling, and employers prevent women from escaping by seizing their passports or identity papers.

The report of the Special Rapporteur draws attention to the fact that there are many international instruments that can be used to prevent abuse against migrant women and suggests some measures to protect the human rights of migrant women.

Superlative Approach

Another concern highlighted in the Special Rapporteur's report is pornography, which represents a form of violence against women that "glamorises the degradation and maltreatment of women and asserts their subordinate function as mere receptacles for male lust." Violence against women by the very people who are supposed to protect them—members of the law enforcement and criminal justice systems—is widespread.

Women are physically or verbally abused; they also suffer sexual and physical torture. According to Amnesty International, thousands of women held in custody are routinely raped in police detention centres worldwide. The report of the Special Rapporteur underlines the necessity for States to prosecute those accused of abusing women while in detention and to hold them accountable for their actions. Rape has been widely used as a weapon of war whenever armed conflicts arise between different parties. It has been used all over the world: in Chiapas, Mexico, in Rwanda, in Kuwait, in Haiti, in Colombia.

Women and girl children are frequently victims of gang rape committed by soldiers from all sides of a conflict. Such acts are done mainly to trample the dignity of the victims. Rape has been used to reinforce the policy of ethnic cleansing in the war that has been tearing apart the former Yugoslavia.

The so-called 'comfort women'—young girls of colonised or occupied countries who became sexual slaves to Japanese soldiers during the Second World War—have dramatised the problem in a historical context. Many of these women are now coming forward and demanding compensation for their suffering from Japanese authorities. "Such rape is the symbolic rape of the community, the destruction of the fundamental elements of a society and culture— the ultimate humiliation of the male enemy," the report by the Special Rapporteur noted. It stressed the need to hold the perpetrators of such crimes fully accountable.

Women and children form the great majority of refugee populations all over the world and are especially vulnerable to violence and exploitation. In refugee camps, they are raped and abused by military and immigration personnel, bandit groups, male refugees and rival ethnic groups. They are also forced into prostitution. In her report, the Special Rapporteur proposes the following measures to be taken for the protection of women and girls in refugee camps: improvement of security, deployment of trained female officers at all points of the refugees' journey, participation of women in organisational structures of the camps and prosecution of government and military personnel responsible for abuse against refugee women.

In recent years some countries have taken significant steps towards improving laws relating to violence against women. For example :

— In July 1991, Mexico revised its rape law in several

important ways. A provision was eliminated that allowed a man who raped a minor to avoid prosecution if he agreed to marry her. Now judges are required to hand down a decision regarding access to an abortion within five working days.

— On 9 June 1994, the Organisation of American States adopted the Inter-American Convention to Prevent, Punish and Eradicate Violence against Women (also called Convention of Belam do Para), a new international instrument that recognises all gender-based violence as an abuse of human rights. This Convention provides an individual right of petition and a right for nongovernmental organisations to lodge complaints with the Inter-American Commission of Human Rights.

— In Australia, a National Committee on Violence against Women was established to coordinate the development of policy, legislation and law enforcement at the national level as well as community education on violence against women.

— In 1991, the government of Canada announced a new four-year Family Violence Initiative intended to mobilise community action, strengthen Canada's legal framework, establish services on Indian reserves develop resources to help victims and stop offenders, and provide housing for abused women and children.

— In Turkey, a Ministry of State for Women was established whose main goals are, among others, to promote women's rights and strengthen their role in economic, social, political and cultural life. Legal measures are being adopted towards the elimination of violence against women. The establishment of special courts to deal with violence is envisaged. Psychological treatment for abused women is also planned, along with the establishment of women's shelters around the country. Specially trained female police officers could provide assistance to victims of violence.

— In Burkina Faso, a strong advertising campaign by the government as well as television and radio programmes on the unhealthy practice of genital mutilation were launched to educate and raise public awareness about the dangerous consequences of such an 'operation'. A National Anti-Excision Committee was established in 1990 by the present head of State. Today, the practice of genital mutilation has been eliminated in some villages of Burkina Faso. In others, there has been an incredible drop in the number of girls excised: only 10 per cent of the girls are excised compared to 100 per cent 10 years ago.

— Some countries have introduced police units specially trained for dealing with spousal assault. In Brazil, specific police stations have been designated to deal with women's issues, including domestic violence. These police stations are staffed entirely by women.

These examples illustrate some steps taken at the national level towards the eradication of violence against women. Combating and eradicating this scourge require enhanced and concerted efforts to protect women at the local, national and international levels.

States have tended to adopt a passive attitude when confronted by cases of violations of women's rights by private actors. Most laws fail to protect victims or to punish perpetrators. Passing laws to criminalise violence against women is an important way to redefine the limits of acceptable behaviour.

States should ensure that national legislation, once adopted, does not go unenforced. State responsibility is clearly underlined in Article 4 of the Declaration on the Elimination of Violence against Women, which stipulates that "States should exercise due diligence to prevent, investigate and, in accordance with national legislation, punish acts of violence against women, whether those acts are perpetrated by the State or by private persons."

Any approach designed to combat violence must be twofold, addressing the root causes of the problem and treating its manifestations. Society at large, including judges and police officers, must be educated to change the social attitudes and beliefs that encourage male violence.

The meaning of gender and sexuality and the balance of power between women and men at all levels of society must be reviewed. Combating violence against women requires challenging the way that gender roles and power relations are articulated in society. In many countries women have a low status. They are considered as inferior and there is a strong belief that men are superior to them and even own them.

Changing people's attitude and mentality towards women will take a long time—at least a generation, many believe, and perhaps longer. Nevertheless, raising awareness of the issue of violence against women, and educating boys and men to view women as valuable partners in life, in the development of a society and in the attainment of peace are just as important as taking legal steps to protect women's human rights.

It is also important in order to prevent violence that non-violent means be used to resolve conflict between all members of society. Breaking the cycle of abuse will require concerted collaboration and action between governmental and non-governmental actors, including educators, health-care authorities, legislators, the judiciary and the mass media.

General Requirements

The human rights of women and girl child are an inalienable, integral and indivisible part of universal human rights. The full and equal participation of women in political, civil, economic, social and cultural life, at the national, regional and international levels, and the eradication of all forms of discrimination on grounds of sex are priority objectives of the international community.

7

Fundamental Rights of Women

As the universality and pervasiveness of violence against women cuts across geographical, cultural and ethnic boundaries, it also persists despite social changes. Difference being of cultural and temporally specific manifestations, and rarely of presence or absence of this violence.

A telling illustration of pervasiveness of violence against women through the ages is of the Indian society and its transition from traditional to modern Indian women have done us proud and have also been revered down the ages.

India probably is the only nation in the world which exclusively enshrines female deities in artistically built temples. The Meenakshi temple at Madurai, Ambabai temple at Kolhapur and the Shantadurga and Mahalaxmi temples at Goa are ample proof of the Hindu reverence for female deities. India has also been proud of women's extraordinary ventures in the field of welfare, politics, art, literature and of late, sports. However, these women who forged themselves undauntedly in a male dominated milieu are exceptions. These women established their identity due to their special upbringing, push of circumstances, familial factors and the motivation of freedom fighters and reformers. India boasted of a woman prime minister.

Currently too, we have women who have made a mark for themselves in fields hitherto reserved exclusively for men, for example P.T. Usha the sportswoman and Kiran Bedi, the Deputy Commissioner of Police. The truth, however, which stares us in the face, indicates clearly the pitiable condition of Indian womanhood trapped in the web of socio-cultural factors such as superstitions and blind faith perpetuated by a male dominated society. The saga of the Indian woman is riddled with cruel, inhuman and pathetic attacks on her physical, emotional, social, political, and even spiritual growth. Her struggle for survival continues from the womb to the tomb without respite.

Rights for Women

In order to state and analyse the various types of violence tampling her human rights beginning with the female foetus and going on till old age, the following rights have been discussed — the right to life, liberty and security of the person, right to education, right to work, the right to be free from torture and the right to knowledge.

Right to Life

Female Abortion and Infanticide : The struggle for survival continues throughout the woman's life from womb to tomb. The advent of amniocentesis in India has given yet another sound blow to this struggle. Prior to the Maharashtra Regulation of Use of Prenatal Diagnostic Techniques Act of 1988, both the municipal and governmental hospitals as well as private practitioners were conducting abortions of female foetuses. Although the Act is a deterrent, private practitioners have continued to conduct abortions with a sex bias. They are safeguarded by the Medical Termination of Pregnancy Act of 1971 which has legalised abortion under specific conditions such as the danger of the health of the mother and/or the child.

The Government of India has implicitly sanctioned female foeticide because, apart from Maharashtra and Goa, no other state has passed legislation against female foeticide following amniocentesis. The dire need of such a law at a national level has often been discussed at various fora but, as yet, there is no universal law banning sex specific abortion. In fact, amniocentesis is propagated through advertisements which influence the psychology of parents. There are advertisements in Delhi such as "Pay Rs. 500 now or Rs. 5 lakhs later (dowry)." It is estimated that between 1978 and 1983 as many as 78,000 female foetuses in India have been aborted.

In certain states, such as Gujarat, Rajasthan, U.P. and Tamil Nadu, female infants in some communities are murdered as soon as they are born. They are drowned in a basin of milk, poisoned by opium applied to the breasts of mothers, strangled to death or sacrificed at an altar to a god. Four out of ten of those killed are murdered with a wet towel. It is pitiable that the mother herself is asked to do these things. No questions are asked.

In the Bhatti community in Jaisalmer, Rajasthan, the sex ratio is 550 women to 1000 men, the all-India ratio being 929 women to 1000 men. There has been no *barat* for decades in this community. Rajendra Singh, a Congressman of Bharatpur, Rajasthan had made a statement that 34 girls in his community had been reportedly murdered soon after birth (*India Today* — October 1988).

Right to Education and Knowledge : Girls' education is generally neglected despite the constitutional provision for compulsory education for all upto the age of 14 years. The percentage of girls attending school varies from state to state, being sometimes ranging between 20-50 per cent.

Female literacy in India is 24.8 per cent as compared to the male literacy of 46.9 per cent. The right to education is indirectly related to violence against women, as it has been observed that education contributes to women's assertion of other rights such as decision-making. There is a direct relation between education of women and adoption of small family norm according to researchers in family planning.

Right to be Free from Torture : The Indian woman is a slave to the so-called institutionalised cultural shackles where she is relegated to right from birth. Her mobility is restricted within the four walls of the kitchen, her self expression is monitored and her thoughts influenced by others in her milieu. She is the victim of suspicion by her brothers, parents, husband and in-laws. The following illustration will suffice to prove the point.

In Dharavi, a large slum in Mumbai, a young man bashed the head of his sister because he suspected her of having an affair with a young man in the neighbourhood. The brother intended to kill his sister but she survived and now is a severely handicapped person totally dependent on him. In marital conflict cases, suspicion of the wife is a common reason. Some wives are brutally beaten, tortured and thrown out of their homes due to the husband's suspicion.

Prejudiced Attitude

Women take on additional responsibility of supplementary family income due to economic constraints and demands of improved lifestyles. Lower class women have, of course, always been working. In this area too, women do not have the freedom to regulate their lives. Research by Dr. Pramila Kapur indicates that earning women from the middle and upper middle classes have no control over their income. They are expected to hand over their salary to their in-laws and forfeit all their rights over it. Coping with the homefront and office the alcoholic husbands squandering away their wives, earnings and the suspicions about the woman's character further aggravate the situation. There was a case of a lady doctor who was given only Rs. 2 daily for her expenses by her in-laws. The male dominance is all-pervading and there are implicit assumptions that the wife should have a lesser designation at the work place and earn a lower salary than her husband. Gender bias at work expects a woman executive to "look like a woman, behave like a lady, think like a man and work like a dog" ("Gender Bias" *Times of India*, 2.8.1993). Junior women lawyers report molestation by male lawyers. Molestations at the work place are reported by a few bold women while others suffer in silence.

Countless cases both in rural as well as urban areas are recorded. Dalit women fall a prey to the lust of the land owners and the other affluent individuals in the rural areas. There are cases of the anganwadi workers being abused sexually or otherwise by the male senior officers. In Mumbai, recently there were two reported cases of women lecturers being harassed by their seniors because of their refusal to satisfy the sexual demands of higher-ups. The case of the air-hostess molested by a senior minister is still fresh in our minds. Discrimination is still prevalent in the matter of wages paid to male and female casual labourers. In the earthquake-affected region of Latur, women were paid Rs. 8 per day for casual labour while men were paid Rs. 20.

Most women have no freedom to select their careers. Elders in the family, neighbours and friends influence young women to take up stereotyped jobs hitherto reserved for women such as nursing and teaching. In the cities the scenario is different. We do observe women gradually coming out of homes. And yet, they have to work doubly hard to prove their efficiency to keep their status. At an interview of women executives on TV it was stated that in order to keep their positions and climb the career ladder, they needed to be consistent, persevering, professional, confident, analytical, objective in interpersonal relationships, patient and continuously strive for knowledge and efficiency. The demands on male executives are not so numerous nor strong.

Marriage in Early Age

In the matter of marriage too, women have no choice. Most marriages are arranged by the families of the groom and bride. In the cities parents of a few communities in the upper middle and upper classes give the freedom to their daughters to select their marriage partners. Even though there are restrictions based on religion, caste and community.

In spite of the Child Marriage Restraint Act passed in the early part of this century, infants are being married in their cradles, in Rajasthan. Early marriage, frequent pregnancies and deliveries take their toll and 13 per cent of deaths before the woman reaches her 25th year are due to complications in child birth. Maternal mortality is the main cause of death among women in the reproductive stage. It is estimated that maternal mortality in India is 500 per 100,000 live births. The danger of death is the greatest when the mother is below 20 years and above 35 years. The average Indian woman becomes pregnant 8 times, produces 6-7 children out of which 4 survive. It seems as if 8 per cent of her reproductive life is gone for pregnancy and lactation (Dr. Shanti Ghosh. *The Girl Child in India*, 1993).

The process of arranging the marriage and the ceremony itself is a humiliatory experience for the prospective bride. In Maharashtra the groom and his family are invited to tea party by the bride's parents. The bride is to be asked to prepare snacks and tea and serve them to their guests. Her culinary and other skills are praised by her parents in order to impress the parents of the potential groom. The girl is asked questions about her education, hobbies, friends and other matters and thus the party ends. The boy is rarely asked any questions. The matter of dowry is finalised at such meetings. The humiliation for a girl is worsened when she is rejected.

Dowry System

Among the cases of violence against women, the problem of

dowry is the most brutal and oft-repeated. It is estimated that a bride is burnt every two days in India, thus giving India the unenviable reputation of being the country with an unbeaten record of bride burning.

The Statistics : The Dowry Prohibition Act of 1961, amended in 1986, was meant to be a deterrent to this evil custom. The reality, however, was different. The number of dowry deaths increased from 1912 in 1987 to 5157 in 1991. It is estimated that one woman is burnt to death every five days in India for not bringing 'adequate' dowry.

Reasons for Non-redressal by Parents : It is difficult to estimate the exact figures in relation to dowry harassment and death because many cases are not reported. Women suffer in silence as they are conditioned to do so from childhood. Parents of the bride who is burnt to death, at times, do not pursue the matter in the court. Some of the reasons for such behaviour are as follows:

1. When the girls reach marriageable age the parents in their desire to fulfil their duties and also to lighten their burdens marry their daughters accepting all conditions of the grooms party. They are forced to borrow money from the moneylender, sell their property such as land in order to 'marry off ' their daughter. As a consequence, they are steeped in debt. They, therefore, are financially too weak to legally pursue the matter of their daughter's death and thus do not seek any redressal.
2. Parents thus resign themselves to fate feeling that it is futile to aggravate the matter as their daughter will not come back to life. They are also worried about the marriage of their other daughters, if any.
3. Being emotionally and physically exhausted in the nexus formed, at times, between the bridegroom's family, lawyers and the police, parents surrender.

4. In case of dying declarations taken in suspicious circumstances generally in cases of deaths due to burns, most women tend to state that their burns are due to an accident or that they have attempted suicide. This is due to the following reasons:
   (i) The victim's husband's family threatens her that if she tells the truth, her parents' family will be murdered.
   (ii) The dying woman is worried about her children's upbringing and future, in case, her husband is convicted.
   (iii) She is weary of the stigma which her children may have to suffer if their father is convicted.
   (iv) She is also apprehensive that if she survives, her husband and in-laws may again try to murder her.
   (v) She is afraid that if she lives, her life would be hell as she accused her in-laws of murder. Generally parents also disown their daughters in such cases.

A girl in India is brought up to be obedient, docile, patient and tolerant and self-sacrificing. In the urban areas girls from the middle and upper middle classes are educated and, at times, given occupational training. Some of them take up jobs before marriage. All this freedom ends with the marriage, which symbolically represents the *lakshman rekha*.

Justifications for Claiming Dowry

1. Most men assume obtaining dowry is their 'birth right'. The groom's parents justify dowry by stating that they have made tremendous financial sacrifices in order to educate their son. Therefore, they expect to recover the expenses by obtaining dowry from the bride.
2. The groom and his parents believe that the bride will be an eternal economic burden on them. They therefore demand dowry to make up for her lifetime expenses.

3. The myth that dowry is considered a monopoly of the affluent classes is not true because the lower classes in the process of identifying with the rich have imbibed some of the unethical customs.
4. There is an impression that only the Hindus demand dowry, in reality except for Zoroastrians, all other religious groups have the custom of dowry. However, there are some sections in each religious group which do not believe in dowry this differs from family and individual beliefs.
5. It is the mother-in-law who demands dowry. We have often heard that woman is her own enemy. In our experiences and observations we find that this is not true. In the 54 cases of dowry harassment studied by the students placed in Sakhya, the Anti-Dowry Guidance Cell, only in 8 cases was the mother-in-law exclusively responsible for demanding dowry and harassing the daughter-in-law. Mothers-in-law are made to do the dirty job representing the wishes of the family, unlike common impression of their villainous role in perpetrating the crime. Their acts are rationalized due to the following reasons:

   (i) Her family coaxes her to demand dowry, stating that since she is elderly and a woman, the bride's family will not reject her demands. This is true in most cases as elderly women are still respected in most homes.

   (ii) The mother-in-law demands dowry so that she, in turn, can give it to her daughter. Who then is the cause of dowry? Only the mother-in-law?

   (iii) The mother-in-law, in most cases, has herself been exploited, suppressed and victimised as a young daughter-in-law. She, therefore, nurtures hostility against those who harassed her and displaces these feelings onto her daughter-in-law. The dynamics can be understood in the theory postulated by Paulo

Freire, namely, that the oppressed internalise the qualities and behaviour of the oppressor.

6. Girls in their desire to take maximum assets and riches at their marriage time which would result in their happiness also welcome taking dowry to their new homes. We cannot generalise because most girls are so conditioned as to adjust to any type of life.
7. Giving large sums of money and expensive presents need not be a ticket to a happy married life. Girls have been harassed regardless of the quantum of dowry.

The Virtual Reality of Dowry

1. Dowry is not a one shot affair. It is an unending ritual taking its toll at every festival and celebration throughout married life.
2. Most people are vaguely aware of the law against dowry. They are, therefore, doubly careful in camouflaging their demands. They suggest that the bride's parents present a 'Honda' or a 'Maruti' car to the groom so that he can return home from work early enough to take his wife out in the evening!
3. Most brides suffer harassment in silence for many years. They do so as they are conditioned to believe that after a girl's marriage her permanent place is with her husband and in-laws. Moreover they fear that their parents would have to suffer social ostracism. There have been incidents of young unmarried girls committing suicide to protect their parents from the burden of dowry.
4. Men who do not take dowry are not thought much of their community. It is felt that they might have some shortcoming in them which could be the reason for their no dowry marriage.
5. In dowry death cases (mostly due to burns) most women give a false dying declaration stating that the burns are

due to an accident or that they have attempted suicide. Appreciations of the future for their children and parents make them prevent their in-laws and husband from being punished by giving false declaration.

Battering of Wife

Wife beating is generally accepted as a cultural phenomenon. Most men take it upon themselves to beat their wives to 'improve them'. Women too tolerate it as a part of life. It is perceived as a token of the husband's affection. The police too, especially of the lower ranks, all view it as a societal norm. The legislation against physical and mental torture (Sec. 498 A) is of recent origin. Unfortunately, there are lapses in its implementation.

Mental torture of the wife is equally injurious. It may be even more devasting than the physical assaults. It is manifested in the following forms — taunting the wife, insulting her in the presence of the children, guests and domestic help, ignoring her completely and cutting off communication with her.

In a case of harassing daugher-in-law, a home visit was paid to conduct a family interview. The wife was not permitted to participate in the interview saying that she was stupid and that he was the spokesman of the family. Insistence to interview was thoroughly criticized saying that 'Women libbers wreck families'.

In another case a marital conflict the working wife stated that her husband locked up all the kitchen gadgets such as the mixer, peeler and pressure cooker so that she had to spend more time in the kitchen and consequently report late for work. This case has now been solved.

Why the Wives Suffer?

The harassed wives suffer in silence because of the following reasons:

(a) They have been conditioned to obey their husbands.

(b) Culturally it is assumed that the wife will silently bear the assaults.

(c) They have no support as such. Their parental family and other relatives refuse to accept them back and bear the burden of supporting them and the children (if any) for the rest of their lives.

(d) They are ignorant of the provision in the law to safeguard their rights, as well as of shelter homes run by welfare organisations and the government.

(e) Even if they are aware of seeking redressal through law, they are brainwashed to keep the *Khandan ki Izzat* unblemished.

Rape by the husband is not as yet a cognisable offence in India. Women are conditioned to play a submissive role especially in the matter of sexual relations. Most husbands feel a sense of exclusive possession over their wives. Hence in sexual relations, the wife's consent is rarely taken. Cases have been reported to deviant sexual behaviour of the husband, for example, beating the wife prior to the sexual intercourse, burning her with cigarette butts or thrusting hard objects in her vagina. Refusal to give in to the insatiable sexual desire of the husband is interpreted as the result of her extramarital relations. She is therefore, 'duly punished'.

There was a case of murder of a young housewife in Mumbai. She had been married for eight months. Her husband was impotent but this was not revealed to her prior to their marriage. In his efforts to cure his impotency, the husband forced her to have sexual relations with his friends in his presence. She was also victimized by her brother-in-law and father-in-law. On one occasion when she strongly resisted her father-in-law's advances, he strangled her and then threw her out of their sixteenth floor apartment. But for the intervention of a passerby nurse, this case would have been registered as suicide because the in-laws made a statement to the police that the woman was mentally deranged. Cases of cruelty by the husband and his relatives have increased from 11603 in

1989 to 15949 in 1991 (*Social Welfare,* Vol. XXXIX, no. 11-12 Feb.-Mar. 1993).

Consumption of liquor is one of the prime causes of domestic violence and misery in the family. Liquor, foreign and indigenous is freely available in most Indian states. The hard-earned money of both the husband and wife is devoured by alcohol. Consequently, the wives resort to taking up extra jobs and hiding their income. Deaths' due to the consumption of alcohol are increasing but there is no statistical data available. It is estimated that the number of deaths due to spurious liquor exceeds the deaths due to communal riots. Many cases, however go unreported. The death of the husband due to liquor consumption places heavy burdens on the wife. She has to shoulder the entire responsibility of supporting her family if she has no grown-up children. At times, men have been blinded as a result of spurious liquor thus leaving the family in unending miseries.

Women Organisations

Passive Role of Women : The average Indian woman has no choice in relation to important events in her life such as marriage, parenthood, family planning, participation in community activities and divorce. "We have mouths but we use them only for crying", a young woman said in a camp conducted for rural women. The family, community and society in general, assume that women have to be told, nay ordered, to behave in accordance with the norms of the family community and society. The in-laws, especially the mother-in-law, play a strong part in the matter of the number of children that the couple has. The wife is often blamed, ostracised and even divorced for her inability to produce sons or in case of sterility. The small family norm has not been effective. Despite India's acceptance of family planning in 1952 as a national issue. There are, of course, regional differences. In the family planning programme it is the woman who is at the receiving end. Men are still reluctant to undergo vasectomy or to use condoms. Women are forced to undergo sterilization despite their ill health and protests. They are not involved neither in the selection of family planning methods nor in the matter of family size. On the other hand they have to suffer all the pain.

Women, especially from the low and middle income groups suffer from ill-health and malnutrition and are the worst suffers from contraceptive services. Women with loops inserted complain of heavy bleeding and backache. Lack of adequate follow-up services is a deterrent to the acceptance. of loops and other contraceptive devices or methods. The Indian Council of Medical Research (ICMR) intended to recruit 20,000 women for experimenting with NORPLANT through the medical college hospital even though a case registered against NORPLANT was still pending in the court (Karkal, July 1992). Men do not want to face any inconvenience and leave that for the woman 'a traditional beast of burden'.

Inadequate medical information supplied to patients, both men and women causes the break up of the family. To illustrate when a man undergoes vasectomy he has to be advised to get his semen tested periodically to ensure that it is free of sperms. In the interim period the couple has to be advised to utilise other contraceptive methods or devices. In some cases that is not done. When pregnancy occurs, the husband accuses his wife of infidelity and throws her out of the house thus causing family break-ups.

Voluntary efforts in the medical field have been geared mostly to women. While one appreciates the concern of the voluntary sector in relation to women and family planning, one wonders why similar efforts are not directed towards the males. Women from the low income groups have no privacy in their homes which prevents them from utilising devices such as the diaphram and jelly. Dr. Billing's ovulation method, though very sound, feasible and scientifically tested also cannot be utilised by all women. This method also requires that women have some privacy to test the vaginal mucous.

By and large, women in slums find it very difficult to stick to the schedule of oral pills. There have been cases when women have forgotten to take the pill for a few days and then have swallowed a whole lot of pills to make up the deficit. Most women do not know that a thorough medical examination is essential prior to the acceptance of this method nor are they aware of the positive and negative effects of the pills.

It is stated that one-fifth of 132 sterilisation camps surveyed by the ICMR had no life-saving drugs, as a result of which there were 180 deaths in Maharashtra, 92 in U.P., 86 in Gujarat, 82 in Kerala, 76 in Orissa and 66 in Andhra Pradesh from 1985 to 1987 (*Times of India,* 27th July, 1989).

In amniocentesis too women are not the ones to take a decision. Most of them are harassed for producing daughters and the choice of amniocentesis is imposed on them. Some are brainwashed to such an extent that they opt for an abortion. In a survey of 100 women at a Delhi clinic who underwent abortion following amniocentesis, most women said that they were taunted continuously by their in-laws for having given birth to a daughter ("Licence to Kill" *Grassroot Action*, 3rd Issue, April 1990).

The eldest male in the family is still the decision-maker in relation to familial issues with a few exceptions. It is only in minor matters such as those relating to the kitchen that the women can have their say.

Lack of Awareness of Methods of Family Planning : Eventhough T.V. has invaded all homes in the length and breadth of the country breaking all information barriers, how many utilise this opportunity? Interests of the rural women are limited to film songs and films. This leaves them ignorant about the functioning of their bodies, especially the reproductive system. Lack of sex education and the consequent faculty attitude towards sex and sexuality increases morbidity in women. Most women are ignorant of the types of contraceptives available, their advantages and disadvantages. An incident related by an institution working in the area of family planning in Tamil Nadu illustrates how women were taken for granted in this programme. The institution spread the word regarding the loop, motivated women in rural areas and inserted loops in a large number of women. It soon observed that the number of women coming for loop insertion decreased day by day. Exploration of this phenomenon revealed the rumour taking rounds that one or two women had large worms due to the loop. Investigations revealed that the loop inserted in these women had fallen out and was viewed as a large worm. One of the reasons for such miscommunication is the fact that the doctors had not explained the process of loop insertion to the women concerned. In the survey mentioned earlier, most women who underwent amniocentesis did not know the names of these tests nor their harmful effects.

Laws for Protection

Women are not aware of their legal rights nor are they aware of the political situation and its effects on the masses. In a study in Bihar it was found that most women knew about the right of inheritance to paternal property. The least known rights were the (MTP) Medical Termination of Pregnancy Act (among the rural and urban women of Gaya). Minimum Wages Act and Child Marriage Restraint Act (among Women of Bhojpur) and Widow Remarriage Act (among urban women of Madhubani) (Sachidananda Sinha, 1984). There is no question of assertion of their rights in respect of these laws. If women are ignorant of the laws passed in their interest.

The Government of India has recently passed legislation reserving 30 per cent of the seats for women in the gram panchayat (GP) and Zilla Parishad (ZP). Orientation programmes for these women at the ZP level are organised by voluntary organisations. In one such programme many of the participants lacked knowledge of the philosophy of reservations for women, the procedures of GP and ZP and their role therein. Some admitted that their husbands represent them at the meetings of GP or ZP. Those who were not educated said that when resolutions are passed at the meetings of GP, papers are sent to the homes of these women members for their thumb impression. Most women representatives do not take an active role in decision-making. They are merely 'nodders' at these meetings. One representative of a GP was beaten up for taking an active role in one of the meetings. She expressed her opinion on an issue very effectively and was applauded by all including her husband who was present at this meeting. When the couple returned home, the husband beat her mercilessly and asked her not to open her mouth henceforth. Some of these women are being monitored by their husbands and are forced to stand for the election of GP and ZP.

The following chart depicts a picture of some women's organisations in Bombay and their main area of work.

Name of the Organisation	Focal Point/Objectives
1. Majlis	Legislation for women and its implications.
2. Stree Hitakarni	Health and its implications for women.
3. Prerana	Problems of prostitutes and their children.
4. Sakhya	Eradication of dowry and management of marital conflicts.
5. Stree Mukti Sanghatana	Women's problems in general.
6. Maitrini	Status of women in terms of employment,
7. Mahila Dakshata Samiti	rights, violence against women, services available, etc.
8. Women's Forum	
9. Swadhar	

There are numerous other women's organizations spread all over India. SEWA of Ahmedabad concentrated on forming trade unions of women handcart-pullers has now expanded its field to women's self-employment as a whole. Similarly, Saheli in Delhi, Sathin in Rajasthan, Stree Adhar Kendra in Pune are some other organisations working towards the improvement of women's status.

All these organisations have shifted from a welfare approach to a development one. The improvement of women being their major thrust.

Role of Commission

Functions covered by the Commission : The NCW was set up on 31st January 1992 as per the National Commission for Women Act 1990. The mandate of the commission covers a wide range of functions which are summarised as under: (i) Investigate and examine the legal safeguards provided for women under the Constitution and other laws and recommend to government measures for their effective implementation. (ii) Review the existing provisions of the Constitution and other laws affecting women and recommend amendments to meet any lacunae, inadequacies or shortcomings in such laws. (iii) Look into complaints and take suo moto notice of matters relating to deprivation of women's rights and take up the issue with appropriate authorities. (iv) Take up studies/research on socio-economic issues. (v) Participate and advise on the planning process of socio-economic development of women and evaluate the progress made. (vi) Inspect jails, remand homes where women are kept under custody and seek remedial action where necessary.

While investigating cases of violation of safeguards for women and complaints relating to deprivation of women's rights the Commission has the powers of a civil court trying a suit. The Commission can summon any person and examine the person under oath.

In order to carry out the functions effectively, eleven expert committees have been set up on women- related issues to tender advice and suggest appropriate measures, for corrective action. A complaints and pre-litigation cell to resolve conflicts outside the legal proceedings is functioning with the active collaboration of counsellors deputed by NGOs.

As an autonomous statutory body, the Commission is working

relentlessly towards its goal and has adopted a holistic multipronged approach towards empowerment of women, taking up cudgels against legal, social, cultural as well as political barriers to their advancement. A number of bills have been proposed, which include the Marriage Bill, 1994 Compulsory Regulations of Marriage, Domestic Violence, etc.

Operative Formats

A number of important recommendations have been made by the National Commission for Women which include inter alia the following: (i) GPC be amended to provide that women should normally not be remanded to police custody; (ii) Bail be relaxed in three cases — where the accused is a woman, is ill, or is a juvenile; (iii) Speedy investigations and speedy trials should take place in respect of women undertrials; (iv) More women should be appointed in the police departments; (v) The investigating officers should not be authorized to publish the name of the victim; (vi) Mandatory training programmes on gender sensitization of the police and all those responsible for administration of justice should be organized regularly; (vii) The Legal Services Authority Act should be amended to incorporate provision for holding Parivarik Mahila Lok Adalats to ensure speedy justice to women; (viii) Sex education be included in the school curricula for adolescent girls and boys; (ix) A fund (statutory or otherwise) should be created for rehabilitation of rape victims. The sources of fund could be fine/penalty imposed on the accused, donations from charitable trusts and contributions from government and local bodies. Further vocational training/skill development centres-cum-production units should be set up by NGOs and local bodies for the benefit of victims of abuse and violence; (x) Community awareness and advocacy campaigns should be conducted for parents and local community members on the importance of girls' education and related needs; and (xi) Support forums should be set up to analyse policies and develop strategies for amending laws related to women and to promote an agenda for the betterment of women.

Nodal Working Agency

Programmes and Schemes : The Central Social Welfare Board established in 1953 and subsequently registered as a charitable company in the mid-sixties, has been serving the cause of women, children and other underprivileged groups through NGOs. In keeping with its objectives, the Central Social Welfare Board provides financial support and assistance for several need-based programmes which facilitate the socio-economic empowerment of women. These include Condensed Course of Education, Vocational Training Courses, Awareness Generation Camps, Voluntary Action Bureaus and Family Counselling Centres. The latter two schemes offer preventive and rehabilitative services to women who are victims of family violence and atrocities. These programmes are providing focal points for evolving social consciousness in respect of violence against women, and are helping them by adopting a "conciliatory approach"

The Voluntary Actions Bureau and Family Counselling Centres run by NGOs with financial support from Central Social Welfare Board follow a policy which leads to better integration of women within the family, rather than a policy which would lead to disintegration of the family as an institution. The family continues to be the basic social unit, with common interests and enjoys the advantage of a common front and can be a catalyst of change for the betterment of all its members.

Targets Ahead

The chart above depicts the area(s) of work selected by different women's organisations. However, all of them adopt different strategies in relation to their objectives. The main ones are as follows:

Micro Level Intervention : This involves dealing with individual cases in the setting of their families and immediate environment. It includes dealing with various types of groups, for example, groups of dowry-affected women.

The micro level is linked with the meso, exo and macro levels. The women's issues (or any other for that matter) are linked with other sub-systems of society, for example, education and health. It is important that the organisations working towards the empowerment of women study the impact of the micro-level system on women's issues and devise strategies to handle it. Issues such as the ineffective educational systems which is not geared to the consistent involvement of the girl child. The atrocious onslaught of contraceptives on women in the family welfare planning programme are raised.

Macro Level Intervention : Unless our efforts are not geared towards changes at the macro level they will go waste. The policy-makers have to be galvanised into action. Changes in the age-old laws, machinery for their implementation, projects for women and their functioning have to be scrutinised and geared to women's overall development. On the whole, most of the women's organisations have been working on the above mentioned lines. The establishment of the National Women's Commission followed by the state level commission is a big step towards the establishment of separate identities for women. These commissions operate at macro level but do take up individual cases if they involve a larger issue, for example rape. The National Commission in its attempt to review the law against rape and to effect changes in it has consulted women's organizations in various parts of India on this issue before final submission of its recommendations to the Central Government.

The problem of alcoholism has driven the village women of Tamil Nadu and Maharashtra to wage a war against this evil. There are distilleries galore in slums and villages. For ages together women have suffered the demonic attacks of alcohol on their families' health, economy and happiness in general. These women have organised themselves and forced the closure of distilleries in their vicinity. They have approached the state government to enact legislation accordingly. Thus, their power lies informing groups of like-minded women fighting for their causes.

International Linkages : Collaboration with international women's organisations is indispensable to effect global change in the status of women. They are one of the most powerful means to effective change in women's status. The Nairobi conference had set the ball rolling, here women all over the world unite once in two years to share their experiences and interventional strategies. The India-Canada conference on violence against women held in December 1993 was also an attempt in the same direction.

Seeking Implementation through Collaboration with Government Machinery : The Government on its part, makes efforts to stem violence against women. The Judiciary and the police system do make all the possible efforts towards this goal. The setting up of family courts and the enactment of Sec. 498A are the concrete forms of these efforts. The role of a women's organisation is that of a vigilant group to see to the proper implementation of these legal provisions. A few years ago, women's organisations in Mumbai observed that cases of mental cruelty against women were not registered by the Police under Sec. 498A. A recent development in the process of women's improvement is the collaboration with the police.

The College of Social Work, Nirmala Niketan, initiated students, placement in police stations in 1983, so as to sensitize the police to the social issues and to their role therein so as to effect good police-public relations. The common issues highlighted are those related to the status of women, prostitution, drugs, AIDS, street children and dowry. Accordingly, we give these inputs in the training of the police at various levels at different training centres. Similarly social work intervention in the area of women police constables (WPC) has also been initiated. Regular workshops are conducted for male police constables and officers and for WPCs. Small surveys are also conducted on the functioning of the police and reports are regularly submitted to the Commissioner of Police.

The Tata Institute of Social Sciences has instituted a special cell for women and children in the office of the Commissioner of Police as well as in one police station in Mumbai. Sakhya, a voluntary organisation has been granted permission to work in three police stations in Mumbai.

The widespread and rampant atrocities against women prompted the State Women's Commission to plan women's security cells in each of the 72 police stations in Mumbai. The Commission called a meeting of all women's organisations and explained the rationale for the Mahila Suraksha Samiti (Women's Security Cells) inviting volunteers to work through the police stations. The members of this Samiti will act as vigilant groups to ensure that the police deal justly in relation to women's issues, for example, dying declarations. The law states that a police officer and a Special Executive Magistrate be present to note the dying declarations of women dying under suspicious circumstances, the presence of relatives being prohibited. However, we find that this is not adhered to and the woman's in-laws force her to tell lies, thus rendering all laws ineffective.

The status and self esteem of women needs to be drastically uplifted and given their due share in all spheres.

There is a dire need to create awareness among different groups regarding the status of women, gender bias and injustice against women generally. The perceptions of youth regarding marriage, women's status and roles in the family need to be revised and changed. Young boys and girls need to develop skills to strengthen the bond of marriage and family life. Young women should learn to assert themselves in their families of origin and matrimony. They should be empowered to take firm decisions in relation to the selection of marriage partners, type of wedding, refusal to give dowry, number of children, type of contraceptives and other familial and non-familial matters. Men, too, need to realise the dignity of women and to appreciate their contribution in various fields.

In a workshop with a group of young girls and boys between the ages of 16 to 22 years belonging to the lower middle class with the above mentioned objectives, there was a question related to their reasons for marriage. The answers of all the boys indicated that they needed a wife to work at home. Their responses were as follows:

> "My mother is too old to do housework and hence I need a wife."
>
> "My parents can't work on our farm any more. Therefore, I want to marry so that my wife can take over from them." "I am the only earning member in my family, and my income is insufficient to support six family members. I, therefore, want to marry a working woman."

It was indeed sad to note that none of them said that they need a companion for life to share their joys and sorrows, to enjoy life's bounty together and to jointly achieve their goals in life. The girls had a more positive bent of mind and were emphatic in their decision to marry someone to share their joys and sorrows. In the subsequent session there was a mutual confrontation and the boys later stated that no one had earlier explained to them the significance of marriage.

Family life including sex education should be introduced in schools beginning with the nursery. The objective of such an education should be to impart scientific facts about sex and sexuality, roles and responsibilities in the family and to shape attitudes conducive to a happy family life without a gender bias.

Women's organisations are also becoming vigilant about the portrayals of women in the audio-visual media. Except for a few art serials, the woman in most commercial movies is portrayed as a sex bomb, a cantankerous wife/mother-in-law or an obedient and dutiful wife. Remarks about violence against women need to be scrutinized. A film named *Damini* portrays the courage of a woman who raises her voice against rape and the unjust judicial system. However, there are two sentences uttered by the barrister in the movie which are shocking.

Regarding a gang rape of a married domestic worker by the employer's son and his friends, he says: *Ladkon ne jo kuch kiya utni badi baat nahi hai. Jawani me to yeh sub kuch hota hi raheta hai.*" (There is nothing objectionable in what the boys have done. Such things keep happening in youth). Unfortunately this has gone unnoticed except for the letter to the Editors of Newspapers written by the author. One would have expected the PTAs of schools, women's organizations and the union of domestic workers to raise a hue and cry. Education of the masses in relation to violence against women could be imparted in the context of human rights.

The focus on women as an exploited, victimised and marginalised group is a recent development in the world. It has been now recognised that despite all their rights being violated, women have been suffering in silence. In India, the concept of Seeta/Savitri (dutiful wives) is imbibed in a girl's mind from the early stages of her life. A vigorous multi-pronged and multi-professional effort is needed to establish the woman as a human being in her own right. It is time to dispel myths, superstitions and misconceptions about woman and her duties and adopt a rational attitude towards the woman as a human being and not a beast of burden.

8

Equality with Men

Recently, a relationship has been established between International law and Human Rights. In fact, international human rights law is a branch of public international law, that is, the law which has been developed to regulate relations between entities having international personality, such as states, international organizations and possibly individuals. In order to understand the functioning of the various institutions charged with the supervision of human rights, it is necessary to have a basic appreciation of the salient aspects of the international legal systems. In the human rights context, international law possesses a dual quality, since it creates both the obstacles to effective human rights protection and provides the means for overcoming such obstacles.

Social Peace

This has been described by Brownlie as 'the constitutional doctrine of the law of nations'. It is also sometimes regarded as synonymous with the term 'independence'. In essence, it represents the totality of a state's rights in the conduct of its external relations and in the ordering of its internal affairs. This does not mean, however, that states are completely free to exercise their sovereignty or independence on both the external and internal planes, since they are subject to various limitations imposed on their activities by international law.

The main feature of the sovereign state is that it is entitled to exercise exclusive governmental control over its territory and persons therein subject to any contrary rules of international law. It is important to note, however, that states, being the pre-eminent subjects of the international legal systems, and the creators of law within that system, have the primary task of participating in the formulation of rules by which their conduct is limited.

One particular consequence of state sovereignty which should be noted here is that since all states are sovereign equals, a state is not bound to submit itself to international adjudication unless it has first signified its consent that it is prepared to do so. Thus, the popular notion that a state can be taken to the International Court of Justice (ICJ) or the European Court of Human Rights (ECHR) for an infraction of the law by another state almost at whim, does not reckon with the impediment of the necessity to produce the delinquent state's consent that it be required to submit to such a course of action.

The rule against intervention is the necessary corollary to the doctrine of state sovereignty. If a state has the right to exclusive jurisdiction over its internal affairs, then it would clearly run counter to this to permit other states to intervene in those affairs. But what exactly is intervention? There has been considerable debate about this. Intervention clearly means something stronger than simple meddling or interference in the way the government of a state orders its internal affairs. It would for, example, have to be more than a critical comment on the pursuit of some domestic policy by another state. Lauterpacht, for instance, stated that in order to constitute intervention, an act must amount to a dictatorial interference in the affairs of another state without lawful justification. A more precise way of putting this might be that it must amount to an attempt by one state to perform state-like functions within the territory of another state. This view is reinforced by the language of the 1970 UN General Assembly Declaration on Principles of International Law concerning friendly relations and cooperation among State in accordance with the Charter of the United Nations, which states:

> No state or group of States has the right to intervene directly or indirectly, for any reason whatever in the internal or external affairs of any other State. Consequently, armed intervention and all other forms of interference or attempted threats against the personality of the State or against its political, economic or cultural elements, are in violation of international law.

This formula, although contained in General Assembly resolution which is technically not legally binding, has been relied upon to such an extent since 1970 that it is now regarded as a precise statement of the rule of non-intervention in customary international law.

The combined effect of the doctrine of sovereignty would seem to preclude the taking of any meaningful action by the international community in the context of human rights abuses by states. If persons within states are subject to the local laws, then surely other states cannot come to their aid if those local laws appear to violate human rights, since this would infringe the sovereignty of the other state and constitute an intervention in its internal affairs. This view would also seem to be confirmed by Article 2(7) of the UN Charter, which provides that the organization is prohibited from intervening in matters essentially within the domestic jurisdiction of any state.

As we have seen, however, sovereignty is not absolute, but it is itself limited by international law. Thus, once human rights have been elevated to a matter of international rather than national concern, states may no longer plead that human rights are a matter essentially within their domestic jurisdiction. It then becomes legitimate for states to make diplomatic protest about human rights violations and to institute sanctions against deliquent state. Some commentators have even argued, as a variation of the nineteenth-century doctrine of humanitarian intervention, that military force may be used against states which violate human rights, since one of the purposes of the UN is to promote and protect such rights. Such an argument runs counter to the major thrust of the UN Charter, which is to facilitate peaceful settlement of disputes and to outlaw the use of force in international relations, and it has also been explicitly rejected by the ICJ in Nicaragua v United States of America. It is not difficult to see that any modern notion of 'humanitarian intervention' would be bedevilled by the same subjectivity and potentially self-serving designs of militarily powerful nations as was the case in the nineteenth century.

Status of Individual

As we saw earlier in this book that before 1945 the individual was simply an object of the law within the international legal system. Individuals were characterized in terms of nationality, that is, the bond which created legal ties between them and their state. States were therefore not generally constrained by international rules concerning the treatment of their own nationals, but they were, as we have also seen, obliged to treat the nationals of other states in accordance with certain international standards if they were not to violate international law. But even here, the individual was merely the vehicle by which an international claim originated; it was the state which suffered the wrong through the maltreatment of its national. Within the international legal system, therefore, individuals were characterized as objects and not subjects of the law. Rules might be made for the benefit of individuals, but they did not confer substantive rights that could be enforced by procedural mechanisms which might be initiated by those same individuals. Exceptionally, however, the Permanent Court of International Justice recognized in the Danzing Railway Officials Case that certain rights created by the treaty could, where such an intention was expressly stated, permit individuals to enforce those rights in the domestic, or as they are known by international lawyers, municipal courts of the states parties. This, however, was a different matter to conferring procedural rights to individuals for enforcement of positive rights by an international tribunal.

In the post-Second World War era, the position of the individual has changed considerably. No longer are individuals seen as rightless objects of international law with no procedural capacity, rather, they are seen as the bearers of rights and correlative duties within the context of the international legal system. To some extent, therefore, they may be classified as limited subjects of international law. Although it had long been recognized that individuals were under a duty not to commit acts of piracy or war crimes under international law, it was not until the judgment of the International Military Tribunal at Nuremburg that it became fully established that international law placed direct obligations on individuals not to commit crimes against humanity, and the superior orders were no defence to the commission of those crimes. As the Nuremburg Tribunal itself observed: 'Crimes against international law are committed by men, not by abstract entities, and only by punishing individuals who commit such crimes can the provisions of international law be enforced.'

Now under international law, individuals may be held personally responsible for war crimes, genocide, torture and furthering apartheid. It is irrelevant that these individuals were following orders by implementing the policies of the state. By making individuals responsible under international law for their acts demystifies the claims that such international crimes are simply an expression of the 'collective will' of the state.

The post-Second World War period is also significant in the development of the individual as a partial subject of international law, not only because of the clear articulation of human rights in an increasing number of legally binding instruments, but also because of the conferring of procedural capacity upon individuals to enforce their rights before a variety of international tribunals. Individuals may now, under certain conditions, initiate proceedings before UN, European, American and African institutions.

While the methods by which individuals may bring applications, petitions or communications, as they are variously known, before the appropriate universal or regional institutions to secure remedies for the alleged violations of human rights will be considered in the appropriate places in subsequent chapters, it is worth remarking here that there is one factor which is common to all such procedures: individuals must in all cases attempt to secure redress of their grievances internally. This is known as the exhaustion of local remedies rule and is of fundamental importance in international human rights law.

The local remedies rule has its origin in the law of state responsibility or the law which governs the circumstances consequences of a violation of international law by states. Violation of the law by a state may be direct as, for example, when a state breaches a treaty, or indirect, such as when a host state fails to afford appropriate redress to an alien who has been injured by the agents of the state. It is in the latter circumstances in which the local remedies rule operates.

Until an individual attempts to exhaust all available local remedies, the state of which he or she is a national is prevented from taking up or espousing the claim at the international level. As noted above, when a state decides to espouse a claim, it does so for itself and not on behalf of the individual, since it is the state which is injured through the wrongful treatment of one of its nationals. In a sense, the identity of the individual is irrelevant, as long as he or she is a national of the claimant state.

In its traditional international law guise, the rule has both theoretical and pragmatic bases. First, it is designed to ensure respect for the sovereignty of other states by not casting premature aspersions on the ability of that state's institutions to afford appropriate redress to the individual in question. As the International Court of Justice said in the Interhandel Case:

> ...the rule requiring the exhaustion of domestic remedies as a condition of the presentation of an international claim is founded upon the principle that the responsible State must first have an opportunity to redress by its own means within the framework of its own domestic legal system the wrong alleged to be done to the individual.

Second, the rule is designed to prevent the proliferation of international claims by aggrieved individuals. Before a claim can be pursued on the international plane, therefore, individuals must attempt to exhaust all effective remedies whether they be judicial, arbitral or administrative. Remedies which are ineffective or illusory need not be pursued. Furthermore, if it is obvious that there are no remedies to exhaust or that the provision of a remedy is likely to be unduly tardy, the need to comply with the rule is obviated.

In its human rights guise, the local rule remedies rule operates in a slightly different context. Here, concern is not with the rule as a precondition to a state pursuing its own claim against another state on the international plane, rather it is with the rule as a precondition to the admissibility of a claim by an individual before an international tribunal against his or her own state. The rationale for the rule is, however, substantially the same: the state must be given the opportunity to redress by means of its own legal procedures any wrong claimed to have been done to the individual concerned before international mechanisms of protection are engaged.

A review of all of the international instruments which provide a right of individual application will demonstrate that exhaustion of local remedies by the applicants is a necessary prerequisite to securing legal standing. What the instruments do not disclose, however, is the attitude taken by the various competent institutions to the interpretation of the provision. Each institution has developed its own approach on such issues as upon whom the obligation lies to prove exhaustion and, indeed, what constitutes exhaustion. Although these matters will be dealt with in detail later, it is appropriate to note here that the requirement to demonstrate the exhaustion of local remedies is much more rigorous in the European Convention system than it is under the universal and inter-American systems. Possibly the major reason for this is that while the social and political conditions in the Council of Europe States are generally conducive to the protection of human rights, in the Americas and certain parts of the world covered by the universal system, they are not. The enforced disappearances of large numbers of individuals within Latin and Central American states in the recent past tends to demonstrate this point.

Legal Concerns

As human rights law is a branch of international law, the means of its creation are identical to that of international law in general. Thus, in order to determine the origins of human rights law, it is necessary to examine the traditional sources of international law. Here, Article 38 of the Statute of the International Court of Justice is generally accepted as the authoritative statement of such sources. It provides -

The Court, whose function is to decide in accordance with international law such disputes as are submitted to it, shall apply:

(a) international conventions, whether general or particular, establishing rules expressly recognized by the contesting states;

(b) international custom as evidence of a general practice accepted as law;

(c) the general principles of law recognized by civilised nations;

(d) subject to the provisions of Article 59 (which provides that the previous decisions of the ICJ have no binding force except in the decided case itself) judicial decisions and the teaching of the most highly qualified publicists of the various nations, as subsidiary means for the determination of rules of law.

Before briefly examining each of these sources of law, it is appropriate to point out that since the international legal system is a decentralized and horizontally integrated legal system having no central legislature, rules are created largely by agreement or emerge through the process of interaction between states. Thus, the law-creating processes of international system have much in common with gemeinschaft societies, although it is doubtful whether the international system is able to demonstrate the cohesion of such societies.

Common Agenda

The principal method of making international law in the modern world is by way of convention or treaty is essentially an agreement between two or more states establishing legally binding rules in a particular area. Article 2(1)(a) of the Vienna Convention of the Law of Treaties 1969 defines a treaty for the purposes of that Convention as 'an international agreement concluded between States in written form whatever its particular designation'. While there is a requirement that a treaty be in writing, the definition makes it clear that it is the form of the instrument which is important, not its title. Treaties are given a variety of names-conventions, charters, covenants, protocols, and so on, but their essential quality is that they are consensual agreements between two or more states under international law. A treaty between two states is generally known as a bilateral, contractual or particular treaty, whereas a treaty between more than two states is known as a multilateral or general treaty, since it seeks to establish rules for a significant number of states parties. Multilateral treaties are also sometimes referred to as international legislation, but this is misleading given the absence of any legislature in the international system. Such a designation simply seeks to convey the idea that a large number of states are party to a particular treaty and conform to the same rules. Treaties have one major advantage over other methods of international law creation: they are accessible and the rules established are more or less clear.

It will already be apparent that the greater part of international human rights law is contained in multilateral treaties. And while it is true that these treaties comprise an accurate index of the individual rights that are protected and the obligations that are assumed by the states which have become parties of the relevant instruments, there are also a number of other matters which must be considered. First, multilateral treaties often allow states to condition their obligations by the entry of reservations. A reservation is defined by Article 2(1)(d) of the Vienna Convention as 'a unilateral statement, however phrased or named, made by a State... whereby it purports to exclude or modify the legal effect of certain provisions of the treaty in their application to that state'. This does not mean that a state may modify its obligations at will. Treaties will often lay down the precise extent to which reservations may be entered.

Article 75 of the American Convention on Human Rights provides, for example, that : 'This Convention shall be subject to reservations only in conformity with the provisions of the Vienna Convention on the Law of Treaties ....' Even where a treaty is silent on the question of reservations, both the Vienna Convention and customary international law demand that a reservation must, if it is to be lawful, be compatible with the object and purpose of the Convention. Thus, for example, an attempt to derogate by way of a reservation from a right in a human rights treaty which is expressed to be absolutely non-derogable, would clearly not be compatible with the object and purpose of such a treaty.

Second, the notion of derogations from certain treaty provisions is one of the distinctive hallmarks of human rights instruments. In nearly all instruments states may, by unilateral declaration, derogate from their obligations under certain clearly prescribed conditions. Such derogations are not only rigorously defined within the particular instruments, but they are also subject to supervision by the institution charged with responsibility for protecting the rights in question. Certain rights, such as freedom from torture, are classified as non-derogable under any circumstances.

A third point to note is that whereas the fundamental breach of a treaty will usually result in the termination of obligations under such an instrument, this is not so in the case of human rights treaties. Article 60(5) of the Vienna Convention provides that the rules concerning termination 'do not apply to provisions relating to the protection of human persons contained in treaties of a humanitarian character'. The rationale behind this rule is clear — if a state could simply discharge its obligations under a human rights treaty by a single violation, it would defeat the continuing protective purpose of such instruments.

Another distinctive feature of human rights treaties, as opposed to other treaties in international law, are provisions which permit denunciation. Here states may withdraw unilaterally from their obligations under a treaty, as long as procedure; established by the treaty is complied with. While most human rights treaties provide for the possibility of denunciation, they also provide that state parties will be responsible for any violations of the treaty committed prior to denunciation. In so doing, the treaties ensure that states are not able to avoid their legal responsibilities simply by choosing to opt out of the instrument when its obligations become burdensome.

Finally, some mention should be made here of the methods by which treaties may be interpreted. The traditional rule is the literal rule, which is expressed in Article 31 of the Vienna Convention. This provides that 'a treaty shall be interpreted in good faith in accordance with the ordinary meaning to be given to the terms of the treaty in their context and in the light of its object and purpose'. Where, however, a literal interpretation of the instrument leaves the meaning ambiguous or obscure or leads to a result which is manifestly absurd or unreasonable, resource may be had to supplementary material such as the preparatory works or the drafting history of the instrument. Institutions which are charged with interpreting human rights instruments seldom adopt such a straightforward approach and frequently apply other techniques of interpretation either separately or in conjunction with those enumerated above.

Here, the process combines with a number of others factors. Of particular importance is the role of the institution, the context within which it functions, the legal, political and social traditions from which the members of the institution are drawn and their perceptions of their own and their institutions' functions. Thus, for example, the European Court of Human Rights has a predominantly teleological or end-orientated approach to interpretation of the Convention. This does not mean that the Court does not apply the standard techniques when occasion demands, simply that they have a conception of their role as that of maximizing the protective function of the Convention. Critics of the teleological approach including some past judges of the Court, have argued that it leads to judicial legislation. This is undoubtedly true, since the court has, on occasion, read rights into the Convention which are not automatically evident at first sight. However, since judges, as a category of decision makers enjoy a broadly legislative function anyway the only objection to the teleological approach might be the extent of their creativity.

Having pointed out some of the distinctive features of human rights treaties, it might legitimately be questioned whether or not they are qualitatively different to other kinds of treaties. Certainly there is a school of thought which argues that they are, and this school of thought is supported by statements of both the European and Inter-American Courts of Human Rights. The former, for example, declared in Austria v Italy that the obligations undertaken by the parties of the Convention were 'essentially of an objective character being designed rather to protect the fundamental rights of individual human beings from infringements of any of the .... Parties than to create subjective and reciprocal rights for the... Parties themselves'. The Court went on in the same case to say that the purpose of the parties to the Convention 'was not to concede to each other reciprocal rights and obligations in pursuance of their individual national interests but ....to establish a common public order of the free democracies of Europe with the object of safeguarding their common heritage of political traditions, ideals, freedoms and the rule of law'. In similar vein, the Inter-American Court of Human Rights declared in Effect of Reservations that 'the object and purpose of the (American Convention on Human Rights) is not the exchange of reciprocal rights between a limited number of States, but the protection of the human rights of all individual human beings within the Americas, irrespective of their nationality'. Thus, as far as the regional systems are concerned, the competent institutions appear to be claiming that their constituent instruments provide the basis for supra-national legal systems or systems of law superior to national law which can be invoked by individuals within those states.

The Customs

Although the majority of international transactions are now conducted through the medium of treaties, custom still remains an important source of law. Indeed, some authors would argue that custom is qualitatively more important than treaties, since it is custom which forms the bed-rock of the international legal system. Even treaties derive their binding force from a prior customary rule which states that treaties are binding must be observed in good faith. Furthermore, while states must signify their consent before they can legally bound by treaties, this is not a necessary prerequisite to a state becoming bound by a customary rule of international law.

What then is custom? The description in Article 38(1)(b) gives a hint of its nature. There it is described as a general practice accepted as law, which indicates that it is created by patterns of interaction between states accompanied by an underlying sense of legal obligation. Thus, custom is traditionally said to consist of two elements: a material element and a 'psychological' element.

The material element is evidenced by what is called state practice or the conduct of states. Such conduct may be evidenced by a variety of factors which impact on a state's international relations. These might include statements by the competent organs of state in a variety of domestic and international fora such as the UN, domestic legislation, the decision of local courts, and so on. Conduct alone, however, is not sufficient for the creation of a binding rule of customary international law; it must also be accompanied by a sense on the part of the relevant state organ that the conduct is underpinned by a sense of legal obligation. This is usually known by its Latin name, *opinio iuris sive* necessitates or, more commonly, simply *opinio iuris*. There has been much debate about whether *opinio iuris* needs to be proved in any given case or whether it can be inferred from a consistent pattern of conduct. The ICJ, however, still insists that it needs to be proved.

There are a multitude of theoretical difficulties associated with proving the existence of customary international law. Many of these arise because customary law is more frequently associated with the development of law within small, tight integrated human communities, usually known by German sociologist Tonnies' term *gemeinschaft*, rather than the development of law between complex corporate entities such as the modern state. Rather than talking of custom in international law, perhaps it would be more appropriate to coin a new term representing the realities of the situation. Nevertheless, 'custom' remains a potent source of contemporary international law. A state which seeks to rely on custom must prove the rule by demonstrating the existence of state practice which is definite, extensive, which has been extant for an appropriate period of time, and which is supported by the necessary *opinio iuris*.

Two matters which are associated with custom should be mentioned here: the legal status of UN General Assembly resolutions and the concept of *ius cogens*.

The legal status of resolutions passed by the General Assembly, the plenary organ of the UN, is frequently misunderstood. 'Housekeeping' resolutions dealing with General Assembly internal organization are legally binding on Assembly members, but resolutions covering other matters are not legally binding per se. Nonetheless, the latter may have certain legal effects depending on their subject matter and manner of drafting.

Here a distinction should be made between resolutions dealing with issues of a general nature, such as those urging member states to promote research into environmental degradation, and those of a 'legal' nature which seek to set down the member states' understanding of the appropriate rules of law in a particular area. The precise legal effect of such latter resolutions is controversial and open to a number of characterizations. Some states such as the USA deny that General Assembly resolutions have any normative effect, and assert that they are simply statements of political aspiration. Others argue that resolutions may, in appropriate circumstances, be authoritative interpretations of the UN Charter by the General Assembly.

Thus, for example, the Universal Declaration might be regarded as an authoritative interpretation of the meaning of 'human rights' in a number of Charter provisions. Still further, some states and commentators argue that resolutions, where they deal with broadly 'legal' issues, are a clear statement of state practice and can therefore be regarded as material element in the formation of customary international law. This indeed has been the position adopted by the ICJ in Nicaragua v United States, where a majority of the Court held that the Declaration of Principles Resolution and Resolution 3314(XXIX) 1974, the Consensus Definition of Aggression Resolution, both evidenced the international community's understanding of the appropriate customary rules in both areas. Thus, while General Assembly resolutions in no way amount to a form of international legislation, they are nevertheless capable of providing the constituent elements for the formation of customary international law.

If one examines Article 38 of the ICJ statute closely, it is apparent that the sources of law appear to be hierarchical, that is, they tend to move from the more specific to less specific. The hierarchy is not, however, immutable. Although under normal circumstances a treaty setting down precise rules of law would override customary international law, there are occasions when the customary rule is of such fundamental importance to the structure of the international system that it cannot be overridden by any contrary agreement.

An example of this would be a treaty between two states to commit an act of genocide, a treaty which international law could not possibly sanction. In many ways, this is analogous to a contract for illegal or immoral purposes under domestic contract law which domestic courts would not enforce on the grounds that it would be contrary to public policy to do so. Indeed, *ius cogens* is occasionally called the international doctrine of public policy or, to use the more precise French term, *orre public*. Article 53 of the Vienna Convention on the Law of Treaties provides a definition of ius cogens and indicates the effects of a treaty which is concluded in violation of such a norm. It states:

A treaty is void if, at the time of its conclusion, its conflicts with a peremptory norm of general international law [ins cogens]... [A] peremptory norm of general international law is norm accepted and recognized by the international community of States as a whole from which no derogation is permitted and which can be modified only by a subsequent norm of international law having the same character.

When this particular provision was drafted by the International Law Commission, the latter gave as examples of ins cogens norms, the rule prohibiting the use of force in international law, and criminal acts under international law such as the commission of acts of slavery, genocide and piracy. Certain members of the Commission also voiced their opinion that the conclusion of treaties which envisaged human rights violations might also be contrary to *ius cogens*. The view that the human rights have a ius cogens character also finds some support from the ICJ in Genocide Conventions Case and the Barcelona Traction Case and from the Inter-American Court of Human Rights in a number of cases. On a general scale, however, it seems clear that treaties which violate rules having a general humanitarian character run the risk of being classified as a breach of ins cogens, with the corresponding sanction that such treaties may be declared void by a competent tribunal.

General Theory

The third potential source of international law is 'the general principles of international law recognized by civilized nations'. This was included in the ICJ's statute in order to deal with the circumstances where the Court might not be able to decide a dispute because of absence of any treaty or customary law dealing with the issue before it. This situation is generally known as *non-liquet*, a situation which is more likely to arise in the decentralized international legal system than it is in hierarchically integrated domestic legal systems.

As with the other sources of international law, there is some dispute over exactly what the phrase means. Some writers take the view that it simply means procedural rules of national or municipal law which have been incorporated into international law, whereas others, such as Waldock, claim that the phrase means that the ICJ is competent to draw from a well of immutable principles of law which are common to all major legal systems. Certainly, the latter view would render this particular source of law more dynamic and better suited to the judicial decision-making process than would the former. It also means that when faced with a *non-liquet*, both the ICJ and other bodies charged with interpreting and applying international law would be able to apply a form of juridical calculus by which they might determine whether or not certain principles possess the necessary qualifications for application at the international level.

It is from the phraseology employed in Article 38 that judicial decisions and the opinions of writers are little more than subsidiary means for the determination of law. None the less, these can be particularly useful, particularly in determining the existence of customary international law. An example of this 'source' of law in action is a Californian court decision in the case of Filartiga v Pena Irala, in which the judge, after reviewing the appropriate international instruments, declared that the commission of acts of torture was contrary to the customary international law, and as such could be applied by the court in pursuance of the US Alien Tort Claims Statute.

Human Rights Honoured

The creation of international human rights law, is as we have seen, primarily a function of the international legal system, and the supervision of human rights is largely undertaken by international institutions created for this purpose. It should be noted, however, that domestic tribunals may also have a substantial role to play in the application of international human rights law. Much depends here upon the nature of the domestic constitution under which the local courts function. Some constitutions permit their domestic courts to apply norms of international law origin directly, whereas others require international law to be transformed into domestic law by legislation before the domestic courts can apply them. Since national and international law are regarded as a single integrated system, whereas constitutions in which transformation of international legal obligations into domestic law is required are called dualist constitutions, since domestic and international law are perceived as two separate and distinct systems. The main feature of monist constitutions is that there is usually some form of direct democratic or legislative control over the transaction of international relations by the executive branch of government, while there is an absence of such direct control in dualist constitutions.

Of course, the monist-dualist dichotomy is seldom as simple

in actuality as the definition would suggest. Even in dualist constitutions, a distinction is often drawn between international rules of customary law origin and those of treaty-based provenance. Moreover, states with dualist constitutions will often differ in their approach to the question of whether international rules of direct application or municipal laws take precedence in the event of conflict between them.

Some constitutions, such as that of Germany, give clear precedence to both customary and treaty rules over domestic federal law, whereas others, such as that of the USA, will only give precedence to particular categories of treaty. The main point to note from this discussion, however, is that some states' constitutions facilitate the direct application by the municipal courts of international human rights law, whereas others do not. In each and every case, the constitution of the state in question must be considered, as indeed must the approach of the municipal courts of the interpretation of the constitution.

Examples of two constitutions might serve to demonstrate the points made above. First, the British constitution, which is often regarded as the archetypal monist constitution. This is perhaps something of a misnomer, since the English courts have always applied rules of customary international law origin where there is no legislative provision to the contrary. However, the appellation 'monist' clearly indicates that, in general, rules emanating from the competent institutions of the European Community excepted, Parliamentary legislation takes precedence over rules of international origin.

Thus, as far as treaty-based obligations are concerned, they will have no domestic application in UK unless they have been transformed into domestic law by legislation. In the absence of statutory transformation, rules contained in an international treaty have no legal force in the UK. The English courts have adopted certain cannons of interpretation to deal with the relationship between statute and treaty, such as, where possible a statute will be construed to give effect to the UK's international legal obligations, but in all cases rules emanating from a treaty will give way to a contrary intention expressed by Parliament in its legislation. In the human rights field, the English courts have consistently refused to allow provisions of the European Convention on Human Rights to take precedence over domestic law, even when the latter has clearly been contrary to the Convention.

This position has recently been reaffirmed by the House of Lords in Brind and Others v Secretary of State for the Home Department. This case concerned certain directives issued by the Home Secretary prohibiting the direct broadcasting of statements made by representatives of proscribed organizations in Northern Ireland. The measures adopted by the Home Secretary were in the form of delegated legislation which the appellants complained violated Article 10 of the European Convention (freedom of expression).

The appellants further contended that the Home Secretary did not take the convention into account when he made the directives and that he had been wrong in law in not doing so. This argument was rejected by the House of Lords, which held that although the UK courts would interpret domestic legislation in a manner which conformed to the Convention where this was possible, there was no corresponding presumption of domestic law that the courts would review the exercise of an administrative discretion on the basis that such a discretion had to be exercised in conformity with the Convention. In responding to a submission that Article 10 of the Convention was a relevant factor to which the Home Secretary ought to have had regard when exercising his discretion in making the directives, Lord Ackner said:

> 'If the Secretary of State was obliged to have proper regard to the Convention, i.e. to conform with article 10, this inevitably would result in incorporating the Convention into English domestic law by the back door. It is apparent, therefore, that the UK constitution,

> as a form of dualist constitution, is not particularly well suited to giving effect to treaty-based international human rights obligations.

An appropriate example of how a broadly monist constitution gives effect to human rights of international law provenance is the constitution of the USA. Article 11(2) of the US Constitution provides that the President has the power to make treaties 'by and with the advice; and consent of the Senate .... provided two thirds of the Senators present concur'.

Article 4 of the constitution further provides that treaties made in such a way 'shall be the supreme law of the land; and the judges in every state shall be bound thereby'. The treaty can therefore be an important legislative device in the USA, but unlike; the UK, the treaty-making power of the executive, in the person of the US President, is subject to clear and direct democratic control. Moreover, treaties which are adopted in conformity with the constitution may produce rules which are directly enforceable by individuals before the municipal courts. These are known as self-executing treaties.

However, in order for a treaty to be self-executing, it must have a precise quality which is capable of giving rise to individual rights. As the Supreme Courts of California pointed out in Sei Fujii v California, the human rights provisions contained in the UN Charter lacked 'the mandatory quality and definiteness which would indicate upon ratification'. If such qualities are in existence in a particular treaty, then the potential for individual protection in the USA would be considerable.

9

Constitutional Protection

Our Constitution makers could foresee the social problems associated with the emancipation of women. They had seen prevailing gender inequality during their time and had visualised that the sex-equality was crucial for the development of the country. In order to do away with the inequality and to provide reasonable opportunities and create awareness for the exercise of human rights and claim, it was necessary to promote with special care, educational and economic interests not only of men but women too and to provide necessary protection from social injustice and exploitation.

The Constitution of India provides the following:

(i) Right to equality (Article 14, 15 and 16).

(ii) Right against exploitation (Article 23).

(iii) Directive Principles of State Policy (Articles 38, 39(a) & (d), 42 and 44)

(iv) Fundamental Duties (Article 51A Q (e))

(v) Elections (Article 325)

Besides the above, the Preamble, which incorporates the chief goal enshrined in the Constitution reflects the spirit of equality. A look into the Preamble will enable us to locate the ideal incorporated into the Constitution.

Constitution of the Country

The Preamble of the Constitution of India, has been expressed in the following words:

> "We the people of India having solemnly resolved to constitute India into a Sovereign Socialist Secular Democratic Republic and to secure to all citizens:
>
> Justice, social, economic and political;
>
> Liberty of thought, expression, belief, faith and worship;
>
> Equality of status and of opportunity; and to promote among them all,
>
> Fraternity, assuring the dignity of the individual, (unity and integrity of the nation);
>
> In our Constituent Assembly, this twenty-sixth day of November, 1949 do hereby adopt, enact and give to ourselves this Constitution."

The expression appearing in the Preamble of our Constitution was then described by Pandit Jawaharlal Nehru in the Objective Resolution which he moved in the Constituent Assembly in its first session and the Assembly adopted the same unanimously. But Nehru's Resolution itself had taken shape out of what had already been said by Mahatma Gandhi in 1931 when Mahatmaji was standing on the deck of a ship taking him to London in the capacity of the spokesman and representative of Nationalist India to the Second Round Table Conference. When asked by a correspondent at that time as to what Constitution he would bring back if he could help it, Mahatma Gandhi offered the following reply:

> "I shall strive for a Constitution which will release

> India from all that dom and patronage and give her, if need be, the right to sin. I shall work for an India, in which the poorest shall feel that it is their country in whose making they have an effective voice; an India where there shall not be high class and low class of people; an India in which all communities shall live in perfect harmony; there can be no room in such an India for the curse of untouchability or the curse of intoxicating drinks or drugs. Women shall enjoy the same right as men. Since we shall be at the pace with all the rest of the world neither exploiting nor being exploited by any of them. We shall have the smallest army imaginable. All interests not to be in conflict with the interests of the millions of dumb that will be respected, whether foreign or indigenous. This is the India of my dream."

The opening words of the Preamble emphasise on the ultimate authority of the people from whom the Constitution emerges. There is no sex discrimination. The words "We the People of India" includes both males and females.

Explanation : The Preamble outlines four objectives of the Indian Republic, viz. justice, liberty, equality and faternity. Justice implies a harmonious reconcilement of individual conduct with the general welfare of the society. The essence of justice lies in the attainment of the common good. It embraces as the preamble proclaims the entire social, economic and political spheres of human activity.

It is in the interest of the society to ensure the maximum liberty of thought and action of the individual consistent with the circumstances and social conditions. 'Liberty' in the Preamble, signifies not only the absence of any arbitrary restraint on the freedom of individual's action but also for the creation of conditions which would provide for the necessary ingredient required for the proper development of the personality of the individual. Since society consists of individuals, social progress depends on the progress of individuals. The two words 'liberty' and 'equality' are complimentary. Equality does not mean that all human beings are mentally and physically equal. It signifies equality of status and equal opportunity.

It is the spirit of brotherhood that is emphasised by the expression 'fraternity'. In a country like ours with diverse religion, language, culture and social system, unity can be achieved through the spirit of faternity. Fraternity ensures two things, viz. the dignity of the individual and unity and integrity of the country.

Constitutional and Legal Rights : Fundamental Rights, receives its treatment under Articles 12 to 35 of the Constitution and includes such principles as right to equality, right to freedom, right against exploitation, right to religion, right to culture and education, saving of certain laws and right to constitutional remedies.

Right to Equality

Art 14. Equality Before Law : "The State shall not deny to any person equality before law or equal protection of laws within the territory of India."

Notes : The Constitution of India guarantees equality before law or equal protection of law to every person irrespective of the fact that he is, or he is not the citizen of India. Both the phrases aim to establish what is called the equality of status and of opportunities as envisaged in the Preamble. Article 14 of the Constitution prevents any arbitrary discrimination.

Interpreting the scope of this Article, the Supreme Court of India held as under:

1. In considering the fundamental right of equality of opportunity, a technical pendantic or doctrinaire approach should not be made and the doctrine should not be involved even if different scales of pay, service conditions, leave, etc. are introduced in different or dissimilar posts.

2. Article 14 forbids hostile discrimination but not reasonable classification. Thus, where persons belonging to a particular class in view of their special attributes, qualities, mode of recruitment and the like are differently treated in public interests to advance and boost members belonging to backward classes, such a classification shall be outside the scope of discrimination having a close nexus with the object sought to be achieved so that in such a case, Article 14 will be completely out of the way.
3. Article 14 certainly applies where equals are treated differently without any reasonable basis.
4. Where equals and unequals are treated differently, Article 14 would have no application.
5. Even if there be one class of service having several categories with different attributes and incidents, such a category becomes a separate class by itself and no difference or discrimination between such category and the general members of the other class would amount to any discrimination or to denial of equality of opportunity.
6. In order to judge whether a separate category has been carved out of a class of service, the following circumstances have generally to be examined:
   (i) the nature, the mode and the manner of recruitment of a particular category from the very start;
   (ii) the classification of the particular category;
   (iii) the terms and conditions of service oı the members of the category;
   (iv) the nature and character of the posts and promotional avenues;
   (v) the specific attributes that the particular category possesses which are not to be found in other classes and the like."

It is rather difficult to lay down a rule of universal application but the circumstances mentioned above may be taken as illustrative guidelines for determining the question.

In its struggle for social and political freedom, mankind has always tried to move forward to the idea of equality for all. The urge for equality and liberty has been the moving force of many resolutions. The Charter of the United Nations records the determination of the member Nations to reaffirm their faith in the equal rights of men and women.

However, fulfilment of complete equality between men and women in all spheres of life has always been proved to be a distant dream. The laws of a country can at best assure to its citizens only a limited measure of equality. The Constitution makers gave only political and legal equality and the status of a fundamental right. Aspects like economic and social equality were included within the scope of Directive Principles of the State Policy.

Article 15 : Article 15 of the Constitution ensures prohibition of discrimination on grounds of religion, race, caste, sex or place of birth. Stated in words, it stands as follows:

1. The State shall not discriminate against any citizen on grounds only of religion, race, caste, sex, place of birth or any of them.
2. No citizen shall, on grounds only of religion, race, caste, sex, place of birth or any of them be subject to any disability, liability, restriction or conditions with regard to—
    (a) access to shops, public restaurants, hotels and places of public entertainment; or
    (b) the use of wells, tanks, bathing ghats, roads and places of public resort maintained wholly or partly out of state funds or dedicated to the use of general public.
3. Nothing in this Article shall prevent the State from making any provision for women.

4. Nothing in this Article or in Clause (2) of Article 29 shall prevent the State from making any special provision for the advancement of any socially and economically backward classes of citizen or for the Scheduled Castes and Scheduled Tribes.

Article 15 guarantees non-discrimination on special grounds, that is religion, race, caste, sex, place of birth or any of them. But, this right is available to citizens only.

Article 15(1) is conferred on a citizen as an individual and is a guarantee against his being subjected to discrimination in the matters of rights, privileges and immunities pertaining to him by virtue of his status as a citizen.

The significance of Article 15 is that it is a guarantee against every form of discrimination by the state on the basis of religion, race, caste or sex. Article 15 strikes at the root of provincialism by prohibiting discrimination based upon one's place of birth. It is also in conformity with the ideal of a single citizenship which the Constitution establishes for the whole of the country.

Article 15, however, has provided a couple of exceptions in its application. Article 15(3) allows the state to make any special provision for women and children. Article 15(4) permits the state to make any special provision for the advancement of socially and educationally backward classes or for the Scheduled Caste or Scheduled Tribes. The treatment meted out to women and children is in the larger and longer range interest of the community. Article 15(e) was included in the Constitution as a result of the First Consitutional Amendment in 1951.

Article 16 : This Article guarantees equality of opportunity in matters of public employment. It is stated in the following words:

1. There shall be equality of opportunity for all citizens in matters relating to employment or appointment to any office under the state.
2. No citizen shall, on grounds only of religion, race, caste,

sex, descent, place of birth, residence or any of them be ineligible for, or discriminated against in respect of any employment or office under the state.

3. Nothing in this Article shall prevent Parliament from making any law prescribing, in regard to a class or classes of employment to an office (under the Government of, or any local or other authority within a state or Union Territory, any requirement as to residence within that State or Union Territory) prior to such employment or appointment.
4. Nothing in this Article shall prevent the state from making provision for the reservation of posts in favour of any backward class of citizen which, in the opinion of the state is not adequately represented in the services under the state.
5. Nothing in this Article shall affect the operation of any law which provides that the incumbent of any office in connection with the affairs of any religious or denominational institution or any member of the Governing body thereof shall be a person professing a peculiar religion or belonging to a particular denomination.

Notes : Under Article 16(1), the general rule laid down is that there shall be equal opportunity for all citizens in matters of public appointment under the State, thereby the universality of Indian citizenship is emphasised.

Article 16(2) prohibits discrimination to any citizen in respect of appointment on grounds of religion, caste, race, sex, descent, place of birth or residence, should that appointment be under the State.

Articles 16(3) to 16(5) are in the nature of exceptions. According to Article 16(3), residence, qualifications may be made necessary in case of appointments under the State for particular positions. The discretion, however, does not rest with the state but within the powers of the Parliament. Article 16(4) empowers the state Government to make reservation of positions in public employment for any backward class. The state is empowered to declare a class of people as backward class. The exceptions embodied in Article 16(5) seek to take out of the scope of the general principle, the management of the affairs of any religious or dənominational institutions under any special law providing for the same.

What Article 15(1) and 16(2) prohibit is that discrimination should not be made only on the ground of sex. However, these Articles do not prohibit the state from making discrimination on the ground of sex coupled with other considerations. In case titled "*Yusuf Aziz* Vs. *State of Bombay* and *Hussainbhoy Laljea,*" sex was held to be a permissible classification. While dealing with this aspect of the matter, the Supreme Court remarked as under:

> "Article 14 is general and must be read with the other provisions which set out the ambit of fundamental rights. Sex is a sound classification and although there can be no discrimination in general on that ground, the Constitution itself makes special provisions in respect of women and children. The two Articles when read together validate the impugned chance in Sec. 497 I.P.C."

Justice Krishna Iyer in the case titled *Ms. C.B. Muthamma* Vs. *Union of India* expressed somewhat similar views in the following words:

> "We do not mean to universalise or dogmatise that men and women are equal in all occupations and all situations and do not exclude the need programatise where the requirement of particular employment, the sensitivities of sex or the peculiarities of social sectors or the handicaps of either sex may compel sensitivity. But save, where the differentiation is demonstrable, the rule of equality must govern."

An example of violation of Article 14 is the case *Air India* Vs. *Nargesh Mirza,* where the Supreme Court observed that having taken the air hostess in service and after having utilised her services for four years, to terminate her services by the management in the event of her becoming pregnant amounts to compelling the poor air hostess not to have any children and thus interfere with and divert the ordinary course of human nature.

The termination of the services of an air hostess under such circumstances is not only a callous and cruel act but an open insult to Indian womanhood, the most sacrosant and cherished institution. Such a course of action is extremely detestable and abhorant to the notion of a civilised society. Apart from being grossly unethical, it smacks of a deep rooted sense of an utter selfishness at the cost of all human values. Such a provision, therefore is not only manifestly unreasonable and arbitrary but contains the quality of unfairness and is, therefore, clearly violative of Article 14.

The Supreme Court while dealing with a rule barring married women from working in a particular firm criticised validity of the rule in the following words:

> "We are not impressed by these reasons for retaining a rule of this type ... Nor do we think that because the work has to be done as a team, it cannot be done by married women. We also feel that there is nothing to show that married women would be more likely to be absent than unmarried women or widows. If it is the presence of children which would account for greater absentation of married women, that would be so with the widows having children. The fact that the work has to be carried out by the workers as a team and presence of all these workmen, is in our opinion no disqualification. So far as married women or widows are entitled to such leave as the rule of the Respondent's Firm provide and they would be availing themselves of these facilities."

Right Against Exploitation : The following expression constitute the relevant portion in Article 23 of the Constitution.

"Prohibition of Traffic in Human beings and Forced Labour"

1. Traffic in human beings and 'begar' and other similar forms of forced labour are prohibited and any contravention of this provision shall be an offence punishable in accordance with law.
2. Nothing in this Article shall prevent the State from imposing compulsory service for public purposes and in imposing such service, the State shall not make any discrimination on grounds only of religion, race, caste or class or any of them."

While comparing Article 23 to the 13th Amendment of the Constitution of America which abolished slavery, it may be seen that in our country, at the time of adoption of the Constitution, there was no such practice like slavery in India but there existed large scale exploitation of forced bonded labour practiced by upper caste people upon the unprivileged section of the society. There existed a practice under which people mortgaged their labour to the upper caste masters in lieu of the interest that would accrue on the principal amount taken as loan and this bondage could continue from generations to generations.

The labour working under this situation had no right to seek employment without his master's approval and consent. His dependence on his master or landlord was so severe that it virtually amounted to slavery.

According to the practice of devdasi women or girls were either sold or dedicated to temples in the name of gods, where they could become an object of lust and instrument of sexual exploitation so long as their youth lasted. The practice of *devdasi, jogan* and other similar practices in Southern, Western part of the country and some of the temples in Orissa particularly bordering Andhra Pradesh were rampant and are still existing.

The ideal of human dignity pervades the entire Constitution and has been expressed in explicit terms in the form of this Article.

The expression 'Traffic in Human Beings' means disposal by way of sale or hire or otherwise of human beings more or less in the same manner as man does with the disposable articles.

The trafficking in women and girls in the male dominated society has been treated as the evil practice since old times. Medieval feudalism brought down the position of women to a very low mark. Prostitution became rampant and flesh trade established itself with agents and pimps and the dignity of women had gone down to the lowest ebb. To counter this, the Parliament enacted "The Suppression of Immoral Traffic in Women and Girls Act, 1956." This Act was renamed as "Immoral Traffic (Prevention) Act, 1956" and was substituted by Act No. 44 of 1986 with effect from Jan 26, 1987. The Act was enacted by the Parliament in persuance of the ratification by India of the International Convention of the Suppression of Traffic in persons and of the prostitution by others, signed in New York in 1950 on May 9. (Detailed study of this problem is being dealt with in the Chapter on Prostitution.)

Cultural and Educational Rights : Under Articles 29 and 30, certain cultural and educational rights are guaranteed.

Article 29 : Protection of Interests of Minorities

1. Any section of the citizen residing in the territory of India or any part thereof having a distinct language, script or culture of its own, shall have the right to conserve the same.
2. No citizen shall be denied admission into any educational institution maintained by the State or receiving aid out of State funds on grounds only of religion, race, caste, language or any of them.

Thus sex is a prohibited ground of discrimination under Article 15 and Article 16, but not under Article 29. Courts, however, have come to settle down with an interpretation which means that sex as a basis of classification may be a suspect but cannot altogether be prohibited. Special laws for women can be made in different kinds of cases notwithstanding the fact whether they are favourable or unfavourable to women. It has only to be seen in such a situation that such orders may not only be reasonable but also seem to be reasonable. The following cases are cited by way of example:

1. In the case titled *Anjali Roy* Vs. *The State*, the fact involved was that after opening of a college exclusively for women, girl students were denied admission into another college which was a co-educational institution. Accordingly one Anjali Roy was denied admission in the co-educational college under the orders of the Director of Public Instruction of the Government of West Bengal. The petitioner challenged the orders of the D.P.I. as arbitrary malafide and unreasonable. The Hon'ble High Court of Kolkata dismissed the Writ Petition holding that the order prohibiting the admission of the girl students to the former co-educational institution was with the intention to make the girl students to take admission in women's college so that the same could be popular and well established and thus, become a self-sufficient. This was thus, a special provision as contemplated by Article 15(3) for the benefit of women and in consequence the provisions of Article 15(1) was not available for this. It was further held that Article 15(1) was of wider implications as compared to Article 29(2) and prohibited discrimination on the ground of sex on all matters and so it included discrimination in matters of admission into educational institutions with the result that Article 15(1) should control Article 29(2).
2. In the case titled "*University of Madras* Vs. *Santhabai and another*. The High Court of Madras took a different view to deny admission to *Santhabai* in a newly opened college. The Court held the view that the University of Madras is not a 'State' as defined in Article 12 of the Constitution and thus its regulation will not be subject to prohibition of Article 15(1) of the Constitution of India. Another point

> is that admissions are regulated within the ambit of Article 29(2) and the regulation of the University required that colleges should have the necessary infrastructure to provide essential facilities for women before they could be admitted. This fact is not discriminatory on ground of sex.

So far as the scope of Article 15(3) is concerned, the High Court expressed that notwithstanding Article 15(1), it was lawful for the state to establish educational institutions solely for women and the exclusion of men students from such institutions does not contravene Article 15(1). The cumulative effect of Article 15(3) and 29(2) is that while male students have no right to get admission in women's college, the women's right to admission to other colleges is a matter within the regulation of authorities. Article 29(2) contains the controlling provisions where the question relating to admission to colleges involves.

The scope of Article 29(2) came up for detailed interpretation before the Apex Court in two cases, both of which were appeals against the judgement and order of Madras High Court relating to admission to Educational Institutions maintained by the state. The Supreme Court, after a threadbare discussion, observed as follows:

> "It will be noticed that while Cl. (1) protects the language, script or culture of a section of the citizen, Cl. (2) guarantees the fundamental right of an individual, who is citizen. The right to get admission into any educational institution of the type appearing in Cl. (2) is a right which an individual has as a citizen and not by virtue of belonging to any community or class of citizen. The right of the citizen is not to be denied to him on grounds only of sex, religion, race, caste, or language or any of them. If a citizen, who seeks admission into any such educational institution but does not possess the requisite academic qualifications and on this account is denied admission

> on that ground only, certainly he cannot be held to complain of any infraction of his fundamental rights under the Constitution within the framework of this Article. In the event of his having the required academic qualifications if he is refused admission only on grounds of religion, race, caste, language or any of them, then it amounts to clear violation of his fundamental rights."

The State, contended that Article 46, charged the state with promoting with special care, the educational and special interests of the weaker section of the people and in particular of the SC/ ST and with protecting them from social justice and all forms of exploitation. But, the court rejected this argument holding that this was a Directive Principle—a non-justiciable right—and it could not over-ride a Fundamental Right which was justiciable. It was the duty of the court to enforce a Fundamental Right.

The passing of the 42nd Amendment of the Constitution of India in 1976, Sec. 3, w.e.f. January 1, 1977 ensured the Supremacy of the Parliament and gave primacy to Directive Principles over the Fundamental rights. In view of the passing away of this Amendment, the aforesaid argument of the Court has little force.

The Right to Constitutional Remedy : The declaration of Fundamental Rights becomes infructuous unless there is an effective instrument for enforcement of the right. Article 32 of the Constitution provides a remedy for the enforcement of the fundamental rights. The remedy is in the forms of specific writs mentioned in the Article. Hence, if there is an aggrieved person who seeks a remedy from the court through a particular writ, the nature of the remedy itself is clear both to the aggrieved person and to the court.

The writs mentioned in the Constitution are:

Habeas Corpus : This is a Latin term which literally means "You May Have The Body". The Writ was regarded in English as a foundation of the human freedom and the British citizen insisted upon this privilege wherever he wanted whether for business or for colonisation. This is how it found a place in the Constitution of the United States when the British colonies in America won their independence and established a new State under the Constitution.

In India, the power to issue a writ vests only in Supreme Court and the High Court. The Writ is a direction of the court to a person who is detaining another, commanding him to bring the body of the person in his custody at a specified time to a specified place for a specified purpose. The writ has only one purpose, that is, to set at liberty a person who is confined without legal jurisdiction; to secure release from confinement of a person detained unlawfully. The writ, in accordance with circumstances can be issued against the State and its authorities as well as private individual or organisation.

Mandamus : This is a Latin expression and means "We Order". The Writ of Mandamus is an order of the Supreme Court or the High Court commanding a person or a body to do that which is his or its duty to do so. For instance an appointing authority is obliged to issue a letter of appointment to a candidate if all the formalities of selection is over and the candidate is declared fit for appointment to the post. But despite the fulfilment of such condition, if the officer or the authority concerned refuses or fails to issue the appointment letter, the aggrieved person has a right to seek the remedy through a Writ of Mandamus.

Prohibition : A Writ of Prohibition is issued primarily to prevent a lower court from exceeding its jurisdiction, or acting contrary to the rules of natural justice. For instance, a judge may be restrained from adjudication upon a case wherein he is personally interested. The Writ of Prohibition is a counterpart of the Writ of Certiorari and an aggrieved person may make an application to the issue of both the Writs, that is 'Prohibition' and 'Certiorari'.

Certiorari : It is a Writ which orders the removal of a suit from any court to another which is superior to the first. It may be used before a trial commences to prevent an excess or abuse of jurisdiction and to transfer the case for trial before a higher court. It may be invoked after trial as well in order to quash an order which has been made without jurisdiction or in defiance of the Rules of Natural Justice.

Quo Warranto : An application for Writ of Quo Warranto seeks an order from the Supreme Court or High Court to restrain a person from acting in an office to which he is not entitled. It may also seek the office to be declared as vacant. What the court has to do is to determine where there has been unsurpation of an office of a public nature. For instance, a member of a Municipal Corporation may, through an application of Writ of Quo Warranto, challenge the authority of the Mayor, if he is of opinion that the Mayor was not properly elected.

The High Court can issue Writ under provisions of Articles 226 and 227 of the Constitution.

Article 226. Powers of High Courts to Issue Writs

1. Notwithstanding anything in Article 32, every High Court shall have power, throughout the territories in relation to which it exercises jurisdiction to issue to any person or authority, including in appropriate cases, any Government, within those territories, directions, orders or Writs, including Writs in the nature of habeas corpus, mandamus, prohibition, quo warranto and certiorari, or any of them, for the enforcement of any of the rights conferred in Part III and for any other purpose.
2. The power conferred by Clause (1) to issue directions, orders or Writs to any Government authority or person may also be exercised by any High Court exercising jurisdiction in relation to the territories within which the cause of action, wholly or in part, arises for the exercise of such power, notwithstanding that the seat of such Government or authority or the residence is not within those territories.

3. Where any party against whom an interim order, whether by way of injunction or stay or in any other manner, is made on, or in any proceeding relating to, a petition under Clause (1), without
   (a) furnishing to such party copies of such petition and all documents in support of the plea for such interim order; and
   (b) giving such party an opportunity of being heard, makes an application to the High Court for the vacation of such order and furnishes a copy of such application to the party in whose favour such order has been made or to the counsel of such party, the High Court shall dispose of the application within a period of four weeks from the date on which the copy of such application is so furnished, whichever is later, or where the High Court is closed, on the last day of that period, before the expiry of the next day afterwards on which the High Court is open, and if the application is not so disposed of, the interim order, shall on the expiry of that period, or as the case may be, the expiry of the said next day, stand vacated.
4. The power conferred on a High Court by this Article shall not be in derogation of the power conferred on the Supreme Court by Clause (2) of Article 32.

Article 227. Power of Superintendence over all Courts by the High Court

1. Every High Court shall have superintendence over all courts and tribunals throughout the territories in relation to which it exercises jurisdiction.
2. Without prejudice to the generality of the foregoing provisions, the High Court may:
   (a) call for returns from such courts;
   (b) make and issue general rules and prescribe forms for

regulating the practice and proceedings of such courts; and

(c) prescribe forms in which books, entries and accounts shall be kept by the officers of any such courts.

3. The High Court may also settle tables of fees to be allowed to the sheriff and all clerks and officers of such courts and to attorneys, advocates and pleaders practising therein.

   Providing that any rules made, forms prescribed or tables settled under Clause (2) or Clause (3) shall not be inconsistent with the provision of any law for the time being in force, and shall require the previous approval of the Governor.

4. Nothing in this Article shall be deemed to confer on a High Court powers to superintendence over any court or tribunal constituted by or under any law relating to the Armed Forces.

Theories for Guidance

The Directive Principles of State Policy constitute the third part of the Constitution and are unique and novel in so far as they depict the ambitions and aspirations of the fathers of the Constitution. It was laid down that these provisions are not enforceable in any court but they are fundamental in the governance of the country and it was the duty of the State to apply these principles in making laws.

Article 39. Certain Principles of Policy to be followed by the State : The State shall, in particular, direct the policy towards securing:

(a) that the citizens, men and women, equally have the right to an adequate means of livelihood;

(b) that the ownership and control of the material resources of the community are so distributed as best to subserve the common good;

(c) that the operation of the economic system does not result in the concentration of wealth and means of production to the common detriment;

(d) that there is equal pay for equal work for both men and women;

(e) that the health and strength of workers, men and women, and the tender age of children are not abused and the citizens are not forced by economic necessity to enter a vocation unsuited to their age of strength;

(f) that the children are given opportunities and facilities to develop in a healthy manner and in conditions of freedom and dignity and that childhood and youth are protected against exploitation and against moral and material abandonment.

The picture, so far as it relates to the Constitutional Provision of equal pay for equal work for both, men and women is concerned is very grim. According to the "Report of the Committee on the Status of Women", wage discrimination is very much practised in the form of fixing lower wage rate for women as compared to their male counterparts. The minimum wages fixed for non-skilled male workers is Rs. 7 to 9 per day for 8 hours a day whereas the wages for women for the same type of work and for the same period is Rs. 4 to 7 per day.

A case came up for consideration before the Supreme Court which involved the question of equal pay for equal work for both men and women. The facts of the case was that Andrey D'Costa, a confidential lady stenographer of the company was being paid remuneration at the rate less favourable than her male colleague doing the same work. The company opposed it by saying that she was not doing the same work. The Supreme Court held that the discrimination between the male and female stenographer of the company was only on the ground of sex and the act does not permit the management to pay to a section of its employees doing the same work or a work of similar nature lesser pay contrary to the provisions of Section 4(1) of Equal Remuneration Act, 1976 (No. 25 of 1976).

Article 42. Provision for just and Humane Conditions of Work and Maternity Relief: The State shall make a provision for securing just and humane conditions of work and for maternity relief.

Article 44. Uniform Civil Code for the Citizen : The State shall endeavour to secure for the citizens a uniform Civil Code throughout the territory of India.

The passing of a Uniform Civil Code is not an easy proposition in a country where the population is composed of diverse religious and ethnic groups and different customs and rituals are being practised by each of them. The passing of the Hindu Marriage Act (1955) and the Hindu Succession Act (1956) are examples of such efforts. However, on the question of giving maintenance to Shah Bano by the Supreme Court in accordance with Sec. 125 of Cr. P.C. (Act 2 of 1974) generated sufficient opposition from a section of the society and the Government of India was pressurised to make a separate Act for Muslim women. Nevertheless, the courts in our country are granting maintenance applying Sec. 125 Cr. P.C. to Muslim women in appropriate cases.

Misuse of Law

The absence of a Uniform Civil Code in India puts Muslim women to disadvantage as according to Shariat, a Muslim male can marry and keep up to four wives as against the Hindus, Parsis, and Christian, etc. Thus, converting to Islam to gain a new spouse is being practised by a few Hindus. The following cases are being cited by way of example.

1. JM, a businessman married to N are having three children out of this wedlock, over a period of fifteen years, changed his religion and embraced Islam. He took a Muslim alias and married a girl friend S and when confronted by N

ended the matter saying that his relationship with S was perfectly justified and legitimate as both had embraced Islam. And after three months of his conversion, JM declared through an oath his decision to become a Hindu.

2. The case of RK, whose marriage to VK dates back to the year 1978 was equally expedient. From the very beginning of the marriage VK alleged harassment by her in-laws over the question of dowry. One day RK brought home another woman 'A' and legitimised their relationship through conversion to Islam and weeks later reconverted to Hinduism in a temple.

Thus, the convenience afforded by the Islamic personal law to opportunistic Hindu men with bigamy in their mind is misused to gain a new spouse as well as to escape payment of maintenance. The thing becomes all the more difficult for the discarded wife as the onus to prove bigamy is on the complainant and where can she get evidence to prove this. Thus, such misuse of religion and conversions should be stopped. Having a Uniform Civil Code can go a long way in propagating this.

Legal Defence

Fundamental rights which every man or woman should be entitled to by virtue of having been born as a human being constitute what are called Human Rights. Human Rights propagate the concept of non-discrimination and equality. Whereas women represent more than half of the world's population and are engaged in work that contributes immensely to the life and wealth of nations, they are subjected to gender discrimination at work, in their homes, and in every sphere of human activity. This situation will have to change one day, else this exploitation and subjugation will continue thus adversely effecting the social fabric in time to come.

In the recent Dravidian and Aryan cultures, women had free access to educational opportunities and discrimination on the basis of sex was unknown. Women rose to high positions during Dravidian and Aryan culture in different disciplines and *brahmaradinis* like Gargi challenged great men and scholars in learned discourses on equal grounds. This was the status of women in the ancient times. Woman was the *sahadharmi* equal partner in the performance of *dharm*, the righteous duties in life.

It has been said by various scholars that only when women are educated and respected will the world emerge prosperous. This world may be as small as the family or as large as the nation— it implies for all. The subjugation of women started in the Smriti period. Manu and Yagna Valkya subscribed a subordinate social role to women. The degradation of women's position was reflected in customs relating to marriage, religion and property where socio-economic freedom was denied to them. They were expected to be under the "protective control" of the father, husband and son. This deterioration continued during the medieval and British periods.

Apart from the Dravidian and Aryan civilization where women were respected, the past of Indian women is the story of subjugation. During India's 5000 years of civilization, its history has to a great extent been "his" story. Women by and large led circumscribed lives. The nineteenth century was one of social reformers who highlighted the problems faced by women — the horrors of *devdasis*, child marriage, child widows and female exclusion, they included Raja Ram Mohun Roy, Ishwar Chandra Vidya Sagar and enlightened Westerners such as Macaulay, William Bentinck and Marcus Puller. A few Indian women writers in the latter part of the nineteenth century and beginning of twentieth century wrote about women and their experiences. But these have been largely about educated women, the elite, the Brahmins, or about women who participated in the political struggle.

The freedom movement brought in a new dimension to this struggle. Gandhiji with his foresight comprehended that only with the active participation of women, could every Indian home be turned into a bastion of the freedom struggle. The manner in which hundreds and thousands of women shed their veils and left their sheltered homes to come into the street to fight side by side in the struggle with their brothers and often put to shame their menfolk was a landmark in the political and social history of India.

The twentieth century, particularly after Independence saw the Indian women bring in a number of achievements to their credit. In all fields of higher learning — engineering, nuclear physics, computer sciences, administration, management, the arts and humanities — women have proved equal to men and have won laurels. It may be a reason to be proud but we cannot ignore the fact that even now 75 per cent of India's over 400 million women are illiterate, invisible and unaware of the going on in the universe. So immersed are they in their daily chores that they have no time to think of what is happening in the world. They are voiceless and subjected to myriad forms of class, caste and gender oppression. Responsible for the pathetic situation of women are the deep-rooted societal and religious traditions. The arbitrary division of male and female roles in society initiate sex-based discrimination and deprivation. Women, by and large have little access to productive resources and control over family income. Ranging from the exclusion of women from development programmes, sex discrimination is seen in wage discrimination and also perpetrates violence against women. A number of laws have been enacted to protect and promote the rights/interests of women, some of which are:

British Law

In the pre-Independence colonial era, the few laws relating to crimes against women were mainly those relating to rape, causing miscarriage, assault on women's modesty, kidnapping/ abduction, etc. and offences relating to marriage (all non cognisable). Social legislation for protection of women was even less and was limited to — Sati prohibition, maintenance laws or some laws enabling widow remarriage, etc. Laws relating to property, adoption, divorce, etc. were heavily subscribed by males keeping their interests in mind furthering the inferior or subordinate position of women in society and confirming their superiority over them in all respects.

Liberal Laws

The post-Independence period witnessed a spate of enactments— criminal, civil and social — besides amendments to some old laws to protect and improve the status of women which came about as a result of the provision in our Constitution on equality in all respects and spheres and non-discrimination on any ground, and even special protection to women and children as part of state policy. The new-found political and social awakening and agitations and movements for women's causes, to which both men and women contributed, gave further impetus to this process of legislation aimed at implementing the philosophy behind the Constitution. (The only exception to this policy would appear to be the Muslim Womens' Protection of Rights on Divorce Act, 1986, apparently an instance of misconceived and miscalculated political opportunism). These enactments can be divided into two broad categories— those directly relating to checking of violence against women and preventing their exploitation and those aimed at improving their legal and social status.

The first category included the laws relating to domestic violence, which for the first time took cognisance of the concept of mental cruelty besides physical violence, changes in rape laws, laws relating to dowry prohibition and prevention of immoral traffic, 'Sati' indecent representation of women, etc., with some changes in evidence and procedural laws to facilitate their implementation.

The second category included laws relating to woman's/ daughter's share in property, adoption laws, changes in divorce laws, etc. In the criminal laws, the emphasis was mainly on stringent punishments and more helpful procedures. The second category of laws were pursued through institutions of family courts, legal aid bureaus, etc.

Lacunae and Loopholes in Laws : Expected to remove various legal lacunae and hurdles, criminal laws were made to provide effective deterrence to violence against women, while those falling in the category of social legislation were meant to work as catalysts for social change. In practice, however, none of the two expectations have been fulfilled. Deterrence in law remains confined to the status book with symbolic convictions and a large majority of cases remaining undisposed of in courts for years together while crimes against women have been showing a continuously increasing trend. Social legislation being relegated to paper only, without any proper awareness about their provisions, either amongst the people or the police. The laws themselves are to be blamed for this ineffective trend in their implementation despite intentions of their framers to the contrary. Often badly conceived and poorly drafted these legislations have many lacunae and loopholes thus exposing inadequacies of the criminal justice system and procedures and lack of public awareness. Generally found missing is the acceptability or support sometimes even positive antipathy — due to the absence of any efforts for public education, either about their provisions or their purpose.

Law against Dowry

With the noble objective of putting a stop to the practice of dowry which had degenerated into one of the worst instruments of exploitation and even extortion, particularly in Hindu society, the Act was brought about in 1961 and was amended twice in 1984 and 1986 to streamline its provisions and make the penalties more deterrent, but continues to be one of the most ineffective laws. Despite the efforts through amendments to remove some of the earlier lacunae several major anomalies still remain. Most of the cases registered fall under the category of Sections (u/s) 4 or 6 of the Act (usually along with Sec. 498-A, IPC) for demand of dowry and harassment or non-return of Dowry/Istridhan by the husband/in-laws reported after the marriage has run aground. A few cases included belong to u/s 3 of the Act for dowry giving and taking before or at the time of marriage even though the Section was specifically amended in 1984 to provide for a stringent minimum punishment of 5 years' imprisonment and Rs. 15,000 or amount of value of dowry (whichever is more) as fine.

Objectives of the Act : The basic objective behind this enactment and subsequent amendments which followed the alarming increase in reported cases of bride burning for dowry in the late seventies and early eighties, was to prevent extortion of dowry.

Lacunae of the Act : Even the definition of dowry "any property or valuable security given or agreed to be given" (Section 2) emphasizes on 'giving' rather than on the 'demand' or 'extortion' aspect. Demand of dowry is specifically punishable u/s 4 but the validity of this section is under a question mark in view of judgements of two High Courts, Calcutta *(Shankar Pd. Shaw and ors. vs State & ors* - 1991 Cr. : L.J. 639 Calcutta H.C.) and Allahabad (Ramesh Chand vs. State of U.P. - 1992 (3) RCR 511), both holding that in view of the very definition of 'dowry' which has 'giving' or agreement to give as its basic ingredients, mere demand cannot be termed as an offence unless there was 'giving' or 'agreement to give'. The Calcutta High Court had, accordingly even suggested a change in the definition of "dowry u/s 2 of the Act in the light of sub clause (6) u/s 498-A of the Penal Code" if demand for dowry or extortion was proposed to be brought under its ambit. Even otherwise, u/s 3 which makes giving or taking of dowry an offence, both the 'giver' and the 'taker' are placed on a par although the giver, in most of the cases, is a helpless victim of extortion under the evil social custom rather than a willful or conscious offender. Despite all the enactments it is not surprising that only a few cases are reported under this section before or at the time of marriage, even while dowry continues to be given and taken extensively and even openly and spread through the fabric of society.

Difficulties also arise because of other provisions. The term "in connection with marriage" and "in consideration for marriage" used earlier need further clarification. That the demand or payment was "in connection with the marriage", particularly in cases of 'extended' dowry demands/payments after the marriage for example, in the garb of customary gifts/presents on occasions of marriages in the natal or marital families, child births, birthdays and other religious or social festivals/occasions, or on grounds of financing foreign education trips, purchase of house or setting up or expanding of business by the husband, etc. is often difficult to prove especially when they are not 'agreed to be given' at the time of marriage. Section 3(3) while exempting the presents given or taken at the time of marriage to the bride/bridegroom if they are: (i) given without any demand with entry in lists as per rules, (ii) of customary nature and not excessive to the financial status of the giver, provide further loopholes for enforcement because of the impracticability and vagueness of these conditions.

Having been obviously made to save customary gifts given voluntarily and within their means by the parents and other persons of the bride's party out of love and consideration for the daughter from coming under its ambit, this provision excludes from its scope any gifts given before or after the marriage (e.g. on the occasion of *Tika, Sagai* or other ceremonies or child birth etc.) even though they may also be given voluntarily as part of tradition/custom. Even this limited provision is exploited to cover forcible demand or extortion of dowry since the desire of parents of girls, keen to somehow or the other fulfil their filial and social obligation of marrying off their daughter ovrrules the complain of demand of dowry. They do not, in any way, wish to jeopardize the marriage itself or prevent the likelihood of future proposals coming their way, thus putting the girls in worse trouble. Regarding the condition of preparation of lists of dowry gifts, there is a provision framed in this connection by the Central Government (Dowry Prohibition Maintenance of Lists of Presents to the Bride and Bridegroom Rules, 1985) which requires these lists to be prepared and signed by the bride and the bridegroom. As the lists are required to be prepared at the time of or soon after the marriage with full details about the presents and the givers this provision is impractical. Most of the giving and taking of presents at the time of the marriage is done by the parents of the bride and not by the bridegroom who should be the proper persons to be fixed with this responsibility.

Unless made mandatory the inhibitions and apprehensions on the part of parents of the bride in asking for such lists to be prepared or signed by the bridegroom will hamper the very objective of this provision. Under the present social ethos in the Hindu society, no such system has generally prevailed so far (unlike the Muslim community where preparation of such lists, particularly for jewellery and other costly presents, is considered to be a normal and acceptable convention). By making it mandatory with specific rsponsibility, particularly of the receiver (parents of the bridegroom even for gifts received on behalf of the bride) this new practice will be effective in its objective. Provision for mandatory filing of a copy of the lists with the area 'Dowry Prohibition Officer' or 'Marriage Registration Officer' could even be considered.

Due to the aforesaid lacunae, this Act does not curb the practice of giving, taking or demand of dowry before or at the time of marriage or even afterwards. It is not taken recourse to as long as the marriage works or the girl is prepared to suffer quietly. Recourse to this Act is sought in case of breakdown of marriaged or death of the girl by violence, with a large majority of cases being registered u/s 6 of the Act often along with sections 498-A/406, IPC) for return of dowry/Istridhan.

The 'matrimonial home' after the marriage concept poses difficulties in seeking redressal after breakdown of marriage. Under this Section (Section 6) for non/return of dowry/Istridhan articles since the proceedings can be initiated only at the place where the dowry/Istridhan was given or was due to be transferred to the wife, normally the matrimonial home after the marriage. Since the wife, after the breakdown of the marriage (when only such complaints are normally filed) is generally not staying in the matrimonial home and usually shifts to another place either to stay with her parents or take up a job, etc. she is hardly in a position to pursue the case in the court at the place of her matrimonial home.

Similar lacunae exist in provision (b) under sec. 6(3) of the Act which provides for the property to "be held in trust" for the children of the woman who dies from unnatural causes within seven years of her marriage, pending its transfer to the children (normally when they attain the age of majority). Due to this provision the aggressor husband or in-laws merrily continue to hold the property and enjoy the fruits of their crime on the pretext of keeping the property "in trust" and indulge in other malpractices, thus further perpetrating such crimes.

Therefore, in spite of the protection provided to "the person aggrieved by the offence" (which would include the "giver") u/s 7(3) of the Act, saving such a person from prosecution on the basis of his statement and shifting the onus of proof on the accused u/s 8-A in case of offence u/s 3 or 4, there has been no case under the Act, which has ended in conviction in Delhi, Mumbai and Bangalore up to the time of the study and the all-India rate of conviction had also been only about 5 per cent (between 28 per cent and 36 per cent of decided cases) from 1988-1991, according to *Crime in India* published by NCRB (cases under this Act were not published separately before 1988).

Provisions of Dowry Prohibition Act : Section 8-B(1) of the Act provides for appointment of Dowry Prohibition Officers and Section 8-B(4) for constitution of Advisory Boards comprising social workers of the area for advising and assisting such officers. The Dowry Prohibition Officers are to be responsible (u/s 8-B(2)) for compliance with provisions of the Act, preventing demand or taking of dowry and collecting evidence for prosecution of the offenders. They may, for this purpose, be conferred with requisite police powers (Sec. 8-B(3)). Rules for functioning of such officers are to be framed by the State Government u/s 10(2) of the Act. These provisions introduced under 1984 amendments, were deliberately meant to involve the social workers of the area in enforcement of the Act rather than depending on the police alone for curbing the evil of dowry. The few officers who have been appointed do not generally perform any duties with regard to prevention of demand or giving or taking of dowry in the absence of rules which should have been framed by the Central or State Governments for their functioning. Similarly there is absence of Advisory Committees and no area social workers have been appointed at most places nor have any rules been framed for their constitution.

It appears that while the Act was framed and later modified twice with a lot of fanfare under pressure from women's groups and other social workers, not much effort has gone into ensuring its proper enforcement therafter, as is evident from this lack of even basic follow up action in these matters.

Due to the Acts being masterminded by men who form the majority of law makers, there are many places which have been deliberately left untouched so as to give vent to their plans and furtherance of social norms whilst ignoring their misgivings.

Suggestions for Effective Implementation

(a) An amendment in definition of dowry so as to bring about a clear-cut picture of demand and giving aspect of dowry. In fact, subjecting the daughter-in-law to threats, harassment or cruelty to coerce her if she does not get 'extended' dowry after the marriage, amounts to 'extortion' which should be treated as an aggravated form of 'dowry demand' carrying a higher punishment. Section 498-A IPC, which covers such cases at present is hardly adequate to deal with this type of crime. A lot of cases where the daughter-in-law is threatened with grievious hurt or death by burning etc. if she does not get further dowry or property, would squarely make out offences u/s 386 or 387 of IPC, punishable with imprisonment up to ten years or seven years respectively, besides fine as against a punishment of up to two years only (with a minimum punishment of 6 months) u/s 4 of Dowry Prohibition Act and three years only u/s 498-A IPC.

(b) Clarification is needed on the term "in connection with the marriage". It should either be deleted entirely or an 'explanation' added to the section. The demand from or giving of any property or valuable security by the party of the bride to the party of the bridegroom 'without any consideration' other than consideration of marriage itself, should be considered as being "in connection with the marriage". The onus for proving any such other consideration being on the receiver/the person demanding such consideration.

(c) Unless and until active initiative or connivance on the part of the given in the transaction is proved, culpability of the "giver" should be limited.

(d) It should be made mandatory for the bridegrooms party to prepare a list of presents to the bride or the bridegroom covered under Section 3 of Dowry Prohibition Act failing which they should be held fully responsible. Incomplete or false lists being made offences. Such lists should be prepared at the time of or within one month of the marriage, signed by both the parties (bride's/bridegroom's) and a copy thereof given to the bride's parents/guardians.

(e) The value of gifts should commensurate with the economic standing of the bride's parents. A maximum limit should be prescribed for such gifts. They should be limited to a prescribed proportion of the gross annual income/wealth in case of those assessed for Income or Wealth Tax and a maximum prescribed sum in case of others. Demand or acceptance of dowry above the prescribed maximum should be deemed to be "Dowry extortion" and punishable as such under law.

(f) There should be in-built incentives for proper listing of such gifts or presents wherein:

  (i) Such presents up to the prescribed maximum limit should be free of any Gift Tax.

  (ii) Source of payment in case of such gifts/presents should not be accountable. A provision for Income Tax rebate u/s 88 of Income Tax Act for such gifts may be made. This suggestion may be opposed on the ground that it will encourage 'black money' as parents could settle for maximum dowry to lighten their tax accruals and also encourage dowry. To fight the tax evaders the government has however, already, been periodically launching schemes for unearthing 'black' or 'tainted' money by allowing declaration or investment in specified schemes without any penal consequences. Relating voluntary gifts to the bride as permissible under the law to a similar scheme would have the merit of making such gifts, which are being given and taken in any case, at least properly accountable and for the benefit and interest of the daughter, not only in affluent but even amongst middle class families, and help in improving social acceptability of the provision, thus making it easier for law to intervene in case of marriage breakups and reclaim for the woman her *streedhan* or any matter connected to it.

(g) As a reimbursement for her share in parental property the gifts should be deductible from her share. Similarly, to put the sons and daughters on a par in this regard, gifts of jewellery or other costly items to the daughter-in-law should be deductible from the share of the son. For this a proper planning of property has to be done so as to prevent problems in the future.

(h) Cognisance of a complaint u/s 6 of the Act should be registered at a place where the wife has been residing continuously for six months or more as it is not possible in case of marriage breakdown for the women to reside in her matrimonial home any more and therefore make her unable to get the case registered there.

(i) To arrest the spirit of unhealthy competition which has entered society regarding dowry gifts, display of dowry should be totally banned.

(j) A curb should be placed on the ostentatious and wasteful expenditure on marriage which is another source of trouble to the not-so-well-off parents of girls. A limit on such expenditure as well as on the size of marriage party/number of guests and entertainment etc. should be strictly enforced.

To implement the Dowry Prohibition Act effectively a team of Dowry Prohibition Officers and Advisory Boards comprising local social workers already provided under the Act should be appointed with proper rules and powers to regulate the functioning of such officers and constitution of the Advisory Boards. The responsibility for preventing any demand or giving or taking of dowry in violation of the provisions of the Act should basically be fixed on such officers.

Police should stay out of enforcement in this regard. This is suggested in order to avoid complaints of malpractices even though they should remain fully responsible for handling cases of dowry-related violence or deaths. Requisite powers of a police officer should be conferred on Dowry Prohibition Officers in terms of section 8-B(3) of the Act. Under Section 7, cognisance of offences under the Act can be taken, inter alia, on a complaint from any 'recognised' Welfare Institution or Organisation. The recognition for the purpose should be accorded by the Central or the State Governments. Proper rules for grant of such recognition should be framed to ensure effective and responsible functioning of such organisations/institutions and provide motivation and incentive to the more active and responsible ones among them.

In sum, 'dowry' as discussed elsewhere in the study, is a complex social problem closely related to the matter of the daughter's share in the parental property. The practice can as such be checked basically through cooperation from society and public education after taking steps to effectively ensure that the daughter actually gets her share. The thrust of criminal law needs to be on curbing 'dowry extortion' through exploitation, harassment and cruelty which is totally indefensible. The above suggestions have been made to facilitate the achieving of this objective. The amendments to the law should be accompanied by an extensive campaign to educate the public, both about the objectives of the law as well as the substance of provisions and punishments provided under the Act, and strict enforcement thereof as part of a well-defined and unambiguous clear public policy. The important role which the media — print and electronic can play in safeguarding and promoting the interests of women is no doubt worth mentioning laws relating to 'Dowry Deaths' and dowry related 'cruelty' by Husband/his Relatives, are discussed below under head 'Domestic Violence'.

Control of Domestic Violence

Domestic violence against married women — wife beating and harassment, sometimes even wife murders — arises from various causes. Legislative measures were introduced as late as 1983 and 1986 to bring domestic violence against married women specifically within the ambit of criminal law. Earlier there were no specific legal provisions for dealing with such gender-related violence within the home which was covered only under the general laws relating to murder, homicide, abetment to suicide, hurt, assault, wrongful confinement, etc. In cases of wife harassment or battering, cognisance and action by the police depended on the nature of physical injury caused or the weapon used. Cases not involving grievious injury as defined under Section 320 IPC or use of dangerous weapon or means or poison in terms of Section 324 IPC fell in the category of non-cognisable offences in which no cognisance or action could be taken by the police except with the magistrate's permission.

The main provisions/amendments are discussed below:

Murders of Married Women by Husband/in-laws or Suicides as a Result of Cruelty or Harassment by them : Such cases were earlier dealt with u/s 302 IPC (murder) or 306 IPC (abetment to suicide). The evidence of the standard as required under criminal law (proof beyond doubt) in such crimes which normally occurs within the privacy of the matrimonial home with no witnesses other than the perpetrators of the crime or their associates present is hard to get. It is sometimes difficult even to establish whether it is a case of 'murder' or 'suicide'. Convictions accordingly u/s 302 or 306 IPC in such cases were an exception, if at all.

The basic strategy followed in legal amendments to get over this problem and facilitate successful prosecutions in such cases has been to shift the burden of proof on to the accused. The amendments made were as follows:

Section 304-B, IPC (Dowry Deaths)

(enacted under Act No. 43 of 1986)

The Section, unique to the Indian penal law to deal with a crime typical to Indian society, introduced a new offence in the penal code viz. 'dowry death'. The term covers any death of a married woman which satisfies three basic criteria:

(a) under unnatural circumstances;

(b) within seven years of marriage; and

(c) preceded by cruelty or harassment by the husband or any of his relatives in connection with demand for 'dowry' (as defined under Dowry Prohibition Act).

The Section provides for a presumption of 'guilt' against the husband/his relatives in case of death of a woman in such circumstances and lays down a minimum punishment of seven years, extendable to life imprisonment. The provision for presumption under this Section was further reinforced u/s 113/B introduced in the Evidence Act in 1986 providing specifically for a statutory presumption of 'causing dowry death' against a person subjecting a woman to cruelty or harassment in connection with dowry demand soon before her death. This Section is in addition to the earlier provisions u/s 302 and 306, IPC, covering both homicidal and suicidal deaths and can be invoked where no direct evidence is available to substantiate a charge of murder against the offenders but 'unnatural' death follows dowry — demand — related harassment/cruelty, evidence basically required being about such cruelty. Cases where specific evidence is available are still to be dealt u/s 302 or 306 IPC, depending on the nature and circumstances of death.

Section 306 IPC (Abetment to Suicide)/113-A Evidence Act : While no amendment was made to Section 306 IPC itself which is taken recourse to for prosecuting the offenders for abetment in case of suicide by a married woman as a result of cruelty or harassment by the husband or in-laws, etc., to get over the difficulty in getting evidence to satisfy the essential ingredients of willful, 'instigation', 'conspiracy' or 'intentional aiding' for constituting 'abetment' in terms of Sec. 107 IPC, and to facilitate successful prosecution under the section, a new section (113-A) was introduced in the Evidence Act in 1983 (Act No. 46) providing for presumption of abetment to suicide against the husband/his relatives where the wife commits suicide within seven years of marriage following cruelty by them. Unlike Sec. 304-B IPC, this section is applicable only to cases of suicide but is not confined to dowry related cases and covers suicides by married women following 'cruelty' or 'harassment' for reasons other than dowry demand.

Section 174(3) and 176 Cr. P.C. (Inquest Reports) : These amendments to the existing provisions were made basically to streamline and further tighten the procedure for enquiries into suicides/unnatural deaths of women within seven years of marriage by making examination of the dead body by a doctor (sub-section (3) of Sec. 174 Cr. P.C.) and magisterial enquiry, either instead of or in addition to police investigation (Sec. 176, Cr. P.C.) mandatory. Amendment to Sec. 176, Cr. P.C. also provided for the relatives of the deceased in such cases to be informed and being allowed to remain present at such enquiries by a Magistrate.

The facilitating provisions and shifting of the burden of proof on the accused and streamlining of procedures for investigations/ enquiries in such cases have not had any positive results. Due to lack of public support and ooperation and loopholes present, there has been no hange in statistics related to dowry.

Convictions and Aquittals : In Delhi, only 4 (0.7%) cases of dowry deaths had ended in conviction with acquittals 20 (4%) and in Mumbai, only in one case (0.3%) there was conviction with 6 (2%) acquittals till the time of collection of information for the study. Bangalore was better with 23 (5%) convictions with 57 (12%) acquittals. In respect of cases under Dowry (Prohibition) Act, and in dowry deaths also, there was heavy pendency — 91 per cent in Delhi, 88 per cent in Mumbai and 76 per cent in Bangalore.

Causes of Failures : The reasons for these failures, however, are not caused by the laws themselves but mostly elsewhere. Even though the amended laws presume guilt against the accused in cases of unnatural deaths within seven years of marriage, the basic requirement for raising this presumption, namely, dowry demand and cruelty or harassment in that connection (or for any other reason u/s 306 IPC) soon before the death has itself been difficult to prove. The reason being the extreme reluctance on the part of the women and their parents to report such earlier demands or cruelty/harassment often till the very end (after the death), and gross lack of awareness of legal requirements of such cases among the public. Besides a substantial number of cases where the main witnesses, mostly the parents and other close relatives of the deceased turn hostile during trials under various pressures, as is evident from case studies of acquitted cases. Indifferent, even shoddy, investigation of cases and inconsistent attitude of the courts sometimes further compound the situation, thus the law is not only to be blamed.

These amended and liberalised laws themselves have come under some criticism from the more radical among women activists. The restriction on the period for drawing the statutory presumption against the accused may by far be fair but it should not be forgotten that eventhough majority of such deaths take place within the period of seven years their occurrence afterwards is not unknown, where the violence starts much earlier. These provisions may not, in fact, be of much help if the woman/her parents have continued to bear the violence/harassment without any resistance or action for seven years. Any further relaxation regarding requirements of evidence can only make a mockery of the judicial system and throw the flood-gates open for exploitation and misuse of these provisions. The remedy would lie not in doing away with all evidence but educating women and their parents to recognise the storm signals of violence and be on their toes in time and take timely action, including reports to the police, the National Commission State Commissions for Women, voluntary organisations, panchayats, etc. before it gets too late. Such action may if not save the victim at least help to provide the required evidence for successful action against the guilty.

The Suggestions

Some suggestions for improvements in laws did, however, emerge during the study which might help in making them more purposeful:

1. To make the provision more rational and avoid any pitfalls arising from the definition of 'dowry' as discussed earlier. It is suggested to substitute the term "any demand for dowry" u/s 304 B(1) IPC by the term "any unlawful

demand for any property or valuable security" (b) for "cruelty u/s 498-A IPC and deletion of explanation of the term dowry under the sub-section.

2. A suggestion for representative of the Social Welfare Department or any recognised non-governmental organization of the area, in addition to other respectables of the neighbourhood, in enquiries both u/s 174 and 176, Cr. P.C. was met with resistance from a majority of police officers during the study but is expected to help in improving the credibility of such enquiries and will improve coordination between NGOs and police. Every care should be taken in associating NGOs with a proven track record and enjoying the trust of the community. They should have transparency and full accountability in their functioning.
3. Regarding post-mortem examinations there were statutory provision under sub-section (3) (v) of section 174, Cr.P.C.; or rules made by the state governments under this sub-section, for the examination of the body in such cases to be conducted by a team of at least two doctors, to replace the executive instructions of the Home Ministry on 22 July 1980 addressed to all State Governments and Union Territory Administrations which are not often complied with. The date of marriage should be given in all requests for post-mortem examination or even a separate colour-coding given to forms in such cases to enable the doctors conducting post mortem examination to know about the applicability of this provision.
4. Specific provision under Cr. P.C. or Dowry Prohibition Act on the lines of Section 5A of Prevention of Corruption Act. The Act provides for Investigation of cases of 'dowry deaths' or suicides (u/s 304-B or 302 or 306 IPC) in case of unnatural death or suicide of a married woman within seven years of marriage, to be conducted by an officer

not below the rank of Inspector. This should replace the earlier executive instructions of the Ministry of Home Affairs for investigation of such cases by officers not below the rank of Dy. S.P. issued on 22 July 1980 referred to above.

Wife Beating and Harassment u/s 498 — A I.P.C. (Cruelty by Husband or his Relatives) : This Section, introduced in 1983 (Act No. 46), makes such 'cruelty' a specific cognisable offence punishable with imprisonment up to three years and fine. The offence is 'non bailable' under the entry in the First Schedule of Cr. P.C. for this section and 'non compoundable' because of non-inclusion of this section in the list of 'compoundable offences' u/s 320 of the Cr.P.C. Even 'mental cruelty' under specified circumstances has become actionable under this provision.

The definition of 'cruelty' in the 'Explanation' under this section is in two parts, part (i) to cover conduct unconnected with dowry demand but depending on its consequences or likely consequences; and part (ii) to specifically deal with harassment relating to 'any unlawful demand for property or valuable security'— 'dowry demand' in common parlance though the use of the term has been wisely avoided.

Cognisance of Offences : Cognisance of offences under this Section by the Court is, however, restricted u/s 198-A Cr.P.C., also introduced by amendments under Act No. 46 of 1983, only upon a police report or a complaint by the aggrieved person or specified relatives (father, mother, brother, sister, father's or mother's brother or sister) or with the leave of the court, any other person related by blood, marriage or adoption. Cognisance by police has also been restricted under Col. 4 of the entry under this section in the First Schedule of Cr.P.C. (amended in 1983) on the basis of report by the aggrieved person or a person related by blood, marriage or adoption, or, in the absence of any such relative by a public servant of the class or category notified by the State

Government for the purpose (No such notification had been issued by the concerned State Governments till the time of the study). Neither the Magistrate nor the police can take cognisance of an offence under this section on their own information or report or information from any other source.

Main Thrust of the Provision : While the provision would appear to cover all types of domestic violence, dowry-related or from other causes, with the background of public and media concern over increasing incidence of 'bride burnings' and suicides by girls and married women, the main thrust of this provision too is on combating property (dowry) demand related harassment and violence.

Attitude of Society : The attitude of ambivalence, both in society and in law towards domestic violence, excepting when it is related to 'dowry demand' or results in serious consequences—death or grievous injury, etc., is the basic reason for efforts and measures to curb such violence remaining ineffective in spite of all the legal amendments. What is required is a clear and unambiguous message that such violence in marital relationship, whatever its nature, extent or causation, is unacceptable. Unless the prevailing social notion of the wife being the husband's property, which can be ill-treated or abused as he likes is removed, there is no chance of ending marital violence against women. The women should ensure proper, timely action and provide ample scope for proof that the crime is being perpetrated only then can be the offender to be punished and discouraged from initiating such violence in future.

Rape : The offence of rape is the ultimate violation of the self and the most humiliating event in a woman's life. This is particularly so when the victim happens to be a young girl raped, within or outside her home, molested and beaten she has no option but to cope in silence. The social dimensions of rape have a special relevance and significance in harbouring such crimes in future. The girl is slienced due to social stigma which makes the offender have no fear whatsoever in repeating such an act. It is not only the victim, but her entire family which suffers in one way or the other deprived of any formal support whether financial, social or psychological; police investigations merely add to the trauma. The end result is that whereas the victim cannot conceal her shame a man can successfully hide his sin.

Mere statistics or laws do not explain the dimensions of this problem. There have been various case studies and interviews with police officers, lawyers and women's groups which have helped in understanding and analysing the various dimensions of the problem. On the persistent demand of women's groups and social activists, the Indian Penal Code was amended in 1983, providing for more stringent punishment for rape.

However, according to government statistics, incidents of rape have over the years reached menacing proportions thereby demonstrating not just the inefficacy of the partly, changed law but also the warped nature of the machinery designed to implement it. While the social stigma attached to rape is deterrence enough to reporting such crimes, the callous attitude of the police which puts the victim through most gruelling and embarrassing interrogation, also prevents women from seeking the help of the law. Men as law makers and in positions of power have been lenient to such crimes and have further helped in perpetrating the crime. The rape victims hopes of getting any kind of justice have further been stifled. It is because of these circumstances that rape is the most under reported crime, "out of every case that comes to light 20 go unrecorded" says Ms. Pramila Dandavate, of Mahila Dakshata Samiti a well known Delhi based NGO.

The Special Cell to deal with crimes against women set up by the Delhi Police at Nanak Pura has no comprehensive data on rape. If this is the story of New Delhi, then where is the hope for smaller towns and villages. This is because rape cases are dealt with by different police stations and not necessarily referred to them. In Mumbai too the number of rape cases has been rising over the years. The police officers believe it is largely the result of love affairs where the young couple indulge in sex on the sly. Some social workers feel that in a majority of cases the rapist is known to the victims. However, it would be wrong to take a simplistic view and evade such gruesome acts.

The Indian Evidence Act, still permits the character of the victim to be used as a defence, and thereby undercuts the positive amendments to the Indian Penal Code. In any case Section 376 of the IPC, which lays down a minimum punishment of ten years' rigorous punishment and even a life term applies only to custodial rape, of a girl under twelve and gang rape.

Punishment, Arrests and Convictions : Shri L.K. Advani, present Union Minister of Home Affairs has suggested capital punishment for rapists. While the National Commission for Women has supported the Minister, several women's organisations and individual activists hold a different view. According to them, if the death penalty is made mandatory, trials will continue for a long time and judges will be reluctant to award the sentence. According to Ms. Indira Jai Singh, a well known lawyer "It is not the severity of the punishment but its certainty that deters a crime. And also the most important view is not how the guilty is punished but to what extent the crimes of rape and other violence against women can be prevented". She is highly critical of the Indian system of administration of justice which is heavily loaded against the victim. Accordingly, to rough estimates, out of an averge of 3,50,000 sexual assault cases filed in courts all over the country the number of accused arrested was less than 2,00,000 and those convicted a mere 33,000.

A review of laws dealing with women has been taken up by the Law Commission and the National Commission for Women with the assistance of lawyers and women's organizations.

A draft is being prepared by the National Commission for Women on the amendments to the obsolete rape laws. The proposals under consideration include public shaming/ostracization of the accused, enhancement of punishment where the accused is also HIV positive and has passed on the infection to the victim. Other suggestions proposed by NCW are insertion of a statutory provision in the rape laws to allow adequate compensation, and provision for counselling for the victims. The exercise is an outcome of years of concerted effort of women activists across the country who have been advocating a complete overhaul of the rape laws. Such suggestions hold weight and have been made after years of research on laws dealing with women. Only if they are kept in mind in future will we have any hope for a change for the better in future.

As many as 20 offences under the Indian Penal Code and Local and special laws are considered broadly to be crimes against women:

A. *Offences Affecting the Human Body*

1. Abetting the commission of suicide (Sec. 306 IPC).
2. Molestation (Sec. 354 IPC).
3. Kidnapping, abduction or inducing a woman to compel her marriage etc. (Sec. 364/366 IPC).
4. Procuration of minor girl (Sec. 366-A IPC).
5. Importation of girls (Sec. 366-B IPC).
6. Selling minor for purposes of prostitution (Sec. 372 IPC).
7. Buying minor for purposes of prostitution (Sec. 373 IPC).
8. Rape (Sec. 376 IPC).
9. Unnatural offence, involving women (Sec. 377 IPC).

B. *Offences Against Property*

10. Chain snatching (Sec. 356 and Sec. 392 IPC).

C. *Offences Relating to Marriage*

11. Marrying again during the life time of wife (Sec. 494 IPC).
12. Adultery (Sec. 497 IPC).

13. Enticing or taking away or detaining with criminal intent a married women (Sec. 498 IPC).

D. *Offences Relating to Criminal Intimidation, Insult and Annoyance*

14. Uttering any word, making any gesture or act intended to insult the modesty of women (Sec. 509 IPC).

E. *Suppression of Immoral Traffic of Women and Girls Act*

15. Punishment for keeping a brothel or allowing premises to be used as a brothel (Sec. 3 of Suppression of Immoral Traffic in Women and Girls Act—SITA).
16. Procuring, inducing or taking a woman or girl for the sake of prostitution (Sec. 5 of SIT Act).
17. Detaining woman or girl in premises where prostitution is carried on (Sec. 6 of SIT Act).
18. Seducing a girl for purpose of prostitution (Sec. 8 of SIT Act).
19. Seduction of a woman or girl in custody (Sec. 9 of SIT Act).

F. *Dowry Act*

20. Penalty for demanding dowry (Sec. 4 of Dowry Prohibition Act 1961).

In all, we selected only five important crimes for our study, viz. (i) Rape or Seduction, (ii) Kidnapping and abduction, (iii) Dowry deaths, (iv) Wife battering, and (v) Eve-teasing which take prominent place in media.

Bibliography

Ahmad, Anis : *Woman and Social Justice*, Royal Publishers, New Delhi, 1997.

Ali, Asghar : *Islam, Women and Gender Justice*, Gyan Books Pvt. Ltd., New Delhi, 2001.

Altekar, A.S. : *The Position of Women in Hindu Civilization*, Motilal Banarsidas, Varanasi, 1962.

Amal, Mandal : *Women in Panchayati Raj Institutions,* Kanishka Publishers, New Delhi, 2002.

Amin, Amina : *Margins of Erasure— Purdah in the Subcontinental*, Sterling Publishers Pvt. Ltd., New Delhi, 1996.

Anand, Meena : *Dalit Women — Fear and Discrimination*, Gyan Books Pvt. Ltd., New Delhi, 2004.

Anand, U.K. : *Working Women and Retirement*, Anmol Publications, New Delhi, 2001.

Anshen, R.N. : *The Family— its Functions and Destiny*, Harper & Row, New York, 1959.

Arora, K.K. : *Women and Career*, Tata Institute of Social Sciences, Bombay, 1963.

August, Bebel : *Women in the Past, Present and Future*, Deep and Deep Publications, New Delhi, 1996.

Auguste, Badel : *Women— Past, Present and Future*, Bone and Liveright, New York, 1918.

Badr, A. : *Economic Rights of Women under Islamic Law & Hindu Law,* Royal Publishers, New Delhi, 1995.

Barooah, Jeuti : *Single Women in Assamese Hindu Society — an Anthropological Study of their Problems and Status*, Gyan Books Pvt. Ltd., New Delhi, 1993.

Barot, Jyoti : *The Indian Family in the Change and Challenge of the Seventies,* Sterling Publishers, New Delhi, 1972.

Bernhard, A. : *Encyclopaedic Study of Women and Love*, Anmol Publications, New Delhi, 1999.

Bhasin, K. : *The Position of Women in India*, Leslie Sawny, Bambay, 1971.

Bhoite, U. B. : *Dalit Women — Issues and Perspectives,* Gyan Books Pvt. Ltd., New Delhi, 1995.

Brian K. Smith : *The Laws of Manu,* Penguin, Delhi, 1992.

Carden, Maren Lockwood : *The New Feminist Movement*, Sage Foundation, New York, 1974.

Chakrapant, C. and Kumar, S. Vijaya : *Changing Status and Role of Women in Indian Society*, M.D. Pub., New Delhi, 1994.

Chattapadhya, Kamladevi : *The Awakening of Indian Women*, Everyman's Press, Madras, 1939.

Chaturvedi, Geeta : *Women Administration in India— a Study of the Socio-economic Background*, RBSA Publication, Jaipur, 1985.

Dabla, B. A . : *Gender Discrimination in the Kashmir Valley*, Gyan Books Pvt. Ltd., New Delhi, 2000.

Dahiya, Manju : *Extension Education and Rural Women*, Anmol Publications, New Delhi, 1998.

Das, Ram Mohan : *Women in Manu's Philosophy*, ASB Pub., Jalandhar, 1993.

De'Souza, Alfred : *Women in Contemporary India and South Asia*, Manohar Pub., Delhi, 1980.

Desai, Devangana : *Erotic Sculpture of India— a Socio Cultural Study*, Tata McGraw Pub., New Delhi, 1975.

Desai, Neera and Patel, Vibbuti : *Indian Women*, Popular Prakashan, Bombay, 1975.

Devi, Laxmi : *Encyclopaedia of Women Development and Family Welfare,* Anmol Publications, New Delhi, 1998.

Dixit, Maitreya : *Women and Achievement —Dynamics of Participation and Partnership,* Kanishka Publishers, New Delhi, 1998.

Dutt, Suresh : *Women and Education*, Anmol Publications, New Delhi, 1997.

Elizabeth, Genovese : *Feminism without Illusions— a Critique of Individualism,* University of North Carolina Press, Chapel Hill and London, 1991.

Everett, J.M. : *Women and Social Change in India*, Heritage Pub., New York, 1979.

Faludi, Susan : *Backlash— the Undeclared War against American Women,* Crown Publishers, New York, 1991.

Gandhi, M.K. : *The Role of Women*, Bhartiya Vidhya Bhavan, Bombay, 1964.

Geetha, R. : *Elderly Women,* Discovery Publishing House, New Delhi, 2003.

Giri, V. Mohani : *Women*, Gyan Books Pvt. Ltd., New Delhi, 2004.

Good, W.J. : *World Revolution and Family Patterns*, Collier MacMillan, London, 1963.

Gupta, A.K. : *Women and Society*, Criterion Pub., New Delhi, 1986.

Gupta, A.R. : *Women in Hindu Society,* Jyotsana Prakashan, Delhi, 1982.

Gupta, Sunit : *Role of Women in the 21st Century,* Anmol Publications, New Delhi, 2000.

Horney, I.B. : *Women in Farly Buddhist Literature,* Buddhist Publication Society, Kandy, 1961.

Horney, Karen : *Feminine Psychology*, W.W. Norton & Co., New York, 1967.

Indra, P. : *The Status of Women in Ancient India*, The Minerva Book Shop, Lahore, 1940.

Irving, M. : *Rethinking Sociology— a Critique of Contemporary Theory*, Appleton-Century Crafts, New York, 1973.

Jain, Simmi : *Encyclopaedia of Indian Women,* Gyan Books Pvt. Ltd., New Delhi, 2003.

Jaya, Arunachalam : *Women's Studies— an Engineering Academic Discipline*, Gyan Books Pvt. Ltd., New Delhi, 1993.

Jayashree : *India and Indian Women*, Granthayan, Aligarh, 1980.

Jung, Anees : *Unveiling India— a Woman's Journey,* Penguin, Delhi, 1987.

Kalawati : *Educational Status of Rural Girls,* Discovery Publishing House, New Delhi, 1994.

Kalpana, M. : *Status of Women in Rural Societies*, Gyan Books Pvt. Ltd., New Delhi, 2002.

Kapur, Promilla : *Marriage and the Working Woman in India*, Vikas Pub., Delhi, 1975.

Karmakar, Sumati : *The Better Half — Mothers, Sisters, Wives and Homemakers,* Dominant Books, New Delhi, 2001.

Kaul, Vanita : *Women and the Wind of Change,* Gyan Books Pvt. Ltd., New Delhi, 2000.

Khan, Wahiduddin : *Woman between Islam and Western Society,* Royal Publishers, New Delhi, 1991.

Khanna, G : *Indian Women Today*, Discovery Publishing House, New Delhi, 1978.

Kidwai, Shaikh M.H. : *Women under Different Social and Religious Law*, Seema Pub., New Delhi, 1976.

Kosambi, D.D. : *Myth and Reality—Studies in the Formation of Indian Culture,* Popular Prakashan, Bombay, 1962.

Lakshmikumari, M. : *The Role of Women in Society,* Sterling Publishers Pvt. Ltd., New Delhi, 1997.

Lal, Raman : *The Western Educated Hindu Woman*, Asia Pub. House, New York, 1970.

Latha, E. V. S. : *Women's Education and Occupational Aspirational,* Discovery Publishing House, New Delhi, 1993.

Madhurima : *Violence Against Women*— Dynamics of Conjugal Relations, Gyan Books Pvt. Ltd., New Delhi, 1996.

Maheshwari, S.C. : *World's Finest Political Wit and Humour,* Kanishka Publishers, New Delhi, 2000.

Mahta, Basant : *Role of Banks in Women Development*, Discovery Publishing House, New Delhi, 2003.

Maithreyi, Krishnaraj : *Women an Society in India,* Ajanta Publication, New Delhi, 1987.

Malhotra, Menakshi : *Dimensions of Women Exploitation*, Gyan Books Pvt. Ltd., New Delhi, 2004.

Mandal, Jotirmay : *Women and Reservation in India*, Gyan Books Pvt. Ltd., New Delhi, 2003.

Manna, Smita : *The Fair Sex in Tribal Cultures— Problems and Development*, Gyan Books Pvt. Ltd., New Delhi, 1989.

Marshall, Katherine : *Employed Parents and Division of Housework*, Oxford, New York, 1993.

Mary, Frances : *Women in India*, Amarka Book Agency, Delhi, 1973.

Mehta, Rama : *Socio Legal Status of Women in India*, Metropolitan Book Co., Delhi, 1982.

Meyer, Johann Jakob : *Sexual Life in Ancient India— a Study in the Comparative History of Indian Culture*, E.D. Dutton & Co., New York, 1930.

Minai, Naila : *Women in Islam— Tradition and Transition in the Middle East,* Seaview Books, New York, 1981.

Minault, Gail : *Secluded Scholars, Women's Education and Muslim Social Reform in Cobaial India*, Oxford Univ. Press, Delhi, 1998.

Mishra, Jyotsna : *Women and Human Rights*, Gyan Books Pvt. Ltd., New Delhi, 2000.

Mishra, Saraswati : *Status of Indian Women,* Gyan Books Pvt. Ltd., New Delhi, 2002.

Mitra, Joyati : *Women and Society —Equality and Empowerment,* Kanishka Publishers, New Delhi, 1997.

Mittal, Mukta : *Women in India— Today and Tomorrow*, Anmol Pub., New Delhi, 1995.

Moddie, A.D. : *The Brahamanical Culture and Modernity*, Asia Pub. House, Lord, 1968.

Moni, Mohan : *Female Education in India*, B.B. Gupta Publication, Kanpur, 1921.

Mujtaba, Sayid, Lari, Rukni Musawi : *Western Civilization through Muslim Eyes*, Ansariyan Publication, Iran,. 1989.

Nancy, F. : *The Grounding of Modern Feminism*, Yale University Press, New Haven and London, 1987.

Narasaiah, M. L. : *Women, Children and Poverty*, Discovery Publishing House, New Delhi, 2001.

Pal, B.K. : *Problems and Concerns of Indian Women*, ABC Pub. House, New Delhi, 1989.

Pandit, S. K. : *Women in Society*, Rajat Pub., Delhi, 1998.

Patel, Vibhuti : *Women Challenges of the New Millennium*, Gyan Books Pvt. Ltd., New Delhi, 2002.

Paul, Diana Y. : *Women in Buddhism*, Asian Humanities Press, California, 1979.

Pinkham, Mildreth Worth : *Women in the Sacred Scripts of Hinduism,* AMS Press, New York, 1941.

Prasad, Sushama Sahay : *Tribal Woman Labourers— Aspects of Economic and Physical Exploitation,* Gyan Books Pvt. Ltd., New Delhi, 1988.

Puri, Jyoti : *Woman, Body, Desire in Past-Colonial India — Narratives of Gender and Sexuality*, Manohar Publishing House, New Delhi, 1999.

Rajgopal, T.S. : *Indian Ideal of Womanhood*, Ramakrishna Mission, Calcutta, 1969.

Rani, K. : *Role Conflict in Working Wives*, Chetana Publications, New Delhi, 1976.